PRAISE FOR CAPABILITY CASES

"I've known the authors of this book for some years, and have used the Solution Envisioning through Capability Cases approach on quite a few major IT engagements for fortune 500 client companies. It's an outstanding technique for ensuring real consensus between stakeholders as to the scope and priorities of an IT project. I heartily recommend this book to anyone involved in creating technology-based solutions to business problems."

—Clive Gee, Ph.D., senior solution architect, IBM Enterprise Integration Services

"Capability Cases clarifies the mysterious process whereby business needs inform, and are informed by, technology. The formalism of Capability Cases provides a way for real-world successes to be abstracted into best practices. The guiding principle is 'clarity,' and the book will be clarifying for any reader concerned with these issues."

—Alexander Morgan, principal research scientist, Manufacturing Systems Research Laboratory, GM R&D Center

"Solution envisioning is critical to the 'learning your way to innovation' that we need for breakthrough performance in e-government public services and the build-out of its target archiecture."

—Brand Niemann, co-chair, Federal Semantic Interoperability Community of Practice (SICoP) and Office of Environmental Information, U.S. Environmental Protection Agency

"The methodologies described in Capability Cases begin to define a structured approach that connects the creative envisioning of potential solutions with a pragmatic process for defining and implementing techniques and technologies. These methods are particularly relevant in the diverse and disparate arena of biomedical sciences and application of bioinformatics in the healthcare and basic biology."

—Dave Parrish, Immune Tolerance Network

"Capability Cases offers hope that mere mortals can rise above the daunting challenge of blending technology and process. Executives hoping to adopt high-performing business models will want to learn this step-by-step approach to designing and implementing IT-enabled organizational change."

—Dr. Jeanne W. Ross, principal research scientist, MIT Center for Information Systems Research

"In this innovative book, Irene Polikoff, Robert Coyne, and Ralph Hodgson have captured deep insights from many years of studying how to get across the 'business/IT gap.' Capability Cases are an invaluable tool for bridging from envisioning to design."

—Steve Cook, software architect, Microsoft Corporation

"This book is a welcome addition to the discussion of the perennial problem of bridging the business/IT gap. The authors bring years of practical experience in addressing such issues as confusing proposed solution attributes with business needs and requirements, balancing the needs and expectations of different classes of stakeholders, and familiar syndromes such as the package will do it and the demo becomes the solution. These issues all too often lead to project failure, as cited in an AMR study of CRM projects, of which only 16% delivered actual business value.

The authors prescribe an approach based on Solution Envisioning and Capability Cases. They provide a compelling rationale for their suggestions, clear instruction for practitioners, and guidance for the incorporation of these methods into existing practice. They make use of such techniques as stories and an emphasis on clear definition of vocabulary to help balance the voice of the user and the voice of the technologist. The book contains galleries of actual Capability Cases and tips for running effective workshops, including techniques for interaction and for creating an effective environment for collaboration. This approach incorporates both standard and innovative methods and tools for recognizing business situations, developing concept requirements, and the application of technology capabilities to realize desired business capabilities.

Based on real-life examples from commercial and public enterprises, and sprinkled with war stories and entertaining cartoons, this book delivers methodical wisdom... and more."

—Doug McDavid, Almaden Services Research, IBM Academy of Technology (mcdavid@us.ibm.com)

"Capability Cases fills in a critical void. Many agile approaches focus on micro-requirements—stories, features, backlog items—assuming that the user community has conducted adequate business or product analysis. We know requirements change frequently and therefore don't want to specify reams of detailed specifications, but what artifacts should we use to guide projects in that intermediate zone between product vision and iteration specifications? The answer: Capability Cases. Capability Cases are one answer to the 'just enough, but not too much' front-end work that's required to link technology to business value."

—Jim Highsmith, senior vice-president, Agile Software Development and Project Management Practice, Cutter Consortium

CAPABILITY CASES

CAPABILITY CASES

A Solution Envisioning Approach

IRENE POLIKOFF, ROBERT COYNE,
RALPH HODGSON

⋏ Addison-Wesley

Upper Saddle River, NJ ▪ Boston ▪ Indianapolis ▪ San Francisco
New York ▪ Toronto ▪ Montreal ▪ London ▪ Munich ▪ Paris ▪ Madrid
Capetown ▪ Sydney ▪ Tokyo ▪ Singapore ▪ Mexico City

Many of the designations used by manufacturers and sellers to distinguish their products are claimed as trademarks. Where those designations appear in this book, and the publisher was aware of a trademark claim, the designations have been printed with initial capital letters or in all capitals.

The authors and publisher have taken care in the preparation of this book, but make no expressed or implied warranty of any kind and assume no responsibility for errors or omissions. No liability is assumed for incidental or consequential damages in connection with or arising out of the use of the information or programs contained herein.

The publisher offers excellent discounts on this book when ordered in quantity for bulk purchases or special sales, which may include electronic versions and/or custom covers and content particular to your business, training goals, marketing focus, and branding interests. For more information, please contact:

U. S. Corporate and Government Sales
(800) 382-3419
corpsales@pearsontechgroup.com

For sales outside the U. S., please contact:

International Sales
international@pearsoned.com

 This Book Is Safari Enabled

The Safari® Enabled icon on the cover of your favorite technology book means the book is available through Safari Bookshelf. When you buy this book, you get free access to the online edition for 45 days. Safari Bookshelf is an electronic reference library that lets you easily search thousands of technical books, find code samples, download chapters, and access technical information whenever and wherever you need it.

To gain 45-day Safari Enabled access to this book:

- Go to http://www.awprofessional.com/safarienabled
- Complete the brief registration form
- Enter the coupon code APPD-YA4O-RYPY-MGOP-J7N3

If you have difficulty registering on Safari Bookshelf or accessing the online edition, please e-mail customer-service@safaribooksonline.com.

Visit us on the Web: www.awprofessional.com

Library of Congress Catalog Number: 2005923980

ISBN 0-321-20576-6

Text printed in the United States on recycled paper at R. R. Donnelley in Crawfordsville, Indiana.
First printing, July 2005

This Book is dedicated to "embattled envisioners" and "change agents" everywhere. May you follow and guide others on interesting trails of possibilities...

CONTENTS AT A GLANCE

Contents

CHAPTER 4   **POSITIONING WITHIN THE SOLUTION DELIVERY CYCLE   141**

PART II   **SOLUTION ENVISIONING PROCESS—DETAILED LOOK**

CHAPTER 5   **BUSINESS CAPABILITY EXPLORATION—PHASE I OF SOLUTION ENVISIONING   155**

CHAPTER 7   SOFTWARE CAPABILITY DESIGN—PHASE III OF SOLUTION
ENVISIONING   249

PART III   CUSTOMIZING AND USING SOLUTION
ENVISIONING

CHAPTER 8   SOLUTION ENVISIONING IN DIFFERENT
SITUATIONS   301

ABOUT THE AUTHORS

Irene Polikoff, partner and co-founder of TopQuadrant, Inc., has more than 15 years of IT experience. Her specialties include technology strategy, IT management, system integration, process reengineering, systems assessment, and technology selection.

Dr. Robert Coyne, executive partner at TopQuadrant, has more than 20 years of experience in the full lifecycle of business development, product design, software development, production, and delivery. He brings integrated knowledge and expertise from business, consulting, academia, and research to solution development processes, methods, and practice.

Ralph Hodgson, partner and co-founder of TopQuadrant, has been a thought leader in the IT industry for some 25 years. He has expertise in enterprise systems design, software engineering, IT consulting, object and ontology modeling, Semantic Technology, logic programming, and methodology development.

FOREWORD

Professor Fred Brooks refers to "thinkers," "do-ers," and "thinker-doers." This book is written by some of the most energetic "thinker-doers" in the business. They are amazingly well-versed in current academic research and leading edge technology. They also get their hands dirty and deliver specifications, designs, and operational software for their customers.

The book adds an important term to our already large catalog of terms that we system builders routinely use—Capability Cases. The essence of the book is that just as we need reusable components to improve our productivity while developing systems, we also need a reusable library of Capability Cases to help explain to our customers what is possible and to comfort them by knowing that "what already exists cannot be impossible."

An envisioned solution—achieved through some suitable activities, such as those defined as the "Solution Envisioning" aspect of the book—then is a collection of Capability Cases. Just like reusable patterns, Capability Cases describe something which already exists from a user's perspective, not a developer's perspective. By combining a collection of Capability Cases a set of users and stakeholders can get a more precise notion of what could be built and what business value that particular solution would provide.

Why is this book important? It is important because far too many business people in the world are simply catatonic at the thought of being responsible for "delivering a custom application." It need not be so. A custom application can be described using a set of reusable Capability Cases; those Capability Cases can be implemented with a set of reusable frameworks or components; and everything is held together with a modest amount of "glue code," which is not very risky to implement. With such a strategy businesses can finally get the applications and systems that they want instead of the systems they are being sold which always require the business to change to accommodate the application or system.

Years ago I had the privilege of managing a collection of remarkable "thinker-doers" at ITT Corporation. We were asked to develop a 10 year projection of software development technologies. We constrained ourselves in our projections by only considering capabilities which already existed, even in a high technology research group. Surprisingly we did a great job of predicting where hardware technology was going and we were a decade optimistic in our view of software technology. So constraining ourselves to think about solutions composed only of Capability Cases is not very restrictive!

If we restrict our thinking about new systems to existing Capability Cases, does this ensure that we will not have failed projects? Of course not. The project may still fail because we attempt to do too much too quickly or with too few developers or with inexperienced developers.

What if we're a startup company and really want to develop something that is substantially different from anything that has ever been built before? It certainly can be done, but some cautions apply. One or two major innovations are all that a single project can accommodate. I have seen companies fail when they try to develop too many fundamental innovations in parallel. But there is nothing wrong with a series of innovations happening in sequence. Companies like Apple and NeXT have demonstrated their ability to do just this. Microsoft has demonstrated spectacular prowess in taking innovations developed elsewhere and commercializing them—with or without the cooperation of the original developer!

Ralph (one of the authors of this book who has been working on software projects as long as I have) and I remember when companies would spend millions of dollars writing meaningless specification documents filled with conflicting vague notions of what some set of stakeholders thought they wanted in a new system. Designers and developers would ponder for days and weeks and sometimes even months trying to figure out what on earth the customer really wanted. Until the solution is completely described in a form that designers and developers can unambiguously understand what

It[1] is, no one can provide an accurate estimate of the time and effort to construct It (using whatever technology).

Capability Cases, in conjunction with the Solution Envisioning process, provide for a more precise way to define It. With such precision, IT organizations can finally start delivering the business value that their stakeholders demand but rarely have received. Irene, Ralph, and Robert have made a fundamental contribution to software engineering. I look forward to seeing a virtual bookshelf full of books describing available Capability Cases. It will happen soon, I predict.

Next will come the tools to assemble Capability Cases with their associated object-oriented components. This is not an easy project and would be quite hard to express using existing Capability Cases. So be prepared to wait a decade or so before our often described building blocks solution can be assembled from Capability Cases.

Tom Love, co-founder and CEO, Shoulders Corporation

---

[1] It is a pronoun and refers to the envisioned solution; IT is an acronym for Information Technology.

PREFACE

Capability.[1] It's a promising word. It sounds, well, *capable*, and it alludes to the delivery of something. We all use capabilities every day in the goods and services by which we construct our lives. We like to be capable; we respect and value capabilities in others. As individuals, we carefully evaluate and compare the capabilities in the products and services we purchase—in everything from cars and houses to palm pilots, digital cameras, and mobile phone services. We look for and expect capabilities in companies we choose to deal with and in the companies we own or choose to be a part of.

As businesses, we also need to purchase or build, deploy and use, offer or consume capabilities all the time—regularly and continuously. It is requisite that we absorb, embrace, employ, and evolve new capabilities—with ever greater speed and agility—simply to remain effective and cost competitive. But, knowing about and successfully deploying the right new capabilities has always been challenging to businesses. In particular, software and technology capabilities are sometimes as elusive, amorphous, and difficult to pin down as they are valuable and essential to the core operations and processes of most modern businesses and organizations.

Most business capabilities today are a combination of human capital, fixed assets (such as facilities), processes, and technology. Forging successful combinations requires proficient orchestration of the interplay between business and technology. In this era of technology explosion (ranging from Web Services to new Platforms for Collaboration and Personalization to Semantic Technologies and Agents), the possibilities are as truly mind-boggling as the challenges of effective action. In nearly every industry and

---

[1] The quality of being capable; capacity or ability needed to do something. (plural) Qualities that may be used or developed; potentialities.

business area, technology capabilities are playing an ever more prominent role—and some business capabilities are becoming identical with technology capabilities.

We are entering a world where the network is the platform and a large amount of business-enabling capabilities will be made possible by assembling commodity software that implements standardized protocols. Indeed, technologies are creating deeper changes in businesses—invoking a disruptive new order that challenges all the rules of business. Business capabilities made possible by technology demolish traditional barriers of geography, law, organization, and time while simultaneously raising new bars for success in terms of connectedness, convenience, quality, and performance.[2]

For instance, capabilities introduced by technology have changed user expectations. Business has become more personal, and customers have (much) more control. Businesses have rapidly become more connected and accessible, and in many cases instantly available all the time. As a result, business has paradoxically become both simpler and more complex. Technologies can simplify transactions, but they also engender more complex transactions and more sophisticated use of data and knowledge. New capabilities create challenges to business models by regularly shifting the value proposition. Many things that were previously sold are given away for free. Business value, to be earned by truly serving customers, has shifted to somewhere else in the value chain.

How hard it is to identify, design, and deploy the right capabilities? Capability, per se, doesn't usually conjure up any nuances or overtones of failure (yet). But, as we all know, as soon as we attempt to acquire and make use of capabilities, there is suddenly a pressing demand for a blend of vision, planning, and know-how to take advantage of and make capabilities actual or realized through their successful application. Further complicating the situation, there is an increasing multiplicity of sources from which to realize (develop, acquire, compose) capabilities. Geoffrey Moore, industry consultant and best-selling author, puts it this way:[3]

[2] We are indebted to Peter Stecher of IBM, EMEA, for insights into this characterization of the revolutionary nature of new technologies in terms of the deeper changes they bring to doing business.
[3] From Gartner Application Integration & Web Services Summit 2005 brochure, highlighting Moore's keynote talk, "The Key to Sustained Leadership: Separating the Core from the Context," where he "shares his latest insights into the software industry challenges and opportunities."

"With service-oriented architecture, integration, composition of applications, open source software, vendor consolidation and the tension between building, buying and outsourcing software solutions—companies are under pressure to change too much and too fast. Risks seem unavoidable. There is not enough budget or time to cover all the bases. The leading enterprises will identify the core of their business and invest in safety and agility of the IT behind this core—first."

Unless we have knowledge of capabilities, the vision to know their worth, and the experience and discipline to apply them, we may get lost somewhere in a "sea of potentials." In our personal lives, in assessing where true capabilities are found, whether they are real, sound, and worth having, we typically use many sources of information, processes, and tools for evaluation—facilities such as *Consumer Reports*[4] for consumer products or recommendations from friends or people who have experience with the capability. This book is an attempt to aid individuals and companies in improving technology-enabled business capabilities by responding to their needs for

- Understanding what capabilities exist—what is out there
- Facilitating the interplay between business and technical ideas
- Understanding the significance and implications of capabilities and the constraints and costs of employing them
- Establishing effective processes for acquiring, adopting, and applying capabilities

We introduce the Solution Envisioning process to help people envision together the needs and possibilities of business. The process is supported by the Capability Case, an aid to understanding and evaluating capabilities. In the everyday sense of the words, the Capability Case is intended to build a case for a capability by illustrating its potential and value. We offer Solution Envisioning with Capability Cases (the approach this book introduces) as a start toward a new kind of essential, comprehensive approach for appreciating and making intelligent decisions about the available technology capabilities that will be powering businesses for some time to come.

---

[4] A source that has its own 'capabilities'—a trusted source of information, knowledge, evaluative mechanisms, and the experience to make useful judgments about the relative promise and value of other capabilities.

Acknowledgments

Many people inspired, encouraged, and supported us in a long journey that preceded writing this book. We trace the beginnings of System Envisioning ideas back to 1991 and Ralph Hodgson's work on the X-Model. The ideas took shape and evolved with the help of many participants of the ACM OOPSLA System Envisioning workshops from 1996 to 2000.

We acknowledge the beneficial experiences and ideas that flowed in the OOPSLA System Envisioning years. Special thanks to Martine Devos who co-led some of the OOPLSA workshops. Martine has always been an inspiration to us as a facilitator and "seasoned envisioner." Her *ConceptCafe* technique is one of the techniques used in our method and described in this book. Our appreciation of the OOPSLA workshops would not be complete without mentioning the contributions of Alistair Cockburn, Branko Peteh, Brian Foote, Bruce Anderson, Carl Ballard, Charles B. Harvey, Chuck Matthews, Clive S. Gee, Dana Bredemeyer, Dave Sapp, Dave Thomas, David Ing, Deborah Leishman, Doug McDavid, Gerald Zinke, Ian Graham, Ian Simmonds, Jack Ring, Jim Salmons, John Daniels, Kal Ruberg, Kent Beck, Lorette Cameron, Mary Lynn Thomas, Marilyn Bates, Mark Simos, Michael Beedle, Mike Karchov, Petri Pulli, Ruth Milan, Steve Johnson, Tom Bridge, Trygve Reenskaug, and Ward Cunnigham.

Our colleague, Dean Allemang, helped us at the start of the writing, and we extend thanks for the many hours over the last two years he devoted to reviewing, discussing, and helping to fine-tune various aspects of the book. We especially acknowledge Dean for his affinity and aptitude for doing the "Envisioning Thing" for semantic technology in our TopQuadrant customer projects. Some people are born to envision. In our view, Dean should be counted among them.

We doubt that any book author ever had a reviewer more conscientious than Larry Levine, who carefully read almost every chapter and provided us with copious notes and valuable feedback. Tom Love, Chris Newlon, Peter Stecher, and Alistair Cockburn provided many insightful observations making it possible for us to sharpen the writing and significantly improve the organization of the book. We also thank Mills Davis for helping shape the introductions for the three parts of the book. And we thank Sidney Bailin for the insights that became part of the storytelling technique.

This book would not be possible without many consulting clients who let us practice Solution Envisioning and learn from them. Many have reviewed the book, and allowed us to use workshop photographs and project examples. Our sincere thanks go to Alec Morgan, Bob Dompe, Christopher Pardy, Con Kenney, Frehiwot Fisseha, Gail Hodge, Gauri Salokhe, Hansen Wu, Harold P. Frisch, Irene Onyancha, Jane Riddle, Jim Cockrell, Johannes Keizer, John Zimmerman, Kafkas Caprazli, Larry Schmidt, Margherita Sini, Paul Keller, Randy Hoffman, Rusty Yates, Stefka Kaloyanova, and Stephen Waterbury.

We feature several Capability Cases and solution stories in the book. We appreciate the cooperation and assistance from the companies and individuals who gave their permission to include these in the book. These include the staff at the iMarkup Solutions, Inxight Software, Inc., Land's End, Inc., London's Transport Museum, Ontoprise and Right Now Technologies, Andrew Bradley of the Hive Group, Dallas Noyes of Cogito, Inc., Professor Jim Hendler of the MindLab and the University of Maryland, John Domingue of the UK Open University, Paul Kogut of Lockheed Martin, Peter Clark of Boeing, Dr. Thomas Vögele of GEIN, and Tony Frazier of iPhrase, Inc.

Artist and visual facilitator Peter Durand of Alphachimp drew all the excellent cartoons you see in the book. Graphic artist James Huckenpahler took many sketchy diagrams we provided and turned them into professional graphics. Finally, our gratitude goes to the staff at Addison-Wesley—to Michael E. Hendrickson for making it possible to start the project and to Paul Petralia, our editor throughout the rest of the process, for helping to make the book a reality.

Finally, we would especially like to thank our families and friends for their understanding and support during the extended time and effort we needed for writing. We could not have envisioned nor realized this book without you.

The Worldwide Institute of Software Architects (wwisa.org)
is a non-profit professional organization dedicated
to the establishment of a formal profession of software architecture and
to provide information and services to software architects and their clients -
analogous to the formation of the American Institute of Architects roughly 140 years
ago. The essential tenet of WWISA is that there is a perfect analogy between building
and software architecture and the classical role of the architect needs to be introduced
into the software construction industry.

The architect, whether designing structures of brick or computer code, forms the bridge
between the world of the client and that of the technical builders. This critical bridge has
been missing from the software industry resulting in the decades-long software crisis.
Entire software structures are dysfunctional or have been scrapped entirely - before
seeing a single "inhabitant." We have simply been building huge, complex structures
without architects, without blueprints.

WWISA was established in 1998 and now has over 4,000 members in 108 countries.
Membership is open to practicing and aspiring software architects, professors, students,
CIO's and CEO's. Members participate to promote training and degree programs, develop
architectural standards and guiding principles, and work toward a standard body of
shared knowledge. We are client advocates; they are our driving force. We hope to
become the clients' bridge to successful software construction by leveraging the full
range of technology in their favor.

○ **WWISA**─○

Membership in the IASA provides:
- Up-to-date architecture content at your level of expertise
- Advancement in the field of professional IT architecture
- Opportunities to grow your professional network
- Training and Education
- A direct relationship with sponsor architects and thought-leaders
- Publishing and speaking opportunities

With over 1500 members, chapters on 4 continents, industry thought-leaders and sponsors world-wide, the IASA represents a unique collaborative environment for driving enterprise, IT and software architecture and representing the interests of practicing architects.

The IASA is the de-facto standard for architecture professionals who wish to expand their expertise, collaborate with peers and create industry accepted levels of qualification.

International Association of Software Architects

Publishing Department
May 2005

www.iasarchitects.org
www.iasahome.org

Don Quixote

Holy Grail

A Quest for Transformation (i.e., a viable business solution):

From a Call for New Business Capabilities ... Through to the Adoption of an Enabling Solution

Characterizing THE QUEST for a viable business solution

Perceiving Problem / Planning Change = THE NEED TO DO SOMETHING	Commiting to Do Something = LAUNCHING AN INITIATIVE	Acquiring / Developing the Answer = FIELDING A SOLUTION		Deploying a Viable Solution = ACHIEVING DESIRED RESULTS	
... Need for Business Transformation / Alignment	Commiting to Begin = "$$"	Beginning ...	Beginning of End	Beginning of End ... END (not really ...)	Maintenance, Evolution, ... yada yada
Business Strategy Development / Realignment	Solution Initiative Formation	Solution Realization		Solution Deployment and Adoption	

... To HERE and quickly!

... BUT, WHAT OFTEN HAPPENS ON THE WAY?

The business just wants to get from HERE

MIND the GAP

What's wrong with this picture?

... Parable I: An 'As-Is' Tale, featuring the usual suspects in their usual roles

The Need to DO SOMETHING

"Do we or do we not have a problem?"

LAUNCHING A SOLUTION INITIATIVE ($$)

LINKING EXISTING LANGUAGES:

TOWER of BABEL

IT
STRATEGY
BUSINESS

Two or more departments (camps), divided by a common organziation, have a bit of trouble understanding one another.

It does not go unnoticed that, as someone says, "What we have here is a failure to communicate."

VOICES

VOICE of BUSINESS

VOICE of TECHNOLOGY

VOICE of the CUSTOMER

SOLUTIONS TEAM

An initiative to DO SOMETHING is launched when funded.

"Hey, if there is going to be $$, we must need a Project Team ... and why not a Task Force to supervise them?!"

The new team is so popular; everyone wants to tell them what to do.

SOLUTION OVERKILL

Once technology is in the picture, a truckload of issues come up.

Determining best matches and making intelligent choices is a BIG problem.

FIELDING A SOLUTION

"What we need here is a disciplined, repeatable process."

After "negotiating" with the methodologists for a while, the project team is shaken, not stirred.

The vendors are always more than willing to put on a "show and tell."

"Each singular solution covers every business stake..."

Finally, a path of action has been decided on and everyone can get on board with making it a reality.

ACHIEVING (DESIRED?) RESULTS
(some possible outcomes...)

Sticker Shock $#

With enough iterations, some part of the originally intended solution gets deployed and works... but, the ROI is not so good. The business results are only partial, behind schedule, and seriously over budget.

OR

Punish the Innocents

The project timeline passes (as all things do!), and the $$ gets spent. But, nothing really useful happens....

Someone will have to be held accountable.

OR

CUSTOMERS Never Know What they Want (until they see it)

What gets delivered to the user is not acceptable. It may be a technical wonder, but....

...it does not solve their business problem in a way that they can use.

...

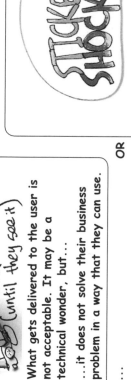

WAITING for the WAVE to PASS

The users may even go along with the adoption rituals and ruse.

But, since it doesn't solve their everyday problems, they don't really use it (not for long anyway).

A Quest for Transformation:

From a Call for New Business Capabilities ... Through to the Adoption of an Enabling Solution

Characterizing THE QUEST with a timely Solution Envisioning intervention

	Committing to Begin = "SS"	Beginning	End of Beginning	Middle to End ... and Beyond
	Solution Initiative Formation		Solution Envisioning	Solution Realization and Adoption

Business Strategy Development / Realignment

... Need for Business Transformation / Alignment

Solution Envisioning Process: Main Phases and Outcomes

THE ENVISIONER

MOTIVATION for SE

Biz Perk · IT Perk

'ACTIONABLE' RESULTS

SHARED VISION → SHARED UNDERSTANDING → SOLUTION REALIZATION

SPARKING IDEAS

STORYTELLING

The SE JOURNEY

ORIENTING QUESTIONS: Where? How? What? Who?

Business Capability Exploration

Capability Envisioning

Capability Design

... **Parable II: A 'To-Be' Future Retrospective** Tale with a timely Envisioning intervention, featuring more than the usual suspects in unusual communication and relationship. This book tells the story....

INTRODUCTION

"The key to every man is his thought. Sturdy and defying
though he look, he has a helm which he obeys, which is
the idea after which all his facts are classified.
He can only be reformed by showing him a new
idea which commands his own."

—*Ralph Waldo Emerson*

TRAILHEAD—WHY THIS BOOK?

In this book, we focus on the interplay between business needs and technology capabilities. Our belief in the following premises has motivated its topic and contents:

- Clarity of the business problem is central to getting results from technology projects. Strong functional fit of business solutions happens when the decision processes are value-driven.

- Innovative solutions emerge from understanding needs and appreciating technology capabilities. Because technology options continue to expand, this is not a simple task.

- Creativity rarely happens on its own. For ideas to flow, they need a supportive environment and skillful techniques to bring real people together to dialogue differently and more productively.

- Capabilities serve as a unifying construct across the lifecycle. A capability-based approach can span from the design of new business capabilities and the envisioning of solution capabilities to the specification of software capabilities.

We present two innovations that work together to better connect business challenges to technology enablers for successfully delivering value:

- **Solution Envisioning** is a business, value-driven approach to designing a system that uses *Capability Cases* and scenarios to foster innovation and to validate and increase confidence in the solution.

- **Capability Case** is a solution idea pattern that makes the "*business case for a capability*." By anchoring solution concepts in a language for business situations and using stories, Capability Cases communicate value. Each Capability Case includes applicable technologies and architecture ideas for realizing the capability.

Central to the effort of formulating solutions is the need to envision a desired future. Forging a shared vision becomes possible when the interplay of technology capabilities and business ideas is encouraged and facilitated. For these reasons, we named our process *Solution Envisioning with Capability Cases*.

Each Capability Case can be seen as a best practice for achieving business results. The Solution Envisioning process provides a way to connect these solution concepts to the business situation. Business objectives and the overall business context guide the selection of capabilities. In the same way an architect presents building designs for consideration, *Solution Envisioning with Capability Cases* offers "designs by example" for IT systems.

WHAT IS THE SOLUTION ENVISIONING PROCESS?

Solution Envisioning is a problem-discovery, situation-assessment, and solution-planning process. It was designed to improve the chances of solution success by addressing the risks and challenges present in the early stages of the implementation process. Solution Envisioning embraces a business-centric approach to designing and realizing technology-enabled business capabilities. It *bridges the gap* between Business and IT through the integration of concepts and techniques from both best-of-breed business strategy methods and software development methods.

Solution Envisioning with Capability Cases is designed for use at the front-end of the software development lifecycle.[1] The process has three phases, with the use of Capability Cases occurring throughout. Figure I.1 illustrates the iterative nature and flow of the Solution Envisioning process. The main deliverable of each phase is shown as the output needed for the subsequent phase. The three phases of Solution Envisioning are

1. **Business Capability Exploration**—Creating the Solution Vision and an initial Business Case

2. **Solution Capability Envisioning**—Creating the Solution Concept

3. **Software Capability Design**—Elaborating and confirming the Business Case and delivering the Solution Implementation Roadmap.

The process supports a consistent, repeatable, and rapid way of progressing from a business-problem understanding to a solution concept. What is often regarded as a mysterious process composed of hit-or-miss activities is transformed into a reliable practice.

Solution Envisioning with Capability Cases has been applied in a number of projects. For example:

- Planning a system to manage engineering designs
- Determining requirements and the technology adoption process for long-term digital archives
- Implementing expertise location and intelligent search for a large services company
- Architecting a wealth management system
- Designing a help desk for a major electronics manufacturer
- Providing citizens with improved access to local and state services

Examples of using Solution Envisioning and Capability Cases in different situations are featured throughout this book. What Solution Envisioning delivers is an agreed solution concept and realization roadmap. These serve as a starting point for building a system using one or more of the well-established software development practices.

---

[1] Leading software development processes and methods call this the *Inception* or *Envisioning* phase.

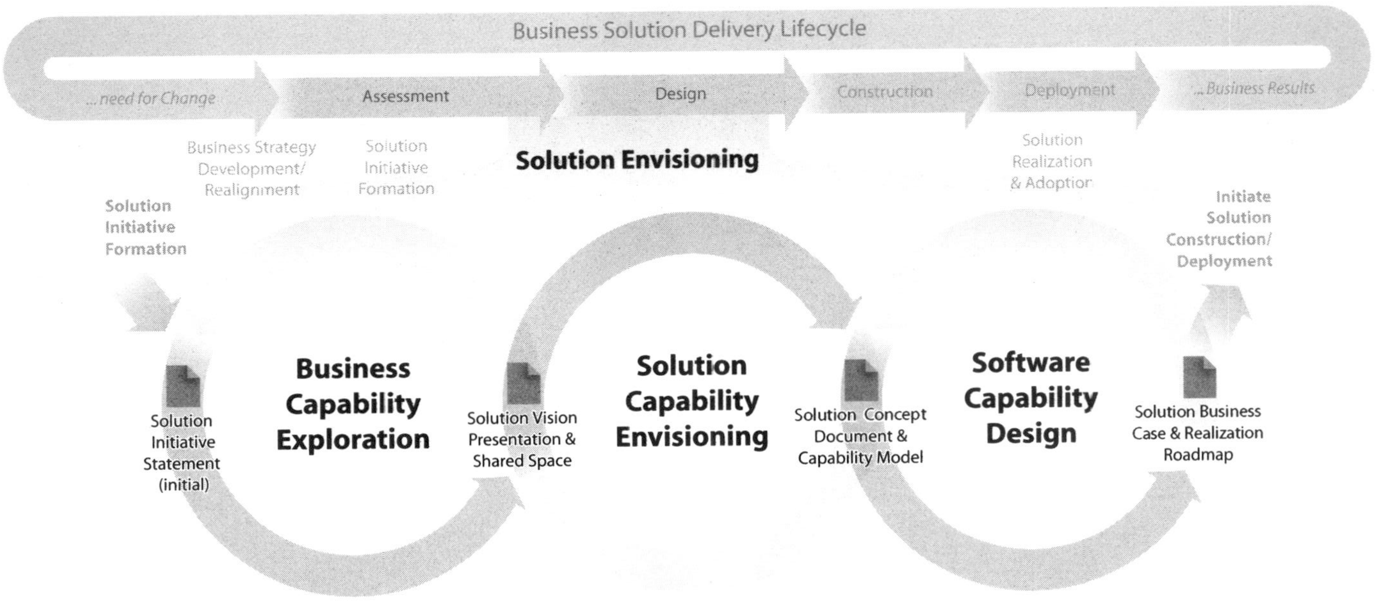

Business Solution Delivery Lifecycle

...need for Change

| Solution Initiative Formation | Assessment | Design | Construction | Deployment | ...Business Results |

Business Strategy Development/ Realignment

Solution Initiative Formation

Solution Realization & Adoption

Initiate Solution Construction/ Deployment

Solution Envisioning

Business Capability Exploration

Solution Initiative Statement (initial)

Solution Capability Envisioning

Solution Vision Presentation & Shared Space

Software Capability Design

Solution Concept Document & Capability Model

Solution Business Case & Realization Roadmap

The overall flow of a complete Solution Envisioning (SE) process can be informally described in terms of these main movements:

Before SE

Pre-a. Formulating a Solution Initiative

Pre-b. Clarifying the business goals and ROI objectives

During SE

1. Confirming business goals and objectives

2. Analyzing the current business situation to understand who is hurting and how

3. Reaching out for someting new – identifying an initial portfolio of capabilities

4. Consolidating an initial solution vision for sharing with a larger set of stakeholders

5. Preparing for and planning a workshop

6. Conducting envisioning workshop to review a solution vision, touring a gallery of capability cases, evaluating and prioritizing capabilities identified for solution

7. Consolidating a Solution Concept as an integrated set of capabilities

8. Determining infrastructure impact; selecting technologies, vendors and products

9. Developing the technical capability architecture for the solution

10. Confirming the business case; producing an implementation roadmap

After SE

Post-a. Constructing, deploying and adopting the solution

Post-b. Realizing ROI; utilizing foundation established for future enhancements

FIGURE I.1. SOLUTION ENVISIONING PROCESS: MAIN PHASES AND OUTCOMES.

WHAT ARE CAPABILITY CASES?

A Capability Case definitively identifies an IT Solution Concept as a cohesive group of software functions that deliver business value. Each solution concept is expressed by using a well-chosen name along with a concise intent statement.

An example is shown in Figure I.2 (a color rendition is included in this book's color insert). The *cases* of the capability are provided as one or more short stories of the capability in action.

Example stories of the capability in use are what warrant our use of the word "case" in "Capability Case." These *solution stories* are presented in a standard template that we have found effective for communicating Capability Cases in a summary form. The template has a short statement of intent, a headline of solution stories, and a featured story. A featured story is illustrated by a graphic along with an explanation, a list of business benefits, products used to build the capability, as well as other applicable products and technology options.

The *Visual Navigator* example is about the potential use of information maps in different situations. The additional solution stories listed illustrate how the same capability takes different forms in different business contexts. What is common is the value of presenting complex information in a visual metaphor. Within a single Capability Case, all stories share the same essential capability or generalized concept. The relevance of Capability Cases is critically dependent on having solution stories, real or envisioned, that adequately communicate the value of software functionality to stakeholders. They help to stimulate interest in how technology capabilities can be used innovatively to generate business value.

Systems are rarely created by one person. They result from the collaboration of several people. Quality systems come from convergent collaboration. A shared vision of the system serves to align the decision making of several people across different disciplines. Capability Cases provide the necessary vocabulary.

When Capability Cases are adopted in an organization, they become a vocabulary for talking about future systems. Like any common language, they provide a means for overcoming barriers between different stakeholders. For example, the "Instant Messenger" capability is immediately understood by everyone. The power of Capability Cases lies in establishing a common vocabulary for all components of the *future system*.

They also provide insight into problems by showing how related problems and solutions have worked. "Instant Helper," "Answer Engine," "Concept-based Search," and Semantic Form Generator" are additional examples of such capabilities. This book includes several collections or galleries of Capability Cases.

Capability Case:	# Visual Navigator
Intent:	Effectively present and summarize large amounts of information by using visualization technologies. Includes ability to navigate and drill-down for more detail.
Solution Stories:	map.net, **The Hive Group's Amazon Product Map**, Smart Money Stock Market Map, Visual Navigation at HighWire Stanford, Infoscape Webmap.

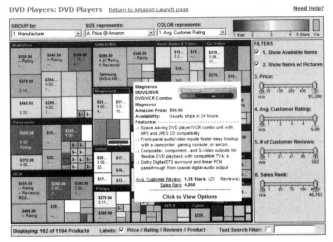

The Hive Group's visual map of Amazon products.

Amazon offers a large number of products. Having to make sense of them all when selecting the right one can be overwhelming. Text browsing of categories and product listings does not produce a pleasant shopping experience. The Hive Group solved this problem by allowing shoppers to use visual maps for exploring product categories using visual cues such as group, size, and color. Shoppers are able to change what group, size, and color represent, thereby selecting the criteria that are important to them. In the example, products are categorized (grouped) by being organized according to manufacturer. The size of the product rectangle corresponds to its price. Colors indicate the popularity of the product as reflected by the number of sales. Maps can be filtered on how good the deal is that's being offered (% of discount), product price, and other attributes. Positioning a cursor over a product displays detailed information.

Business Benefits:	Improved user experience, ability to find the right product among a large number of offerings, increased sales, shortens the discovery process, ability to intuitively guide users to relevant information.
Featured Products:	Honeycomb from The Hive Group
Other Applicable Products:	BrainEKP from The Brain Technologies Corporation, DataVista Spectrum from Visualize, Inc., Inxight Star Tree SDK from Inxight Software, Inc., KartOO from KartOO SA, Metis from Computas, WebMap Server from WebMap Technologies.

FIGURE I.2.   VISUAL NAVIGATOR.

PREVIEW OF IMPORTANT TERMS FOR MODELING THE BUSINESS SITUATION

To facilitate the process of communicating the nature of the situation and to enable root cause analysis, Solution Envisioning requires a business situation to be expressed in terms of core, characterizing elements. These include *business forces* (or drivers), *challenges*, and desired *results* as seen by multiple stakeholders. Another important element is *essential business activity scenarios*.

Together, with Capability Cases, these concepts form the main vocabulary of terms we use for Solution Envisioning with Capability Cases. Sidebar I.1 gives a brief illustration and explanation of each term.

Forces, results, and solution capabilities become meaningful when connected to the work of the business. It is important that stakeholders are helped in the envisioning and capturing of future business activity scenarios. Forces and results are used to describe and situate the scenario steps they affect and to map to relevant Capability Cases.

Sidebar I.1   A Vocabulary for Characterizing the Business Context

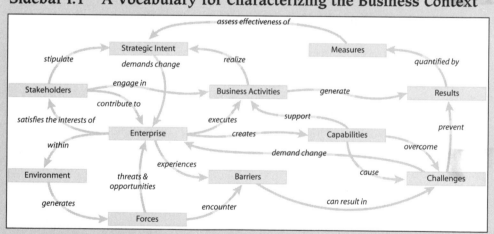

FIGURE I.3.

An enterprise operates within a business environment. A number of parties populate this environment, including the enterprise's investors, customers, suppliers, partners, solution providers, competitors, regulators, and other influencing bodies. Adding in one more vital group—the employees—this environment is the source of the *forces* that determine the business situation. To counter these forces, the business must have the capabilities and configuration to achieve necessary *outcomes*.

Outcomes derive from the desired *results* the business achieves, but also the contributions that are needed from various stakeholders. The design chosen is the enterprise's *business model*. How the business chooses to bring about these outcomes is its *strategic intent*. To deliver this intent, the business must identify and understand its own *barriers* that stand in the way of certain possibilities for operating. These barriers, together with the new possibilities that the business wants to develop, combine to cause key *challenges* that the business must overcome. The business does this by performing processes that use its *capabilities* and *competencies* in the most optimal ways.

HIGHLIGHTING THE MAIN IDEAS AND THREADS OF THE BOOK

For those who may not read every chapter in order, we hope that the following executive summary, which outlines some of the main ideas and threads, will be useful:

- The role of IT has changed. To fulfill their mission, today's IT departments must become trusted intermediaries between technology providers and business units.

- The failure of business, IT, and users to communicate effectively is responsible for many types of IT project failures, including the failure to realize true business value.

- With the wealth of technology options available to business today, making the right technology selection decisions has become a key challenge.

- Successful solution development using components, packages, and Web Services calls for new methods and new ways of working together.

- Technology decisions are best made by interdisciplinary teams with multiple viewpoints present.

- Effective collaboration requires a common language. Establishing this language between business and IT realizes enormous dividends.

- Capability Cases were designed as a precise communication vehicle between stakeholders. When Solution Envisioning with Capability Cases is adopted in an organization, it establishes a vocabulary for talking about future systems.

- Solution Envisioning is a process for working with Capability Cases to design business solutions. It provides a consistent, repeatable, and rapid way of progressing from a business problem understanding to a solution concept.

- By supporting a dialog on *"What the system could be, and what it could do for the business,"* Solution Envisioning becomes an effective enabler of business–IT partnering.

- The deliverable of Solution Envisioning is a conceptual blueprint that serves as a starting point for implementing a business solution using any of the well-established software development practices.

Solution Envisioning with Capability Cases in a Nutshell

The Solution Envisioning process starts with a model of the business situation. Business forces, desired results, and their measures and key business scenarios are identified. Candidate Capability Cases are nominated as a starting point for the solution. Serving as a portfolio of possibilities and solution ideas, Capability Cases encourage creative exploration. Expressed in business terms, the identified solution ideas are mapped to business activities and serve as a shared vocabulary of capabilities, meaningful to all stakeholders. Solution Envisioning continues with the forging of a shared understanding of a solution concept. Technology selection and implementation architecture work then follows.

The Problem Addressed

The business–IT gap is hardly a new topic. Its impact on business and the various approaches for resolving it have been well-chronicled over the last two decades. Many methodologies have come and gone. Structured methods were superseded by object-oriented methods, the waterfall lifecycle by the spiral lifecycle, and informal tools by Computer-Aided Software Engineering (CASE).

Although these approaches to systems analysis and design helped technical people translate requirements into code, they did little to ensure that the right problems were being addressed. Everything rested on the quality of requirements. Verification—"Are we building the system right?"—was more the focus than validation—"Are we building the right system?" Many of these techniques had the reputation of being too cumbersome, slow, and static even at the time they were first introduced. Since then, business expectations of rapid IT solutions have changed by orders of magnitude.

Not surprisingly, a keen interest developed in Rapid Prototyping, Joint Application Development (JAD), and Rapid Application Development (RAD).[2] Each was motivated by the desire to have business people and developers work together to identify what the users really need. These techniques were all designed for custom software development. Today, Agile Methods,[3] in some ways, can be seen as following in the tradition of RAD and JAD [Beck, 1999; Cockburn, 2001b].

Solution Envisioning, having the same motivation for "Rapid Validation" and "Shared Understanding," adopts techniques from JAD and the Agile Methods. What is new is the creative, connective, and expressive power afforded by our use of Capability Cases—*creative* in that they provide a rich space of solution possibilities and stimulate innovative thinking; *connective* because they bridge the worlds of business and IT by using business language to connect solution concepts to business situations; *expressive* because they use solution stories to convey "the case for the capability."

While software development methods were maturing, business strategy and business design methods were also evolving. Porter's Five Forces and Value Chain models gave business people a language for talking about business contexts and for exploring how networks of value could inform business strategy [Porter 1985]. Senge's *systems thinking* work provided techniques for understanding business dynamics [Senge, 1990; 1994]. Kaplan and Norton introduced a business performance measurement approach called the *Balanced Scorecard*, developing their ideas into a method called *Strategy Maps* [Kaplan, 2001; 2004]. Because business today is inseparable from the technology that enables it, these approaches began to enter the world of IT.

In another space, the field of management science, two notable developments for problem understanding and structuring emerged: Checkland's SSM (Soft Systems Methodology) [Checkland, 1981; 1990, Wilson 1984] and Eden's and Ackermann's use of mapping techniques in SODA (Strategic Options Decision Analysis) [Rosenhead, 1989]. SSM has endured well into the present day. Its ideas on conceptual models of the problem and root definitions of viable solutions are used within our Solution Envisioning Method. SODA has evolved into a method for business strategy formulation [Eden, 1998]. We adopt some techniques from these approaches in our work.

---

[2] JAD overcame the slow and faulty communication and feedback that causes a traditional process to fail. Rapid Prototyping uses prototypes to explore what is of interest to the stakeholders. RAD incorporates principles from Tom Gilb's Evolutionary Development [Gilb 1988] with RP and JAD to support fast iterations.

[3] www.agilealliance.org.

Taken on their own, none of these software development, problem-modeling, and business methods addresses "bridging the gap" between business and IT. We found that we had to combine elements from a number of these approaches along with pattern language ideas and decision support techniques for technology selection to build our Solution Envisioning approach.

Today, the acceleration of business and technology change has made it a challenge to choose and become proficient in a development method that will assure timely business results. Because today's technology offers the ability to quickly deploy very powerful solutions, organizations often elect to jump directly into these solutions rather than go through a traditional business requirements process. Simply stated, businesses cannot justify the benefits and do not have the time to use rigorous methodology.

One response is component-based approaches and Web Services. These have simulated a renewed interest in a dynamic reuse-based approach to constructing IT solutions. We are motivated to bring reuse to the earliest part of the development lifecycle and present *Solution Envisioning with Capability Cases* as a method for the appreciation, reuse, and adaptation of solution concepts. Of particular relevance is the way Capability Cases are useful for component-based strategies for developing solutions, such as Service-Oriented Architectures with Web Services.

When Can Solution Envisioning Be Used?

Simply stated, any project that has to consider how technology can make a difference is a perfect candidate for Solution Envisioning with Capability Cases. The process can be used both to create new solutions and to improve existing solutions. For assembling pre-made (packaged) components, it offers an effective way to identify, select, and establish an integration plan. For defining new capabilities, it invites stakeholders to consider a more comprehensive set of solution possibilities.

The problems that Solution Envisioning addresses are the key to the success of any technology project. However, we note that there are projects where these problems are especially critical—in fact, where they dominate the effort. These are the projects that target the creation of new business capabilities through the adoption of emerging or "breakthrough" technologies. With the increasingly rapid evolution of technology, these cases are becoming more of the norm than the exception. Here, we find ourselves inventing new names for capabilities, envisioning stories of their potential value, and inviting stakeholders into creative discourse. A current example is Semantic Web Technology,[4] a disruptive technology that is emerging rapidly.[5] This book includes a number of Capability Cases that use Semantic Technology.

A Trail Map for the Book: The Journey Ahead

Structured as three integrated but separable parts, this book is accessible to readers ranging from business executives to practitioners to change agents and practice leaders:

Part I explains the rationale for and business value of using Solution Envisioning. The intended audience includes C-level executives, IT managers, business analysts, and solution architects responsible for making decisions about technology investments.

Part II is a practitioner's handbook that provides a step-by-step guide in three progressive phases: *Business Capability Exploration*, *Solution Capability Envisioning*, and *Software Capability Design*. Practitioners include those responsible for organizing, conducting, and participating in solution envisioning engagements: business decision makers and analysts, enterprise architects, project managers, technology specialists, and software developers.

Part III answers the question: "How do we set up, tailor, and implement Solution Envisioning as a practice?" Through example cases, it shows how Solution Envisioning can be adapted to the needs of different situations. For change agents, champions, and others charged with implementing best practices, it provides additional guidance for planning, setting up, tailoring, and implementing Solution Envisioning.

The chapters in Part II of this book include a collection of techniques that are part of the Solution Envisioning method. These include critical thinking, root cause analysis, and exploration of known solution examples. We have also included a number of templates to assist the reader in developing key work products, such as a business case, concept of operations, architectural decisions, and non-functional requirements.

---

[4]   Key W3C standards, OWL and RDF/S, that support the Semantic Web became official recommendations on 2/10/2004.

[5]   One of the authors, Ralph Hodgson, co-authored a book with Jeff Pollock that featured many Capability Cases for Semantic Technology [Pollock, 2004].

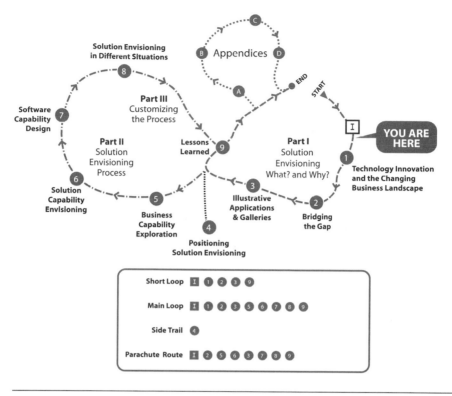

FIGURE I.4.

The end of this book provides indexes for techniques and templates. Although these techniques are an integral part of Solution Envisioning method, they can be (and have been) used productively on their own.

There are a number of ways to approach this book. Some suggested routes are depicted in the following trail map:

The core sequence of chapters is represented in the trail map as the "Main Loop."

Senior IT managers and business people may want to focus on the Introduction, Chapters 1, 2, 3, and 9—a "short loop." For a more a comprehensive overview, we recommend also reading Chapters 4 and 8. Some readers may also want to consult Appendix A.

Some readers may want to quickly jump into a more in-depth exposure to the process and techniques. They are likely to be experienced practitioners very familiar with the issues surrounding the business–IT gap and the recent changes in the world of business technology. We recognize these readers could become frustrated by the fact that we do not get into the details of Solution Envisioning and step-by-step instructions of applying it until Chapter 5. We suggest these readers take the "parachute route." This covers Chapters 2, 5, 6, 3, and 7, in that order, and, optionally, Chapters 8 and 9 for tips on getting started. Many of these readers may also want to consult the extra material in Appendices B and C.

Chapter 4 is an optional side excursion that may provide useful insights to many readers, whether taken in order or revisited. It explores the intent and design of Solution Envisioning, examining what makes it different and where it fits in the overall solution delivery process.

PART I

SOLUTION ENVISIONING: WHAT? AND WHY?

CONTENT

PURPOSE

To explain what Solution Envisioning with Capability Cases is, the rationale for creating it, and the business value of using it.

KEY QUESTIONS ADDRESSED

Why do we need Solution Envisioning, and what is it?

ORIENTATION

Solution Envisioning with Capability Cases focuses on the front-end of developing information technology (IT) solutions. Mistakes made here about "what to build" carry the most cost and risk penalties. As business and technology change accelerates, attention on the front-end becomes more important, but more demanding. The role of IT has changed from a pure technology role to a business solution provider role. Technology choices are increasingly diverse. IT and business people, although they don't call it by this name, increasingly engage in "Envisioning Solutions"—looking at new technology and envisioning the results that will come from technology initiatives. This book provides a process and methods for that essential work.

Solution Envisioning is a problem-discovery, situation-assessment, and solution-planning process that uses Capability Cases to achieve connections between Business and IT. In Solution Envisioning, two key questions are addressed: "Have we identified the right business opportunities and challenges?" and "Have we fully appreciated how technology can help us?" Two key innovations are at work: *interplay of technology possibilities with desired business outcomes and a language for business situations linked to capabilities*.

For enterprises grappling with changing business and technical realities, Solution Envisioning provides an approach needed to explore powerful new solution ideas, apply them cost-effectively to solve core business problems, deliver value, and realize opportunities.

PRIMARY AUDIENCE

The main audience for this book is business executives responsible for making decisions about technology investments and others responsible for identifying and communicating the value of technology to the business, hence influencing decision-making.

1

TECHNOLOGY INNOVATION AND THE CHANGING BUSINESS LANDSCAPE

"Our Age of Anxiety is, in great part, the result of trying to do today's jobs with yesterday's tools."

—Marshall McLuhan

FIGURE 1.1.

CHAPTER PREVIEW

This chapter explores risks and consequences that arise from miscommunication between business and IT. Many readers may find the situations described by the following questions all too familiar:

- If you are a businessperson, have you been in situations where communicating your business needs, strategies, and goals to technical people meant having to translate them into unfamiliar notations and models?

- If you are a technologist, have you ever found yourself striving to explain to non-technical people the merits of your proposal?

- As an architect or developer, have you had to implement requirements without fully understanding the reasons behind the need for the functionality?

- As a business executive or program manager, have you ever been responsible for choosing between technical solutions that you couldn't distinguish from one another?

These challenges are not new, but the acceleration of business and technology change in the last decade has raised them to a different level. Therefore, they are examined in the context of the recent changes in the role of IT—from a pure technology role to a business solution provider role—and the accompanying rapid evolution of technology. These changes have taken solution developers from the simpler world of making decisions about what programming language to use to a much more complex world of making mission-critical choices about components, solutions, platforms, architectures, and standards.

The communications gap between business and technical people arises because of the differences in perspectives, languages, and vocabularies used by business strategists, solution users, IT, and technology evangelists. By using the languages of both business and technical communities, Solution Envisioning with Capability Cases provides a way to connect solution concepts to the business situation and supports the new role IT is required to play in today's enterprise. We conclude the chapter with a story that begins to illustrate how Solution Envisioning can make a difference in the communication, planning, and realization of business solutions.

UNDERSTANDING BUSINESS CHALLENGES AND IT REQUIREMENTS

The twenty-first century started not with the much-feared year 2000 systems breakdown, but with continued struggle to use technology effectively to support the business. With information technology now an integral part of most business operations, what effect is this having on the economy overall and on individual businesses? The Standish Group report talks about IT project cost overruns of $55 billion in 2002.[1,2] Gartner estimates a total of $75 billion losses a year. Others cite even larger numbers. Ravi Kalakota and Marcia Robinson say in their book, *Services Blueprint: Roadmap for Execution* [Kalakota, 2003]:

> *"Execution is the science of turning multi-million dollar application and infrastructure investments into results. This is proving to be harder than expected....more than $100 billion per year is flushed down the drain because of poor execution. Poof! It is gone."*

In any large company, it is easy to find examples in the millions of dollars. In many cases, companies can't say how fruitful their IT investments really are because they don't have ways to define and measure successes or failures. Is this a situation that businesses just have to accept? We think not.[3]

There are effective ways for business and IT to partner on successful business solutions. Our motivation for writing this book is to offer practical guidance and techniques for the creation of value-driven IT solutions, including the following:

- A strategy for achieving competitive advantage through effective linkage of technology and business strategies
- A well-defined approach for making strategic decisions that guarantee more efficient spending on technology

---

[1] According to the Standish Group's most recent CHAOS research on project success and failure in the U.S., just 34% of the 13,522 IT projects tackled in 2002 were considered a success. Just over half (51%) of projects were challenged, and 15% were failures. The research firm estimates projects, on average, yielded cost overruns of 43% and time overruns of 82%. In addition, only 52% of required features and functions made it into the released product. Findings are reported at http://www.nwfusion.com/news/2004/1012ibmsys.html.

[2] There is no question that many improvements in software development and project management methodologies introduced in the 1980s and 1990s have resulted in significant progress. A Standish Group report published in 1995 estimated the cost of overruns at the time to be $78 billion per year.

[3] This team of authors first met at IBM while working on major application development projects for external customers of IBM Global Services.

- A common framework for communication and working relationships between business and IT
- A process designed to accelerate selection and configuration of available IT solutions and integration of new component capabilities
- A reliable set of techniques for reducing the risk of failure of business initiatives and for maximizing return on investment (ROI)

The word "solution" implies there is a business problem to solve or a business opportunity to realize. Requirements help us understand the nature of problems and opportunities. The word "requirements" often means different things to the various people working together to realize business solutions. Types and levels of requirements have been categorized and defined in many ways.

Linda A. Macaulay [Macaulay, 1996] gives a simple definition of a requirement as "something which a customer needs," noting that, from a designer's point of view, a requirement could be defined as "something that needs to be designed." Karl E. Wiegers [Wiegers, 1999] distinguishes between business requirements, user requirements, functional requirements, and non-functional requirements (See Sidebar 1.1).

The broad and growing availability of packaged solutions, components, and web services brings a need to differentiate between business requirements, component selection requirements, and requirements as blueprints for component construction. These differing types of requirements satisfy different goals. Their clarification and specification may need to be undertaken in different ways. We define these three types of requirements as follows:

- **Business requirements**—Clearly defined and measurable goals and objectives a solution must realize. Business requirements are captured in the documents describing the vision, the scope, and the concept of an enterprise system. Today, with the increased attention on business value and ROI from enterprise systems, these documents form an integral part of a business case. Business requirements determine the design of the system.

- **Component selection requirements**—These include key capabilities, decision criteria, and constraints necessary for making selection and purchase decisions for business solution components. These may include large-grained components like CRM (customer relationship management) packages as well as small to medium components such as web conferencing, credit-card authorization, and package shipment service ala FedEx or UPS.

- **Component construction requirements**—The specifications that are necessary for realizing solution architecture as a software system constructed from components.

This book addresses what might be termed "conceptual requirements" for enterprise business applications—requirements that express the conceptual essence of the IT solutions being sought. Conceptual requirements cover both business needs and component selection needs. They clarify the nature of the business problem and identify attributes of the solution. When the concept of the solution is clear, it then can be designed.

With Solution Envisioning, we show how to turn solution concepts into designs that realize business capabilities. The three phases of Solution Envisioning are

I.   Business Capability Exploration

II.   Solution Capability Envisioning

III.   Software Capability Design

As indicated by the names and progression of phases, the process encompasses the following: gaining an understanding of needed Business Capabilities (Phase I), mapping these to enabling technology capabilities or Solution Capabilities (Phase II), and finally, converting the solution concept into a Software Capability Design that can be implemented (Phase III). These three phases are discussed in further detail in the three chapters that make up Part II of this book.

Informing Business Strategy with Views of Technology Possibilities

In the past, companies too often looked at technology as an answer, choosing it before understanding their business needs. They struggled to design their business around technology. This approach didn't work well. An equally costly mistake is to ignore technology when designing a business model. Knowing what is possible through the use of technology shapes our thinking of the problem.

In *24/7 Innovation*, Stephen Shapiro [Shapiro, 2001] offers many examples of new technology inspiring ideas for business processes that lifted the respective businesses to an entirely new level of excellence. On enabling business innovation through technology, he offers this advice:

> *"Make sure that new processes and new technology solutions are designed in tandem. Start exploring technology options early in the process redesign stage."*

To strike the careful balance needed for this kind of "tandem design," Solution Envisioning uses exploration of the possible solution space as one of the primary means for getting a better understanding of the business problem that needs addressed and the possibilities of new business ideas. A theme also addressed by Peter Weill and Jeanne W. Ross in the book *IT Governance* [Weill, 2004] is *how new information technologies bombard enterprises with new business opportunities.*

Sidebar 1.1 Speaking of Requirements—Use Cases and Capability Cases

Many of the well-known requirements books are about methods and techniques for developing system use cases. These methods expect that the business value, the concept, and the high-level design of the system—the main topics covered in this book—have already been well-defined by the time use case development starts.

In defining the business concepts of enterprise systems, we use the construct of the *Capability Case*. Capability Cases serve as a common language used by the different stakeholders—Business and IT—to discuss, evaluate, and make commitments to solution capabilities. Why introduce Capability Cases as a way to define business requirements and solution concepts?

Readers knowledgeable in software development methodologies may assume the application area of Capability Cases is similar to that of *Business Use Cases* and *Essential Use Cases*. However, use cases are not designed for capturing the concept of a system or its business value. Alistair Cockburn in his book *Writing Effective Use Cases* [Cockburn, 2001a] points out that: "A use case only documents a process, it doesn't reengineer or re-design it. In creating the design, the designers take a leap of invention. The use cases do not tell them how to do that."

The goal of a Use Case is to describe in some detail the interaction between a user and the system—to capture both normal or successful flows of interaction events and abnormal or exceptional flow of events as alternative paths through the use case. A Capability Case, on the other hand, is designed to capture the business value of different aspects of the system—its capabilities. Its focus is very different from the use case focus and, therefore, deserves a construct of its own.

The idea of distinguishing *capability* for business requirements was first established in the "Sense and Respond" work of Steve Haeckel.[4] This work views an enterprise as a composition of its capabilities to respond to situations in the business ecology in order to deliver desired business outcomes. Such an enterprise is adaptive—it can re-configure its capabilities to meet changing demands. Haeckel's Sense and Respond work is about business capabilities. The focus of this book is on IT capabilities that support and enable businesses. These are known as *capability enablers* in the adaptive enterprise approach.

---

[4] Steve Haeckel. *Adaptive Enterprise: Creating and Leading Sense-and-Respond Organizations* [Haeckel, 1999].

The Changing Role of IT

In the last decade of the twentieth century, IT professionals have traveled a difficult road amid the rapidly changing landscape of business technology and *expectations creep*. At some point during the journey, expectations that businesses placed on their IT departments changed. In the past, IT was the main developer and maintainer of a company's applications and systems. The most crucial responsibilities of today's IT executives and managers are

- Identifying enabling technology that will deliver business capabilities and value

- Performing their role at minimum cost with maximum fidelity

- Presenting recommendations to business decision makers in the most effective way for making the right decisions

- Managing projects, not only to meet the budget and schedule, but also to deliver expected business benefits

What has caused these changes in responsibility for IT managers and departments? Among many trends, some key influences stand out, all reflecting changes in expectations of what technology does and can do for businesses:

- Maturing of the software industry with many business solutions and components available out-of-the-box

- An increasingly complex range of technology options

- Expansion of the Internet and its new business models and solutions that provide capabilities to users

The pace of change has been accelerating over the last five years with new technology options, solutions, and capabilities appearing daily. To fulfill their new role, today's IT departments must become trusted intermediaries between technology providers and business units. They must continually enhance the capabilities of the business by harnessing the potential of technology.

The gap between business and IT is now a key obstacle in fulfilling the IT department's organizational mission. Figure 1.2 illustrates the changing role of the IT specialist in terms of the change in demands that IT personnel must fulfill in 2005 compared to 1989.

1989 IT Specialist	2005 IT Specialist
Somewhat aware of the gap, but really doesn't care about it or "mind it"	Can not be effective in his job without a way to cross the gap
Developer	**Provider of Business Solutions**

FIGURE 1.2.   A GROWING GAP BETWEEN IT AND AGILE, TECHNOLOGY-EN-ABLED BUSINESS SOLUTIONS.

Table 1.1 identifies some key changes in the business and technology environment that have caused a profound shift in the role of IT.

TABLE 1.1.   THE CHANGING ROLE OF IT

IT Competencies	1989	2005
Technology Skills	**Narrow, but deep**	**Broad, but relatively shallow**
	A homogenous computing environment means that IT departments need to have deep knowledge in a relatively small number of technologies. The majority of IT departments are self-sufficient in the breadth and depth of technical skills required. Subcontract labor is used for tactical extensions of the workforce.	A heterogeneous computing environment requires a broad range of technical skills few IT departments can afford. This results in transitioning IT from a technology developer and implementer to technology recommender and manager. Subcontractors are viewed as strategic partners.
Technology Evaluation	**Manageable choices**	**Diverse choices**
	Choices are limited with the standard computing platforms firmly established.	There is a wide choice of solutions and options (for example, we know that CRM products are being offered by over 400 vendors) and little time to make sense of them. Often, crucial capabilities are overlooked or misunderstood.
Project Management	**Not recognized as a profession**	**Central to IT**

TABLE 1.1. THE CHANGING ROLE OF IT—CONTINUED

IT Competencies	1989	2005
Communication	An afterthought	A key competency
	Most of the day-to-day work is about building and supporting large custom-built systems. IT professionals communicate primarily with one another.	Required not only to work effectively with lines of business, but also with numerous vendors, partners, and suppliers. Communications skills are tested to the extreme with IT systems often being built by distributed teams.
Generating Ideas	In narrow technical domains	In broader business domains
Business Acumen	IT is viewed as a cost center	IT is expected to drive business
		We have encountered a growing body of supporting evidence for this shift. One example is a 2003 Forrester Research Technographics Study. It found that 59% of business unit executives view customer acquisition and retention as a top priority for their IT.[5]
Research	Limited	Extensive

IT Imperatives and Governance

The state of affairs outlined in the previous sections can also be framed in terms of key IT imperatives that must be mastered to succeed in the world that governs today's business environment. The problems described in the following four imperatives are widespread in the industry. To deal with the implications of these imperatives, CIOs need to ensure they have the right processes in place to support making more optimal decisions around launching, managing, and delivering value from solution initiatives. Additionally, we strongly suggest that CFOs refrain from authorizing any spending on implementing or improving business applications until they know these processes have been adopted and are being practiced. The following are some recommendations we make in this book.

---

[5]   *VarBusiness Magazine*, April 28, 2003, page 60.

1: Find an Optimal Way to Present Technology Possibilities to Non-Technical People

It is interesting to note that most of the process improvement initiatives in IT have been about furthering Project Management methodologies. This is an important step, but one that doesn't address core requirements of the new role: business innovation, ability to communicate complex technical concepts in business terms, technology research, and a framework for making decisions and recommending solutions.

According to Robert Reich's[6] analysis of economic trends surrounding IT work in the United States:

> *"Millions of people around the world can and will learn the necessary computer language. In order to justify their high salaries, America's future IT workers will need to be more like management consultants, strategists, and troubleshooters."*[7]

Yet today, IT departments are still using methodologies from the time when requirements engineering and solution design were about creating a detailed specification for writing code. The main focus of software requirements processes and workshops remains trying to capture business ideas in the highly structured languages of IT-oriented models. Too often, this work is not about understanding business goals, exploring technology potential, and creating solutions together, but instead about trying to capture specific details of the future system using notations established by software development methodologies.

2: Implement Effective Collaboration Between Technical and Non-Technical People

The distance between a business idea and a detailed data model or an interaction diagram is huge, so this imperative is a tall order. In some cases, business people are not able to answer highly specific questions asked by technical people. Answering these questions requires "living in the future." This means envisioning the new ways of working and the changes in the business environment that will invariably result from implementing a solution.

In other cases, requirements specification documents quickly become too prescriptive and detailed in describing interaction flows of the future system. In counterpoint, they are typically too brief about the business reasons for the system and the

---

[6] U.S. Secretary of Labor during President Clinton's administration.

[7] *CIO Magazine*, Fall/Winter 2003; this was a special issue featuring the theme "technology's impact on everything."

business results to be accomplished. This often results in a large volume of documentation that is too complex to communicate well to either the business or the development team. It is no wonder that business people and developers alike are too often perplexed and unhappy about the mutual work process! And, it is no surprise that the results leave a lot of room for improvement. Karl Wiegers[8] describes a project where a development team was faced with a dozen three-inch thick binders of requirements specified by the requirements team. The developers just shuddered in horror, turned away, and started to write code. They effectively ignored requirements documentation. The project did not go well.

One of the authors of this book had a similar experience while working on a large order-tracking-and-billing system that took two years to implement. The requirements document was a two-foot high printout. Developers who were part of the project from the beginning were not well-versed in the document. They found it too daunting and preferred to rely on their own memory. Developers who were added to the team mid-stream preferred reading the actual code and talking to solution users and other technical team members instead of trying to understand the requirements document. Wiegers also talks about how often business sponsors commit similar "sins"—for example, they sign off on requirements documents without truly reading them.

This brings up a topic that scientists characterize as "cognitive affordances." In simple terms, it means the type and degree of communication that can be successfully achieved by an artifact as determined by how well it matches the cognitive needs and styles of the intended audience. Requirements documentation, including text, models, graphics, and so on should offer a high-degree of cognitive affordance to the people who must understand and use it—otherwise, they won't! The greater the gap between the languages and vocabularies of the people on the "receiving end" and the people on the "transmitting end," the larger the document must become. Unfortunately, in most situations, the communication value of the document decreases as its size grows.

3: Avoid the "Build One to Get Agreement" Syndrome

In a recent conversation, a Project Manager we know (we'll call him "Dave"), said:

> *"I know that there is no other way to build software than to just start building it. I know that I will get the capabilities wrong. When that fact is brought to my attention, I will fix it. I realize that I may be doing things three or four times over, but there is no other way."*

---

[8]   Karl E. Wiegers. *Software Requirements* [Wiegers, 1999].

Dave is using a "build one to throw away" approach[9]—create something, then see if it is the *right* thing. This is the basic *fallback* approach (generate-and-test) to solving problems when we really don't know how to solve them. Such practices indicate a very immature state of the art in software design and underlay some of the reasons why billions of dollars are being wasted on unsuccessful IT projects.

The conclusion can be drawn that software technology and its potential capabilities are maturing faster than existing IT integration, development, and management processes can support.

Dave "solved" the expensive problem of software rework by involving an offshore development firm. He now pays 60% less for a developer and can run more "build one to throw away" cycles for less money.

> *"With on-site developers, we would sometimes redo things 3 times. With offshore, the communication problems are greater, so we may end up redoing it 4 or 5 times, but I am still ahead because I am paying less per hour."*

Because he is only responsible for the cost of development, any extra time his business sponsors must spend to test and catch what is wrong with the solution is not part of his budget. The time elapsed, and the possible loss of business opportunity resulting from this implementation approach, is also not included in his narrow cost calculation.

4: Component, Package, and Web Services Developments Call for New Methods

Today, with many pre-built business applications available, the "build one to throw away" approach carries another kind of exposure. Significant risks are entailed in

---

[9]   The need for iteration in software development was first introduced by Fred Brooks [Brooks, 1974] and developed further by Tom Gilb with his work on "Evolutionary Development." Elaborated in recent times by "Extreme Programming" and the "Agile Methods" community, iteration has now become an essential part of most development projects. It is important to remember that iteration is not a goal in itself. It is a necessary activity in the presence of uncertainty and is one way to support a convergence of understanding and obtain agreement about what is needed. Unnecessary or unproductive iterations can be both expensive and risky. The more iterations of the goal or desired solution that you can achieve using less expensive media—different from the target media (for example, code) but which are sufficient to represent the solution—and the more options you can explore quickly (preferably at the same time), the less overall risk and the greater overall value return. There is one aspect of iteration that can operate as an end in itself—the degree to which it creates a space for people to interact.

committing to a packaged application. Often, this requires large upfront expenses for software purchases early in the cycle of understanding business needs and the right solution capabilities.

Later in the cycle, it is often the case that the real requirements finally become clear. Then it is realized the solution cannot be customized or integrated to meet these requirements. In this situation, the upfront expenses are either money lost or the initial investment in a continued struggle to make the compromised solution work. For these reasons, technology selection has become a key early activity in the development process. To be effective, it must cover platform technologies, processing engines, small and large business applications, and components. All these implementation choices are faced early and may be critical to the success of the solution.

Coupling Business Vision to Technology Enablers

According to a recent survey,[10] the number-one priority for CIOs is finding best practices for partnering with business units and delivering the greatest value to the organization. In fact, CIOs reported spending 26% of their time meeting with their business counterparts. This means that the CIO role has expanded beyond driving the strategy for IT to driving the strategy for the business. The economic forces described by Robert Reich are already transforming IT departments, bringing significant business benefits.

One such example is International Sugar's amazing journey out of bankruptcy [Ferranti, 2003]. The only surviving manager in the company was the CIO. He helped transform the way International Sugar works with its customers. The company used to have people who spent all the day on the phone with customers. Now the customers use the web portal. As a result, the company won business for its commodity product simply because it used technology to make it easy to work with.

Some forward-thinking CIOs recognized early on the Internet's transformative capacity as an infrastructure for realizing new business models. A case in point is the story of how the CIO of Transamerica Leasing used the Internet in 1997 to create new revenue for the company. He was the driving force behind an exchange network between companies in the container shipping business. The idea of the exchange was to identify and dynamically utilize surplus inventory. At different ports around the globe, each network member could match their needs against the available pool of containers. This and many stories like it are clear examples of how technology can be an inspiration for new ways of doing business.

---

[10]   *CIO Magazine*, April 2003.

What do these stories tell us? For one thing, they suggest the book shelves of this new breed of IT managers are just as likely to have books on business strategy as they are books on the latest technology. They also highlight the need for new approaches that can help technology-driven business innovation to happen more effectively. This book provides concrete methods and guidance for addressing this need.

Making Decisions Within a Growing Universe of Technology Choices

A view of today's technology landscape leads inescapably to the realization that somewhere around the mid-1990s, we experienced the equivalent of a Big Bang. An entire new universe of technology options exploded onto the scene. For instance, focusing on just a typical customer service problem (see the example story later in this chapter), we see an expanding variety of technology options, as illustrated in Figure 1.3.

People who have to make business technology decisions today typically find themselves in a situation not unlike that of the proverbial kid in a candy store. With so

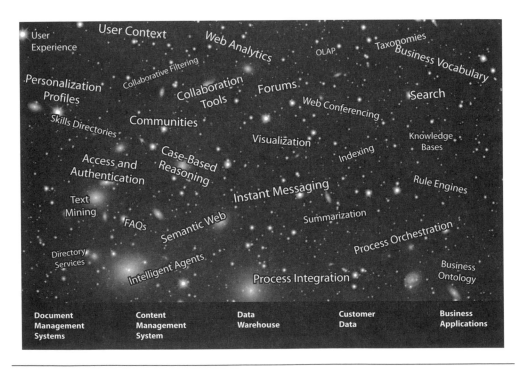

FIGURE 1.3. AN EVER-EXPANDING UNIVERSE OF INFORMATION MANAGEMENT TECHNOLOGIES.

many options to choose from, how does a company know the best way to move forward? This is a point well made by Steven Shapiro:[11]

> *"Today the problem is one of choice. There is such a wealth of technology available with the potential to revolutionize whole industries that evaluation and selection have become the first potential pitfall. No one person can be sufficiently expert to take advantage of all the opportunities that new technologies present."*

Today, business technology decisions have to be made by interdisciplinary teams with multiple viewpoints present. As hard as it is for one person or a group of people with a common point of view to choose among many options, the situation becomes infinitely more complex when a diverse group of people must formulate a solution. A decision now has to be made by a team where each tcam member understands a different part of the puzzle that is involved in making the best choice.

FIGURE 1.4.

---

[11] Steven Shapiro. *24/7 Innovation: A Blueprint for Surviving and Thriving in an Age of Change* [Shapiro 2001].

When decisions are hard to make, many non-optimal patterns of behavior begin to emerge, for example:

- **Follow the Market Leader**—A safe choice based on the motto that "no one was ever fired for choosing IBM"
- **Get the Most Complete Solution**—Going after all the bells and whistles in the growing selection of available features
- **Align with the Infrastructure**—A decision based on the infrastructure compatibility and the existing technical knowledge

With business stakes so high, one more pattern often prevails that can lead to less than desirable results—not making a decision. When decisions are forced, blame and disappointment soon follows.

Supporting the New Role of IT

Even for established, well-adopted technologies, it is difficult for decision makers to determine the business value of a technology in a particular situation simply through an explanation of the technology. It is necessary to see candidate technologies in a context where they are providing business value. This need becomes even stronger when there is an emerging technology that is introducing new capabilities and paradigms. Some of the risks include the following:

- If business determines the solution without establishing a shared vision with IT, it may not take full advantage of what is possible through technology and available solution frameworks and components.
- If IT makes solution decisions without fully understanding the business context and objectives, results will not deliver expected value.
- When architectural thinking is not present in the design process, the resulting system will not hold together.
- With so many solution options and ideas readily available—some in a directly executable form such as web services—specifying solutions in a vacuum, without being informed by what already exists, is a luxury few businesses can afford.

To address these problems, you need a powerful communication vehicle able to bring together business and technology perspectives. It must facilitate the interplay of problem/situation understanding and the formulation of solutions, including software, hardware, communications, people, and information. Research and reuse should be at the core of the approach. Finally, it needs to be supported by a way of working that ensures each party can make its contribution and be heard in the most effective way.

AN ILLUSTRATIVE STORY OF SOLUTION ENVISIONING

Backdrop—Consequences of Communication Failures

Whoever said, "We spend a lot of time *communicating*, but very little *in communication*," might well have been speaking about the communication breakdowns that happen in software development.

The advice frequently given for addressing communication issues is to bring business people and IT people closer—have them at the same table, in shared conversations—in short, working together. Yet, the right advice without a powerful way to establish a common understanding and a shared language is likely to result in the conversations that are frustrating for both groups.

Story: "A Quest for Self-Service"

We illustrate the communications challenge with a story involving a business executive at Secure Investments, a major financial services firm. He was charged with optimizing his company's customer service and support operations.

The executive decided that to reduce costs the company must improve its web-based self-service capabilities. Soon after making this decision, he called on the IT department and explained that in order to move more customers to the self-service channel, the search options and results delivered on Secure Investments' website must be greatly improved.

"Why," he wondered, "do I find things on Google, but I never get the right information when I search through our content? Surely, our problem is much smaller than the one Google has to deal with. I've heard that we can now buy a Google appliance. What do you think?"

Two alternative versions for the story's outcome are given in Sidebars 1.2 and 1.3. The first is the all-too-common unhappy outcome and the second has a successful outcome for the business.

Sidebar 1.2 First Alternative—Take One

...The IT manager was not sure; he wanted to consult his staff and do some research. They decided to meet in a week; later, the IT Manager brought along one of his technical specialists to the meeting. The business executive was told the technical reasons why Google would not work in their situation. The IT specialists talked about hyperlinks, page ranking algorithms, and dynamic, database-driven content. Five minutes into the presentation, the executive wanted to move away from the technical explanation because it didn't make sense to him. He always half suspected that all the technical jargon was just a way to justify the high costs of IT. The IT manager suggested creating a team including support desk, marketing, and technical experts to choose the solution. A project was born.

The team started by identifying requirements, but they couldn't come up with much except for "the search must be better." Realizing that many self-service solutions were available, they decided to identify and interview vendors. Soon, a short list of eight products was created. One vendor offered a complete content management solution with a robust search engine. Another featured customizable frameworks for building CRM applications. A third vendor had a full solution for managing and capturing support desk interactions with customers based on associative technology and so on. One of the vendors even volunteered to create a demonstrator. After talking to vendors, the team created a large spreadsheet with all kinds of features. The spreadsheet grew and became more complex with rankings and ratings.

FIGURE 1.5.

Two months had passed, but the team was not getting any closer to making a decision. They were not sure how to decide: The solution capabilities were all very different; the claims about the unique advantages of each vendor technology were confusing. Each vendor had success stories that looked impressive, but which solution would work best for them? IT liked the customizability and Java-based architecture of one vendor. The support desk liked the content authoring tools and rich features of another vendor.

The project got stuck for months with no one wanting to make a decision. Finally, pressured by the business executive, the team chose a solution that the support desk people felt was best for authoring content and linking potential questions with answers. The package was procured, the training completed, the migration was being planned.

One day, during the final stages of the migration, the business executive came back excited after a trip to a customer service conference and said that he became aware of some issues that come along with the improved self service as well as potential solutions:

"You see, if we get more people using self-service, then the greater proportion of calls to the support desk will be about solving complex problems. We need to be ready to deal with this change. Otherwise, our current help desk operation will not be able to take advantage of better self-service and we will not realize expected savings. How about we add to our new search an ability to route the requests to the right service person, the one with the most expertise on the topic, and we also post the self-service dialog into a call center application screen so the customer-service rep knows what has been explored before?"

The IT manager promised to investigate the idea.

A week later, the IT manager and one of his technical specialists explained to the business executive that the package they were implementing didn't have the capability he was looking for. Furthermore, given the solution's technical architecture, which they explained in great detail, it was hard to add functionality or integrate it with another solution that had the desired functionality. In addition, this request would require integration with the mainframe-based call center systems. It was not impossible; however, for a number of highly technical reasons, it was a complex and expensive undertaking. In fact, this addition would cost more than the entire project they were about to finish. The business executive felt like he was experiencing déjà vu. Frustrated, he asked:

"Why would you implement a system that doesn't allow me to do what I need?"

The IT manager quickly pointed out that this new request was not part of the original requirements. A stalemate ensued.

Sidebar 1.3   Second Alternative—Cut and Retake

...The IT manager was not sure; he wanted to consult his staff and do some research. They decided to meet in a week. A week later, the IT manager and the business executive met. The IT manager said:

"I am sure there are ways for us to leverage technology. Google may be one of the options, but first let me ask—have you thought of how much you want to save by improving self-service?"

The business executive talked about how much it cost to service phone requests and his conclusion that moving an additional 10% of customer calls to the self-service channel would save about $150,000 a month. He also shared a number of interesting facts about operating the support desk. After a half hour, the IT manager was able to say:

"Now that I know more about your objectives, let me put together a portfolio of technology capabilities that can work in our environment and deliver the kind of results you are looking for."

FIGURE 1.6.

They agreed to review the portfolio and use a workshop setting to select the capabilities together with a team of support center and marketing experts. Two technologists prepared for the workshop by researching solution options and assembling a portfolio. They were responsible for conducting and facilitating the session.

The business customers (for the solution) were also busy preparing. They started by creating a list of changes in the business environment that became evident over the last few years. They listed possible effects of deploying a new self-service solution, such as work process changes. Finally, they defined the results that they were looking to see from the new solution and identified a measurement for each result. The IT manager explained that this information would help the workshop discover and design the best solution—one that focuses on results and takes into account the needs and changing dynamics of the business.

The portfolio presented during the workshop featured about a dozen different capabilities known to reduce customer service costs. The IT team was able to reuse some of the capabilities they had identified two months ago as candidates for the new financial advisor portal. Even though these "Capability Cases" represented solutions that were possible to realize by using technology and products from a number of different vendors, they were all presented in one common format. Illustrated by the stories of how the capabilities were being used, they were easy to understand, assess, and compare.

The team found one capability most fitting their immediate situation and needs—"Answer Engine." This capability is shown in the galleries of the case studies in Chapter 3, "Illustrative Applications and Galleries." During the discussion about business environment changes, one point kept coming up—how the product lines they were servicing had grown and become more complex in the past couple of years. Specialization had incrementally increased resulting in the situation that few reps were able to handle all the questions. "Instant Helper," one of the capabilities featured in the portfolio, gave the team the idea of capturing self-service interactions and routing the request to the right people according to their specialization and expertise. They also realized how many different products and technologies were available, and they talked about the importance of architecting a solution that would allow them to leverage existing capabilities as well as expand and add new capabilities as their needs grew. Finally, they discussed appropriate measures that would enable them to assess the success of the solution and the respective data they would need to collect to make the assessment.

With desired capabilities selected and a phased approach to implementation identified, the IT specialists worked on choosing among a few vendors that offered an "Answer Engine" type of capability while ensuring that there was a framework for incorporating future capabilities. The selection process only took a couple of weeks, and two months later, the solution went live. After the first three months, the solution exceeded the expectations with a 12% increase in the self service. The IT team was working on integrating the rule-based "Instant Helper" into the next release. The business executive was as impressed by the breadth of solution options and the understanding of the problem displayed by the IT department as he was by the quick execution. He decided to include the IT manager in his business unit's monthly management meetings and is now looking forward to hearing more ideas on how technology could be helpful.

What We Have Here Is a *Failure to Communicate*

What makes the first and the second stories so different?

In the first story, the business and IT people at Secure Investments tried to work together. They formed an interdisciplinary team. They attended meetings together, and they talked to each other. The missing ingredient was having a way of working together that would allow the team to take advantage of each others' strengths while working towards a common vision. They talked, but they did not communicate.

A key insight from the story is that solution requirements might be best explored by using stories to explain technology possibilities in a business context. Stories are one of the most potent means by which people make sense of our world and share ideas about it. Our needs are made clearer by being shown examples. Software developers are often taken by surprise when they deliver an application to a user and are greeted by remarks like "that's not what I was expecting, but now I can tell you what I need" (as illustrated in Figure 1.7).

"Users never know what they want...   ...until they see what they get!"

FIGURE 1.7.   EXAMPLES HELP US TO DEFINE AND COMMUNICATE OUR NEEDS.

In our experience, users frequently are surprised by the solutions they are asked to use, and, far too often, don't like them. The good news is that faced with a solution they don't like, they seem much better able to articulate what they do want.

Enabling and Enhancing Communication Pays Enormous Dividends

In the second scenario, business people and IT worked together, each contributing what they were best at. The key enabler was a portfolio of capabilities and the process for using them. It helped to create a common way of working and a common language that allowed each party to concentrate on the steps they were best capable of doing:

- Business people provided context and objectives for the solution.
- Technical people conducted technology research and used their analytical skills to identify and describe capabilities as examples of what is possible with technology. They took the care to connect their ideas to business drivers and results.
- Business people used the portfolio to envision the way the future system could operate in order to guide them in the selection of capabilities.
- Technical people assessed the technical implications of these choices.

TRAIL MARKER I: APPRECIATION OF THE PROBLEM AND TRAIL AHEAD

In this chapter, you have become familiar with issues surrounding the business-IT gap, recent changes in the world of business technology, and the new role that IT is expected to play in fulfilling the goals of businesses and organizations.

This sets the stage for Chapter 2, "Bridging the Gap with Solution Envisioning," to help you understand the intent and design of the two key innovations introduced in this book for bridging the business-IT gap. These are a repeatable process for *envisioning* (Solution Envisioning) and using reusable *solution ideas* or patterns (Capability Cases).

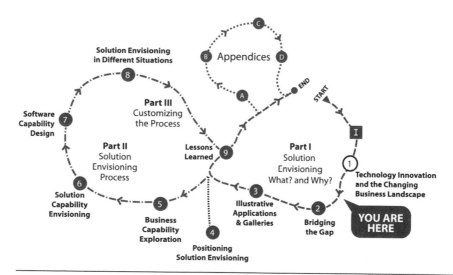

FIGURE 1.8.

Beyond Chapter 2, the route continues in Chapter 3 with case studies of where the process has been applied, including galleries of Capability Cases.

2

BRIDGING THE GAP WITH SOLUTION ENVISIONING

"Vision without action is a daydream. Action without vision is a nightmare."

—*Japanese Proverb*

"A vision without a plan is an hallucination."

—*Jack Ring*

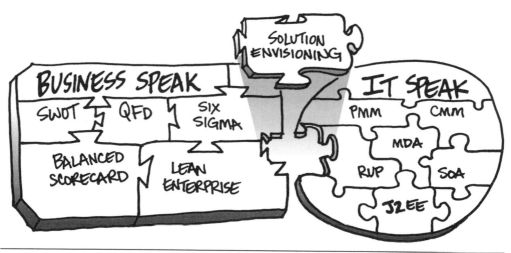

FIGURE 2.1.

CHAPTER PREVIEW

This chapter introduces Solution Envisioning with Capability Cases by covering these topics:

- The complete Solution Envisioning process is outlined by giving a short overview of each of its three phases.

- Capability Cases are described in terms of their role and value in the envisioning process. Templates used for summary and extended views of Capability Cases are presented and illustrated with examples.

- To lay the foundation for understanding how the Solution Envisioning process and Capability Cases work together, we include a section on the shared vocabulary that integrates them. We show how key concepts and terms are used to connect possibly relevant Capability Cases to the business situation of interest. We also outline the relationship of these terms to business strategy approaches.

- Finally, we briefly discuss situations where Solution Envisioning can be used and how long it takes.

The material in this chapter is introductory in earlier sections on the process and Capability Cases. It becomes more challenging in the later sections on the concepts and vocabulary used for understanding and capturing the business context for which an IT solution is sought. This understanding is needed for the deeper treatment of the process provided in Part II and for certain insights given through examples in Part III of the book. Some readers may want to scan the later sections of this chapter on first pass and return to them if or when they want further detail on the concepts or practice. The following is a high-level preview of the main threads regarding the fusion of a repeatable process for *envisioning* with reusable *solution ideas* or patterns.

Upstream, in the "fuzzy space" where new business solutions are created, diverse interests need to be brought together. Business people, technology vendors, solution users, and IT people each have their own way of seeing and speaking about the world. Solution Envisioning is a process for using a new type of solution pattern—Capability Cases—to effectively bridge the gap between business and IT.

While the idea of solution patterns for matching business problems to relevant technology capabilities is very powerful, it has little impact without a practical way to apply it in situations where multiple stakeholders and their work practices must be brought together. Practicing Solution Envisioning with Capability Cases required us to establish an approach that would connect business strategy, technology trend assessment, solution design, and IT system development concerns.

Scenario 2 at end of Chapter 1, "Technology Innovation and the Changing Business Landscape," showed us how such an approach makes it possible to find effective ways for business decision makers and technologists to work together. Emphasis is placed on staged exploration and solution design involving both business and technical people. First, characterizing features of the business context and desired outcomes are agreed. Relevant capabilities are identified. Using scenarios, these capabilities serve as triggers for breakthrough thinking and innovation. The creativity comes from "design by analogy" grounded in the needs of the business situation.

Solution Envisioning with Capability Cases

A Timely Intervention—in the Quest for a Business Transformation

In the cartoon story in the *Preamble* of this book, we characterized the attempt to successfully enable a business with a technology-based solution as a *Quest*—a complex journey with many twists, turns, and unforeseen difficulties. People often embark on the quest without appreciating some of these challenges. There is a tendency toward oversimplification, at least at the beginning. The cartoon storyline portrayed some of the many things that can go wrong—despite best intentions—in an initiative to create a solution.

This book is based on more than 70 years of collective experience. Over the course of many projects, we noted patterns in the ways people get stuck, don't progress well, fail to finish, or arrive at a different destination than was intended. We realized there were common underlying causes. In developing Solution Envisioning, we had a goal to provide a well-founded set of interventions that deal with these recurring challenges. Activities of Solution Envisioning address an early part of the bigger journey as shown in Figure 2.2. They help to facilitate an exploratory but convergent process of collaboration, decision making, and organizational commitment that improves the odds of successful quest.

The Goal: Matching Business Challenges to Proven Solutions

Before solutions can be envisioned, problems need to be understood and agreed upon. In the Solution Envisioning approach, we place strong emphasis on an inquiry into the nature of the business situation and the strategic intent of the enterprise.

By the business situation we mean the forces that act as threats or drivers that present new opportunities and the resulting challenges for the enterprise.

A Quest for Change
Changing the Business Through Adoption of a Technology-Enabled Solution

Business Solution Delivery Lifecycle

...need for Change → Assessment → Design → Construction → Deployment → ...Business Results

Business Strategy Development/ Realignment | Solution Initiative Formation | **Solution Envisioning** | | Solution Realization & Adoption

Addressing Questions We Have Heard Repeatedly

- How can we complete this quest successfully?
- Is there an approach we can use that will guide and support us?
- What kinds of intervention and facilitation would help our process in making the right decisions?
- How can we as change agents/champions make the case for improving upfront planning of an initiative?

Solution Envisioning with Capability Cases is designed to address these kinds of questions and fill this gap.

Filling a Critical Gap in Development Methods

Leading Software Engineering Process Models and Methods concentrate on this phase. They specify a prior, essential phase to set up the development project that is called Envisioning or Inception.

However, they do not provide much detail or support for how to effectively accomplish that phase, thus leaving a *critical* gap in the process to successfully realize solutions that acheive business goals and provide value.

FIGURE 2.2.   SOLUTION ENVISIONING AS A TIMELY INTERVENTION IN THE QUEST FOR A SOLUTION.

Specifying a future business model is itself an act of envisioning. This first phase of Solution Envisioning—Business Capability Exploration—deals with both the current state-of-affairs and the early ideas about desired possibilities for the future. Interplay of technology and business strategy is facilitated by the use of solution stories that can inspire the business people to consider new business designs and capabilities.

Following this phase, the IT capabilities needed to support the new business model are decided on in a phase we call *Solution Capability Envisioning*. In the first two phases, Solution Envisioning is a scenario-driven approach to experiencing a future system through analogies and examples using a set of relevant *Capability Cases*. The third phase, *Software Capability Design*, focuses on translating selected capabilities into solution blueprints.

As briefly outlined in the book's Introduction, Capability Cases are designed to work hand-in-hand with the envisioning process. They are structured to make apparent the potential role and business value of specific technologies. The term "Capability" in Capability Case is meant to indicate the potential to deliver business functionality.

A Capability Case (CapCase) presents solution concepts in a way that they can be connected to the business situation. In the same way that an architect presents building designs for consideration, Solution Envisioning with Capability Cases offers *designs by example* for IT systems. What do we mean by this?

The underlying idea is simple. Business people are shown building blocks, or solution capabilities, from a catalog of solution concepts illustrated by stories. Being anchored in the context of business drivers, challenges, and desired results, Capability Cases operate as concepts-at-work. We find that they appeal to the imagination of decision makers, when they are exploring the intersection of requirements and possibilities. They ignite ideas and cause connections to happen. For example, a "Virtual Store Assistant" CapCase might trigger the idea of a virtual librarian for a records archive application. This is what we mean when we talk about Capability Cases fostering *design by example* and *design by analogy*.

Each CapCase can be viewed as a best practice for achieving business results. Business objectives and the overall business situation guide the selection of capabilities. A key element of the process is the collaborative dynamic of deciding on solution capabilities through exploration of a wide range of solution possibilities. Equally important is the creation of a shared vocabulary for naming conceptual parts of the solution. For instance, consider the name of a capability "Instant Messenger." The name intends to convey an implicit understanding of the solution idea. One of the strengths of using CapCases is the ability to create the same conceptual recognition and shared meaning for all components of a solution.

A shared experience of possibilities is a central idea in Solution Envisioning. Other design goals we have tried to accommodate in the process are:

- Providing a rapid means to fully explore the solution space
- Being both exploratory and convergent while *bridging the gap* between a diverse set of stakeholders and a large number of indistinct value propositions
- Creating a framework for navigating today's jungle of technology options
- Communicating best practices in the way that makes them catalysts for innovation and fosters a shared vision
- Providing a traceable decision flow from business objectives to solution capabilities

Process Overview: From Vision to Plan in Three Phases

Figure I.1 illustrated the three major phases at the core of Solution Envisioning:

- **Business Capability Exploration** (BCE) that results in an initial Solution Vision to be communicated and shaped by a larger set of stakeholders in subsequent phases.

- **Solution Capability Envisioning** (SCE) that creates a documented Solution Concept as a set of capabilities that collectively enable and embody the desired business solution.
- **Software Capability Design** (SCD) that validates the Business Case, establishes an actionable Capability Architecture for the Solution, and delivers a Solution Realization Roadmap.

In addition to these, an important first step of Solution Envisioning is a briefing that orients all the participants to the working approach. The process is discussed, tailored to the situation, and communicated to participants. Fine-tuning of the agreed methods, activities, and ways of working continues throughout the Solution Envisioning process. This serves as a running reflection on how the process is working and an opportunity to adjust it.

Figures 2.3–2.5 show a more detailed view of each phase at the level of *Activity Clusters*. These ten high-level groups of activities are

BCE-I	Establish Business Situation and Resources
BCE-II	Identify Business Needs as Forces and Results
BCE-III	Explore Possibilities Informed by Technology
BCE-IV	Consolidate Initial Solution Vision for Sharing
SCE-I	Prepare for the Solution Envisioning Workshop
SCE-II	Conduct Solution Envisioning Workshop
SCE-III	Perform Post-Workshop Assessment and Consolidation
SCD-I	Select Implementation Technologies
SCD-II	Develop Software Capability Architecture
SCD-III	Develop Business Case and Solution Roadmap

A detailed explanation and discussion of these activities are provided in the three chapters that form Part II of this book. In the next sections, we give a short overview of each phase.

Business Capability Exploration

The nature of Business Capability Exploration is to do the necessary *pre-work* of laying the foundation for the solution. Its purpose is to understand the nature of problems in the existing context of the business and to support a select, core team of stakeholders who are initially driving the initiative as they produce a preliminary Solution Vision. We say preliminary because it will be shared and shaped in successive phases.

To arrive somewhere new, there is the need to understand where you are, what is causing the need to move, and what results the move needs to achieve. Business Capability Exploration has a number of framing and focusing activities guided by these objectives:

- Assessment of business dynamics and predicaments
- Expression of root causes and their analysis—a relationship between cause and effect in the business environment
- Initial scan of potential solutions
- Agreement over business objectives

Figure 2.3 shows the four main clusters of activities that drive the work of Business Capability Exploration. For a more detailed view, see Figure 5.2 in Chapter 5, "Business Capability Exploration—Phase I of Solution Envisioning."

FIGURE 2.3. FOUR MAIN CLUSTERS OF ACTIVITIES THAT DRIVE BUSINESS CAPABILITY EXPLORATION.

The phase is completed when an understanding is reached on the nature of the business problems and the specific results the solution needs to bring about, and when a vision is reached for how the solution might be realized. This understanding is documented as a *Solution Vision Presentation*[1] and is made available to a broader set of stakeholders within a suitable collaborative portal or workspace.

Solution Capability Envisioning

The nature of Solution Capability Envisioning is to facilitate a series of collaborative interactions or *envisioning workshops*.[2] These sessions are structured to make it possible for a broad set of stakeholders to forge a shared understanding about the intent of the initiative and the details of the solution vision.

Having understood and represented the problem in the activities of the previous phase, an exploration of solution alternatives proceeds with the confidence that there is now a framework for evaluation of proposed solution ideas or concepts. The purpose of Solution Capability Envisioning is to identify the main functionality blocks for the solution by nominating, evaluating, and prioritizing an integrated set of capabilities that will collectively support the business vision.

Figure 2.4 shows the three main clusters of activities that comprise the work of Solution Capability Envisioning. For a more detailed view, see Figure 6.2 in Chapter 6, "Solution Capability Envisioning—Phase II of Solution Envisioning."

The phase is completed when the Solution Vision has been refined and confirmed by a broad, representative set of stakeholders. The result—an integrated set of capabilities—is captured and communicated in the form of a *Solution Concept Document*.[3] A solution concept should be thought of as the optimal set of capabilities that

---

[1] **Solution Vision Presentation**—A presentation that provides (a) a summary of the business situation; (b) a vision of one or more possible solution concepts; (c) motivating future scenarios and supporting capabilities; and (d) value propositions that serve as input to making a business case. (See the BCE Table in Appendix D for this definition along with those of all the workproducts of Business Capability Exploration.)

[2] Chapter 6 describes how Solution Envisioning workshops are conducted and provides further detail on techniques used during these sessions.

[3] **Solution Concept Document**—The Solution Concept workproduct conveys the vision of the solution. It is a description of the business context with forces and motivating scenarios, stakeholders and their desired results, capabilities that enable new ways to work, future scenarios that illustrate new ways to work, and a road map that addresses risks, impacts, and the options and plans for the solution design work of the next phase. (See the SCE table in Appendix D for this definition and those of all of the workproducts of the Solution Capability Envisioning phase.)

supports realization of business objectives. Solutions need to be understood in terms of their effects on how people and systems will work. The Solution Concept is created through:

- Matching the problem at hand to known solution capabilities (through CapCases)

- Collaborative sessions to envision how solution capabilities will overcome challenges and bring about the desired results

- Storytelling to establish shared understanding of the roles that the business side and technology side will play in the future world

- Arrangement of the capabilities into the various solution concept views of the conceptual architecture

- Agreement about business priorities for the implementation of capabilities

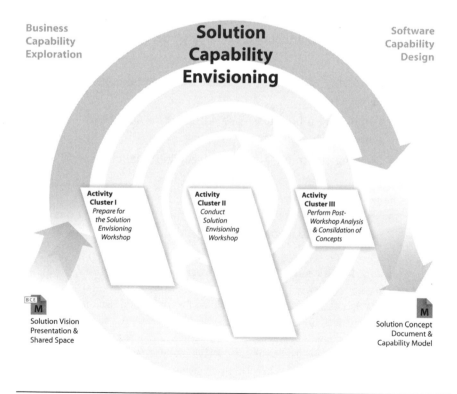

FIGURE 2.4.   THREE MAIN CLUSTERS OF ACTIVITIES FORM THE WORK OF CAPABILITY ENVISIONING.

Software Capability Design

The nature of Software Capability Design work is converting the results of envisioning into an actionable set of high-level designs and plans for building the solution. Its purpose is to complete the development and documentation of a Solution Realization Roadmap.[4] These deliverables must be sufficient to scope, fund, and launch an efficient final phase for assembling, deploying, and adopting the solution.

Figure 2.5 shows the three main clusters of activities that complete the work of Software Capability Design. For a more detailed view, see Figure 7.2 in Chapter 7, "Software Capability Design—Phase III of Solution Envisioning."

When the capability view of the conceptual architecture has been developed, the technical components of the solution can be identified. It is at this stage that technology decisions are made and implementation architecture defined. The organizational impact of the solution is understood and planned for. Priorities for implementation guide the creation of a roadmap, including a solution blueprint and plans for its realization.

In summary, the Capability Design work entails the following:

- Making commitments to technology decisions
- Elaborating the capability architecture of the solution
- Specifying evolvable solutions using component and service-oriented architectures
- Completing a business case sufficient to support the final development of the solution
- Creating communication and organizational change strategies
- Building a solution realization roadmap

The phase is completed when the work of Solution Envisioning has been packaged as an actionable shared memory in the organization.[5] This means that the business

---

[4] **Solution Realization Roadmap**—A package of deliverables, including Solution Architecture (comprised of the Vendor Short List, Architectural Decisions, IT Impact, Interface Specification, and Non-Functional Requirements). **Business Case**—A presentation that provides (a) a summary of the business case; (b) a roadmap to implementation; and (c) a description of key risks and risk mitigation decisions. In addition, the implementation plan may also be packaged as a high-level Microsoft Project plan. (See the SCD table in Appendix D for this definition along with those of all the workproducts of Software Capability Design.)

[5] By "shared memory," we mean they are documented in an accessible and understandable form. By "actionable," we mean that sufficient consensus and commitment has been achieved in an organization to warrant action.

goals, justification, high-level designs, and plans have been clearly articulated and documented in a form directly usable in the construction phases. The construction can be accomplished in a number of ways. Whether the approach is to buy, build, or both, the goal is to set the stage for an efficient and successful realization and adoption. The Solution Envisioning deliverables are designed to provide a seamless connection to popular software engineering methods by providing the input they specify and require.

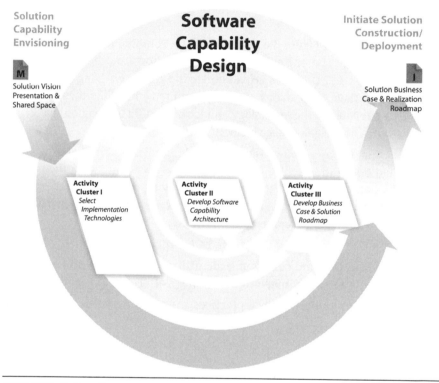

FIGURE 2.5.   THREE MAIN CLUSTERS OF ACTIVITIES COMPLETE THE WORK OF CAPABILITY DESIGN.

THE ROLE AND VALUE OF CAPABILITY CASES

A Capability Case is the *Case for a Capability*. By "Capability," we mean the potential to deliver business functionality. The word "Case," in this context, has a different meaning from its use in the construct "Use Case." It is borrowed from two places:

- In the case-based reasoning[6] world, the word "case" has a long es-tablished meaning of defining a problem-solution pair for reuse and adaptation in new problem contexts. In this sense, CapCases are reusable solution concepts.

- Additionally, in the business world, "case" has a well-established meaning of making a business justification (making the case) for spending effort or money. In this sense, a CapCase stimulates inter-play between what is possible with a technology and how a business might overcome a problem or gain a market advantage.

As illustrated in Figure 2.6, to implement a solution, a lot of questions arise—the business why's on one end and the technical how's on the other end. How do you match these up? CapCases help to bridge the gap by enabling solution stakeholders to evolve their expectations about the requirements while they are both exploring the capabilities of the technology and looking to fill application needs that are cur-rently feasible using the technology.

In a similar way to how Use Cases facilitate discussion about "what the system should do for the user," CapCases support a dialog on "what the system could be and what it could do for the business." They represent a *case of use of a technol-ogy* (CapCase) rather than a *case of use of a system* (Use Case). They serve as so-lution catalysts in several possible ways by:

- Communicating the vision of technology enablement for an enterprise

- Guiding and confirming identification and selection of technology platforms by mapping technology offerings to business needs

- Communicating best practices for realizing value from technology

---

[6]   Case-based reasoning (CBR) is a problem-solving paradigm that, in many respects, is fun-damentally different from other major artificial intelligence (AI) approaches. Instead of re-lying solely on general knowledge of a problem domain, or making associations along generalized relationships between problem descriptors and conclusions, CBR is able to utilize the specific knowledge of previously experienced, concrete problem situations (cases). A new problem is solved by finding a similar past case and reusing it in the new problem situation. As evidenced in our everyday behavior and supported by results from cognitive psychological research, reasoning by reusing past cases is a powerful means by which humans frequently solve problems. Part of the foundation for the case-based ap-proach is its psychological plausibility. Over the last decade, CBR has grown from an iso-lated research area into a field of widespread interest and use, making it one of the most successfully used AI approaches.

- Stimulating concept-driven requirements elicitation by enabling business users to convey what results they want to achieve through examples and stories

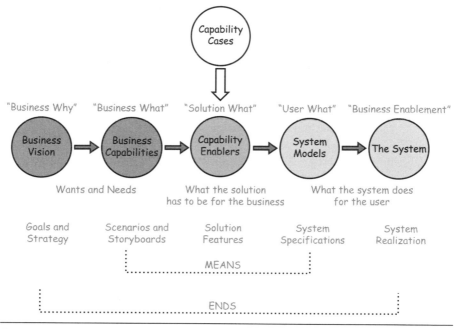

FIGURE 2.6.   CAPABILITY CASES IN THE CONTEXT OF REALIZING NEW BUSINESS SOLUTIONS.

Harnessing the Power of Stories and Tangible Examples

Communicating with other people is probably one of the hardest tasks one has to do in life. Connections, interpretations, and decisions are made in the mental domain that operates predominantly on images and concepts, not on words. Verbal communication provides the main way of sharing images and concepts between people. It works quickly and reliably when there is a shared vocabulary. Without it, communication becomes a long and torturous process.

Imagine trying to explain the concept of a car to someone who has never seen or experienced one. Without a shared vocabulary, representations of a desired system in text form are not helpful. Design decisions are made in the mental domain, where it is important that a concept or image of the system be created in the minds of each of the stakeholders.

Visual images are critical to making the intention of a system explicit to all stakeholders. Identifying the benefits and telling stories of how a system will be used to deliver them are essential steps toward creating a shared image. Once the image is established, it needs a name so it can become a part of the vocabulary. With a name, it can live on and grow richer in meaning. For example, recall the story in Chapter 1 ("A Quest for Self-Service" at Secure Investments). The capabilities *Answer Engine* and *Instant Helper* became a part of the company's vocabulary. As a result, the company acquired shared *design memes.*[7]

In our search for a repeatable way to establish common meaning and shared vocabularies, which can be used to design solutions, we looked for approaches that worked in the past. Surely the communication problem was not new. Stories are one of the important means (along with pictures and music and songs) through which human beings understand the world. We relate to one another's experience through the narrative themes and images that a good story conveys.

We also observed what was happening in the "trenches." What tools and techniques were already being used to close the gap? The search resulted in the creation of an asset-based approach for designing systems in which solution and technology capabilities shape the realization of the system. It provides a way to connect solution concepts to the business situation using a "Business Problem–IT Solution" *pattern* that we named "Capability Case." The principle of looking for commonality across independent cases of solutions was well established by the Design Patterns community.[8] When a number of independent stories line up and suggest a common solution, we have the basis for a CapCase. The CapCase is named as such so it conveys the intent of this general idea.

---

[7]   As described in http://en.wikipedia.org/wiki/Meme: "In casual use, the term meme is sometimes used to mean any piece of information passed from one mind to another... Memes can represent parts of ideas, languages, tunes, designs, skills, moral and aesthetic values, and anything else that is commonly learned and passed on to others as a unit. The study of evolutionary models of information transfer is called memetics." A smiley face is an example of a visual meme. Running jokes are an example of a verbal/textual meme— for instance, "Knock knock, who's there?" sets up the whole structure and expectation of a joke.

[8]   See Appendix A for more on the relationship of Capability Cases to the Patterns Movement and community.

Capability Cases—A Summary View

A CapCase is described using a template that expresses the commonalities of one or more solution stories. At its most basic—we call it a summary or identification level view—the CapCase template is simple (see Table 2.1).

TABLE 2.1. INFORMATION INCLUDED IN THE SUMMARY-LEVEL VIEW OF A CAPABILITY CASE

CAPABILITY CASE SUMMARY TEMPLATE

Name:	Naming a capability is a first step in defining it. There is a long-standing tradition in the pattern movement of collaboration and discussion toward finding the "right" name, the one that best describes what the capability is about. Having two or three people brainstorm about a name is quite useful. In our work, we've found that the more often you use the name, the more meaningful it becomes to the group.
Intent:	This is the "elevator pitch"—one or two sentences describing the essence of the capability. Expect to take some time and apply careful consideration to create a statement of intent.
Solution Story Example:	This is the "for example" piece—a story of a capability in action. The story should include a short description of the situation, the challenges present, and how the solution helped. We find that a screenshot or other graphic illustrations are essential to get a story better understood. The story could be real or envisioned.
Business Benefits/ Results:	The value to the business in solving a problem or seizing an opportunity. By describing how the organization in the story benefited from the solution, a critical match is made between technology possibilities and business goals.
Applicable Technologies and Products:	When people are intrigued by the capability or see a possible application of it in their own context, they will invariably want to know how it was done or how it could be done. A list of products or a brief description of the technology used completes the Capability Case.

Figure 2.7 shows a completed summary-level template.

Capability Case:

Answer Engine

Intent:

Interpreting a question asked in a natural language, it checks multiple data sources to collect knowledge nuggets required for answering the question. Instead of returning a list of relevant documents, it provides a direct reply, sometimes creating it on the fly by combining relevant knowledge nuggets.

Solution Stories:

OneStep at Charles Schwab, OneStep at LexisNexis

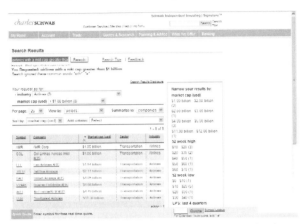

OneStep understands what it means to "compare" values and recognizes the particular values requested.

Charles Schwab clients often needed fairly simple, but precise and timely, information to help them make financial decisions. To get the information, they would call the support desk. Charles Schwab found that the information needed to answer many of the inquiries was readily available in the documents and databases accessible through its website. Yet, the majority of clients didn't want to search through the website; they routinely turned to customer service for the answers.

Schwab implemented an Answer Engine capability that allowed web visitors to ask detailed questions in natural language and get back simple, comparative reports. Answer Engine ensured that Schwab's clients could easily and quickly access the information they needed for critical financial decisions. Many requests are now being serviced by the website without the need to call customer service.

Business Benefits/Results: Reduced cost of customer support (Charles Schwab estimates that this capability saves the company $125,000 per month), improved customer service, and increased utilization of self-service access to information

Featured Products:

iPhrase OneStep from iPhrase

Applicable Products:

InQuira 6 from InQuira

FIGURE 2.7.   SUMMARY-LEVEL VIEW OF THE ANSWER ENGINE CAPCASE.

Capability Cases in Action

The conversations that follow the presentation of a Capability Case are a key part of the Solution Envisioning process that bridges the gap. Indicative comments and insights often exchanged by participants include the following:

- **"How can it (the system) do this?"**—The conversations usually start with business people wanting to know more about the technology. Often, there is some disbelief about technology's ability to deliver the functionality, especially if the technology is relatively new or business people are not sophisticated in their use of technology. This offers an opportunity to identify any misconceptions, differences in understanding, or concerns.

- **"It will not work here."**—This often-heard statement can elicit valuable input, and it may indeed be true! The ensuing conversation must cover an explanation of why. Such conversations can offer a lot of insight into the business situation and identify additional areas of misunderstanding.

- **"Can it also do 'this'?"**—This statement is an indication of growing interest. Additional needs start to be identified. Creativity begins to flow.

- **"We could use it to…"**—As the conversation progresses, more creative ideas are shared. Connections to business needs and goals are fostered.

In an organization, such stories have the power to catalyze change and enable the organization to re-invent itself. Stephen Denning calls these kinds of stories "springboard stories" [Denning, 2001]:

"A springboard story has an impact not so much through transferring large amounts of information as through catalyzing understanding. It can enable listeners to visualize from a story in one context what is involved in a large-scale transformation in an analogous context. … In effect, it invites them to see analogies from their own backgrounds, their own contexts, their own fields of expertise."

Sidebar 2.1—Igniting Action Through the Art of Storytelling

The ability to tell a compelling story is the key to authoring effective Capability Cases. Through stories, we share meaning about the world. We make and exchange sense of the experienced world and we create future worlds through stories. Stories are potent because they captivate the listener by engaging their attention. A story becomes powerful when the listener identifies with the story, enters into its world, and makes his or her own understandings and connections that transcend the story. Using the power of storytelling to communicate, influence, and teach is a well-accepted practice. It is, in fact, an integral part of human culture.

"The narratives of the world are without number...the narrative is present at all times, in all places, in all societies; the history of narrative begins with the history of mankind; there does not exist, and never has existed, a people without narratives" (Barthes):

Stories communicate but they also illuminate. They create a space in which people can share an understanding or envision a new reality. We identify with each other through stories. A good story with a protagonist facing challenges and achieving success captures our imagination.

In his book, *The Springboard—How Storytelling Ignites Action in Knowledge-Era Organizations*, Stephen Denning describes the ways in which stories can catalyze change and enable an organization to re-invent itself. The book grew out of his work in transformative knowledge management, which he is credited for, at the World Bank. As noted in the quote from his book in the text before this Sidebar, it describes particular kinds of stories that Denning calls *springboard stories*.

Solution examples in CapCases are intended to act as mini-springboard stories. Taking a leaf from Denning's work, they emulate best practices for creating powerful narratives that communicate, connect, and inspire. A well-written case study has the same power. When a CapCase is well-expressed and connected to business forces and results, it makes the case for a solution idea in a compelling and substantive manner. The evidence is there—in the forces and measured results. The ability to communicate is there—in the independent stories of adoption.

In summary, a Capability Case:

- Facilitates a shared understanding of forces, challenges, and desired results
- Enables business and IT to do joint creative work towards a shared vision
- Expands the space of solution possibilities through its use as an "innovation catalyst"
- Builds confidence and commitment towards implementing the shared vision
- Helps communicate a solution vision to other parties

Capability Cases—An Extended View

Summary-level CapCases are sufficient very early in the solution exploration phase when high-level design ideas and concepts are first discussed. To determine relevance of a capability to a specific business context, typically, more details are needed. To translate it into an implementable blueprint, yet another level of detail is required. The template for an elaborated CapCase is detailed in Table 2.2.

TABLE 2.2. INFORMATION INCLUDED IN A FULLY ELABORATED CAPABILITY CASE

Elaborated Capability Case Template

Name:	(Same as in Summary-level View in Figure 2.7.)
Intent:	(Same as in Summary-level View in Figure 2.7.)
Description:	An explanation of how the capability works. Such explanations can range from a short statement to an extended overview.
Solution Story:	One or more Solution Story Examples (see description in Summary-level View in Figure 2.7).
Vintage:	The maturity of the capability. Vintage can be "conceptual," "research prototype," "early commercialization," "mature commercialization," or "general industry adoption."
Challenges:	A challenge is an obstacle or predicament that the business is facing that stands in the way of realizing some desired improvements or transformation of the business. Challenges are often revealed by barriers or *pains* that users and stakeholders are experiencing.
Forces:	Business forces that indicate the need for the capability. By business forces, we mean any new or existing condition that is affecting the business.
Business Results:	Results business wants to accomplish. For each key result, we identify measurements that could be used to assess effectiveness of the capability toward achieving it.
Capabilities:	A list of functions that the Capability Case provides. These can be thought of also as "responsibilities" (in the CRC[9] sense) and can be related to Use Cases.

---

[9] CRC stands for Class-Responsibility-Collaborator. CRC cards facilitate a brainstorming technique that is often used in object-oriented design to walk through, explore, and review design alternatives. See the paper where they were introduced by Ward Cunningham and Kent Beck at http://c2.com/doc/oopsla89/paper.html. Ward Cunningham's Wiki page on the topic can be found at http://c2.com/cgi/wiki?CrcCards. Allistrair Cockburn provides a useful concise tutorial on using CRC cards at http://alistair.cockburn.us/crystal/articles/ucrcc/usingcrccards.html.

TABLE 2.2.   Information Included in a Fully Elaborated Capability Case—continued

Typical Use Scenarios and Guidance:	Best Practices and Lessons Learned for guidance in implementing the capability. This provides some information on obstacles—technical or organizational—that an enterprise may need to overcome to successfully deploy the capability.
Applicable Technologies:	(Same as in Summary-level View in Figure 2.7.) For each technology, it may be necessary to list separate implementation considerations.
Implementation Effort:	An order of magnitude estimate of implementation costs and complexity to help in prioritization and decision making.
Integration:	Capabilities are building blocks for business solutions. Two perspectives of integration are of importance: mechanism and strategy.
Integration Mechanism:	Mechanisms define ways in which a capability is invoked as a part of the overall solution. The following four mechanisms are distinguished: **UI Integration**—The simplest form of integration. Examples include making a capability accessible through a link on the web or as a "portlet" in a portal. **Task-centric Integration**—One example of this mechanism is an Instant Helper screen with a "Can I help you?" message popping up when a user hesitates at a check out in the e-shop. **Data-centric Integration**—When data is shared, aggregated, or exchanged. **Process-centric Integration**—When a capability is triggered by events in a process or has to generate events for other capabilities or processes.
Integration Strategy:	Strategies represent different architectural approaches for integrating capabilities. The following distinctions are made: **Proprietary Plug-ins**—Used when integrating additional capabilities into large grained functional components that offer some degree of openness through proprietary APIs. The style could operate on multiple levels. **Cooperative Applications**—An example is a cooperation of MS Word and Groove where each serves a clearly separate function and operates independently. At the same time, a MS Word document can be stored and version controlled by Groove. Another example is two custom business applications that serve separate business functions where one sends a weekly data extract to another. **Common Integration Framework**—Requires a set of agreed protocols used by different applications to communicate. Examples include various Enterprise Application Integration (EAI) platforms, Service-Oriented Architectures (SOA) for Web Services, COM/DCOM, J2EE, and CORBA platform and architecture frameworks. Interoperability is achieved through an application profile.

When a CapCase is first identified, it is described, at a minimum, by an intent statement, one solution story, and some information on benefits and technologies. If the capability is of interest to the business, it is typically elaborated to include more information on the business situation it addresses and specific implementation-related details. It may also include additional solution stories. In the chapters that follow, we describe the motivation for and use of some of these richer aspects of the Capability Case template. CapCases are considered fully elaborated when all the fields are completed and measures of effectiveness for the Results associated with the capability are identified.

For illustration, an elaboration of the Answer Engine CapCase is shown in Figure 2.8—this is a more detailed view of the same CapCase shown in the Summary-level View in Figure 2.7.

A Vocabulary That Integrates Envisioning and Capability Cases

In this section, we introduce selected key terms and associated concepts of Solution Envisioning. They incorporate and *connect* techniques and terminology used by both business and technical people within the envisioning process.

The business environment or context has a number of dimensions, including:

- **Stakeholders**—Whose interests we are addressing
- **Business activities**—Actions of stakeholders to use, support, or engage in the business
- **Forces**—The business drivers that are affecting the stakeholders
- **Vision**—Where the enterprise sees itself in the future
- **Strategic intent**—What the enterprise will do to realize the vision
- **Results**—Objectives that stakeholders need to accomplish to realize strategic intent
- **Outcomes**—How the results bring benefits to the business
- **Barriers**—Obstacles the business experiences that stand in the way of its objectives
- **Challenges**—The improvements the enterprise must make to its core competencies
- **Processes**—Activities needed to carry out the work of the business
- **Capabilities**—Required people, competencies, technologies, and infrastructure

Capability Case: # Answer Engine

Intent:	Interpreting a question asked in a natural language, it checks multiple data sources to collect knowledge nuggets required for answering the question. Instead of returning a list of relevant documents, it provides a direct reply, sometimes creating it on the fly by combining relevant knowledge nuggets.
Solution Outline:	Solution uses natural language-parsing capabilities backed up by a conceptual model (ontology of a business domain). You can connect to different sources of information through APIs. Different APIs accommodate a structured and unstructured information repository. Special APIs may be needed for specific content management packages, such as Documentum or Livelink. Templates are used for formatting and presenting the information in different ways.

Solution Stories:

   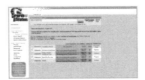

OneStep at Charles Schwab   *OneStep at LexisNexis*

Elaboration State:	Full description
Vintage:	Early commercialization
Challenges:	• How to allow people to use natural language to find information • How to have systems that interpret and distill information pertinent to a specific situation and task • How to maintain and deliver information in a consistent way to multiple audiences with differing needs • How to make expertise more readily available to a broader audience • How to provide accurate and relevant search results using easily specified, dialog-driven or natural-language queries • How to provide users with the timely and targeted information based on their interests and needs • How to use the Internet for a quick and easy response to customer inquiries
Industry:	Cross-Industry
Industry:	Customer Service, Marketing, Product Design, Research
Forces:	**Customer:** • A large percentage of the inbound support calls are procedural inquiries as opposed to specific account inquiries. • Increasingly, customers are using the Internet as their source of information. • Sites with a lot of information can overwhelm and drive away users. • Users would rather ask questions than type in key words.

	Marketplace:	
	Enterprise:	• Call-avoidance from customers and staff results in significant savings.
	Technology:	• Growing number of disparate information repositories including unstructured (HTML pages, Word documents, etc.), semi structured (XML, RDF), structured (databases) • Traditional keyword search technology is outdated.
	Regulatory:	
Results:	**Financial:**	• Lower cost of customer service
	Customer:	• Brand recognition and company reputation • Customer satisfaction • Effective web presence • Self-service access to information • Users have a more engaging experience of the website and are more likely to return.
	Internal:	• More time available for staff to perform high-value work
	Learning and Growth:	
Capabilities:	• Know knowledge sources. • Relate knowledge sources to an ontology. • Interpret a question asked in a natural language. • Query knowledge sources. • Maintain answer templates. • Collate relevant pieces of knowledge to provide answers.	
Typical Use Scenarios and Guidance:	When precision of the search is important and users are unforgiving of broad, general search results. There is a well-established domain vocabulary, for example, government, law, financial, and product-centric areas. Information includes detailed, volatile, quantitative data, such as finance information and tax regulations. Content is in a variety of formats from different sources.	
Applicable Technologies:	Semantic Analysis, Ontologies for concepts extraction, Natural Language Processing, Categorization and aggregation, Dynamic (template-driven) presentation.	
Applicable Products:	**OneStep from iPhrase, InQuira 6 from InQuira**	
Implementation Effort:	Low to Moderate	
Integration Mechanism:	Data-centric	
Integration Strategy:	Proprietary API Plug-in, Common Integration Framework	

FIGURE 2.8. ELABORATED VIEW OF THE ANSWER ENGINE CAPCASE.

Some of the relationships between these key elements of a business situation are illustrated in Sidebar I.1 in the Introduction of this book. By design, Solution Envisioning and Capability Cases share this vocabulary. For example, in the Solution Envisioning process, *business forces* and *results* are elicited from the business situation and are used to represent some of its core aspects. The same key constructs—forces and results—are used to help catalog and index Capability Cases as useful candidates for business situations.[10] In this section, we show how the vocabulary is used to connect possibly relevant Capability Cases to the business situation of interest. We also outline the relationship of these terms to well-established business strategy and planning approaches from which they were derived.

Forces

A *force* is a business driver, internal or external to the business, that requires a response. By force, we mean a new or existing condition that is affecting the business. A force can be an issue, where the business is failing in some way, or an opportunity to realize new benefits.

Forces can arise from a number of different sources that we categorize as: regulatory, customers, enterprise, marketplace, and technology. Forces can be constant or dynamic. For example, existing government regulation can be considered a stable force. On the other hand, "the increasing availability of wireless infrastructure" represents a dynamic force that is on the increase. Such dynamic forces can be thought of as trends.

Michael Porter's Five Forces [Porter, 1985] model, illustrated by Figure 2.9, is well known in the industry as a way to distinguish between forces according to their sources. Porter's work established the "Five Forces Model" as a tool for formulating action as a response to business drivers. The Porter model distinguishes buyers (customers), competitors, suppliers, new entrants, and substitutes.

Recognizing that the industry has changed since Porter's work, we have adopted different categories: *regulatory*, *customers*, *enterprise*, and *marketplace*. Porter's competitors, suppliers, and substitutes are subsumed in our marketplace category. In the networked economy, value nets also bring into play the notion of a "complementor"—a partner with complementary services and products. The marketplace category also subsumes this idea. In acknowledging that technology can change business direction, we have added one more category of forces—*technology*. Figure 2.10 shows the resultant Five Forces model that we adapted from Porter's model and developed for use specifically with the Solution Envisioning Process.

---

[10] A specific example of matching forces in Capability Cases is illustrated in Figure 2.11.

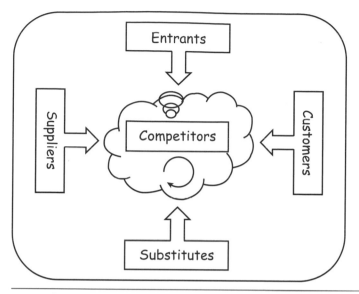

FIGURE 2.9.   Porter's Five Forces model.

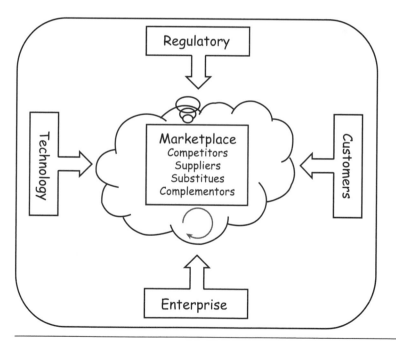

FIGURE 2.10.   Five Forces model as adapted for Solution
Envisioning.

Table 2.3 presents examples of forces in each category.

TABLE 2.3.   EXAMPLES OF FORCES FROM THE FIVE FORCES MODEL ADAPTED FOR SOLUTION ENVISIONING

Category	Force
Regulatory	Deregulation in the financial services industry enables banks to offer insurance products.
Technology	Increasing availability of wireless infrastructure.
Customers	Customers expect personalized information.
Enterprise	Employees expect to be able to work from home. Lack of resources to deal with new technology.
Marketplace	Concerns over privacy and security on the web.

Business forces and drivers are used interchangeably. It is beneficial if forces have been identified during business strategy work that precedes Solution Envisioning. Forces are also identified during Solution Envisioning, especially in its first phase, *Business Capability Exploration* (see Chapter 5 for more details on the activities that focus on eliciting and refining forces). These, and any forces that may have been identified in prior business strategy work, are refined and transformed as needed to align with the Five Forces categories adapted for use with Solution Envisioning.

When identifying forces, we are concerned with the following information:

Category

Category identifies the source of the force. As previously described and illustrated in Figure 2.10, we differentiate between the five categories of forces.

Volatility

Forces can be constant or dynamic. For example, existing government regulation can be considered a stable (or constant) force. On the other hand, "the increasing availability of wireless infrastructure" represents a dynamic (or unstable) force that is on the increase. Dynamic forces are often called trends.

When identifying a force or business driver, we consider if it represents a trend and if the trend is increasing or decreasing. The kinds of questions that can be used to determine this are

- Is the force likely to grow or diminish?
- How certain are we that it is here to stay?

Implication

Forces represent business opportunities or threats. For example, "the increasing availability of wireless infrastructure" could be seen as an opportunity to offer new services in the direct-to-customer business model. Depending on the stakeholder viewpoint, the same force could be seen as a threat or as an opportunity. For banks, the force "deregulation in the financial services industry" is an opportunity because it enables banks to offer insurance products. For insurance companies, it is a competitive threat.

Significance

How important the force is to solution stakeholders.

Evidence

Evidence consists of facts and supporting data that confirm the presence of the force. Evidence can be obtained from industry research as well as from company-specific data, such as business intelligence reports or customer surveys.

Results and Measures

A *business result* is a statement of a desired outcome—something the business wants to accomplish. A result is a change in the state of some aspect of the business or in the impact of the business in its environment.

Capability Cases make use of Kaplan and Norton's Balanced Scorecard framework for distinguishing four categories of results: financial, customer, internal, and learning and growth [Kaplan, 1996].

Like Balanced Scorecard, Solution Envisioning with Capability Cases places a strong emphasis on measurable results. Four categories or business perspectives for results are taken into account:

- **Financial**—"How do we look to our shareholders?"
- **Customer**—"How do our customers perceive us?"

- **Internal Processes**—"How do we gain operational excellence?"
- **Learning and Growth**—"How do we innovate and create value?"

Using the Balanced Scorecard approach, results are expressed with two kinds of measures: *outcome measures* as lagging indicators of the result being accomplished and *performance drivers* as leading indicators. The point of view is taken from the perspective of only one group of stakeholders, albeit a very significant one—the company's shareholders.

Neely, Adams, and Kennerley's work on the Performance Prism extends the Balanced Scorecard framework to take into account today's reality of multiple stakeholder groups: end users, employees, suppliers, regulators, pressure groups, and local communities [Neely, 2002].

The Performance Prism has five perspectives:

- **Stakeholder Satisfaction**—Who are our key stakeholders, what forces surround them, what are their challenges, and what do they want and need?

- **Stakeholder Contribution**—What do we want and need from our stakeholders in order for us to operate with efficiency, effectiveness, or an edge on the competition?

- **Strategies**—What broad action plans do we need to implement to satisfy the wishes of our stakeholders while satisfying our own needs?

- **Processes**—How should we organize our activities in order to execute our strategies?

- **Capabilities**—What capabilities do we need to have in place to allow us to operate our processes?

Solution Envisioning adopts the Balanced Scorecard approach of distinguishing four categories of results: *financial, customer, internal processes*, and *learning and growth*. Like Balanced Scorecard, it places a strong emphasis on measurable results.

From Performance Prism, Solution Envisioning adopts support for the perspectives of multiple stakeholders. It also takes a strong *capabilities*-oriented approach to understanding what enables the business to operate—both in its current state, and in a future, transformed state where *new capabilities* are established through a solution initiative.

Measuring Results

Some results are easier to quantify than others. Consider the difference between "decreased inventory" and "improved employee morale." The measurement for the first result is readily understood, while the measurement for the second result requires more thinking. In all cases, results can and should always be measured. Therefore, a firm Solution Envisioning rule emerges: *If you cannot say how a result will be measured and what its expected values should be, further work is needed to analyze the result until it can be expressed in measurable terms.* (It should be noted that, in this book, we sometimes use the words "business objective," "outcome," or "benefit" interchangeably with "result.")

For identifying measures, we recommend using a template suggested by the approach of the authors of the Performance Prism approach—see Table 2.4.

TABLE 2.4. A TEMPLATE FOR IDENTIFYING AND DESIGNING MEASURES

Measure:	What will the measure be called?
Purpose:	Why is it being introduced?
Relates to:	What other measures will it closely relate to?
Metric/Formula:	How will it be calculated?
Target Level(s):	What level of performance is desirable?
Frequency:	How often should the measure be made and reported?
Source of Data:	Where will the data come from?
Who Measures:	Who will be responsible for collecting and analyzing the data?
Who Acts on the Data (Owner):	Who is responsible for initiating actions and ensuring that performance along this dimension improves?
What They Do:	Exactly how will the owner use the data?

Defining and agreeing on measures is hard work. Many companies delay identifying measures and their targets. This creates a serious obstacle for business solution design because measures clarify the nature of expected results. When a solution is designed without knowing what it needs to accomplish—specifically, in terms of measurable results—the solution will be found wanting when the measurements are identified.

Table 2.5 lists examples of business results and potential measures. Results are grouped according to the type of business strategy they can support. In addition, we have used the Performance Prism approach of identifying the main stakeholder perspective to show who benefits from a result.

TABLE 2.5. CATEGORIES OF BUSINESS RESULTS AND POTENTIAL MEASURES

Business Strategy	Result	Stakeholder Perspective	Representative Measures
Marketing Excellence	Ability to better predict demands for products or services	Customer satisfaction	New product revenue Return on capital employed Sales win/loss ratio
Marketing Excellence	Improved brand recognition and company reputation	Investor satisfaction	Price premium Additional cash inflows resulting from the brand Consumer awareness and preference data Historical cost of brand development
Cost Reduction	Decreased inventories	Investor satisfaction	Cash-to-cash cycle Items-in-stock versus planned Inventory
Operational Excellence	Adherence to company policies and procedures	Regulator and community satisfaction	Standard operating procedure exceptions Average value of repeat penalties for non-conformance
Technology Enablement	Flexible IT infrastructure	Investor satisfaction	Cost to add new functionality to IT applications Time to add/modify IT functionality
Customer Centricity	Consistent interactions with customer through multiple channels	Customer satisfaction	Customer call center interactions to self-service ratio Cost of content re-purposing to multiple channels Customer complaints

In many cases, we list several measures for each result. Why? Often, a focus on one measure creates behaviors that actually undermine desired results. In one example, an insurance company wanted to improve customer satisfaction through quicker problem resolution. It decided to measure the speed of problem resolution based on how much time each customer call took. Sure enough, customer support representatives were motivated to end the calls as quickly as possible. As a result, customer satisfaction went down. The bottom line—you get what you measure; therefore, a balanced and carefully thought-out system of measurements is needed.

Anchoring Capability Cases in the Business Context

How do the concepts we have just introduced—*forces* and *results*—relate to Capability Cases? They are part of an extended model of the CapCase introduced earlier in this chapter (as shown in template form in Table 2.2). Table 2.6 shows mapping of some of the results listed in the previous table to selected CapCases.

TABLE 2.6. MAPPING RESULTS TO CAPABILITY CASES

Result	Capability Case
Ability to predict better demands for products or services	Alert Me Brand Portal Customer Personalization Profiler
Consistent interactions with customer through multiple channels	Consolidated Customer View Customer Interaction Advisor Semantic Data Integrator
Improved brand recognition and company reputation	Answer Engine Ask an Expert Brand Portal Tell a Friend Promotion and Offering Targeter

Similarly, forces can be mapped to specific CapCases that provide a response to those forces. We find these types of maps, which show forces or results connected to a relevant Capability Case, to be very useful views. Figure 2.12 illustrates an example of a map for forces. More maps are shown in Chapter 5.

A Brief Illustration of Selecting Capability Cases

One of the first projects on which we used Capability Cases was at a large professional services firm. The firm was establishing a support center called PSN (Practitioners Support Network) for thousands of consultants in the field. The center was to be small and highly networked throughout the global organization. It was expected to quickly respond to a variety of requests, including:

Technical, such as

- I have a technical problem with a product or a piece of code. Can you help me?
- Does anyone have experience with product X? Have we ever implemented it?
- Can product Y work with product Z?

Procedural, such as

- Can I share this information with the customer?
- What is our standard procedure for dealing with this type of situation?

Requests covered a wide range of technical products and project types. The management team charged with creating a technical infrastructure for the center wanted to know how emerging technologies, ranging from intelligent search to virtual collaboration, could help the center be more effective. In one week, 20 different Capability Cases were identified.

The names and intents of a selected sampling of these CapCases are listed in Table 2.7. After the workshop review, the team prioritized six capabilities to be further researched and developed into a first release of the system.

TABLE 2.7. CAPABILITY CASES FOR PRACTITIONERS SUPPORT NETWORK

Capability Case	Intent
Ask an Expert	To provide a forum through which questions can be directed to known experts, and answers collated, so that frequently asked questions can be answered automatically from a knowledge base.
Browse with a Buddy	To enable co-browsing where a colleague, friend, or customer support representative can remotely drive your web browser or you can be served the same web pages.
Concept-based Search	To provide precise and concept-aware search capabilities specific to an area of interest using knowledge representations across multiple knowledge sources both structured and un-structured.
Instant Helper	To enable website visitors to ask for immediate help by integrating chat or email sessions. Using business rules, requests can be routed to the most suitable person according to the customer's history, preferences, area of the site they are currently in, and other factors. Website monitoring can be used to identify when visitors are looking at certain items so it can pop up "Can I help you?" chat sessions as appropriate.

TABLE 2.7. CAPABILITY CASES FOR PRACTITIONERS SUPPORT NETWORK—
CONTINUED

Capability Case	Intent
Interest-based Information Delivery	To filter information for people needing to monitor and assess large volumes of data for relevance, volatility, or required response. The volume of targeted information is reduced based on its relevance according to a role or interest of the end user. Sensitive information is filtered according to the "need to know" basis.

Soon after the completion of this project, we were asked to help with the design of a supply chain collaboration portal for a major manufacturer. Although, the business context was different from the previous project, several Capability Cases created for the support center proved to be highly relevant for the portal. We were able to re-use them. A number of new capabilities were also identified.

After a catalog of Capability Cases is established, opportunities for the re-use of already identified capabilities keep growing. A process for selecting capabilities becomes important. Figure 2.11 illustrates one of the workproducts we often use as part of the envisioning workshop conducted during the Solution Capability Envisioning phase of Solution Envisioning (see Chapter 6 for details). During the workshop, we often run a session to position each of the proposed Capability Cases with respect to their value and effort. The figure shows the capabilities that were nominated in such a session for the supply chain portal project; they are positioned according to their perceived business value and implementation effort.

The implementation effort and maturity of a capability play a key role in the selection process. Often, enterprises will stage the implementation of the capabilities according to their implementation effort. Some businesses are risk-averse and will not consider capabilities that are still in conceptual, research, or early commercialization stages. Others will proactively seek competitive advantage through the use of emerging technologies and the *establishment of new capabilities*.

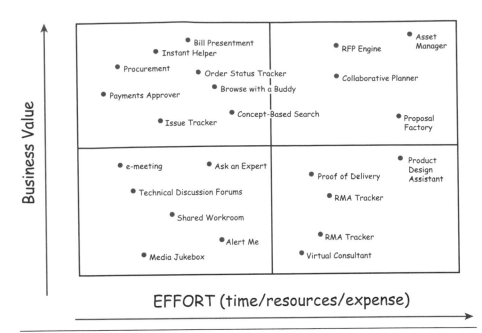

Business Value

EFFORT (time/resources/expense)

FIGURE 2.11. MATCHING AND EVALUATING CAPABILITY CASES BASED ON BUSINESS VALUE AND EFFORT.

Using Forces for Matching Candidate Capabilities

One way to derive a portfolio of candidate capabilities is by matching the forces that are impacting an organization to the forces relevant to a specific CapCase. Forces are the motivators and constraints that surround the problem and the solution.

Referring to the "A Quest for Self-Service" story presented in Chapter 1, several of the forces surrounding the "Answer Engine" (as shown in Figure 2.12) were evident in the company's (Secure Investments) business environment. Its customers were increasingly using the web, yet they didn't find the search engine on the company's website effective enough—hence, a large number of telephone inquiries. The questions called into Secure Investment's help desk were often procedural or asking for general information. The sources of the information were readily available online. They were, however, dispersed between different repositories and formats. The matching of forces provided an indication that the Answer Engine capability may be a good fit for the situation.

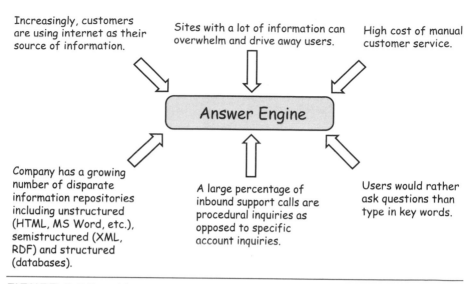

FIGURE 2.12.   MATCHING FORCES EVIDENT AT SECURE INVESTMENTS SUGGESTS ANSWER ENGINE.

Using Results for Matching Candidate Capabilities

A complementary approach is to identify capabilities by looking at the benefits—business results—that they bring to an organization. Secure Investment's main objective was lowering the costs of customer service, but it was also interested in some of the other results Answer Engine was known to accomplish. Because Secure Investments wanted to make sure that the lower cost was a direct result of improved self service features—as well as being interested in understanding how Answer Engine affected customer satisfaction—it decided to measure several results. For example, it elected to use the Self-Service Index to track how much the new capability improved online customer service.

Sidebar 2.2   #1 Project Risk: Confusing Business Problems and Objectives with the Solution

It is our experience that solution capabilities are frequently expressed as results or even as challenges. This tendency is a project risk. Mixing the problem being solved with the solution and the solution with the desired business benefits creates confusion that compromises a shared vision.

Such confusion is an early warning sign that the project may not be successful. It often indicates that the analysis of the business situation has not been completed. It can also indicate that the people responsible for requirements have done both the analysis and the design work, but they haven't captured their line of thought on how solution capabilities connect to the surrounding business context.

In such a case, because there is no foundation for bridging the gap between the business' understanding of its needs and the technical requirements to fulfill them, no shared understanding of the solution is established between the business and the technical people. So any proposed solution is likely to miss the mark.

As an example of not distinguishing between the business problems, desired results, and the required solution capabilities, consider the following experience. At the time of writing this chapter, we were asked to review a business case for a proposed project in a large government organization.

The business case, as presented to us for review,[11] was a nine-page PowerPoint presentation proposing a content management system and a supporting taxonomy/metadata development project. This business case serves as salient example of not distinguishing between business problems, the desired results, and the solution capabilities available. It illustrates the importance of identifying challenges, forces, results, and measures to analyze a business situation and formulate a solution.

The proposal was requesting a multi-million dollar, three-year spending plan based on the following customer benefits statement:

Original Benefits Statement

- Enables projects to create their own web pages
- No HTML skills needed; faster deployment of content

---

[11] Our understanding was that this presentation represented the most complete view or record of the business case at that time, and no other supporting information or documentation was given to us or available. The content of the presentation was conveyed to us as *the business case*. The analysis in Sidebar 2.2 is meant only to suggest that this representation of a business case was lacking in clarity, focus and content sufficient to support an effective solution initiative.

- Version control and "snapshots" of site states
- Better search results from embedded metadata

Workflow Used For

- Accuracy and conformance to standards and policies
- Archiving for long-term access

After analyzing this statement and the rest of the presentation, we identified the following as (implicitly) proposed solution capabilities:

Proposed Solution Capabilities (our logical extrapolation from the listed benefits)

- Self-authored project web pages
- Content version control at a file level
- Site configuration management
- Metadata enhanced search
- Content authoring workflow

We surmised a few possible benefits the proposal could be looking to attain:

Projected Results

- Faster deployment of content
- Improved precision of search
- Greater standardization of content
- Decreased time IT spends to support content publishing

Analysis of the Consequences

Because of the limited input statement, our analysis was guesswork to some extent. For example, the statement "workflow used for archiving for long-term access" could be addressing one or more goals:

- By removing invalid or outdated content from the active index, it could improve search precision.
- Reduction in content could also decrease the amount of real time access storage needed (cost benefit).
- The benefit of archiving could also be seen in the improved ability to recover content.
- The workflow could help minimize mistakes in the archiving process.
- Finally, the new archiving capabilities could help to ensure adherence to the government regulations not supported by the currently deployed solution.

Even with these benefits identified, we couldn't state with any certainty their relative importance, priority, or urgency to the business. Nor could we guess what expectations the organization might have for each of the possible results. Without a treatment of challenges, benefits, or forces, there was no indication as to why investing in the proposed solution was the right thing to do. The business case was left incomplete.

Conclusions

Did the proposed solution make sense? We couldn't tell. It was not possible to evaluate the proposal from the business perspective because the justification for the solution and the thought process used to derive it were not provided. If approved in its present form, it was likely to become an IT project not properly connected to the business' strategy and goals—that is, it exhibited the classic symptoms of the "gap" between business and IT as illustrated in the cartoon that opens this chapter, Figure 2.1.

By enforcing a formal separation between solution capabilities and challenges, drivers, and the results that define the business situation, Solution Envisioning with Capability Cases overcomes this critical project risk.

WHEN CAN SOLUTION ENVISIONING BE USED?

In the same way that Use Case descriptions facilitate discussion about "what the system should do for the user," Solution Envisioning with Capability Cases supports a dialog on "what the system could be and what it could do for the business." Capability Cases serve as solution catalysts in several possible ways:

- By communicating the vision of technology enablement for an enterprise.
- By guiding and confirming the identification and selection of technology platforms by mapping technology offerings to business needs
- By communicating best practices for realizing value from technology
- By stimulating concept-driven requirements elicitation by enabling business users to convey what results they want to achieve through examples and stories

We have used Solution Envisioning with Capability Cases in a number of situations where it has proven to be of value. Based on our experience in practice, we briefly outline ten common uses. In Chapter 8, "Solution Envisioning in Different Situations," we cover tailoring Solution Envisioning for use in varying situations. Figure 8.2 depicts these same ten uses according to the business solution lifecycle and organizational focus area that they characterize. The following is an overview of the ten common uses.

1. For *"Seeking Innovation"*—We have found that Capability Cases provide a convergent way to understand technology potential by evaluating it from the business perspective.

2. When *"Formulating a Solution"*—We use Solution Envisioning with Capability Cases to explore a broad range of solution possibilities. This overcomes the tendency to limit solution concepts to only the ideas previously experienced by designers.

3. To *"Gain More Confidence"*—Business people need solution stories that anchor ideas in a business context to commit to proposed solution ideas. This is especially true if such stories include measures of effectiveness.

4. To express *"Conceptual Architectures"*—We use Capability Cases for communicating to a development team and other stakeholders. CapCases capture a set of selected solution concepts along with the business reasons for implementing them.

5. For *"Communicating Best Practices"*—A set of Capability Cases represents a registry of available business components, best practices, and lessons learned.

6. To *"Ignite Change"*—The Solution Envisioning process helps bring this along by helping to identify a "solution champion." It also helps communicate a vision of the solution to all the stakeholders.

7. For *"Enterprise IT Capability Management"*—Capability Cases provide a way to document and communicate existing IT capabilities in the context of their use.

8. To *"Validate Benefits"*—We use Capability Cases because they carry a set of measures that quantify business results. These measures provide the means to assess the effectiveness of IT solutions and their benefits.

9. To *"Promote Technology Potential"*—Technical visionaries have used Capability Cases to package and market the business capabilities that communicate the potential of technology.

10. In preparation for *"Deployment of a Solution"*—Solution Envisioning with Capability Cases develops and presents a preview of what is coming and an explanation of why it is important to the business.

Depending on the situation, the role of Solution Envisioning with Capability Cases varies. In the early stages of the solution design, they define the conceptual components of the solution. Later in the lifecycle, they communicate the solution's results to a broader audience. Not only do Capability Cases serve as a vehicle for exploration and discovery, but they also provide a way to institutionalize or promote the adoption of best practices.

Opportunities abound for the application of Solution Envisioning, but there is a key pre-requisite: An organization embarking on Solution Envisioning must be both aware of the gap and committed to engaging in a process for bridging it. This commitment must be present on the business side of the organization as well as the technology side.

To serve as a bridge, the Solution Envisioning process is anchored half in the world of business and half in the world of technology. After all, a bridge has two ends, and if anyone is going to cross it, it had better have a solid foundation on both sides! With this in mind, to successfully execute the process, the Solution Envisioning team needs to be

- Composed of members representing all relevant areas
- Sponsored by an executive of the company
- Committed to communication and establishing a shared understanding
- Able to engage in dialog, synthesize differing perspectives, and stay open to discovering synergistic connections

HOW LONG DOES IT TAKE?

Solution Envisioning has proven to be a thorough, yet rapid way to conceptualize a solution. The process typically takes anywhere from a couple weeks to as long as a couple of months. In some situations (such as *gaining confidence in a technology* and *validating its benefits*, which are discussed in the previous section), it is neither practical nor necessary to engage in the full Solution Envisioning process. However, it is possible to do something valuable. Depending on the goals and the amount of input available (how much usable pre-work has already been done), it is usually possible to do something meaningful with Solution Envisioning in a very short time—not in one day, but a few days.

Do we complete the whole process in such cases? No. However, very productive groundwork is laid and vital communication is established between business and technical stakeholders. Generally, it takes a minimum of about three weeks to even partially cover the work of all three phases of Solution Envisioning.

Examples of tailoring the scope and focus of Solution Envisioning are given in Chapter 8. These range from examples of a very condensed version of the process, which we are sometimes asked to facilitate in just a couple weeks (a few days on-site plus a few days each of pre-work and post-work), to an intermediate version (four to six weeks) to a full version that extends over two to three months.

As shown in Figure 2.13, on average, full Solution Envisioning projects deliver comprehensive solution blueprints in four to eight weeks. The projects are typically

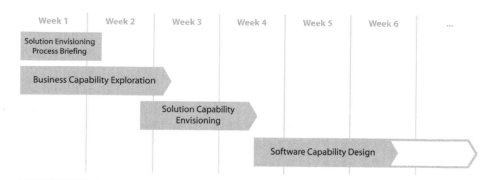

FIGURE 2.13.   FROM BUSINESS VISION TO SOLUTION BLUEPRINT IN FOUR
TO EIGHT WEEKS.

carried out by a small, full-time team (three to four people) that engages and facilitates the involvement of a larger group of part-time participants—namely, key solution stakeholders from the company or organizations involved.

In our experience, Solution Envisioning makes several contributions toward a more rapid and agile design method:

- **Avoiding rework** (not going down the wrong path)—Situation modeling techniques accelerate understanding of the nature of the problem and desired results. CapCases speed up the process of agreeing on the essence and important features of the solution, as well as identifying the appropriate technologies.

- **Reuse rather then reinvention**—CapCases accelerate requirements work through the reuse of solutions, technology, and capability ideas.

- **Communicating the solution vision more effectively**—CapCases create a shared language through which solutions can be expressed and understood.

TRAIL MARKER II: ENVISIONING SOLUTIONS WITH CAPABILITY CASES

If you are reading this, you (probably) just made it through one of the most challenging segments of the book. In this chapter, we covered the Solution Envisioning process, Capability Cases, and the concepts and vocabulary we use to connect them.

Let's recap the highlights of this chapter:

- Solution Envisioning bridges the gap between what the business needs and what technology promises to deliver by allowing stakeholders to see technical solutions in action.

- Capability Cases are a new type of "Business Problem–IT Solution" pattern that has been created to provide a way to connect IT solution concepts to particular business situations.

- The practices, processes, and methods of business and IT communities are very different. Because effective collaboration requires a common language, Capability Cases and Solution Envisioning share a few key concepts and terms. Terms like "forces," "challenges," and "results" form a common language between business and IT. Such terms are used to ask questions about the business situation and understand its needs so that, working together, business and IT can index and match Capability Cases as useful candidates.

- The Solution Envisioning process is intended to optimize decisions made in early stages of the solution lifecycle. It also ensures they are carried forward into implementation.

- Solution Envisioning is an agile process, customizable to a situation. Solution Envisioning projects typically deliver solution blueprints in four to eight weeks.

Chapter 3, "Illustrative Applications and Galleries," offers material that may be easier to navigate and should be of special interest to business decision makers. Portraying accounts from Solution Envisioning projects that we have conducted, it gives a feel for the experience and value of the process, along with tours of the accompanying Galleries of Capability Cases.

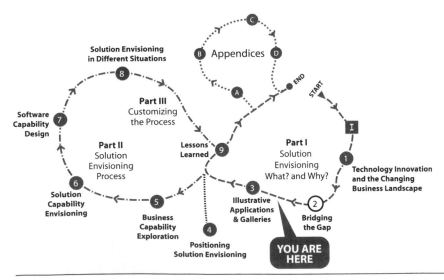

FIGURE 2.14.

3

ILLUSTRATIVE APPLICATIONS AND GALLERIES

"All invention and progress comes from finding a link between two ideas that have never met."

—**Theodore Zeldin, An Intimate History of Humanity**

FIGURE 3.1.

CHAPTER PREVIEW

This chapter describes two Solution Envisioning projects—the State Government Self-Service Project and the NASA Digital Shuttle Project. We explain how and why the Capability Cases we present were selected as candidate matches for their respective solutions to these projects. For each project, Capability Cases are presented within "galleries" explored during Solution Envisioning workshops.

The chapter begins by explaining the general role of galleries and *gallery tours* in the Solution Envisioning process. It continues with a description of two projects, with an account of the following for each:

- An introduction to the project and the format chosen for the Solution Envisioning workshop
- An overview of the Business Capability Exploration phase
- An outline of the starting point for Capability Envisioning, including an overview of the relevant technologies and a summary of selected capabilities
- A tour of the Capability Case gallery
- Workshop results

CAPABILITY CASE GALLERIES

In Solution Envisioning, a gallery of capabilities and solution stories serves at least three major purposes:

1. The gallery of capabilities stimulates ideas and fosters creative conversations and interactions between stakeholders about emerging solution concepts.

2. Capability Cases serve as an "existence proof" that progress can be made in concrete situations, using available technology.

3. Solution stories provide a context of use that can be compared to current stakeholder interests.

A structured approach for discovering and assessing solution capabilities comes from identifying forces and challenges that are affecting a business situation and agreeing on the specific business results to accomplish. The result of this process yields a set of candidate Capability Cases. On further evaluation, some of these capabilities may become a core basis of the solution, while others will be considered "nice to have, but not essential" and deferred or eliminated from consideration.

Presenting candidate capabilities as a *gallery* of solution options exposes the decision makers to a broad range of possibilities. The gallery experience is typically conducted in the envisioning workshop setting. Capability Cases are mounted on walls and a *gallery guide* is often distributed to the workshop participants with a description of each. Having a gallery of solution ideas sets the stage for a highly interactive experience—one where joint inquiry can lead to joint commitments.

Having all the key stakeholders of the future solution present for the workshop is a critical factor to success. The goal is to gain a shared understanding of each capability and its response to the business situation.

An effective way for the workshop to experience the gallery together is to conduct a guided *gallery tour*. The guide defines the essence (or intent) of the capability, talks about the solution story, and explains why it was selected—how it relates to the forces, challenges, and results at hand. Illustrative solution stories help participants understand the way a capability delivers value. They also help spark ideas, and new capabilities are often proposed during the workshop.

During the tour, a lively conversation typically ensues between the team members where many insights into the nature of the solution can occur—often prompted by questions for the guide. Assumptions and predispositions about the nature of the problem and possible solutions are surfaced, informing the decision-making process. Names of capabilities become a shared vocabulary for the session, allowing workshop participants to express their needs and concerns in a way that is understandable to the other stakeholders in the room. Typically, what results is a common view of a possible solution. A vision of a solution is gradually defined by taking pieces of solution stories and combining them in a way that satisfies the needs of the stakeholders in the session.

The case studies in this chapter convey some experiences from gallery tours conducted during Solution Envisioning workshops.

CASE STUDY I: SEARCH TECHNOLOGY WORKSHOP FOR THE STATE GOVERNMENT

A Search for Self-Service

Situation

Surveys conducted in 2000 indicated that 58% of the state's citizens thought it was harder to deal with local government than with the average business. Though most government agencies had websites, more than half of the population had never taken advantage of them. This was not surprising because the websites offered few capabilities beyond access to general information, as shown by the survey results presented in Table 3.1.

TABLE 3.1.   Results of Surveying Citizen's of the State—Services Available On the Web

Which of the following services, if any, does your local government's website offer?
Multiple responses permitted

	Percent
Provides general local government information	30.3%
Register online	6.2%
Pay utility bills	4.2%
Renew your driver's license	3.7%
Pay property taxes	3.3%
Vote online	3.1%
Pay speeding/parking tickets	2.2%
Renew your professional license	1.6%
Pay for a building permit	1.3%

Forces and Desired Results

Citizens of the state wanted access to more government services on the web. As indicated by the survey results in Table 3.2, almost 90% said that, given the option, they were likely to perform transactions online. State residents also said they were interested in seeing richer content on the sites, including state and federal information in addition to local information, petitions, political news, and a government glossary of terms.

TABLE 3.2.   Results of Surveying Citizens of the State—Services Wanted by Citizens

Using a scale of 1 to 5, where 1 is extremely interested and 5 is not at all interested, how interested would you be in using an online service for each of the following transactions:

	Average Interest Level
Paying speeding/parking tickets	3.2
Paying for building permits	3.1

TABLE 3.2.   RESULTS OF SURVEYING CITIZENS OF THE STATE—SERVICES WANTED BY CITIZENS—CONTINUED

Using a scale of 1 to 5, where 1 is extremely interested and 5 is not at all interested, how interested would you be in using an online service for each of the following transactions:

	Average Interest Level
Renewing your professional license	2.8
Paying speeding/parking tickets	2.6
Paying utility bills	2.2
Voting online	1.85
Online voter registration	1.84
Renewing car tags	1.74
Renewing your driver's license	1.7

If a website were available that offered you the ability to handle the transactions listed above online, how likely would you be to use that website?

	Percent
Extremely likely	39.8%
Very likely	32.7%
Somewhat likely	17.8%
Not likely or unlikely	4.2%
Somewhat unlikely	1.4%
Very unlikely	1.2%
Not at all likely	2.2%
Total	100%

The state's IT department knew that expanding content on government sites would require improvements in accessibility and searching. IT personnel did not have expertise with search technologies and wanted to learn more about them. Potential savings through self-service programs is well-documented, so the state decided to have select personnel participate in a Solution Envisioning workshop.

Workshop Objectives and Format

The main goal of the workshop was to have a better understanding of what was possible through the use of search and portal technologies. Additional goals included the following:

- Establishing a common understanding of the current business challenges and business context
- Developing a capability model to reflect the needs of the state
- Exploring how to go forward with the implementation of new capabilities

The workshop was designed to enable participants to understand and explore a broad set of technology options. The session was conducted over the course of two days. During the first day, gallery tours were used to present current search and portal technologies, their capabilities, and relevant trends. During the second day, workshop participants outlined a scenario for commercial vehicle registration and selected and ranked technology capabilities to support the scenario.

Business Capability Exploration

For this project, Business Capability Exploration was accomplished as a one-week exercise that took advantage of the work already performed. Existing materials, including survey responses and the analysis results of many types of stakeholders, were studied. This is summarized in Table 3.3.

TABLE 3.3.   STAKEHOLDER INTERESTS

Stakeholders	Expectations and Interests
Any Stakeholder	One-stop shop, assembly meetings
Citizen	Single point-of-contact, personal service, agency transparency, proactive notification, privacy, participatory government, proactive reminders, state information (services, hospitals, schools, attractions, events, and so forth)
Business (as a customer)	Efficient handling of regulatory obligations (one-time entry of details), simplified forms, process visibility, low costs, proactive notification
Business (as a partner)	Proactive notification, simplified forms, process visibility, low costs, efficient bid handling, electronic data exchange at low cost (email, WEB), prompt payment

TABLE 3.3.   STAKEHOLDER INTERESTS—CONTINUED

Stakeholders	Expectations and Interests
Employee	Higher quality interaction (reminders, information exchange, history of interaction), proactive reminders (regarding citizen service), fewer inter-agency barriers, automated timesheets and other admin functions
Commission	Demographic reports, tracking of specific legislation (progress of bill), federal mandates, agency status
Legislator	Demographic reports, tracking of specific legislation (progress of bill), federal mandates, agency status
Advocacy Council	Demographic reports, tracking specific legislation (progress of bill), federal mandates
An Agency	Participatory government—public forums through WEB, local news
Local Government	More integrated services (local news, court cases and decisions, tax information, and so forth)
Federal Government	Demographics, minutes from selected meetings
State Government	More integrated services (state news, court cases and decisions, tax information, and so forth)
Governor	Participatory government
Elected Official	Participatory government
Judiciary	Legislation progress

Analysis revealed that access to government services was the main interest of citizens and business stakeholders. Therefore, the search capabilities of interest were those that could take into account a user's goals and context of search. For example, locating the right vehicle registration form is not possible without knowing the type of vehicle, how it was acquired, and other factors. Several business scenarios in which this type of search would happen were discussed.

This example is one of the first Solution Envisioning projects we performed. We did not have many pre-existing Capability Cases at the time. So, the pre-workshop effort included creation of a broad range of CapCases that showcased search technologies and had the potential for responding to the following:

- Expressed interests of the stakeholders as described in Table 3.3
- Identified business forces, challenges, and results

Forces

As explained in Chapter 2, "Bridging the Gap with Solution Envisioning," you must express a business situation in terms of its relevant forces, results, and challenges to reliably identify solution capabilities. Table 3.4 shows an example of how some of the business forces discovered during Business Capability Exploration were used to nominate Capability Cases for the gallery.

TABLE 3.4.   MAPPING OF FORCES TO CAPABILITY CASES

Force	Suggested Capability Case
Some web content is in a graphical form, including images and Flash pages	Image Finder
A large percentage of the inbound support calls are procedural and routine inquiries as opposed to specific account inquiries	Location Finder and Personalized FAQ Agent
Availability of news syndication services	Featured Topics and News

In addition to the forces shown in Table 3.4, a number of other forces were found to be impacting the situation. The following *marketplace* forces were identified:

- Increasing need to resolve differences in vocabularies that exist and evolve in a specific social context
- Reducing the number of calls from customers and staff results in significant savings
- High cost of manual customer service
- Effective web content management lowers costs for developing and maintaining high-quality content

Challenges

A number of common challenges were found across several business processes within the scope of the project. Table 3.5 shows a mapping between some challenges and suggested capabilities.

TABLE 3.5.   MAPPING CHALLENGES TO CAPABILITY CASES

Challenges	Suggested Capability Case
How to allow people to better describe the information they're looking for on the web	Retrieval Assistant
How to find information stored across multiple repositories, often with connections and inter-dependencies	Federated Search
How to provide real-time or nearly real-time help/advice to customers visiting the government's website	Instant Helper

Other challenges that were often mentioned include

- How to help users narrow in on the general location of the information they seek
- How to maintain and deliver information in a consistent way to multiple audiences with differing needs
- How to quickly assess the relevance of a large corpus of information
- How to find information stored in multimedia form
- How to make sure your interactions with customers are consistent across all channels
- How to present the full range of services you offer in a way that makes it easy for users to find exactly what they need
- How to handle large volumes of routine email inquiries

Results

During Business Capability Exploration, the team identified an initial set of desired results:

- Consistent interactions with the customer through multiple channels
- Content delivery to multiple devices and channels while maintaining a single source
- Customer satisfaction
- Effective web presence
- Efficiency of operational processes
- Faster response to customer inquiries
- Flexible IT infrastructure—ease of integration and modification

- Improved information flow between individuals, departments, and systems
- Improved knowledge of customer preferences
- Improved precision of search results
- Improved quality of process execution
- Lower cost of customer service
- Lower operational costs
- Shift customers to more effective channels
- Single point of retrieval for information from multiple sources
- Speed and accuracy of customer problem-resolution
- Users have a more engaging experience of the website and are more likely to return

At the workshop, business results were further examined, prioritized, and used to analyze and rank presented capabilities.

Solution Capability Envisioning

Enabling Technology Overview

The state government is just one example of the many organizations interested in how search technologies can help solve some of their business problems. There has been an unprecedented growth of electronic content available not only on the web, but also behind corporate firewalls on Intranets. As these facts indicate, some form of information-finding is becoming mission-critical for many enterprises and types of work:

- There are several billion public web pages on the Internet.
- An ever greater amount of content is generated on-the-fly from databases.
- This already immense amount of information doubles every three months.
- Behind the public Internet, a similar situation exists for most corporations. The body of information contained in a variety of private document repositories and databases is already enormous and growing quickly. Many companies argue that this is the information they care about most—key knowledge about their products, services, skills, and capabilities.

As a result, professionals working in fields as varied as customer service, marketing support, sales, product development, and company operations often find themselves drowning in a sea of information. Delphi Group found that many of today's knowledge workers spend 50–60% of their time trying to locate information. Customers are not immune from this problem either. According to recent surveys conducted across a large, representative selection of websites, visitors couldn't find what they are looking for 60% of the time.

When employees can't find information, their productivity suffers. When customers (or in this case, citizens of the state) can't find the information they seek, one of the following things happens—each carrying a considerable cost—they

- Send an email or a snail mail to a help desk
- Phone in with the inquiry
- Visit state offices to receive support
- Give up in frustration

Next generation search technologies have matured to the point where locating information doesn't have to be a constant struggle. Revamped search and navigation capabilities have been reported that result in up to a 50% decline in customer service calls. When used for e-commerce, the result is up to a 400% increase in sales. What is stopping organizations from adopting advanced search technologies?

Search is often associated with the Boolean or Key Word type of searches made popular by Alta Vista and Lycos. Most business users today are very familiar with the way Internet search works. They have come to expect search queries to be performed in a certain way. They also have come to expect that results are usually imprecise and unpredictable. In reality, search is a complex combination of emerging technologies that include pattern recognition, collaborative filtering, natural language processing, image recognition, semantic analysis, and knowledge representation approaches. Different technical approaches are better suited to different business situations.

Google was launched on an innovative approach to search. The idea was simple—combine key word search with the cross-referencing aspect of the web. Web pages to which other pages are linked often get a higher rating. If the web pages that link to the page are themselves popular destinations for the search topic, the rating goes even higher. The approach works so well on the Internet that many companies wanted to use it on their own Intranet. Depending on the content and format of the Intranet, however, this attempt can lead to disappointment. The power of Google is not as evident on Intranets, for a number of reasons, such as:

- A higher percentage of typical Intranet content is in documents (MS Office files, PDF files) and in databases as opposed to static HTML pages.
- Intranet content evolves in ways different from the open web. As a result, popularity rating does not have the same meaning.

Similarly, auto-categorization technologies often perform better on the websites of content providers where documents are of similar length, style, and structure than they do on a typical Intranet. Knowledge representation technologies, on the other hand, are currently more feasible on an Intranet or a company's website than on the open web. This is because they are model-driven, making it easy to optimize for specific types of search queries (most popular or most important).

Often, IT departments lack personnel with specific expertise in the areas of search and information discovery technologies, as well as lacking a familiarity with the kind of capabilities that can be delivered. More importantly, they usually lack understanding of the multiple approaches afforded by these technologies, their pros and cons, and the applicability of each. This was true for the state project discussed earlier, so Capability Cases were used to educate the IT team on the technical options and the strengths and weaknesses of the different approaches.

Nominated Capabilities

A varied set of Capability Cases was nominated for the presentation and discussion at the workshop. Listed in Table 3.6, these CapCases illustrate different ways search technology could deliver value. We also provide brief descriptions for some CapCases that were part of the gallery but are not included in this book.

TABLE 3.6. Capability Cases Presented at the State Government Workshop

#	Capability case	Shown on Page
1	Concept-Based Search	97
2	Navigational Search	100
3	Visual Navigator	102
4	Retrieval Assistant	104
5	Personalized FAQ Agent	106
6	Instant Helper	108
7	Browse with a Buddy	110
8	Virtual Time Machine	112

TABLE 3.6. Capability Cases Presented at the State Government Workshop—continued

#	Capability Cases Not Included in This Book	
9	Federated Search	To enable search of multiple information repositories and consolidate results. Federated search can interface with a number of search engines, consolidate their results, apply its own relevance rules, and present them as a single view.
10	Image Finder	To enable search through indexing, categorizing, and ranking images. Often allows users to perform a query by choosing an image that is somewhat similar to the desired images. Image Finder might take into account a variety of meta data including the image's filename, META tags found in the HTML page, or META tags embedded in the image itself. It might also look for clues from the image's context, for example, the words or phrases that are close to the image. Some approaches can "see" inside images to discern shapes and colors. They use this information to find images similar to the one the user is starting with.
11	Location Finder	To give customers the ability to use a company's website to find nearest stores, branches, and other locations that carry required products or provide required services.
12	Email Response Agent	To completely automate email responses to customer inquiries or to assist agents to respond to new or unique issues by automatically suggesting response templates and possible answers based on the content of the inquiry.
13	Document Normalizer	To increase the utility of an archive of small documents by identifying redundant items (for example, a user's group for exchanging maintenance tips).
14	Customer Analyzer	Use WEB and traditional data sources (internal and external to an organization) to identify customer product preferences, customer profitability, demographic information, credit history, and other information.
15	Opinion Monitor	To collect data from diverse groups of people in the form of electronic surveys and feedback questionnaires. Support design and publishing of surveys and viewing of results in text and graphical reports.
16	Featured Topics and News	To feature articles and industry news related to a company's products and services.

In the next section, we replicate many of the CapCases that were in the gallery and attempt to give a feel for the gallery tour experience (as much as is possible to do in a book) by describing some of the key discussions that took place.

Envisioning Workshop Gallery I: State Government Self-Service

A summary view of each Capability Case is presented along with a brief discussion.

Capability Case I.1

Concept-Based Search

Intent:

To provide precise and concept-aware search capabilities specific to an area of interest using knowledge representations across multiple knowledge sources both structured and un-structured

Solution Story:

Empolis SmartCooking, IBM Practitioner Support Network, Integrating Text Databases with SKIP, Intelligent View Thyssen-Krupp, Onigo.com, **Simatic Knowledge Manager**

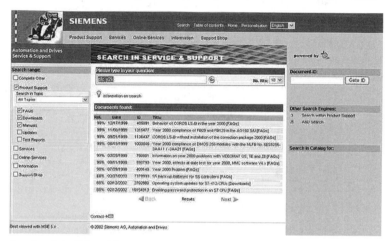

Results of the "plc y2k" query

Siemens Simatic system is a self-service WEB application for Siemens Industrial Control Products. In the screen shot above, the "plc y2k" query returns a number of documents even though none of them contain the specified text string. The system understands the concepts of "y2k" (Year 2000) and "plc" (Programmable Logic Controller) and finds documents that contain these or similar concepts. A knowledge model or a map of concepts used by the system operates as a unifying intelligent index seamlessly integrating information located in different repositories. Simatic is available on the web and on CD as an intelligent knowledgebase.

Benefits:

Improved self-service, better search precision

Featured Products:

Livelink from Open Text Corporation, Orenge from Empolis

Applicable Products:

Arisem KM Server from Arisem, ClearResearch from ClearForest, ClearSight from ClearForest, CoBrain from Invention Machine, Kaidara Commerce from Kaidara Software, Kanisa ServiceWeb from Kanisa, K-Infinity from Intelligent Views, Ontobroker from Ontoprise, Semetric from Engenium, SKIP from SemanTx Life Sciences, TripleHop Recommendation Engine from TripleHop Technologies, TurboSearch from LingoMotors

Discussion

This capability could also be called a *knowledge-enhanced search* because the words of the search query are examined to identify specific concepts that the search engine knows about. Concepts, their synonyms, and their relationships to each other are typically modeled for a given area or domain.

This capability would not be very effective as a general-purpose, Internet-wide search system because it requires a model of knowledge that the Internet cannot currently provide. (Growth of the *Semantic Web*[1] may change this situation.) It can be extremely effective as a specialized search engine, as illustrated by the Siemens Simatic solution story.

Siemens' Power and Automation division uses *Concept-based Search* for its self-service customer support. The knowledge model contains information about "plc," or Programmable Logic Controller, as well as known problems associated with these and other products made by Siemens. The model serves three purposes:

- Insures precision of the search.
- Improves user interaction—both natural language and dialog are possible.
- Federates across multiple repositories of information serving as a common denominator.

Siemens estimated that it reduced calls into its technical assistance center by 40% and saved   3 million annually by using Concept-based Search for customer self-service through the web.

Similarly, the state could build a knowledge model of services offered by the state and local governments and use it to provide access to forms and other information needed by citizens wanting to take advantage of services.

Federated Search is a related capability. It is especially useful when many heterogeneous sources of information exist. It serves as a single point of access, consolidation, and aggregation. The gallery featured Federated Search with a solution story from a Department of Defense project where it was used to unify access to several government sites and systems. As in the Concept-based Search, queries are

---

[1]   "The Semantic Web is an extension of the current web in which information is given well-defined meaning, better enabling computers and people to work in cooperation." From "The Semantic Web." Tim Berners-Lee, James Hendler, and Ora Lassila. *Scientific American*, May 2001.

run against a knowledge model (such as a taxonomy or an ontology[2]) that interprets and extends them. The interfacing system then passes it to one or more systems that it is federating. The system providing the Federated Search capability knows the requirements and capabilities of these systems—what information they can provide and what information they expect to receive. It consolidates the returned results prior to displaying them to the user.

[2] A semantic model in which relationships (associations between items) are explicitly named and differentiated is called *ontology*. Because the relationships are specified, there is no longer a need for a strict structure that encompasses or defines the relationships. The model essentially becomes a network of connections with each connection having an association independent from any other connection.

Capability Case I.2   # Navigational Search

Intent: To help people narrow in on the general neighborhood of the information they seek using topical directories or taxonomies. A taxonomy should be created taking into account user profiles, user goals, and typical tasks performed. To optimize information access by different stakeholders, more then one inter-related taxonomy is needed.

Solution Story: HighWire Stanford Electronic Library, **Tax Map on IRS Intranet**

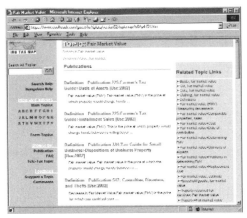

Subjects from different documents are grouped together

IRS information is complex, extensive, and spread across many unconnected documents. The IRS wanted to improve the quality of answers provided by its call centers by creating an integrated view across all diverse sources of information. It used semantic technology in the form of Topic Maps to create a "Tax Map" application. IRS call center personnel use Tax Map to quickly and reliably access various information pieces available for a given subject. Navigation is fine-tuned by tax law experts. Two means of navigation are available: using integrated main topic and form topic indexes and using resource type. The application uses existing document sources. When sources are updated, the navigation system is automatically regenerated. Conformance with the Topic Map standard (ISO/IEC 13250:2003) guarantees long-term preservation of the links between information items.

Benefits: Increased productivity of call center personnel, increased quality and reliability of call center services, bringing new hires on board faster.

Featured Products: Topic Map Loom from Infoloom

Applicable Products: Applied Semantics Auto-Categorizer from Applied Semantics, Arisem KM Server from Arisem, Autonomy IDOL from Autonomy, Inxight Categorizer from Inxight Software, K-Infinity from Intelligent Views, LingoMotors TurboCat from LingoMotors, Semio Tagger from Semio, Seamark from Siderean Software, Stratify Discovery System from Stratify, Zycus AutoClass from Zycus

Discussion

Another popular way to find information is by browsing a hierarchy of categories or topics while converging on an area of interest. We call this capability *Navigational Search*. Yahoo! is an example that often comes to mind when we think of browseable topics. Websites like Yahoo! use taxonomies[3] to create navigable categories of information. Every page on the web can fit into at least one of Yahoo!'s categories. Categories are organized in hierarchies with multiple levels of subcategories. Each category describes the content of the pages that can be filed under it without reference to the particular words that may appear in the pages.

Traditionally, electronic documents have been classified under a taxonomy by manually reading and coding each file. Yahoo!, for example, is known for employing librarians who categorize pages by hand. However, this method lacks scalability and flexibility. Few organizations can justify maintaining a large staff of knowledge classifiers. An alternative is using categorization software to automate a process of populating the taxonomy with the relevant content. This CapCase highlights several vendors that offer auto-categorization software.

Taxonomies may also be used to suggest additional relevant (related) topics and documents. This is illustrated in the featured solution story about using Navigational Search to access IRS publications. Documents are considered related, but not because of key words (for instance, in this example, the terms "fair," "market," and "value" are often repeated in documents). Instead, they are determined to be related because they belong within the same topics as determined by a semantic model, such as taxonomy. This means that the effectiveness of Navigational Search is highly dependent on the quality of the model it uses.

---

[3] A *taxonomy* is one of the simplest forms of semantic model. A taxonomy offers a way to categorize or classify information within a tightly defined tree-like hierarchical structure. Taxonomical hierarchies provide an ordered connection between each item in the structure and the item or items below it.

Capability Case I.3	# Visual Navigator
Intent:	Effectively present and summarize large amounts of information on one screen by using visualization technologies. Includes ability to navigate and drill down for more detail.
Solution Story:	map.net, The Hive Group's Amazon Product Map, Smart Money Stock Market Map, **Visual Navigation at HighWire Stanford**, Webmap at Infoscape

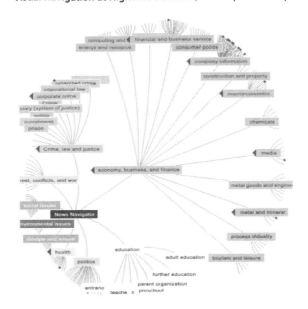

Dynamic access to detail on scientific topics through visual navigation

Stanford's online medical library contains thousands of scientific articles categorized according to their topics. Users can browse collections of topics using a visual tree. Clicking on a topic moves it to the center of the display. Clicking and dragging moves topics of interest toward the center and exposes new topics which had previously been minimized. Double-clicking on a topic will show a list of the documents in the original web browser window. Typing a term in the "Search for Topics" box will highlight all topics that have a topic name that contains the search term. The highlights appear as red triangles next to the topics. Hovering over a topic (without clicking) triggers a popup window that gives the full topic name and the number of documents in the topic (if that count is greater than zero).

Benefits:	Improved access to information, ability to discover new information, ability to see and understand relationships between different topics and concepts
Featured Products:	Inxight Star Tree SDK from Inxight Software
Applicable Products:	BrainEKP from TheBrain Technologies Corporation, DataVista Spectrum from Visualize, Inc., Honeycomb from The Hive Group, KartOO from KartOO SA, Metis from Computas, WebHeatmaps from NeoVision, WebMap Server from WebMap Technologies

Discussion

Navigating through large amounts of information, even when it is well-organized, can be confusing and difficult. One way to improve the browsing experience is by supplementing hierarchical text lists with visual maps that depict relationships between topics, or by showing a richer summary view not possible with text. Maps present more information on one screen so the user doesn't need to click back and forth to see all the data. Often, positioning a mouse over the map will pop up a small display describing details of the selected item.

Several types of visual maps are possible, including the following:

- **Linked trees, mind map-like diagrams**—These show relationships between topics and areas that provide a dynamic overview of all the topics and their relationships, and they include the ability to expand and zoom in on different branches. This is the visualization approach chosen by Stanford's online medical library, as featured in the solution story for this capability.

- **Plotted maps with different colors, sizes, and positioning**—These indicate the relative number of documents or special properties of the documents. These maps don't show relationships, but they offer additional informational value through the use of map features.[4]

---

[4] For an example of this map type, see the *Visual Navigator* Capability Case, Figure I.2, in the Introduction. Also see it in this book's color insert.

Capability Case I.4

Retrieval Assistant

Intent: Uses ontologies to extend, enrich, or focus search queries

Solution Story: Using Ontology to find Information at the German Environmental Portal

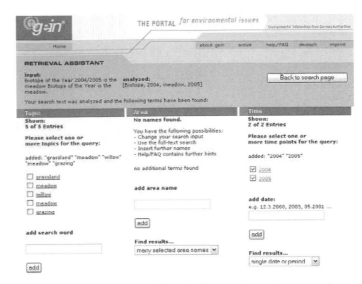

The German Environmental Portal aids users' search requests by suggesting additional terms to clarify the query

Users of the German Environmental Information Network can search content using semantically enhanced queries. Search strings are parsed to find and suggest related topics to the user. In addition to a broad range of topics, the content is matched against location and time dimensions of ontology.

Benefits: Improved relevancy of search results

Featured Products: Custom-built Topic Map engine

Applicable Products: Orenge from Empolis, Siderean Seamark from Siderean Software, Topic Map Loom from Infoloom

Discussion

The *Retrieval Assistant* capability can clarify search requests by suggesting additional terms to add to the query. In the gallery example that featured the German government portal of environmental information, the original search request was *biotope of the year meadow*. Retrieval Assistant asked if the term "meadow" should be expanded to include its synonyms, such as "grassland." Understanding that "meadow" may refer to a specific physical location, Retrieval Assistant presented the user with an opportunity to specify the geographic location relevant to the search. Finally, understanding the notion of "biotope of the year," it asked to specify a year, in this case, 2004.

As with some of the previous capabilities, *Retrieval Assistant* relies on a specific type of knowledge model. In this example, the model describes aspects important to environmental information.

Capability Case I.5	# Personalized FAQ Agent
Intent:	An intelligent bot that uses a company's knowledge of the customer as well as information about its products, services, known problems, and ways to resolve them to answer customer questions online. Customer knowledge may include information on products the customer bought from the company, the status of their relationship to the company, and the query context, such as from which point on the company's website the FAQ session was initiated.
Solution Story:	Blue Horizon—FAQ, Nissan's Virtual Agent, **Self-Service at Remington**, Simatic Knowledge Manager

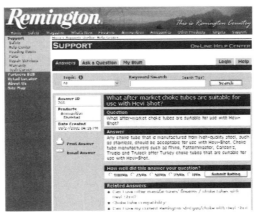

Remington customers are able to directly get answers to many of their frequently asked questions using a convenient, self-service website.

When Remington created a simple information website, they were flooded with email questions that threatened to overwhelm call center agents. In response, they implemented RightNow software for email management and providing self-service answers to customer inquiries directly on the website. The knowledge base behind the system grows based on the questions customers ask. It takes input from all channels including email interactions and live chat sessions. When the customer can't find the answer, they are automatically guided to send an email or to initiate a live session. During the first 6 months of operation 120,000 people visited the FAQ section and fewer than 1% had to direct their questions to a Customer Service Representative. Remington opted for a hosted solution that was deployed in two weeks.

Benefits:	Improved customer service and satisfaction while maintaining customer support costs. Reduced email-related and telephone-related support and time to respond to email inquiries, while increasing visibility.
Featured Products:	RightNow Self Service from RightNow Technologies
Applicable Products:	ActiveBuddy BuddyScript Server from ActiveBuddy, Inc., AskJeeves from AskJeeves, EasyAsk from EasyAsk Inc., KANA RESPONSEIQ from Kana Software Inc, NeuroServer from NativeMinds Inc, Orenge from Empolis.

Discussion

Personalized FAQ Agent is a self-service capability that uses a knowledge base of possible questions and answers to find the most appropriate response to a customer's online queries. Some implementations take the customer context into account—for example, what page the customer is on when he submits the query, what action he is trying to perform, and so on.

Each customer interaction is, in turn, represented in the knowledge base enabling it to grow and become more comprehensive over time.

Capability Case I.6

Instant Helper

Intent:

To enable website visitors to ask for immediate help by integrating chat or email sessions. Using business rules, requests can be routed to the most suitable person according to the customer's history, preferences, area on the web they are currently in, and other factors. Website monitoring can be used to identify when visitors are looking at certain items and pop up "Can I help you?" chat sessions as appropriate.

Solution Story:

Ask the Expert at Prudential Securities, Chat with an Agent at ATT WorldNet, **Chat with an Agent at LandsEnd**

Having problems?
Need questions answered?
Click the button to talk to us.

Land's End website conveniently offers a 'live help' option to the user.

On the Land's End website, the "Instant Helper" button is always present. Any questions a customer may have regarding shipping policies, sizes, exchanges, or any other information can be immediately responded to by a live representative accessible through a chat window. A customer representative understands the context of the question because she knows the exact location of the shopper on the website. A shopper does not need to dial Land's End on a separate line.

Benefits:

Decreases the likelihood of a customer abandoning the shopping cart; makes it possible for the customer service rep to assist with complex online transactions; increases customer representatives productivity

Applicable Products:

Chordiant Assisted Response from Chordiant Software Inc., E.piphany Real-Time from E.piphany Inc., E.piphany Service Center from E.piphany Inc., Facetime Instant Message Director from FaceTime Communications, Firepond Converse from FirePond, Inc., Groopz from Digi-Net, Kamoon Smart Engine from Kamoon, KANA RESPONSEIQ from Kana Software Inc., NeuroServer from NativeMinds Inc., RightNow Live Chat and Collaboration from RightNow Technologies

Discussion

Today, many websites have the capability to invoke live help either through an instant messaging dialog or by using voice over IP. Usually, a website user requests live help. However, some websites pop up an instant messaging dialog if they determine the user is hesitant or may be getting stuck in some interaction on the site.

Capability Case I.7	# Browse with a Buddy
Intent:	Provide a means to allow co-browsing where a colleague, a friend, or a customer support representative can remotely drive your WEB browser or you can both be served the same web pages.
Solution Story:	**Shop Together at Land's End**

The Land's End website offers a co-browsing facility to allow two shoppers to shop together and assist each other.

This implementation allows two shoppers to browse together and add items into a single shopping basket.

Benefits:	Brings communal and social aspects of the real world shopping to the online world, allows shoppers from different physical locations to make purchase decisions together and to seek each others' advise
Applicable Products:	Groove from Groove Networks, PageShare from PageShare Technologies, SysMaster from SysMaster Corporation, BrowserFor2 from Matthewssoftware

Discussion

Co-browsing is another name often associated with the *Browse with a Buddy* capability. This capability is not a direct application of search technology, though one can envision situations where a person's browsing partner and guide is an intelligent agent using search technologies to understand the person's context and goals.

The solution story features the Land's End web catalog where two shoppers can browse the site together: one shopper being in a driving role while the second shopper gets served the web pages accessed by her "buddy." Shopping is one area where this capability may be attractive. Other areas include help desk, sales, and any collaborative work situation. In the workshop, it was determined that the state could use this capability in a number of ways. It could, for example, invoke co-browsing to help citizens fill out a form correctly or to lead them to the right area on the state's website.

Capability Case I.8

Virtual Time Machine

Intent:

To enable display of a virtual history of events without having to store multiple snap-shots of data that hasn't changed. In the simplest case, each item just has to be tagged with "first appeared" and "last seen" timestamps. Visualization is the key factor[md]there is a need for fast forward and rewind facilities, in the mode of a DVD player.

Solution Story:

London Transport Museum

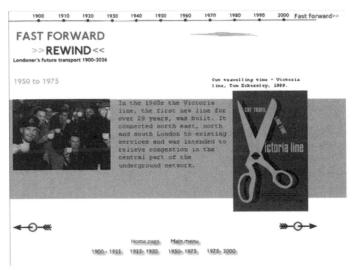

The London Transport Museum website allows visitors to explore how transportation has changed over time using a time travel metaphor.

This site uses a timeline metaphor so users can select a time over a period of a few years, and the site shows what events happened during these years. Visitors get to learn about the time period and understand which museum exhibits reflect the time they are interested in.

Benefits:

Effective web presence, inviting and exploratory user interface metaphor, adds an extra dimension for organizing the information[md]time frame as well as subject area

Applicable Products:

N/A, this is a public organization using internal technology platforms.

Discussion

Participants in the workshop had several solution ideas that were sparked by the *Virtual Time Machine* CapCase. Virtual Time Machine is based on the observation that trends are only visible when you can explore changes over time. While we do not yet know how to travel into the future, we should be able to revisit the recent past and compare it with the present. The intent of the capability is to store a series of "snapshots" of historical data, so it becomes possible to recreate an accurate picture of opinions, links, and perceptions as they existed at a specific date.

In the workshop gallery, the capability was illustrated by a timeline metaphor used at London's Transportation Museum website. While the Virtual Time Machine solution story was about exploring "soft" aspects—how people's perception and use of transportation evolved over time—one workshop participant used this concept to create a hard-data-driven *Demographic Predictor* capability concept for his state. Demographic Predictor would use past demographic data for different regions in the state to help businesses make decisions on locating and re-locating their offices.

We call the process by which Demographic Predictor came about *reasoning by analogy* and *design by example*. Too often, creative explorations can be open-ended journeys that don't converge on real possibilities. The design by example strategy is used within Solution Envisioning in a way that fosters creative thinking while keeping the focus on business capabilities and business goals.

Workshop Results

The workshop was successful in meeting its objectives by facilitating realization of the following insights and results:

- Appreciation of a broad range of capabilities that could be used to build a government portal
- A shift from thinking of the problem as "better search" to a more informed position—search technologies could be used in a number of ways to enable self-service
- The realization that an important key to providing users with assistance is knowing where they are in a process (for example, in a process of applying for a license) and what the next step is
- Understanding how intelligent advisors and recommenders can provide visibility into the state of the process that a user is engaged in
- Insight into how personalization for specific types of users (role-based) and even individual users was an important consideration

CASE STUDY II: SOLUTION ENVISIONING AT NASA

The Starting Point

Situation

Many large and small companies work together to make the NASA Space Shuttle Program possible. As a result, the Space Shuttle engineering processes extend across various enterprise systems with numerous heterogeneous data sources. They are difficult to navigate and use effectively. Integration and synchronization of information is a constant problem requiring manual audits to ensure information integrity. This situation creates risks and inefficiencies in working practices.

While budget pressures require NASA and its subcontractors to do ever more with less, they are faced with difficult existing conditions, such as the following:

Stove-piped, legacy engineering processes that result in high management overhead.

- Paper-based and manual procedures prevail.
- Low visibility across organizational boundaries.

Programs (NASA and its contractors) are going through significant changes in the workforce.

- Large numbers of workers are retiring or nearing retirement age.
- More work is being moved to contractors.
- Most of the work is about maintenance and less about design and innovation.

The overall goal of the Digital Shuttle Project, as stated by NASA AMES[5] in conjunction with the Space Shuttle Vehicle Engineering office, is the "*Application of KM technologies to specific Agency problems to retire risk in the near term.*"

---

[5]   Located in California's Silicon Valley, NASA AMES is a premier research lab in support of NASA Missions and the nation's Vision and Space Exploration. http://www.nasa.gov/centers/ames/home/index.html

Forces and Desired Results

The Shuttle Drawing System (SDS) was a key focus area for this project. Over one million engineering drawings and Engineering Orders (EOs) define the Space Shuttle Orbiter. Drawings are a primary means of communication across lifecycle areas of design, engineering, and maintenance. The existing SDS required mental processing of multiple drawings and EOs to reconcile differences between the "as-designed" and "as-built/maintained" drawing sets. This is inefficient, tedious, and subject to misinterpretation by the various lifecycle practitioners.

Budget pressures require the Space Shuttle program to do more with less. Safety concerns require rapid access to complete information necessary for decision making. Because many organizations work on the program, workgroups are geographically dispersed and work efforts are partitioned. This leads to many cultural, contractual, integration, interoperability, and efficiency issues. The situation is further compounded by the fact that both NASA and its contractors have been experiencing mass corporate knowledge loss through retirement and attrition of key staff.

In many interviews conducted during the Business Capability Exploration phase of the project, positive comments were heard about people, processes, and the organization.

Dedication and pride in working for and with NASA remains high as the following quotes illustrate:

- "People are dedicated and committed."
- "It still amazes me that people will come back from vacation or even from retirement and work 24/7 if there is a problem."
- "We are working on something that matters."
- "There is a sense of mission."

Workshop Objectives and Format

The central objective of the Digital Shuttle Project was to integrate knowledge representations and information sources to reduce the uncertainty of interactions between design specifications, maintenance changes, and upgrades. The strategy for accomplishing the objective was to

- Transform engineering drawings into a form that can represent the current state, eliminating ambiguity, uncertainty, and misinterpretation
- Create models and metadata in a form more directly usable for current engineering tools and practices

- Provide a method of incorporating additional lifecycle information—attributes, design notes, assumptions, manufacturing details, test results, process requirements, classification, historical and tracking data, and contextual use—through a knowledge capture technique
- Increase sharing of engineering data and systems across NASA and its contractors' sites
- Evaluate aspects of integrating social and technical models

An additional objective was to evaluate how explicit representation of risk and subsequent knowledge capture, characterization, and reuse could enhance the useful life of integrated engineering models.

The workshop's goal was to introduce Space Shuttle program engineers and managers to different IT capabilities that can be used to satisfy these objectives. One of the challenges we needed to overcome was that workshop participants were mechanical and electrical engineers, program coordinators, and controllers who had limited knowledge and understanding of software technology. Many of the internal systems they were using were dated and did not take advantage of the rapid technology advances of recent years. Often, their knowledge of what was possible with new technology came from their personal use of the web rather than from the software they used in their everyday work environment.

The workshop was first conducted with the core Digital Shuttle team of about 12 people, with the aim of fine-tuning the presentation and messages, before taking it to a broader audience and, ultimately, to the top management.

Business Capability Exploration

For this project, the Business Capability Exploration phase lasted several weeks and included extensive interaction with staff representatives from NASA Kennedy Space Center, NASA Johnston Space Center, United Space Alliance (USA), and Boeing. Findings confirmed the following needs:

- **The need for more effective education and learning**—Workforce structures and processes are undergoing significant changes. As a result, there is a need to bring new Space Shuttle Program personnel on-board more effectively and also to achieve more efficient mobility within the organization for existing staff.
- **The need to find knowledge more effectively**—Knowledge in many forms exists within the Space Shuttle Program but cannot be found. Time is wasted on finding information located in disparate systems and silos of documentation. Relevant tacit knowledge needs to be

captured and incorporated into the institutional memory in a knowledge framework for easy access.

- **The need to capture knowledge more effectively**—A strong reliance on informal networks, well-established among long-time employees of the Space Shuttle Program, to solve problems results in a high risk of loosing critical knowledge when key people leave. Creating a mechanism for locating people in the organization with relevant knowledge will reduce time, costs, and errors.

- **The drivers for greater efficiency and organizational effectiveness**—The Space Shuttle Program has matured and is now in the operational phase. With the design phase complete, budgets are smaller, driving the need to be more cost-effective.

Throughout the interview process, there was confirmation that significant benefits would derive from this initiative. A few of these benefits include reduced risk/fewer mistakes, cost reduction, faster decision making, faster and more accurate access to information, faster learning curves for new people, greater efficiency, more reuse, enhanced processes, the ability to "know who knows what," and reduction of time wasted looking for information.

Seamless knowledge transfer and collaboration between NASA and its contractors is a key goal. New contractual language and intent can foster new behaviors between NASA and its contractors.

- **The need to recognize the extent of organizational change**— Communications and participation are the keys to overcoming resistance to change. Without addressing problems in these areas, there will be barriers that will inhibit the success of the Digital Shuttle Project and limit what it can become. Implementing a mobilization and communication strategy will lessen the resistance to change and create the desire to try out new tools by identifying benefits.

In the interviews, we asked people to rank the challenges they had in meeting their work objectives, with a scale from 0 to 5 (most challenging). We also asked them to rank business results that they viewed to be important to the program. From a list of 16 challenges, six challenges emerged as the most critical to satisfying the important objectives. These had a median value of 4. Figure 3.2 illustrates how the challenges map to objectives.

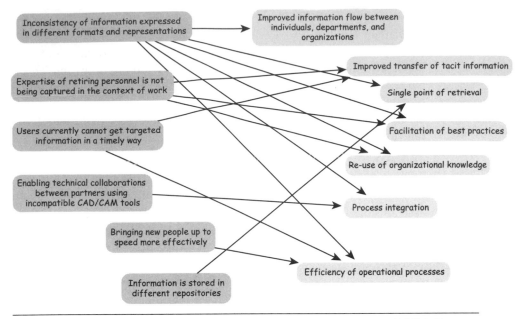

FIGURE 3.2. MAPPING OF CHALLENGES TO KEY OBJECTIVES—NASA DIGITAL SHUTTLE PROJECT.

Other barriers to meeting the business objectives included the following:

- Inability to effectively integrate information in the current Shuttle Drawing System with other models/data/systems
- Ineffective methods of working with modern engineering tools
- Difficulty in knowing whether you have all or enough of the relevant drawings

Figure 3.3 shows some of the common themes encountered during the interviews.

FIGURE 3.3.   INTERVIEW RESULTS—NASA DIGITAL SHUTTLE SOLUTION ENVISIONING PROJECT.

Capability Envisioning

Technology Overview

New standards recently approved by the World Wide Web Consortium (W3C)[6] are making it possible to represent information in ways that make information smarter and more autonomous and, therefore, far more accessible and adaptive. These standards—in conjunction with new tools and infrastructure components built to support them—are driving the development of adaptive computing within the enterprise as well as the growth of the next generation of the web, called the Semantic Web.

The vision of the Semantic Web is to extend the current web by enriching the information transmitted and accessed over the Internet with well-defined meaning, thus enabling computers to do more of the work in assembling and processing data to turn it into relevant information and knowledge. In other words, the initiatives

---

[6] W3C is an international standards body directed by Tim Berners-Lee, the creator of the World Wide Web.

underlying the Semantic Web establish a set of protocols and technologies that promise to improve the categorization and association of data, thereby enhancing the ability to create relationships and generate inferences between diverse systems and data.

Still, in its research and development stage, the term "Semantic Web" is perhaps new to many of us. However, the problems it aims to address are the very ones we have been struggling to solve for decades, such as information overload, stovepipe systems, and poor content integration.[7] The fundamental roots to these problems are lack of semantic definitions in individual systems, lack of semantic integration between data, and lack of semantic interoperability across disparate systems.

Disparate IT systems and information used by the NASA Space Shuttle program result in the following barriers:

- Knowledge exists but is hard to find.

- Information is in databases, but it is often not synchronized and is impossible to integrate.

- Complex processes, non-user-friendly documentation, and systems that require long learning curves.

NASA's problems are not unique. Most companies today rely on the data structures and databases that are not extendable, reusable, or amenable to integrated models—in particular, organizational models expressing *"who needs what from whom and why."* Semantic technology offers a solution by allowing the meaning of and associations between information to be expressed in such a way that it can be understood and processed at execution time by different systems.

The semantic definitions of concepts are captured in two new knowledge representation markup languages from the W3C—RDF (Resource Description Framework) and OWL (Web Ontology Language). RDF provides a protocol for establishing relationships between data whereas OWL enhances RDF with the ability to specify business rules and constraints on different data elements and their relationships to one another. Building on XML, these languages are beginning to be woven into the fabric of web-based tools and the World Wide Web.

W3C has also defined initial architectures and logic required to implement semantic solutions alongside existing applications and data sets. A wide range of companies have adopted semantic approaches and the vision of the Semantic Web, and

---

[7] *The Semantic Web: A Guide to the Future of XML, Web Services, and Knowledge Management.* Michael C. Daconta, Leo J. Obrst, and Kevin T. Smith. Wiley Publishing, 2003 [Daconta, 2003].

[8] *Adaptive Information: Improving Business Through Semantic Interoperability, Grid Computing, and Enterprise Integration.* Jeff Pollock and Ralph Hodgson. Wiley Publishing, 2004 [Pollock, 2004].

they are actively pursuing technology strategies that further advance the field.[8] These technologies and approaches are being used today by a growing number of early adopters. Initial applications clearly demonstrate that solutions based on these approaches can be implemented incrementally and can deliver ROI-supported value.

How is semantic technology distinguished from more conventional applications?

- Semantic technologies represent meaning through connectivity. The meaning of terms, or concepts, in the model is established by the way they connect to each other.

- A semantic model expresses multiple viewpoints.

- Semantic models represent knowledge about the world in which the system operates. Several interconnected models can be used to represent different aspects of the knowledge. The models are consultable (accessible) by applications at run time.[9]

- A semantic application uses knowledge models in an essential way as part of its operation. Use of a model is often referred to as "reasoning over the model." Reasoning can range from a very simple process of graph search to intricate inferencing over the model.

- Semantic applications are thin because they work with "smart" data. All the business rule logic is held in the models shared across applications.

Semantic models are intended as a way for different agents (applications or people) to interoperate and share meaning. The variations and commonalities semantic models represent are not of a single entity or stakeholder. By definition, semantic models support multiple viewpoints. This makes them especially suitable for solving interoperability problems.

The Semantic Web extends beyond the capabilities of the current web and existing information technologies, enabling more effective collaborations and smarter decision-making. It is a deployment platform in which an array of semantic technologies and conceptual frameworks are integrated to define and harness information semantics.

---

[9]   A useful characterization is that, for a semantic technology to be truly at work within a system, there must be a knowledge model of some part of the world that is used by one or more applications at execution time.

Nominated Capabilities

We will now take a look at the gallery of capabilities that was used during the workshop. Selected Capability Cases are listed in Table 3.7. Again, brief descriptions are provided for some that were part of the gallery but are not included in this book.

TABLE 3.7.   CAPABILITY CASES PRESENTED AT THE NASA DIGITAL SHUTTLE WORKSHOP

#	Capability case	Shown on Page
1	Product Design Assistant	124
2	Generative Documentation	126
3	Content Annotator	128
4	Expert Locator	130
5	Concept-Based Search	132
6	Automated Content Tagger	134
7	Interest-Based Information Delivery	136

Capability Cases Not Included in This Book

#	Capability case	Description
8	Ask An Expert	To provide a forum through which questions can be directed to known experts, and answers collated, so frequently asked questions can be answered automatically from a knowledge base.
9	Context-Aware Retriever	To retrieve knowledge that is highly relevant to an immediate context, from one or more systems, through an action taken within a specific setting—typically within a user interface. A user no longer needs to leave the application they are in to find the right information.
10	Distributed 3D Modeler	To enable engineers' work on product designs in a distributed environment, using different CAD tools as needed. Engineers need the capability to view and edit 3D models and associated information without needing to have access to the CAD system that created them.

Envisioning Workshop Gallery II: NASA Digital Shuttle

FIGURE 3.4.   TOURING CAPABILITY CASE GALLERY DURING NASA WORKSHOP.

Capability Case II.1

Product Design Assistant

Intent:

To support the innovative product development and design process by bringing engineering knowledge from many disparate sources to bear at the appropriate point in the process. Possible enhancements to the design process include: rapid evaluation, increased adherence to best practices, and more systematic treatment of design constraints.

Solution Story:

Audi Semantic Testcar Configurator, Sharing Engineering Knowledge at Ford

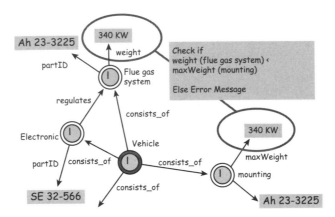

Constraints on possible configurations recorded as rules in an ontology.

Audi manufacturing engineers design, build, and test new prototypes as part of the innovation process. The faster this cycle can be completed, the greater the number of innovations that can be brought to market, and sooner. Audi uses a semantic engine from Ontoprise to represent complex design knowledge in electronic form. The engine brings together knowledge from many different sources and draws logical conclusions from the combined information. Audi uses this capability to provide a computational representation of complex dependencies between components of research test vehicles. These dependencies play a key role in the configuration and development of new vehicles. For example, for testing to proceed smoothly, the engineer must know whether a selected engine can be built into the chosen chassis, if the brakes are sufficient for the engine performance, or that correct electronics are present in the vehicle.

"We expect a shortening of the development cycle, while at the same time improving development quality," said Thomas Syldatke of Audi. "The electronic advisor shall take care of routine tasks, allowing our engineers to concentrate on creative efforts."

Benefits:

Reduced the overall prototyping cycle time for new car designs, improved development quality, automation of routine tasks, increasing innovation as engineers gained time for creative efforts.

Featured Products:

Ontobroker from Ontoprise, OntoEdit from Ontoprise

Applicable Products:

Cerebra Inference Engine from Network Inference, e2KS from Emergent Systems

Discussion

The gallery contained two examples of *Product Design Assistant* in use. Both solution stories are from the automobile manufacturing industry.

One company represented knowledge of the car design in a semantic model. Product Design Assistant uses the model to integrate information about components and configuration of new vehicles being designed, and it provides engineers with advice on dependencies between design decisions. Engineers are happy because they get help with routine tasks of information gathering and consistency checking. The company benefits because this capability improves speed-to-market and the quality of designs.

In the second solution story, car design knowledge is collected during the engineering work and then made available to all the processes in the workflow. The delivery of knowledge into work processes raised an important discussion during the workshop. One of NASA's major subcontractors was in the midst of a knowledge capture effort. It has conducted lengthy videotaping sessions with retiring engineers. Each engineer's story of their work on the space shuttle, problems they encountered, and design decisions they made were captured in a movie. The company has amassed a large video library, but it was not useful because collected knowledge was not connected to the work environment where that knowledge was needed. The discussion raised the possibility of supplementing or replacing the established knowledge capture process with a Product Design Assistant type of capability.

Capability Case II.2

Generative Documentation

Intent:

Maintain a single source point for information about a system, process, product, and so forth, but deliver that content in a variety of forms, each tailored to a specific use. The form of generated documents, and the information they contain, is customized to a particular audience.

Solution Story:

Automatic Schematic Generation with 3-D Models, **Meeting Minutes Butler for a German Financial Company**, Sharing Engineering Knowledge at Ford

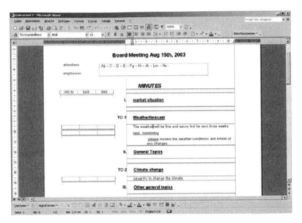

Agendas and meeting minutes are created with MS Word and automatically annotated.

Meeting minutes taken in board meetings at a German bank contain helpful information for the organization. Unfortunately, parts of the meeting minutes are confidential. This made the process of creating and distributing excerpts of board meeting minutes a very complex task.

The Minutes Butler supports the board's assistants by automatically capturing the written information and organizing the distribution of excerpts according to recipients' responsibilities. Assistants write documents with MS Word using templates. Contents of released documents, like agenda items, tasks, or decisions are automatically sent to the server, which generates excerpts of the meeting minutes by using a set of rules. The assistants save time, because they don't need to physically create excerpts with the copy machine, and all employees get access to essential knowledge (according to their profile). While writing the minutes, the assistants are also offered hints to whether a similar decision or task has already been made or what other decisions are affected.

Benefits:

Higher productivity for board assistants, faster dissemination of essential knowledge, higher quality of workproducts

Featured Products:

Ontobroker from Ontoprise, OntoEdit from Ontoprise, OntoOffice from Ontoprise, Zope Webserver from Zope Corp

Applicable Products:

Cogito Knowledge Center from Cogito, Inc., e2KS from Emergent Systems

Discussion

The *Generative Documentation* capability addresses a problem many of us experience—the problem of reducing the burden of documenting and repurposing information for different audiences.

The need to present information in a different format or from a different perspective is common to all business areas and industries. In product design, different formats are often needed to present information in a variety of drawing and diagramming standards.

The Generative Documentation capability generates different presentation formats on demand from the information made available to it.

The second solution story for this Capability Case, "Meeting Minutes Butler for a German Financial Company," shows generation of different documents from the same source. Here, the presentation format stays the same (MS Word), but the content changes depending on the audience.

The Space Shuttle Program has many regular meetings, including engineering board meetings, review meetings, and scheduling meetings. The meetings are attended by a wide variety of personnel from different disciplines and departments. Meeting decisions and minutes are sent by email to an even broader audience. These often remain unread or just scanned by receivers due to information overload. Focusing the dissemination of the information more precisely to the needs of receiving parties could help remedy this.

In the first solution story listed in CapCase II.2 "Automatic Schematic Generation with 3-D Models," the system is capable of generating design, construction, and maintenance views in a variety of standards for schematics (see this version of the CapCase, *Generative Documentation* in the color insert).

Capability Case II.3	# Content Annotator
Intent:	To provide a way for people to add annotations to electronic content. By annotations we mean comments, notes, explanations, and semantic tags.
Solution Story:	**iMarkup Solution Story**, OntoAnnotate Collaborative Aircraft Maintenance, RDF Annotation for Inline Comments

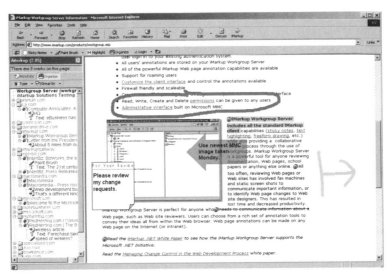

Collaboration is enabled through the markup of digital contents and its exhange over the web.

The example illustrates how a group of people can collaborate and communicate by means of digital content exchange using a browser. Annotations made by each person are stored on an annotation server indexed against specific content. For example, a highlight, an arrow, or a sticky note can be added. The markups can be organized and viewed in many ways, for example, by author, date, or type of annotation. Pre-defined markup forms are available, such as draft status memos.

Benefits:	Improved capture of decision rationale, work comments and discussions, better ability to collaborate remotely
Featured Products:	iMarkup from iMarkup Solutions
Applicable Products:	Annotation Delivery Platform from OntoText, Annotea from W3C Annotea Project, eReview from Web4, OntoAnnotate from Ontoprise, PhotoStuff from Mind Lab, SWAP RDF Editor from Mind Lab

Discussion

Often, it is as important to capture comments on documents and other digital assets in an electronic form as it is to store the documents themselves. The best way to capture these comments is in the context of the document by highlighting, redlining, and identifying issues and suggestions. This is where the *Content Annotator* capability comes in.

An implementation of the Content Annotator capability might also be used to mark up images. For example, a photograph showing wiring of an avionic system could be marked up to specify which area of the image shows which type of a wire or to point out the specific location where the work (such as reconnecting the wires) has been performed and what engineering order authorized the work. The markup is stored as metadata and could be used to find an image and integrate images with other systems.

Capability Case II.4	# Expert Locator
Intent:	To provide users with convenient access to experts in a given area who can help with problems, answer questions, locate and interpret specific documents, and collaborate on specific tasks. Knowing who is an expert in what can be difficult in an organization with a large workforce of experts. Expert Locator could also identify experts across organizational barriers.
Solution Story:	**Technical Expert Locator at Boeing (TEL)**, ReferralWeb at the University of Washington

Tecnical experts within Boeing can be located rapidly and conveniently.

Boeing has a large workforce of experts, which makes it difficult at times to find the right person for the right job. It developed the web-based TEL system to provide Boeing employees with convenient access to an enterprise-wide network of qualified experts from diverse technical areas with experience through the lifecycles of all Boeing products. It enables rapid identification and contact of the company's experts in specific technical areas who can help resolve complex technical problems, answer questions, locate and interpret specific documents, and collaborate on specific tasks. Currently, all employees who are pursuing a technical career path (the members of the Boeing Technical Fellowship Program) are registered in the system, thereby allowing the company's foremost technical employees to be utilized accordingly. The Boeing technical thesaurus was harnessed by the TEL developers to create profiles for the experts. It incorporates 70,000 concepts, with an additional 50,000 synonym concept names, and 300,000 links including broaderTerm, narrowerTerm, and relatedTerm. TEL developers used techniques from artificial intelligence to refine the thesaurus by automatically adding missing links in the semantic network. It provides a standardized vocabulary for describing expertise and "semantically close" topics, based on links between concepts, which can be used for performing intelligent searches.

Benefits:	Significant reduction in cost and time when there is a need to identify and contact employees across the Boeing enterprise who are qualified experts within specific areas of technology
Featured Products:	Ontobroker from Ontoprise
Applicable Products:	Arisem KM Server from Arisem, AskMe Enterprise from AskMe Corporation, Entopia Quantum from Entopia, KnowledgeMail from Tacit, ReferralWeb from University of Washington

Discussion

The *Expert Locator* capability and another capability used in the gallery (*Ask an Expert*, not shown in this book) both address how the *social networking* required to accomplish the everyday work of maintaining the shuttle could be improved through the use of technology.

Many people interviewed during the Business Capability Exploration phase said that their best and most immediate source of help is their co-workers and colleagues. Solving problems, seeking advise in decision making, and finding information is all about "who one knows." Long-time employees know exactly who to call. The problem is that new employees don't have the same knowledge. Furthermore, with people retiring, the dynamics in the program are changing. Systems and procedures used by the program are complex. New engineers need a "buddy" to walk them through the process each time they start working on a different problem.

The solution story featured in the Expert Locator CapCase is from Boeing Corporation, where a semantic model of expertise associated with the different areas of the aerospace industry was developed. This model was used to index the relevant employee directory. The team that prepared the CapCase thought an Expert Locator would be quite useful for NASA, but the concept was immediately challenged. Some of the workshop participants pointed out that this is not how NASA and its subcontractors are used to working. Comments included the following:

- "We know exactly who to call with a problem."
- "We have been around long enough to know who knows what."

Other participants pointed out that everyone in the workshop was a senior employee with many years in the program. Could it be that the newer members would have a different opinion? One of the workshop participants was assigned to investigate this.

The second CapCase in the area of social networking is not shown in this book. Named *Ask an Expert*, it is concerned with the ability to post questions and receive answers online. Question and answer pairs are stored in the knowledge base for future re-use, so the next time the same or similar question is raised, the system can reply to it without needing to consult a human expert. The Ask an Expert capability depends on people using it not just to ask questions, but also to answer them. Different approaches exist to ensure that questions are answered. One approach is based on recognizing, rewarding, and celebrating experts. Recognition is given to people who answer the most questions in a way that solves the problem that triggered the question. Another approach is to assign experts who will reply to different types of problems. Questions are emailed directly to these people. Providing answers becomes their job responsibility. This requires knowing the right person to whom the given questions should be addressed. The Ask an Expert capability responds to this need.

Capability Case II.5

Concept-Based Search

Summary View: See Capability Case I.1 in the State Government gallery.

Discussion

Concept-based Search is described in detail in the State Government gallery (see the Discussion section under Capability Case I.1). This capability was ranked highest in terms of interest and priority at the Digital Shuttle workshop.

Some of the key indicators of where Concept-based Search could be used effectively are when:

- A large volume of information already exists.
- There is a need to build a corporate memory and transfer expertise among personnel.
- Experience is as valuable as textbook knowledge.
- The accuracy of the results of knowledge searches is important.
- The content is valuable: for example, FAQs, news, manuals, and product documentation.
- Many users will use the capability when it becomes available.
- More than just keywords are needed to drive search: for example, detailed knowledge on products, customers, markets, and terms.

Capability Case II.6

Automated Content Tagger

Intent:

To provide a way for people to add annotations to electronic content. Annotations can be comments, notes, explanations, and semantic tags. Content annotation provides metadata that is becoming increasingly important to improve the precision of search as well as context-based information retrieval and repurposing.

Solution Story:

AeroSWARM Automated Markup, HighWire Stanford e-Library

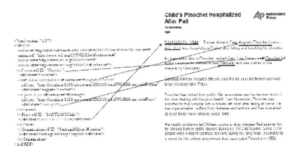

AeroSWARM finds references in a news story and renders them as semantic mark-up.

The creation of markup from unstructured text sources, such as web pages, is tedious and time-consuming. Anyone who produces documents on a regular basis (such as, intelligence analysts and commanders) or who has a large quantity of legacy documents needs some form of automated markup assistance. Lockheed Martin built a tool called AeroSWARM, which reduces the effort required for markup. It automatically generates OWL markup for a number of common domain-independent classes and properties. The author can then manually do markup additions and corrections to the output of AeroSWARM.

A user can specify the set of web pages to mark up and choose a target ontology. Then, AeroSWARM generates OWL markup like that shown in the figure above. The sample markup includes entities (for example, person, place, organization), relations (for example, Pinochet persToLoc Santiago) and co-references (for example, Pinochet sameIndividualAs Augusto Pinochet). A table on the AeroSWARM site describes all the entities and relations that can be automatically identified and marked-up.

Benefits:

Reducing the workload for annotated markup to a level manageable by human effort. The markup enables valuable business capabilities such as improved search, information discovery, and retrieval.

Featured Products:

AeroSWARM from Lockheed Martin

Applicable Products:

ClearTags from ClearForest, Enigma 3C Platform from Enigma, Semio Tagger from Semio, SKIP from SemanTx Life Sciences, Stratify Discovery System from Stratify

Discussion

The *Content Annotator* capability showed how content could be annotated or marked up by people to capture information in context and create metadata. The *Automated Content Tagger* capability shows how metadata can be created automatically.

Capability Case I.7

Interest-Based Information Delivery

Intent:

To enable filtering of information for people who need to monitor and assess large volumes of data for relevance, volatility or required response. The volume of targeted information is reduced based on its relevance according to the role or interest of the end user. Sensitive information is filtered according to a "need to know" protocol.

Solution Story:

Cerebra Biotechnology Information Monitoring and Filtering, **KMI Planet Personalized Newsletter**, Meeting Minutes Butler for a German Financial Company, Personalized News and TV Program Guide, Personalized Recommendation at Amazon, SemanTx Autoreader

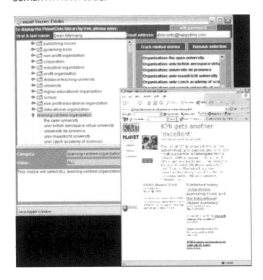

Search for "Learning-Centered Organizations."

People interested in the activities of the Knowledge Media Institute can customize a newsletter to their interests. Someone who is interested in Learning Organizations will be presented stories related to any such organization.

Benefits:

Reducing the workload for annotated markup to a level manageable by human effort. The markup enables valuable business capabilities such as improved search, information discovery and retrieval.

Applicable Products:

Autoreader from SemanTx Life Sciences, Cerebra Inference Engine from Network Inference, Net Perceptions from Net Perceptions, Inc., Ontobroker from Ontoprise, Orenge from Empolis

Discussion

One of the dangers of information overload is that key information may get lost in a sea of noise. The *Interest-based Information Delivery* capability ensures that important information gets delivered only on a need-to-know or want-to-know basis.

A related, although different, CapCase is *Context-aware Retriever*. It improves integration of information into a user's workflow. With the Context-aware Retriever capability, users don't need to interrupt their work to look up information because it is made available to them within any of the tools that support their work processes. This type of capability would make it possible for NASA engineers to access all the information directly from the CAD tools they use. Managers could get such access from PowerPoint or an email client, while inspectors may be enabled to access the information from their test and configuration management environments. The gallery featured two examples of Context-aware Retriever.

Workshop Results

The workshop resulted in greater appreciation of the potential of semantic technology through stories. The team established a shared understanding of what the technology could do for them. A key outcome resulted from the ranking of capabilities and commitment to creating a solution based on the concept that was named "Knowledge Hub." Knowledge Hub would use a Concept-based Search type of capability for better, integrated access to multiple sources of information within the Space Shuttle Program.

The importance of creating a scenario that would show capabilities in action became evident. It was decided to prepare such a scenario for the next workshop. The scenario would show how new capabilities would assist in an investigation of an in-flight anomaly.

Finally, a number of key success factors surfaced, including the need to create a staged roadmap for the implementation of the Knowledge Hub solution concept. It was pointed out that its implementation would have an impact on the standard contract between NASA and its subcontractors. The nature of this impact and the necessary contract changes were discussed. It was agreed that the roadmap should include a plan for implementing contractual changes.

Capability Cases as Solution Design Assets

This chapter described projects that used galleries of Capability Cases. Design is a collaborative experience. The gallery tours enable collaboration by providing a neutral space where people feel free to speak openly and share their explorations into the solution space. They create an environment where it is possible to "discuss the undiscussables"—a key to more effective solution design.

Solution Envisioning with Capability Cases is an asset-based approach to developing solutions. Many of the Capability Cases shown in the galleries were created just in time for a specific project. However, without exception, we have been able to successfully re-use them in later projects. Having libraries of forces, results, and Capability Cases helps to stimulate thinking about what is happening in a given business situation under consideration. Unlike use cases, which tend to shift the attention to defining what a system *should do*, Capability Cases invite a dialog on what a system *can be*. This supports a more complete and accelerated approach to exploring the problem and solution spaces.

Trail Marker III: Exploring Capability Case Galleries

This chapter described two projects that used galleries of Capability Cases—the State Government Self-Service project and the NASA Digital Shuttle Project. Additionally, we reviewed the three major purposes served by having a gallery of capabilities and solution stories as a central part of the envisioning process. We discussed how Capability Cases function as reusable solution design resources across projects.

Chapter 4, "Positioning Within the Solution Delivery Cycle," contains optional material that positions Solution Envisioning as a process and set of methods that link to business strategy approaches and complement software development approaches.

If you are a business executive or manager, you may want to scan Chapters 4–8. However, you can complete a short tour of the book by proceeding directly from here to Chapter 9, "Conclusion—Lessons Learned and Looking Ahead with Envisioning."

Practitioners, and those interested in more detail, will want to study Chapters 5–7 on the three phases of Solution Envisioning and continue with Chapters 8, "Solution Envisioning in Different Situations" and 9 for insights on tailoring and getting started with using Solution Envisioning.

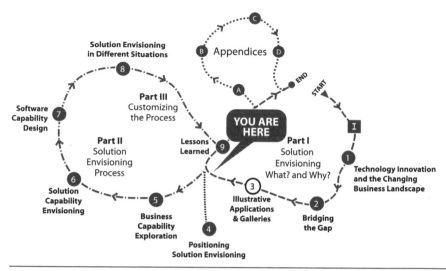

FIGURE 3.5.

4

Positioning Within the Solution Delivery Cycle

*"Since our problems have been our own creation,
they also can be overcome."*

—*George Harrison*

FIGURE 4.1.

CHAPTER PREVIEW

This chapter examines how Solution Envisioning is designed to create a direct bridge between business needs and technological promise by allowing stakeholders to appreciate technical solutions in action. We describe what makes Solution Envisioning different and where it fits in the overall solution delivery process. We examine in what sense design is, by nature, an iterative process. The chapter concludes by presenting how Solution Envisioning is designed to enable meaningful and productive iteration as needed. It describes how Capability Cases (CapCases) support the iterative process by operating initially as solution sketches and later as vehicles for specifying solution blueprints.

The following is a brief preview of other concepts and topics covered. It is well known that non-optimal solution decisions made early in the design and planning stages become major obstacles to success. Reversing such decisions later in the project is very costly. Despite this, too often, people just want to get going with some implementation. The value of a technology rarely can be determined simply by understanding the technology itself. The *Package Will Do It* and the *Demo Becomes the System* syndromes are understandable but problematic responses directly related to the urgent need to see the technology in a context in which it provides business value.

Solution Envisioning and CapCases establish a business value for different technical solutions, in a real work setting, while avoiding the pitfalls of these syndromes. CapCases provide an experience of solution ideas at work ahead of working prototypes. In this way, they act as catalysts for creativity and encourage strategic conversations.

Often, we are asked to explain how Solution Envisioning is different from well-known software development methods. For example, "We are already using RAD (Rapid Application Development) and RUP (Rational Unified Process); how is your approach different?" The answer is that it is not about being *different*, but about providing a *complementary* approach. By design, Solution Envisioning borrows and builds on processes and deliverables suggested by leading business strategy and software methodologies. It adds a missing element—an effective linkage between business and IT processes.

WHAT MAKES SOLUTION ENVISIONING DIFFERENT?

When considering the dynamics that happen between business and technology personnel, it becomes apparent the working methods of these communities fail to bring them together.

Business strategy and planning work is supported by a number of established techniques. They include SWOT (Strength, Weakness, Opportunity, Threat) Analysis, Balanced Scorecard, Strategic Planning, and other approaches. Though they can be highly successful for creating business plans and strategies, they do not specify how the results of these techniques can be taken up by the established software development processes.

Two of the most commonly used software development methods are RUP and MSF (Microsoft Solution Framework). An "envisioning" phase is viewed by both methods as absolutely crucial to the success of any software project. However, no proven, repeatable means are provided or evidenced for executing this essential phase. No actionable connections with the business strategy deliverables are specified. (See Figure 4.2 for an illustration.)

The lack of linkages creates an impetus to experience something working early, because it is known that ideas about what is needed are often triggered by and then evolve from seeing something tangible. In some situations, a package solution is bought prematurely, while other times demonstrators and prototypes end up becoming the delivered system. The former is an example of the Package Will Do It syndrome and the latter is an example of the Demo Becomes the System[1] syndrome. In both cases, the problems of scaling up or evolving the solution to meet the business' needs arise.

The issue is well-stated by Bob Galliers in *Re-orienting Information Systems Strategy: Integrating Information Systems into the Business* [Stowell, 1995]:

> *"...organizations find difficulty in achieving success in their information systems strategy formulation and implementation efforts. This is partly the result of a lack of awareness by managers and their information systems colleagues: the former are often happy in the mistaken belief that information technology can be left to technologists, and many of the latter are happier to have an information systems strategy and an information systems development that are more concerned with technological issues than with business imperatives—with as little as possible involvement from business executives. It is also partly due to the very nature of the two processes, as currently practiced: the one creative and synthetical; the other mechanistic and analytical."*

---

[1] We want to make clear that we believe in using evolutionary prototypes in the early delivery of functioning solutions. We define evolutionary prototypes as software built on a sound architectural foundation. "Demo Becomes the System" refers to situations when such foundation is not in place. Instead, a "paper house" intended as a sketchy model keeps being elaborated and invested in to the point that people begin to expect it to serve as the "permanent residence."

In this quote, Galliers makes two key points:

- Achieving success in formulating strategy for IT solutions and their implementation depends on bringing together business managers and technologists.

- The practices, processes, and methods of these two communities are very different.

Galliers wrote about the differences in practices and the consequences of their disconnect in 1995. Now fast forward to 2003. Two of the leading e-business strategists strongly echo Galliers' words in their assessment of the situation [Kalakota, 2003]:

- *"Top Management talks the macro language of Competitive Strategy, SWOT and Balanced Scorecards*

- *The different operational lines of business speak the process languages of Lean Enterprise or Six Sigma*

- *IT departments converse in the micro language of enterprise application portfolio models, software maturity models, and software engineering methods (like the iterative development methods).*

So, yes, everyone is busy planning, but no one is linking activities. This often leads to an alignment problem. This point can not be overstated. Most companies have alignment issues between the strategy, operations, and IT because they all rely on different methodologies. There is no common language that incorporates all three. As a result, it is important to understand the relationship between these various methods and place them in the context of a blueprint that integrates these multiple perspectives.

Making all these methods talk to each other is going to be a significant part of your job, Mr. VP. Your corporation does not need another new management method; it needs a better way of linking the existing ones to create value."

Solution Envisioning is an augmented process that incorporates insights and requirements for effective action from all sides of the gap. It connects best of breed business strategy methods with software development methods.

In the fifth article in a series called "The Top Ten Reasons Projects Fail,"[2] Frank

---

[2] http://www.gantthead.com/article.cfm?ID=165885. This article says that modeling is the right tool for defining detailed (system) requirements. However, it is not a good tool for defining high-level business requirements because models are not good vehicles for communicating with senior executives and business managers—"the people the team needs to get in sync with as the project charter is built." Also, with system modeling tools like UML, it is difficult to completely separate requirements from design, and "it is critical to define high-level business requirements separately from design and design considerations. This is the only way to keep design assumptions that have not been confirmed from coloring the nature of what is really required."

Winters stresses that, to progress successfully from business needs to a solution that achieves desired results (*that is, avoid project failure*), you have to start at the right level using the right language and accomplish two key transformations:

> *"The first transformation is from ambiguity—fuzzy, vague folklore about what's needed as might be the case—to a high-level business requirements document that clearly defines what is needed in business English, the language of choice at that point.*

> *The second transformation is from that document to a set of models—modeling being the language of choice for much of the way forward—that can be used to drive and control system development throughout the lifecycle.*

> *No one has the definitive advice on how to do these transformations."*

Solution Envisioning with Capability Cases responds to Winters' last statement. It attempts to optimize decisions made during the critical early stages of solution lifecycle by

- Utilizing systems thinking ideas to explore the systemic nature of business situations

- Formulating relevant problem analogies to achieve a shared understanding of the business situation and possible technical solutions

- Realizing opportunities for reuse of conceptual and technical assets at various levels of scale and granularity

- Synthesizing the solution concepts of intended software systems in conceptual architectures

WHERE DOES IT FIT IN THE SOLUTION DELIVERY PROCESS?

Chapter 2, "Bridging the Gap with Solution Envisioning," described the Solution Envisioning process as follows:

- *Beginning* (ideally) when an explicit business strategy has been formulated and is ready to be realized through a technology-enabled solution initiative.

- *Completing* with a clear vision of what system(s) and technology-base needs should be built or acquired to realize and deliver the solution.

Seen within a much larger effort, Solution Envisioning is only a part of the Quest for a successful business solution.[3] It expects certain inputs. These are possibly

---

[3] Clearly, we believe it to be a critical part as evidenced by the existence of this book!

developed and modeled with leading business planning and strategy approaches. It produces outputs that, based on our experience, are much needed by software development processes and methods.

Recognizing its place as a bridge between upstream and downstream processes, what happens before and after Solution Envisioning is employed? What are the decisions that lead up to using Solution Envisioning? What makes it possible? Or precludes using it? What are the consequences of envisioning? Or not doing it? What follows a Solution Envisioning intervention? These questions will be addressed in subsequent chapters.

In Chapter 5, "Business Capability Exploration—Phase I of Solution Envisioning," we cover the first phase of Solution Envisioning. It deals with the inception of the process where upstream interactions are directly encountered. There, we discuss some of the implications and dependencies that Solution Envisioning has on the activities that come before it—namely, Business Strategy Development and Solution Initiative Formation. Likewise, in Chapter 7, "Software Capability Design—Phase III of Solution Envisioning," we return to the issue of what happens after Solution Envisioning. We describe how executing it provides a platform for solution realization and adoption.

Solution Envisioning (and possibly other related approaches) can be regarded as the next logical stage in the continuing maturation of solution delivery methods. Over the past 10–15 years, system lifecycle methodologies have matured and converged significantly on effective practices for system development. However, they are still *weakest on the front-end*.

As consultants over the years, we have learned the hard way that when the goals, decisions, and key artifacts are not in place for the next downstream phase, the activities of a given phase must go upstream to fill in the gaps. This is frustrating at best, but at worst, it is a key determinant of project failure. Historically, this has been happening at many levels (and, by necessity, continues) as in the following *stop-gap* approaches:

- Instead of business strategy and business modeling, work out the market and business strategies and envisioned new processes in the system development process.
- Instead of capability design, work out the business goals and solution objectives while doing the use cases.
- Instead of doing use cases, work out the user tasks/workflow in the objects.
- Instead of object-oriented analysis, work out the business logic in the code.
- Instead of doing even light object-oriented design, work out everything in the code.

Best practices have slowly evolved to close these gaps. Nearly all best practices now reflect the need to perform fundamental *business strategy*, *modeling*, and *envisioning work* as indispensable input to software requirements and development. However, no proven, repeatable means are provided or evidenced for executing these essential activities. In Figure 4.2, this is illustrated for RUP[4] and MSF.[5] Solution Envisioning was created to address this need. Our experience and gathered evidence shows that it works, as documented in the case studies in Chapter 3, "Illustrative Applications and Galleries," and Chapter 8, "Solution Envisioning in Different Situations."

As something new in the world, Solution Envisioning must fit within an overall *engagement strategy* for realizing a solution. Change agents are often the people who recognize the need for envisioning. To proceed, they have to convince other stakeholders of the value and effectiveness of the approach. This has required support, including educational briefings about Solution Envisioning and the problems it addresses; process and method guidance and collaterals; case studies; and clear evidence of value and payoff. Providing this information in a rich form was one of the main motivations and goals for this book.

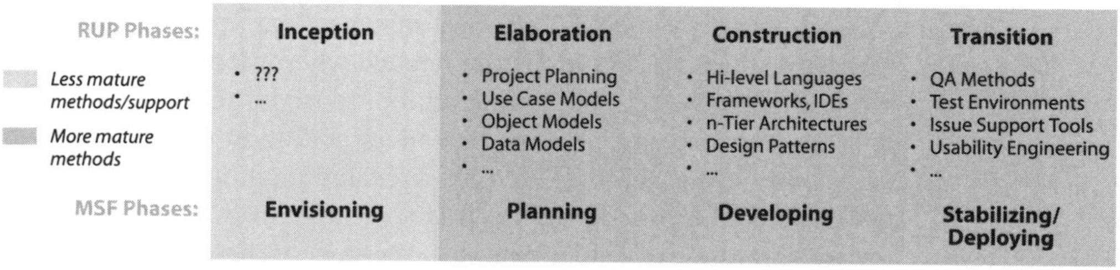

RUP Phases:	**Inception**	**Elaboration**	**Construction**	**Transition**
Less mature methods/support	• ??? • ...	• Project Planning • Use Case Models • Object Models • Data Models • ...	• Hi-level Languages • Frameworks, IDEs • n-Tier Architectures • Design Patterns • ...	• QA Methods • Test Environments • Issue Support Tools • Usability Engineering • ...
More mature methods				
MSF Phases:	**Envisioning**	**Planning**	**Developing**	**Stabilizing/ Deploying**

FIGURE 4.2.   THE WEAKNESS AT THE FRONT-END OF SOFTWARE DEVELOPMENT PROCESS METHODS.

---

[4] RUP, Rational Unified Process, is a widely used software development method created by Rational Corporation, which is now a part of IBM.

[5] MSF, Microsoft Solution Framework, is a well-adopted system development method from Microsoft.

ENVISIONING, CAPABILITY CASES, AND THE ITERATIVE NATURE OF DESIGN

It has long been understood that the design of software system solutions (and that of any human design effort that deals with complex or ill-formed problems[6]) benefits from practices that support iterations, especially in activities associated with problem understanding and requirements.[7]

In recognition of this, there are many established variations of iterative development process models, methodologies, and practices. Some lifecycle models put significant emphasis on deliberation and review in order to "do it right the first time" so as to avoid mistakes and failure. With experience bringing a deeper understanding of the constraints and essential nature of design, software development practices today consist increasingly of staged and agile ways of working. These allow for learning cycles and knowledge generation about the intended result within smaller, well-managed *"try-it; test-it; fix-it cycles."*[8]

Two points of connection to Solution Envisioning with Capability Cases are important to bring out in relation to lifecycle considerations:

1. **Iteration is not an end in itself; it is a means to an end.** It is one means (perhaps the best known) to support convergence on understanding and agreement about what is needed in a process of progressive realization. Iterations are needed when there is choice, uncertainty, and risk. So, the essential purpose of iterative software development is to engender better understanding of the problem and inclusion of more of the desired features and qualities (requirements) in the delivered product. It is a mistake to be enamored with iterative processes for their own sake because unnecessary or unproductive iterations can be very expensive and risky.

2. **Early representations of a solution (or product) are essential to get a reaction from people.** Prototypes are the common way of providing this early experience (though not the only way, depending on how inclusive one's definition of *prototype* is). The more iterations

---

[6]   Herbert A. Simon. *The Sciences of the Artificial*, Second Edition. The MIT Press, 1981.

[7]   "The hardest single part of building a software system is deciding precisely what to build. ...Therefore, the most important function that the software builder performs for the client is the iterative extraction and refinement of the product requirements. ...it is necessary to allow for an extensive iteration between the client and the designer as part of the system definition[...]" From, "No Silver Bullet, Essence and Accidents of Software Engineering," Fred Brooks, *Computer Magazine*, April 1987.

[8]   As described in *Lean Software Development: An Agile Toolkit for Software Development Managers*, Mary Poppendieck, Tom Poppendieck [Poppendieck, 2003].

and exploration of options that can be achieved using inexpensive media, the better. It is here that Capability Cases as *sketches* of possible solutions have a role to play. They offer a way to visualize and, in some ways, experience possible solutions very early on so the business requirements can become explicit, important technical decisions can be made, and the development can proceed.

Concerning the design of physical products (such as cars), Michael Schrage [Schrage, 2000] in *Serious Play, How the World's Best Companies Simulate to Innovate* has this to say:

> *"As a rule, the more prototypes and prototyping cycles per unit of time, the more technically polished the finished product."*

This applies to the design of all artifacts. The intensive use and high value of prototypes may reflect core psychological and social needs of human beings to move together through the process of envisioning and creating something new (that is, the design process). People prefer and are much better able to see their requirements *"embodied in the design of a possible solution"* rather than inspect and refine the details of any kind of requirements model.[9] In fact, visualization and interaction with possible solutions are central to the process of eliciting the elements and properties of the solution. Most people call these *the requirements*, but many of them are often not explicit until after the solution is experienced. Thus, some requirements can only be fully articulated in retrospect.[10]

Solution Envisioning Is an Iterative Process

As will be seen in Chapters 5, 6, and 7, which detail the three phases of Solution Envisioning, the Solution Envisioning process embraces iteration in an essential and positive sense. Moreover, it provides practical means to ensure that iteration is productive. This is achieved through interlocking activities, incremental evolution of workproducts, and most importantly through a guided, convergent set of decisions about what the solution should be.

---

[9] This is well understood in architectural practice, where architects have long used the progressive detailing and precision of sketches to elicit client desires (requirements) and responses to alternative solutions. Even in the earliest stage of rough sketches, they are representations of possible solutions (with reflected requirements) rather than requirements per se. At the right stage, sketches are translated into and exchanged for blueprints that are used to actually build the artifact(s).

[10] "I would go a step further and assert that it is really impossible for a client, even working with a software engineer, to specify completely, precisely, and correctly the exact requirements of a modern software product before trying some versions of the product" [Brooks, 1987].

In addition to driving toward clarity about a design, all iterative processes also allow for or enable *a space for people to interact* and communicate over time. Whether this is a side-effect or a legitimate goal of iteration in general, we will not argue here. Solution Envisioning recognizes and explicitly values such sustained communication. It orchestrates this kind of critical interaction as an essential means for shared understanding and agreement about the solution concept, as well the commitment needed to realize it.

A primary goal of Solution Envisioning is to encourage *good iterations* while avoiding and discouraging bad iterations. As a core part of Solution Envisioning, CapCases are particularly useful in this regard.

Capability Cases—Initially Solution Sketches and Later Blueprints

Capability Cases enable people to experience possible solutions and possible futures in a joint envisioning process. They provide another way (akin to prototypes, but different) to interact with real solutions and designs—not like a working system, but conceptually complete enough that people can start to see and feel the requirements they are interested in. In the spirit of the following statement by Michael Schrage [Schrage, 2000], CapCases help to stimulate and shape critical conversations about an emerging solution concept:

> *"In world class companies, an interesting prototype emits a social and intellectual equivalent of a magnetic field, attracting smart people with interesting ideas about how to make it better. ... the value of prototypes resides less in the models themselves than in the interactions—the conversations, arguments, consultations, collaborations—they invite."*

By design and in practice, CapCases function in two distinct but connected roles in progressing from envisioning to design—and this is a vital part of their strength as envisioning and design tools.

Initially, CapCases function more as *solution sketches* and allow multiple possibilities to be explored in parallel. We want to carefully differentiate this primary role of CapCases as views of possible solutions used to stimulate imagination and thinking about the needed solution, from their premature use as direct, candidate solutions.[11]

---

[11] A superficial appraisal of a Capability Case might presume that it operates as another variant of *a solution in search of a problem*. The misperception may be that by using Capability Cases early (in the requirements or problem-modeling stage), there is a danger of leading with technology and prematurely foreclosing a real understanding and exploration of the business problem and needs. We do not present Capability Cases this way. Rather, we encourage analogical thinking using solution stories and their associated technology and product commitments.

Later, in the Software Capability Design phase, when the business needs and solution concept have been well-established, selected Capability Cases—often, specialized and further developed to suit the specific context—also function as rapid pathways to specify technical *blueprints* for the solution (or parts thereof). This role is also intended and evidenced in the connection of specific fields within the extended Capability Case template (refer to Table 2.2) to technology and product options, integration strategies and mechanisms, and support for selection of a suitable implementation strategy.

TRAIL MARKER IV: RATIONALE FOR SOLUTION ENVISIONING OUTLINED

The value of this chapter is in positioning Solution Envisioning within the larger cycle of moving from recognizing the need for change to realizing a solution that delivers the desired results. The new system(s) are incorporated into business operations and lead to new opportunities and needs—launching a new cycle.

Bracketing the beginning and end of such a business change cycle are effective and mature processes and methods for honing the business strategy and for developing the software systems. Solution Envisioning provides a well-founded process and set of methods for connecting these two domains with their well-established, but widely differing, cultures, languages, and techniques.

The material just covered gives extra insight into the intent and design of our approach, but it is not essential to get a basic understanding of Solution Envisioning with Capability Cases (which is covered in Chapter 2), nor is it critical in examining details in order to begin practicing it (covered next in Chapters 5, 6, 7).

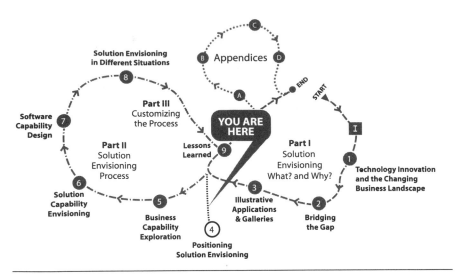

FIGURE 4.3.

PART II

SOLUTION ENVISIONING PROCESS—DETAILED LOOK

CONTENT

PURPOSE

To provide a practitioner's handbook in the form of a step-by-step guide for practicing Solution Envisioning with Capability Cases.

KEY QUESTIONS ADDRESSED

What are the details of the Solution Envisioning process, and how is it performed?

ORIENTATION

The Solution Envisioning approach for supporting the development of solutions that deliver business value is based on two key innovations: *Solution Envisioning* and *Capability Cases*.

Solution Envisioning engagements have three iterative but progressive phases that clarify and target needed *business capabilities*, map these to possible technology-enabled *solution capabilities*, and finally, specify an architecture and implementation roadmap for realizing them as *software capabilities*:

- Business Capability Exploration
- Solution Capability Envisioning
- Software Capability Design

Beyond current methods and processes, which address capabilities from only one side or another of the business–IT gap, Solution Envisioning synthesizes and connects best practices from business strategy methods, such as Balanced Scorecard, Strategy Maps, Performance Prism, and Return on Investment analyses, with best-of-breed software development methods and techniques such as RUP, MSF, and XP.

PRIMARY AUDIENCE

Practitioners include all those responsible for organizing, conducting, and participating in Solution Envisioning engagements.

5

Business Capability Exploration—Phase I of Solution Envisioning

"If you can imagine it, you can create it."
—William Arthur Ward

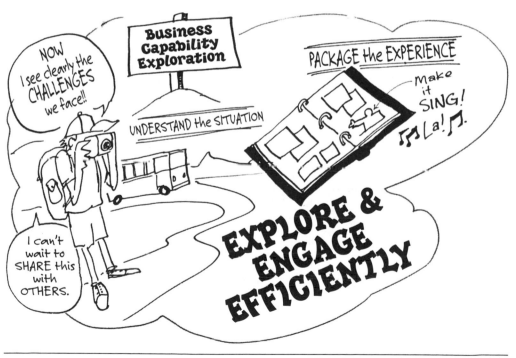

FIGURE 5.1.

CHAPTER PREVIEW

This chapter is an in-depth view of the first phase of Solution Envisioning, *Business Capability Exploration (BCE)*—exploring the context and nature of the business problem or opportunity. Gaining clarity of the business situation lays a foundation for the journey that follows. A critical understanding of the business need and challenges is required to proceed with the discovery of the nature of the solution that is needed.

BCE plays an important role in the success of Solution Envisioning projects by establishing the following:

- The context and scope of the business situation
- Dynamics (drivers) that motivate something new to happen
- Root causes behind business predicaments
- A set of candidate solutions
- Agreement over goals and objectives

The phase is completed when an understanding is reached on the nature of the business problems and on the specific results a solution will need to bring about. This understanding is documented in a preliminary vision of the proposed solution that can be communicated to a broader set of stakeholders for evaluation and further decision making within an envisioning workshop.

TO BEGIN ENVISIONING—BUSINESS CAPABILITY EXPLORATION (BCE)

As shown in Figure I.1 of the Introduction, Business Capability Exploration comes early in the quest to change a business through adoption of a technology-enabled solution. The purpose of Capability Exploration is to get clear on the business problem that is being addressed, the context that surrounds it, and the space of concepts that may be needed to formulate a solution. By framing the situation and possible directions, BCE also establishes a readiness for informed decision making and begins the process of envisioning (designing) a solution.

The new (transformed) business reflects a business design. The goals of Business Capability Exploration are to inform the thinking about possible designs by exploring a broad set of Capability Cases. BCE lays the foundation for enabling stakeholders from all stages of the solution lifecycle to forge and communicate a shared understanding of the intended solution.

As the first phase of Solution Envisioning, BCE has to deal with the pre-work of helping frame a solution initiative. This often requires aligning the initiative and the work of Solution Envisioning to the Business Strategy.

The Work of Business Capability Exploration

To provide a consolidated overview of BCE and a convenient reference, Figure 5.2 shows *Activities*, *Workproducts*, and the supporting *Techniques* of this phase. The figure is intended to be self-explanatory, but these points may assist in reading it (and the similar diagrams in Chapters 6, "Solution Capability Envisioning—Phase II of Solution Envisioning," and 7, "Software Capability Design—Phase III of Solution Envisioning"):

- A legend is provided to distinguish key items: Main Input Workproduct, Activities, Intermediate Workproducts, supporting Techniques, and the Main Output Workproduct.

- The circular background is meant to evoke the exploratory and iterative nature of the work and to counter the notion (that can too easily be read into any representation of actions) of it being a prescriptive sequence.

- The general flow of the work is indicated going left to right.

- The input workproduct (shown at the left coming into the phase) launches the work of the phase. Clusters of related activities follow with the last cluster to the right producing the main output workproduct.

- The output workproduct must tie together the cumulative outcome of the work of the phase in a form sufficient to move on to the next phase of Solution Envisioning.

- Activities are marked with the following indexes or references:

- Numeric index (for example, 1') of the Activity in the upper-left corner. This is used to reference the Activity and indicates only the relative order of its execution in the phase.

- Alphabetic reference (for example, A) to any workproduct(s) created or changed.

- A leading tool icon indicates and references any Techniques (for example, T1) used to support the work of the Activity.

- The Main Input Workproduct—the Solution Initiative Statement—is shown as the entry point to the work of BCE (shown to the left of the circle with an incoming arrow).

- The Main Output Workproduct—the Solution Vision Presentation & Shared Space—is the exit point for the work of BCE (shown to the right of the circle with an outgoing arrow projecting to the initiation of the next phase).

- Intermediate Workproducts are shown in the stacks below. These are ordered relative to the respective Activities that impact them, and indexed with the letters used to reference them from the Activities.

- Referenced Techniques are shown with respective indexes from Activities.

We want to stress that the coverage given here of Business Capability Exploration is meant to provide a *comprehensive* record of all the Activities and Workproducts that we have ever needed and used in all the situations we have come across. In any given situation, only a subset of these are typically used:

- In some cases, certain Activities may not be necessary given the goals of a specific Solution Envisioning effort.
- In other cases, some of the outcomes or Workproducts needed have already been accomplished and are available for direct incorporation into the Solution Envisioning project.

Without noting this, the detailed exposition of all the possible Activities may appear too daunting and time-consuming to execute. Our experience has been that Solution Envisioning can always be performed as a flexible and productive intervention that delivers high value in a short timeframe. Chapter 8, "Solution Envisioning in Different Situations," provides guidance on tailoring the process to different situations to ensure it is a practical and efficient.

The Four Activity Clusters of BCE

BCE Activities are grouped in four clusters. These clusters of related Activities are shown as groupings or *staircases* in Figure 5.2:

I.   **Establish Business Situation and Resources for the Initiative**—Structure and represent the overall context for the desired business transformation by establishing the current business situation. Gather relevant information and make it accessible to the initiative team. Understand the business goals and ROI objectives. This cluster consists of Activities 1 through 7.

II. **Identify Business Needs in Terms of Forces, Barriers, and Results**—Determine the specific business needs (who is hurting and how) by analyzing the business situation in terms of forces, barriers (impacts on stakeholders), results, and measures. This cluster consists of Activities 8 through 10.

III. **Explore Possibilities and Refine Results Informed by Technology Capabilities**—Explore future business possibilities in terms of supporting technology options and available capabilities (reach out for something new). Nominate capabilities in relation to stakeholder benefit, and refine results with measures. This cluster consists of Activities 11 through 15.

IV. **Consolidate Initial Solution Vision for Broader Sharing and Evaluation**—Consolidate and package initial solution vision (including mapping of selected capabilities to forces, barriers, challenges, and results) in preparation for sharing with a larger, representative set of stakeholders within an envisioning workshop setting. This cluster consists of Activities 16 and 17.

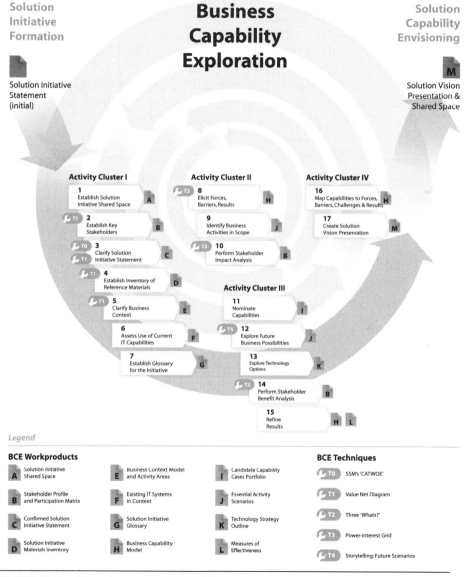

FIGURE 5.2. THE ACTIVITIES AND WORKPRODUCTS OF BUSINESS CAPABILITY EXPLORATION.

In subsequent sections, we explain and discuss each of the Activities in some detail. We also cover issues and insights that pertain to the clusters as a whole. For some Activities or particularly important issues or topics, we provide more extensive material and guidance.

The Nature and Goals of Business Capability Exploration

Business Capability Exploration starts with *what matters to an enterprise* and concludes with linking *what matters* to *what can be done*. It is designed to focus on and establish a shared understanding of what matters. It also engages stakeholders (and potential adopters of a future solution) by allowing them to *experience a future state of the business*. This is accomplished by doing an initial scan of candidate solutions to gain a better understanding of the business situation and goals. In this way, the work of Capability Exploration orchestrates a key dynamic—that understanding the problems to be solved and developing a concept of the solution are highly iterative and mutually informing activities.

Capability Cases play a central role by enabling decision makers to experience (and thus reuse) the situations being represented in those Capability Cases. Solution ideas are surveyed to inform an emerging vision of the solution and to comparatively examine its value proposition by understanding what is possible and what has been done by others. Discussions prompted by the Capability Cases often help clarify what is happening in the business context. The participants can assess the match of available and potentially useful capabilities against the demands and requirements of their situation.

It is important at this stage to get "buy-in" from stakeholders—not just on a solution vision, but also on the process they are engaging in to get there. The participants must have confidence that if they wander off track, which often happens in any exploratory process, that this will be noticed. Built-in mechanisms, such as collectively constructing a shared line of reasoning, will put them back on track. This line of reasoning is progressively built up from statements that express relationships between stakeholders, the forces and barriers that impact them, and the challenges they face in creating the capabilities needed to accomplish their business goals (results).

Who Does Business Capability Exploration?

Business Capability Exploration is best done by an interdisciplinary team led by business people who know and understand the "problem space" well. Industry experts ensure that there is new thinking about what changes should be made and these decisions are informed by market trends and new business models. Technologists and IT people are involved, not only to experience what the business leaders are thinking, but also to influence thinking on how technology can change the business.

It is important for IT to play a strong supporting role. A way to accomplish this is by assigning a Solution Architect from the IT department. This person will participate in all activities and will take a primary responsibility in performing a "Solution Scan" and assessing the infrastructure impact. In the next phase, IT people can begin to assume the lead.

The Timeline

The work of Business Capability Exploration is rarely completely new. A principle of Solution Envisioning is to build upon decisions already made. These decisions act as business constraints and "IT givens." Business strategy and goals may already be established. A decision may have been made to enhance the technology infrastructure already in place. When a lot of previous work has happened, Capability Exploration can be performed very quickly as a validation and packaging of the information needed for the next phase. Experience shows this can be finished in as little as two weeks.

When Solution Envisioning is used to design a brand new product, the Business Capability Exploration work may become a project in its own right that may take several weeks to complete. For an initiative that requires a new business model or significant changes to the existing model, this is especially true.

Where Does Solution Envisioning Start?

A Solution Initiative Statement in some form is the right starting point. In some cases, a kind of initiative statement exists in some form, and it may just need some honing. In others, we find that there is a need to help key stakeholders (for example, change agents) to develop one. Based on our experience, we find that Solution Envisioning must acknowledge the often-fuzzy state of incubation of business strategies and their conversion into a call for a business transformation (that is, a defined solution initiative).

When a Solution Initiative Statement does not exist, creating one is the starting point of this phase and the initial focus of the work. Without this prerequisite, it is difficult to bring together the necessary commitments, sponsorship, and access to and use of resources.

Connecting the Work of Business Capability Exploration to Business Strategy

We start by assuming some kind of business strategy exists. This is a useful presumption. It mitigates the risk that the envisioning work might find itself having to "swim too far back upstream." Why should this risk be avoided? Solution Envisioning should not be seen or used as a complete substitute for business strategy methods. There are many good approaches for doing market research and examining and planning business strategy.[1]

With that said, Solution Envisioning must start by connecting to the business strategy. In some cases, this could mean back-filling some of the strategy work or its articulation if it has not been done. Possible starting places in order of desirability are

1. Business strategy work has been done and well-articulated in a way that can be readily communicated and understood.

2. Business strategy work has been done, but not articulated in an actionable way needed to properly launch BCE.

3. Business strategy work has not been done—and, therefore, not communicated or understood.

In the ideal situation of case 1, it is likely the business strategy work will have produced one or more calls for solution initiatives. If a well-articulated solution initiative statement exists, the work can begin directly. In the other cases, we recommend the use of certain techniques as *pre-work* for starting Business Capability Exploration, such as S.W.O.T. or CATWOE.

S.W.O.T. stands for Strengths, Weaknesses, Opportunities, and Threats. Stakeholders articulate concise responses to the individual questions, "What are the Strengths? Weaknesses? Opportunities? Threats?" that the organization is currently facing.[2]

The questions posed by the CATWOE framework (see Sidebar 5.1 for an overview) also serve to connect to (or unearth) the business strategy when asked in a way

---

[1] We have mentioned, a few such as Balanced Scorecard and Performance Prism, from which we learned and adopted important concepts. We designed Solution Envisioning to connect to these approaches in a direct way.

[2] These questions are quite similar to those of a technique *Three What's?* that we suggest for supporting other early activities of Business Capability Exploration (see Sidebar 5.3). The first question in that technique, *"What's Working?"*, maps directly to *Strengths*. The second question, *"What's Not Working?"*, maps directly to *Weaknesses*. The third question, *"What's Changing?"*, can be mapped to both *Opportunities* and *Threats*, so S.W.O.T. has more differentiation in this area, but elicits similar content.

that both frames the current situation and acknowledges the search for a future business model. CATWOE is a technique that can be used with different focuses at various stages in the *quest*—from very high levels concerned with business strategy to more downstream, technical concerns. At this stage, it is used to explore alternate ideas of future systems—so-called *root definitions* in the Soft Systems Methodology (SSM).

Both of these techniques ask core questions from which a picture of what is going on in the current business quickly emerges.

Sidebar 5.1 Technique (T0): CATWOE

Problem Context Understanding the nature of a problem situation or the systemic behavior of an envisioned solution to a "human activity system."

Approach SSM, the Soft Systems Methodology created by Peter Checkland, is an "enquiry" into a real-world situation in which people take purposeful action. The perceived situation is seen as a number of purposeful holons. These purposeful holons, or "human activity systems," as they are called in SSM, are defined and modeled in such a way that their *comparison* with perceptions of the problem situation not only enables an understanding of the situation as such but, more importantly, leads to the emergence of a structured and coherent debate about intended change [Checkland 1981, 1990; Wilson 1984].

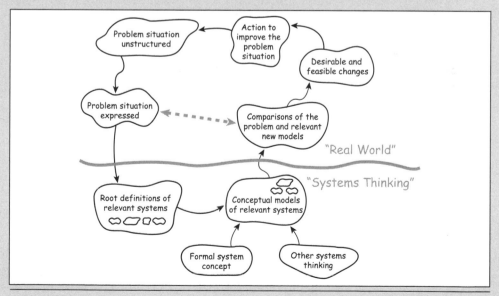

FIGURE 5.3.

With SSM, the process is as important as the outcome. The experience itself of applying an SSM approach will change the organization. This will arise from changed views about the problem and possible solutions. SSM proceeds by formulating definitions of "purposeful systems"—building conceptual models of problem situations using a framework that "appreciates" the interests of different stakeholders. The approach considers a number of dimensions summarized in the acronym CATWOE:

C—The *Clients*, those who more or less directly benefit (or suffer); for example, customers.

A—The *Agents*, those who will perform the work to make the transformation happen.

T—The *Transformation* itself, which can be thought of as the difference the system will make.

W—The "Weltanschauung" or *Worldview*. That which is going on in the wider world that is influencing and shaping the system and need for the system to adapt. The shared set of beliefs that underpin the initiative.

O—The *Owner*. The sponsor or the person who can stop the project.

E—The *Environment*. That which is assumed to be given and cannot be changed. Encompasses the political, legal, economic, social, demographic, technological, ethical, competitive, and natural environment.

CATWOE is very effective as a framework for scoping and framing a solution initiative (or system) definition. CATWOE helps to agree a *root definition* of the solution, surfacing assumptions about who and what is important.

Initial Solution Initiative Statement

An existing solution initiative statement can vary in precision, degree of focus, clarity, and format. Clarifying a solution initiative statement is critical to surfacing assumptions and focusing the intent of a solution. Without such a clarification, the starting point consists of a vague statement that is believed to identify a problem and may falsely commit people to inappropriate solutions. Often, politics stand in the way. An organization's "immune system" may resist attempts to clarify the solution initiative—with certain stakeholders, who have too much to lose, fearing that it might actually succeed. A number of techniques for surfacing and dealing with these issues exist.[3]

The following are three examples of initial solution initiative statements where the names of the companies have been made fictitious:

> I. **Solution Initiative Statement (initial version).** An improved Data Management system is needed to more cost effectively support maintenance and sustain engineering operations of Space Shuttle Orbiter's electrical wiring systems. A set of tasks has been defined that will prepare for developing any new Wire Data Management System. These tasks include development of a database management system Concept of Operations Document (ConOps), a User Requirements Document, and Recommendations for Follow-on Tasks Document before the end of FY04.

The statement above is both specific and unspecific—in the sense that a system (WDMS) is named but in terms that no one knows what this system is yet and what it would do.

This is typical for initiatives where there is a clear need to explore the problem before nominating a solution, yet some general way of talking about a solution is needed. In this case, it is accomplished by naming the system.

Contrast this with a situation where a preconceived commitment is expressed, as illustrated in the following example:

> II. **Solution Initiative Statement (initial version).** Secure Investments is interested in improving the delivery of information to its financial analysts through its corporate intranet. To accomplish this goal, it is undertaking a study to identify the benefits of modern search and categorization technologies. A specific piece of work has been targeted to develop a taxonomy that will serve as the foundation of a "Knowledge Architecture" for an improved unified framework to organize Secure Investments' knowledge artifacts.

Cases I and II talk about solution goals. The following example is more specific about the nature of the problem:

> III. **Solution Initiative Statement (initial version).** Order Management is currently being performed on three separate, non-integrated systems within ACME Corp. Depending on the line of business and other characteristics, an order could be taken and managed on one

---

[3] When these fail, projects invariably opt to operate in stealth mode by flying "beneath the radar screen." Adoption becomes a matter of engendering grassroots support. Few succeed, success being undermined by inadequate funding.

of three systems or on multiple systems. ACME identified the need to have one OMS as part of a new IT strategy and framework.

In recognizing the variability of the starting points, BCE includes techniques and activities that can be used to ground the initiative and confirm the nature of the problem and solution.

BCE ACTIVITIES I: ESTABLISH BUSINESS SITUATION AND RESOURCES

This cluster consists of BCE Activities 1–7 (see Figure 5.2 for reference):

1. Establish Solution Initiative Shared Space
2. Establish Key Stakeholders
3. Clarify Solution Initiative Statement
4. Establish Inventory of Reference Materials
5. Clarify Business Context
6. Assess Use of Current IT Capabilities
7. Establish a Glossary for the Initiative

References to Activities and associated Workproducts use the indexes and labels given in Figure 5.2. This group of activities establishes the general foundation and workspace for the entire Solution Envisioning effort and, possibly, the continuing work beyond for delivering the solution. It identifies and assembles a wide variety of information and people resources. It clarifies the definition of the initiative and its business context. It also surveys the IT infrastructure in which a future solution will co-exist.

Although this cluster consists of seven Activities, the work can often be accomplished in two to three days. For example, Activities 2, 3, and 4 can be completed in a two-hour meeting where

- Each team member brings a list of relevant documents to the meeting.
- Lists are reviewed and compiled in an overall inventory.
- The CATWOE technique is used to clarify the solution initiative statement and identify an initial set of stakeholders.
- Going through a checklist of possible stakeholders and using a technique such as "Value-Net" (see Sidebar 5.2 in Activity 5) ensures that no stakeholder is forgotten.

The diagram in Figure 5.2 and the corresponding listing show a *logical* (but not re-quired) order for the initiation of each of these activities—but not necessarily their completion. An iterative and interwoven execution is more typical, guided by the dependencies and opportunities that emerge in context.

Activity 1   Establish Solution Initiative Shared Space

BCE-1
Establish Solution Intiative Shared Space

Create an accessible shared space and "marketing chan-nel" for project information.

This is an important early activity that helps establish the solution initiative. A shared space (a website, a portal, or a collaborative environment like Lotus Notes or Groove) focuses the work of gathering, organizing, relating, creating, and pre-senting relevant materials and workproducts. As Solution Envisioning for the ini-tiative unfolds, it will contain a progressive history and justification for decisions and actions taken.

This resource will grow in importance through the rest of the phases of Solution Envisioning. For instance, the main outcome of Capability Exploration, an initial Solution Vision, has to be placed in a prominent, well-structured, and appealing lo-cation for easy sharing with a broader set of significant stakeholders. Similarly, the Solution Concept Document will be placed here after Capability Envisioning, and the Business Case and Realization Roadmap after Capability Design.

Just as the work of these phases builds upon the previous—indeed the readiness criterion to start each phase depends on the proper version of the input being available in this shared space—the space will contain the cumulative record and outcomes of Solution Envisioning. We suggest, if possible, the continued use of this shared space—or at least clear reference and access to it—should be carried over beyond Solution Envisioning into the construction, deployment, and adoption phases. This continuity will benefit the completion of the overall initiative and help to assure its success.

Workproduct A   Solution Initiative Shared Space

Solution Initiative Shared Space

A shared workspace such as a website, portal, or collaboration space that provides information and news about the project.

Activity 2   Establish Key Stakeholders

Stakeholders are the different parties who have an interest in the solution—those that benefit from the solution and those affected by the solution. Stakeholders can be customers, partners, users, sponsors, and other affected parties. The first part of this activity is to identify a core set of key stakeholders in relation to the initiative. A second part of this activity is to define how each stakeholder participates (is affected by) the initiative, and whether they need to be involved.

This is the first in a series of activities that will iteratively identify and examine the relation of stakeholders to the solution initiative. In determining the required business capabilities to fulfill the initiative, the active involvement of stakeholders is the primary means to refine the desired business outcomes into objectives with measurable results. The stakeholders, in their various roles, are accountable for achieving these results.

Due to the fundamental importance of stakeholder involvement and fulfillment to the success of any business activity, subsequent activities in this phase will analyze both the impact (Activity 10) and benefits (Activity 14) of the projected solution with respect to stakeholder interests and roles. In particular, Activity 10 has an extended discussion and guidance regarding interviewing stakeholders. It introduces additional techniques for capturing the multiple dimensions of the relationship stakeholders have to the work of the business and possible changes to it.

This focus of the current activity is the early identification and active engagement of a core set of key stakeholders who are critical to the foundational work of the initiative. They are needed to help shepherd and continue championing the initiative (and its funding), as well as the credibility, quality, and value of the Solution Envisioning intervention. They can help introduce facilitators and other stakeholders to one another and identify and secure access to a wide variety of relevant information sources and other resources. Sometimes, they are critical to clearing the way or providing political cover for more sensitive aspects of the Solution Envisioning work. It is, after all, about change, and in most cases, some parts of an organization and people within it do not welcome change.

A stakeholder is anyone inside or outside of the organization who will or may be affected by the planned solution. At minimum, consider the following roles:

- Solution Sponsor
- Leader of Related Initiative
- Lines of Business Executive
- Chief Technology Officer

- IT Manager
- Operations Manager
- Solution User
- Solution User's Customer
- Supplier Representatives
- Customer Representatives

Drawing a "Value-Net" (see Sidebar 5.2 in Activity 5) of the business is helpful in profiling the key stakeholders. After the Value-Net is defined, the stakeholders who participate in it can be identified and their current roles and responsibilities established.

Workproduct B   Stakeholder Profile and Participation Matrix

BCE B Stakeholder Profile and Participation Matrix

Stakeholder Profile and Participation Matrix (initial version)— This is a composite workproduct that will eventually cross-index the list of stakeholders with a specification of how each stakeholder benefits and is impacted by the solution initiative (see Activities 10 and 14). The initial version may contain only a list of each stakeholder identified, their role in relation to the business, whether the initiative is likely to affect them, and if they should be solicited for involvement.

Activity 3   Clarify Solution Initiative Statement

BCE-3
Clarify Solution
Initiative Statement

BCE C

Clarify the business transformation being considered by (1) establishing the current business context, (2) assessing related activities and stakeholders, and (3) agreeing on the solution initiative framing.

This activity takes as input the initial version of a Solution Initiative Statement used to launch BCE and the overall Solution Envisioning intervention. In conjunction with the work of the other activities in this group—working with key stakeholders, gathering materials and documents, and clarifying the business context and IT infrastructure—the Solution Initiative Statement is progressively framed, clarified, and confirmed. When there is sufficient shared agreement that it is complete enough, the Confirmed Solution Initiative Statement is placed in a prominent place in the Solution Initiative Shared Space for communication to a broader set of stakeholders. In some cases, it may be necessary to produce and carry forward some variants of the Solution Initiative Statement or even alternative statements into the next phase—Solution Capability Envisioning (SCE). In all cases, in Activity

6 of SCE (Review Solution Vision), a final Statement will be selected and refined as needed to complete the work of Solution Envisioning.

The Solution Initiative Statement(s) may continue to be shaped and refined through subsequent activities and phases. It may be considered confirmed for the purposes of this phase when the core team of stakeholders agree that it provides clear guidance regarding the motivation for and goals of the initiative. This serves as an important milestone in the work of BCE and helps to move the work forward to the next levels that will be undertaken in the next clusters (II-IV) of the Activities. Drawing a "Value-Net" (see Sidebar 5.2 in Activity 5) of the business may also be helpful in clarifying the scope and concise statement of the solution initiative.

Workproduct C Confirmed Solution Initiative Statement

Confirmed Solution Initiative Statement

Confirmed Solution Initiative Statement—A specification of the intent of the solution in terms of the problem that is being addressed, who benefits and how, motivations for the solution, constraints that surround the solution, and who the sponsor is. This serves as a concise statement of a program that will create and deploy IT capabilities needed to achieve the required business transformation.

Figure 5.4 presents an example of an elaborated and confirmed Solution Initiative Statement from a recent project where Solution Envisioning was used at NASA. The Wire Data Management System (WDMS) project worked with Orbiter wiring stakeholders, relevant work activities, purposes for which they need wire information, and how current and future IT capabilities support their needs.

Who Is the Customer?

KSC OP-F Orbiter Electrical ground processing division at Kennedy Space Center.

Who Are the Users?

Engineers who test, troubleshoot, repair, and upgrade Space Shuttle wiring.

What Business Improvement Is Envisaged?

More cost-effective and efficient maintenance, repair, and upgrade of the existing fleet of Orbiters through improved wire data management, systems, and services.

What Do We Believe Is Possible?

- Modern technologies can be readily deployed to improve Orbiter wiring fault diagnosis and maintenance work.
- Efficient access to dispersed information is essential to isolate, identify, repair, replace, or make improvements to orbiter wiring.
- Considerable engineering time can be reduced by automating wire data extraction, formatting, and document generation drudgery.
- 3D models of wire harnesses and their routings may be valuable for effectively planning engineering work and for determining damage prevention measures.

Who Is the Project Sponsor?

NASA AMES ECS.

What Are the Constraints and Givens?

- Procedures
  - Standard Practice Instruction procedure (SPI)
- Workproducts
  - Problem Report (PR)
  - Test Preparation Sheet (TPS)
- Systems
  - Work Authorization Document (WAD)
  - Orbiter Maintenance Instruction (OMI)
  - Orbiter Maintenance Requirement Specification Document (OMRSD)
  - Problem Reporting and Corrective Action database (PRACA)
  - Avionics Damage Database (ADD)
  - Automated Wire List (AWL)
  - Cable Design Fabrication and Test Data System (CDF&TDS)
  - Shuttle Connector Analysis Network (SCAN)
- Other
  - Web-based document retrieval system (Documentum)

FIGURE 5.4.   SNAPSHOT OF A CONFIRMED SOLUTION INITIATIVE STATEMENT AT NASA DURING BCE.

Activity 4   Establish Inventory of Reference Materials

Create an inventory of artifacts relevant to the Solution Initiative. These typically include reports, presentations, white papers, memos, and memorandums of understanding, statements of work, and other reference materials.

Some types of documents that may be important to review when gathering business situation facts include:

- Business Strategy
- Company Direction (statements of intent)
- Marketing and Customer Satisfaction Surveys
- Backlogs of Issues
- Vision Documents
- Executive Presentations (internal and external)

Workproduct D   Solution Initiative Materials Inventory

 Solution Initiative Materials Inventory The collection of reference materials relevant to the project. The inventory should either be placed in the solution initiative shared space or be accessible from links in the workspace. It is useful to be able to support discussions about inventory materials.

Activity 5   Clarify Business Context

Before Solution Envisioning work can begin, there is a need to explore or validate the business environment and the future intent of the business as seen by a number of key stakeholders. The activity establishes the business context related to the Solution Initiative and identifies relevant activity areas.

The goal of this activity is to answer questions, such as:

- What is the boundary of what we are considering?
- Who is in this context; why do we care about them?
- What problems need to be overcome?

- How do these problems arise?

- What forces are at work, and how are we challenged by their causes?

- What models of cause-and-effect explain what is going on?

When these questions are explored, what emerges is a picture of what is going on in the current business. The current business situation of an enterprise can be expressed as:[4]

- A business context diagram that bounds the scope of the situation being addressed, and surfaces forces and challenges

- A business model of the value-net of the enterprise that maps to stakeholders and their roles and responsibilities

- An analysis of the dominant systemic issues that the business faces

Context always bounds the scope of any situation being addressed. This is always in flux at the start of any problem understanding. But used effectively, attention on the *right* business situation will home in on the stakeholders, what forces are at work, outcomes to be realized, and the challenges to be overcome. As organizational entities are named, so are the stakeholders along with their roles and responsibilities. A business model, either of the *As-Is* or the *To-Be* world emerges. Value-Net diagrams are powerful ways to focus attention on the business context. Our preferred way of drawing these diagrams on a whiteboard is shown in Sidebar 5.2.

---

[4] Checkland's Soft Systems Methodology (SSM) introduced the idea of depicting situations with diagrams known as "rich pictures." A rich picture is a free-form diagram showing who is involved, their goals, interests, challenges, and complaints. They show how people and things are affected by conditions in the business environment and how interests agree or are in conflict. Think of rich pictures as a kind of cartoon—they can be funny, sad, political—preferably all at once. For an introduction to SSM, where these concepts are described in greater detail, see [Checkland, 1981], [Checkland, 1990], [Wilson, 1984].

Sidebar 5.2   Technique (T1): Value-Net

BCE T1 | Value Net Diagram — A Value-Net depicts the enterprise or its organizational units in a network of value creation with the ultimate recipient of value being the end-customer.

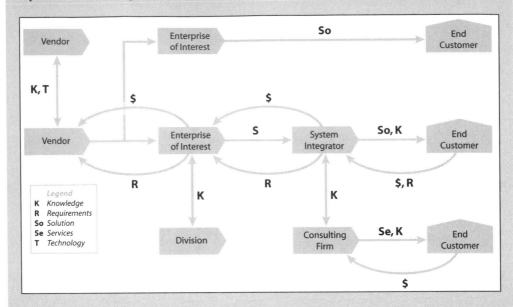

FIGURE 5.5. VALUE-NET.

Building a value-net requires the following questions to be answered:

- What products and services do we provide to others?
- What products and services do we require of others?
- What information passes between parties?
- What knowledge do we share with others?
- Who looks after that knowledge?
- How does revenue flow in the value-net?

Until the business model and context are set, it is unwise to do too much analysis of the issues that the enterprise is facing. The bigger picture will ensure that all stakeholders are being considered and that all sources of forces have been considered. After the context set, an analysis of causes and effects can be undertaken. Techniques for doing this are described in subsequent Activities.

Workproduct E   Business Context Model and Activity Areas

 Business Context Model and Activity Areas   A model of the business environment that depicts the key activity areas in a value-net showing the relationships between business units.

Activity 6   Assess Use of Current IT Capabilities

 Assess how current applications, systems, and databases are used to support the activities of different organizational units affected and within the scope of the solution initiative.

Workproduct F   Existing IT Systems in Context

 Existing IT Systems in Context   A specification of the dependencies of current business activities to existing IT systems indicating which systems and databases need to be considered as *IT givens* for the solution initiative.

Activity 7   Establish a Glossary for the Initiative

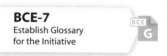 Create a readily accessible list of definitions of terminology for project personnel and other interested parties.

Workproduct G   Solution Initiative Glossary

 Solution Initiative Glossary   Definition of terms used by the project and pointers to where to find more information if necessary.

BCE ACTIVITIES II: IDENTIFY BUSINESS
NEEDS AS FORCES AND RESULTS

"The wrong kind of problem statement...can effectively stop problem solving."[5]

This cluster consists of BCE Activities 8–10 (see Figure 5.2 for reference):

8. Elicit Forces, Barriers, Results

9. Refine Forces and Barriers

10. Perform Stakeholder Impact Analysis

The structured representation of a business situation follows from the practice and methods of *problem understanding*. Within Solution Envisioning, this constitutes the first part of the journey from problem to solution.

"In searching for a process that could mediate among competing solutions without simply favoring the most articulate or most adamant argument, it became evident that the problem itself would self-select the best solution if it were sufficiently understood."[6]

As the quote suggests, solutions are fundamentally dependent on and conceived out of understanding and conceptualizing a problem space. Understanding the problem must be approached in a way that reliably progresses decision making about what can be done that can be shared among the maximum number of constituents who will be impacted.

The desire for something new to happen in the support of a business arises from many situations, such as those characterized by the following, typical kinds of statements:

- "Our systems are not able to cope with our customers' expectations of us."

- "We just can't partner effectively with all the new channels that are appearing."

- "Our competitors are realizing more market share; we need to get ahead of them."

- "We have so much pain with those packages we bought; they just don't work for us."

---

[5] *Design for the Real World.* Victor Papanek [Papanek, 1985].

[6] *Solutions Looking for Problems.* Rick Dove [Dove, 1999].

Earlier in this chapter, we stated that the Solution Envisioning approach begins in the Capability Exploration work by structuring the business situation shared cause-effect framework. This is composed of simple sentences that express important causes and related effects about *stakeholders, forces, barriers, results, challenges,* and *strategies* pertaining to a proposed solution and its adoption. The activities in this cluster focus on how situations, such as those expressed in the preceding bulleted list, are scoped and framed in a consistent way that is appropriate to begin envisioning IT solutions.

Central to this framing of the business context and the possibilities for transforming it are the concepts within the vocabulary of Solution Envisioning and Capability Cases. The elements of this vocabulary were introduced in the Introduction (see Figure I.3) and explained in more detail in Chapter 2, "Bridging the Gap with Solution Envisioning." The definition of these terms and an understanding of the role they play within Solution Envisioning set the stage for the next groups of Activities.

Activity 8   Elicit Forces, Barriers, Results

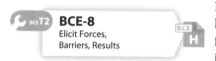

BCE-8
Elicit Forces,
Barriers, Results

For each stakeholder, determine the underlying forces, barriers, and results that surround the business transformation under consideration. Force is a new or existing condition that is affecting the business. Barrier is an obstacle within the business context that prevents business objectives from being realized. Result is a change in the state of the business that allows business transformation to take place. Forces and barriers must be supported with marketplace evidence.

There are a number of ways to elicit forces and barriers that are impacting stakeholders in the performance of their activities. Analysis of documents collected (see Activity 4) may produce initial lists of business forces, barriers, and results. The interview guides or questionnaires shown under Activity 10, Perform Stakeholder Impact Analysis, are designed to elicit forces and barriers. For example, questions like 1.4 in Table 5.2, "What are the issues, problems, and complaints that we have?," are intended to directly identify barriers. In a similar way, the questions in 2.1, "What are the new market conditions and forces?," and 2.4, "What is threatening us or what are the most urgent things for us to do?," in Table 5.3 explicitly ask stakeholders to articulate forces.

In a workshop setting, a powerful technique that we call the "Three What's?" (see Sidebar 5.3) is used to help stakeholders discover forces and barriers. It asks people to tell stories about *what's working, what's not,* and *what's changing in the business.*

The eliciting and capturing of forces, barriers, and results from stakeholders tends to be a very interactive process. Reusable lists of *canonical* forces relevant to industry and business area offer a way to stimulate discussion. A useful exercise is to rank them according to relevance and importance. Having evidence for forces and results can be of great help. Examples of such evidence are observations, facts, or industry statistics that support or counter the statement.

People will make statements about similar forces or barriers phrasing them in different ways. To complete this activity, the informal set of collected forces and barriers needs to be "normalized." The goal is to express them in a consistent way that resonates with the organization. Similar statements are merged. Repeating statements are removed. Some statements are abstracted. Some statements may need more refinement and details. Results are refined in a later step (in Activity 15).

Sidebar 5.3   Technique (T2): "Three What's?"

BCE T2 — Three 'What's?' Stakeholders are requested to answer the following questions. This can be done on an individual basis, but is usually more effective in a group session where the insights, courage, and ability to articulate real concerns build with the interaction of stakeholders. The questions can be drawn up on a whiteboard or flipchart in a plenary session or in breakout groups, and the responses discussed, organized and grouped, refined, and documented.

What's Working?	**What's Not Working?**	**What's Changing?**
This question allows people to start on a positive footing. This builds confidence in their willingness to speak and trust in the process—to confirm that it is not one-sided or fundamentally critical.	This question goes to the heart of their personal stake and responsibility in the business operating effectively. The responses here map directly to barriers that the stakeholders experience in meeting the business objectives or that stand in the way of new possibilities.	This question asks stakeholders to express their insights and understanding of new pressures, threats, and opportunities in the marketplace. What new possibilities (and technologies) are others taking advantage of? What must our business do to remain competitive—at a minimum to survive? Or better, to thrive? The responses here map directly to an informal statement of forces.

Figure 5.6 shows an example of the final list of *forces* from the Capability Exploration phase of a project that focused on an Electronic Records Archive (ERA) system.

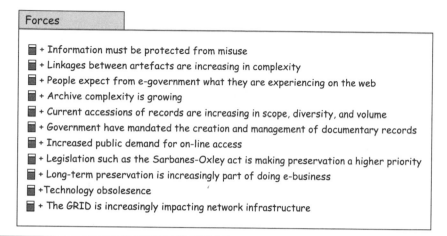

FIGURE 5.6.   LIST OF REFINED FORCES FROM A PROJECT ON ELECTRONIC RECORDS
ARCHIVING.

When business situations are very "messy," more extensive problem modeling is
required. Cognitive mapping techniques are useful for analyzing root causes [Eden
1998]. Exploring the dynamics of the problem in either Systems Thinking[7] models
or System Dynamics Models[8] may also be of value. By looking at the systemic nature of the phenomena in the business situation, the real nature of problems can
be revealed.

Workproduct H   Business Capability Model

Business Capability Model (component): Stakeholder to Challenges
List—A list of the forces, barriers, and results relevant to each stakeholder, along with evidence from the marketplace and business environment. This
workproduct will be later transformed into one of the Capability Maps within the
"Business Capability Model."

Business Capability
Model

---

[7] The reader is referred to Peter Senge's books on Systems Thinking for system archetypes
for common problem situations and causal modeling techniques [Senge, 1990, 1994].
Also recommended is Jamshid Gharajedaghi's book on applying the Systems Thinking approach to Business Architecture [Gharajedaghi, 1999].

[8] System Dynamics models are simulation models that allow the systemic nature of a problem situation to be analyzed. See John D. Sterman's book on *Business Dynamics* for a detailed guide [Sterman, 2000].

Activity 9 Identify Business Activities in Scope

BCE-9
Identify Business
Activities in Scope

Identify business activity scenarios in the current business (As-Is) that are in-scope for the solution initiative for all stakeholder roles. Capture the work sequence at the generic level for each activity by creating essential activity scenario diagrams. The scenarios should reflect the essential sequence of work steps that characterize the business activities.

As a first step, essential business activities in scope are identified for each stakeholder affected by the initiative. Table 5.1 shows a template for identifying and documenting this information *per stakeholder*. In addition to "required" fields—Activity Name and Brief Description—the template also has fields for capturing other useful information that places the activity in context, such as Improvement Areas and Metrics. These fields support the scoping exercise by identifying areas of improvement to be addressed by the solution initiative. Assessment of the stakeholder work continues through the next steps—sequencing and diagramming the activities. It then becomes the central focus of the next cluster of Activities that explore future possibilities for the business.

TABLE 5.1. TEMPLATE FOR IDENTIFICATION OF ACTIVITIES IN SCOPE PER STAKEHOLDER

Activity Name	Brief Description	Frequency	Improvement Areas	Evidence and Metrics

When enough of the stakeholder activities in scope for the solution initiative have been identified, the next step is to explore each activity. Activity sequence diagrams need only capture enough detail to understand the essential steps in the activity—sufficient to explore and examine possibilities for improvement. Figure 5.7 shows a simplified example of a business scenario taken from a project to build a Wealth Management Portal.

In some situations, there will be a need to focus more intensively on an understanding of the As-Is state. With a large number of activities to identify and diagram, more time will need to be spent in the Capability Exploration phase. As a mini-project in its own right, it may last several weeks. A situation analysis workshop where a number of key stakeholders are brought together to discuss and create a shared understanding of the current state of the operations of a business or organization becomes important.

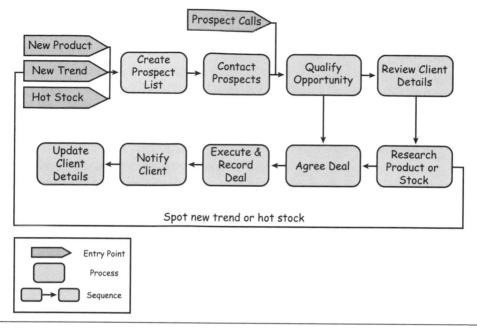

FIGURE 5.7.   A SIMPLIFIED BUSINESS SCENARIO—THE FINANCIAL ADVISOR'S SELLING CYCLE.

In other situations that focus more on a new product or new initiative of a business, comparatively little time may be spent on charting and diagramming As-Is activities. In these cases, the essential business activities will consist more of projected scenarios of future operations or use. These take the form of story-boards or narratives more than activity diagrams and are covered under Activity 12.

Workproduct J   Essential Activity Scenarios (Initial Version)

 Essential Activity Scenarios   Stakeholder essential business activities are identified by Name and Brief Description. The identified activities are detailed to a useful level as scenario diagrams.

Later, these scenarios are used as the basis for creating storyboards of transformed scenarios (To-Be) for how the business can operate with the new capabilities selected in the solution initiative. See Activity 12 for more details.

Activity 10   Perform Stakeholder Impact Analysis

BCE-10
Perform Stakeholder
Impact Analysis

For each stakeholder, information is collected to profile him or her with respect to the solution initiative. A description of the impact on the stakeholder is captured based on how his world will potentially change as a result of the initiative.

The different groups of solution stakeholders may have conflicting interests, but common ground has to be established. Analyzing stakeholders will help to surface issues and assumptions. It also provides insights on the situation. Many stakeholders can be categorized as either protagonists or antagonists of the solution. A Power–Interest grid is a good tool for performing such analysis (see Technique (T3): "Power–Interest Grid" in Sidebar 5.4).

The analysis helps to determine:

- Who to interview
- Who to invite to the Solution Envisioning workshop (to be conducted in the Capability Envisioning phase)
- How to structure the Communication Strategy

Another technique is to discuss stakeholder impact according to their types or groups. According to the ideas derived from the Soft Systems Methodology (see Technique (T0): "CATWOE" in Sidebar 5.1), we distinguish the following types of stakeholders:

- **Customers**—Those who will benefit from the system or be affected by the system
- **Agents**—Those who will build and operate the system
- **Owners or sponsors**—Those who can stop or authorize the project

Sidebar 5.4   Technique (T3): Power-Interest Grid

 Power-Interest Grid

In this 2-by-2 matrix, stakeholders are positioned according to their level of interest in the solution and by how much influence they could potentially have over the project. For example, a few fictional stakeholders identified at Secure Investments might be positioned on the grid in the following way:

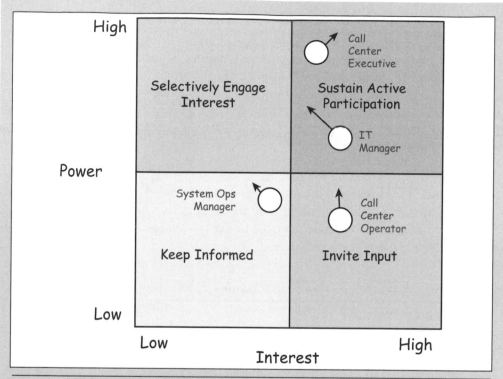

FIGURE 5.8.

Each stakeholder's position on the grid provides an indication of the type of involvement they should have in the project:

- High-power, high-interest stakeholders should be actively engaged in the Solution Envisioning activities.

- High-power, less-interested stakeholders should be at a minimum well-informed about the work. Consider including some of them in the interview process during the BCE phase. If the goal is to raise their level of interest, consider inviting them to the Solution Envisioning workshop.

- Low-power, high-interest stakeholders can play an important role in Solution Envisioning activities. Their needs must be balanced against the high-power, high-interest group.

- Low-power, less-interested stakeholders may need to be informed about the project and their relationship to the project checked from time-to-time to make sure no major issues surface.

In making these considerations, it is important to consider how each stakeholder's power and interest may change over time. This is shown as a vector on each stakeholder.

Stakeholder Interviews

When the stakeholders groups are large and there is insufficient information from any previous work, interviewing key stakeholders should be combined with a questionnaire to a wider audience. Tables 5.2 and 5.3 present a template for an interview guide. It is based on the two contrasting perspectives with reinforcing sub-questions:

    I. "Where are we now?—Where is the organization today?"

    II. "What is happening in our environment?—How is our world changing?"

The questions explore the problem space using a *Future Search Conference* approach[9] for exploring past, present, and future. As noted in Activity 8, these guides repeat themes and are informed by the techniques *Three What's* and *S.W.O.T.* Depending on the situation, they can be used to complement and reinforce or substitute the use of those techniques.

TABLE 5.2.   STAKEHOLDER INTERVIEW GUIDE—TEMPLATE 1

I.	WHERE ARE WE NOW?	
1.0	Where is the organization today?	What is the perception we have in the marketplace by our: (use one sentence, for each) ■ Customers? ■ Suppliers? ■ Competitors? ■ Investors and shareholders?
1.1	What are our distinct competencies?	List the top-ten business capabilities that distinguish us. For example, is it our use of leading edge technologies, innovation in our products, and comprehensiveness of our service offerings, our pre- and post-sales support, or the quality of our relationships with our customers, suppliers, and partners? Consider the attributes of your organization that differentiate you from your competitors in the eyes of your customers.

---

[9] "Future Search Conference" is a workshop approach to achieving common ground by inquiring into the past, exploring the present, and envisioning alternate viable future scenarios [Weisbord, 1993; 1999].

TABLE 5.2.   STAKEHOLDER INTERVIEW GUIDE—TEMPLATE 1—CONTINUED

1.2	What are our vulnerabilities?	Where are we weak? Where could we easily be attacked? What could we improve easily? List the top-ten.
1.3	What do we feel proud and sorry (rant and rave) about?	List the top-ten "Rants" and "Raves" that you hear yourself or others making.
1.4	What are the issues, problems and complaints that we have?	List the top-ten barriers that you think can stop us from achieving our goals.

TABLE 5.3.   STAKEHOLDER INTERVIEW GUIDE—TEMPLATE 2

II.   WHAT IS HAPPENING IN OUR ENVIRONMENT?

2.0	How is our world changing?	What captures the shift that is happening in our business environment? Try to express that shift as a change vector from the world we knew to the new world. For example: A shift from "Standard value propositions to known customers" to "Value propositions that need to be created dynamically for new and unforeseen customers"
2.1	What are the new market conditions and forces?	List the top-ten business drivers that we have to respond to. Think about how your customers' demands/needs for your product and solution offering are changing. Consider the values that you compete on: price, cost, quality, distribution, brand loyalty, product functionality, choice, availability, product/service, and so on.
2.2	What are the new ways to win?	List three to ten ideas for winning in the changing environment.
2.3	What are others doing?	For each of these new ways to win, give an example of what others in your market are doing. Consider emerging competitors and who your competitors will be in the future.
2.4	What is threatening us or what are the most urgent things for us to do?	Rank each of the above in terms of what are the most threatening. Do this by writing the list of new ways to win in the order of most to least threatening (for example: 5, 3, 2, 4, 1). 5 being most, 1 being least.
2.5	Who do we want to be like?	List players in different (maybe related) marketplaces that we would most like to be like. Give some reasons.

The impact of the initiative on each of the stakeholders can be described using a template shown in Table 5.4.[10] The *Impact* field identifies how the stakeholder's world will change—their day-to-day activities, responsibilities, interactions, and so on—as a result of this initiative.

The Stakeholder Impact Summary will help the initiative project team in several ways:

- It facilitates having conversations with stakeholders about the initiative.
- It identifies who the key players to focus on are (those who will be impacted most).
- It provides a context for creating value propositions for the key stakeholders.
- It influences the solution design by identifying features needed to address some of the concerns of the stakeholders.

Workproduct B (component) Stakeholder Profile and Participation Matrix

RCF
B
Stakeholder Profile and Participation Matrix
Stakeholder Impact Summary—A tabular specification of how each stakeholder is impacted by the solution initiative. A template is used to document the following information about the stakeholder with respect to the initiative: Attitude, Temperature, Influence, Risk Tolerance, Expectations, and Impact.

TABLE 5.4. TEMPLATE USED FOR THE STAKEHOLDER IMPACT SUMMARY

Stakeholder	Attitude	Temperature	Influence	Risk Tolerance	Expectation	Degree of Impact	Impact
(Values used for these fields are shown below)							
Name / Contact Info.	Positive / Neutral / Negative	Hot / Warm / Cold	Strong / Moderate / Minimal	High / Moderate / Low	{text field}	Marginal / Moderate / Significant	{text field}

---

[10] Some of the fields and values in this stakeholder profile template are adapted from the "allPM.Com" checklist by Tom Welch.

BCE Activities III: Explore Possibilities Informed by Technology

This cluster consists of BCE Activities 11–15 (see Figure 5.2 for reference):

11. Nominate Capabilities

12. Explore Future Business Possibilities

13. Explore Technology Options

14. Perform Stakeholder Benefit Analysis

15. Refine Results

A number of forces are at work in the early stages of systems development. Not least is interplay of the expression of business needs and the early intuitions about future designs. Such ideas will often stimulate new needs, and requirements are generated in the process. Requirements become agreements or commitments to an envisioned future. An overall assessment of the projected business transformation needs several perspectives, identified through questions such as

- What do we have to change?

- What impacts will that have on our IT systems and organization?

- What will it cost us to make this change?

- Are we ready to doing this, or do we need more analysis?

Quality Function Deployment (QFD)[11] introduced the powerful idea of the *Voice of the Customer* as a means for focusing on the needs of the customer. Solution Envisioning introduces the idea of the *Voice of the Technologist* to inform and stimulate requirements, based on what technology makes it possible to become. In parallel with understanding the issues an organization is facing, a scan of what technologies can do is conducted. This approach facilitates finding ways in which an organization can take advantage of these capabilities. Two key questions are addressed by this scan:

1. With the diverse choices of solution ideas available, which ones can support viable business architectures?

2. With these ideas, what is it possible for an enterprise to be?

The activities in this cluster, especially Activities 11–13, *Nominate Capabilities*, *Explore Future Business Possibilities* (through future scenarios), and *Explore Technology Options* are performed in a parallel and highly iterative manner. The

---

[11] See Chapter 8 for more information on QFD and an example of integrating QFD with Solution Envisioning.

sequential order shown is for convenience of explanation and reflects the initial pass-through often taken. Any of the activities may be initiated before the completion of others. These activities are mutually reinforcing and performed simultaneously and iteratively until satisfactory results for each and the set as a whole are reached.

Activity 11   Nominate Capabilities

BCE-11
Nominate
Capabilities

Based on essential business activity scenarios (created in Activity 9), nominate organizational and IT capabilities that could support the enterprise of the future.

Capability Cases are the primary vehicle and asset used in Solution Envisioning to help perform a solution scan and effectively communicate its results to the business. Capability Cases help ensure that the business decisions on the solution are informed about what is possible. Critical thinking, root cause analysis, and looking at solution examples is used to identify *candidate capabilities* needed to deliver goals stated for each scenario step.

Figure 5.9 illustrates the process of "nominating" or proposing potentially supportive capabilities for steps within the Financial Advisor's Selling Cycle scenario. We showed the creation of this scenario diagram as an example in Activity 9, "Identify Business Activities in Scope," and Figure 5.7. Note that each of the Capability Cases named here is further described in Chapter 3, "Illustrative Applications and Galleries," and some are shown at a summary-level in the accompanying galleries. These include

- "Interest-based Information Delivery"
- "Instant Helper"
- "Customer Analyzer"
- "Expert Locator"
- "Ask an Expert"

Capability Cases can be indexed using *forces* and *results*, as shown in Figure 2.11. Using these indices, we can show why a capability is relevant—what benefits it can bring and what forces and challenges it responds to.

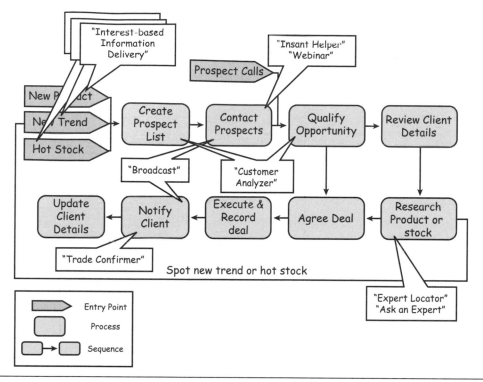

FIGURE 5.9.   Nominated Capability Cases for Financial Analyst activities.

When there is an existing catalog of Capability Cases for the domain, indices can be used to select a portfolio of candidate capabilities—for example, by matching forces in the business situation to forces that the Capability Cases address. Similarly, we can identify capabilities by looking at the benefits—business results—that they bring to an organization. Figure 5.10 illustrates the use of forces and results to match potentially applicable capabilities to generate an initial portfolio of candidate capabilities.

These candidate capabilities are further assessed as to their relevance and importance—and additional capabilities may be uncovered—in the iterative work of this activity and the complementary and parallel Activities 12 and 13.

Forces, results, and solution capabilities become meaningful when connected to the work of the business. As we have seen, Solution Envisioning does this systematically. It helps stakeholders envision and capture essential business activity scenarios that future solution users will execute, and then to connect forces, results, and capabilities to the scenario steps they impact or support.

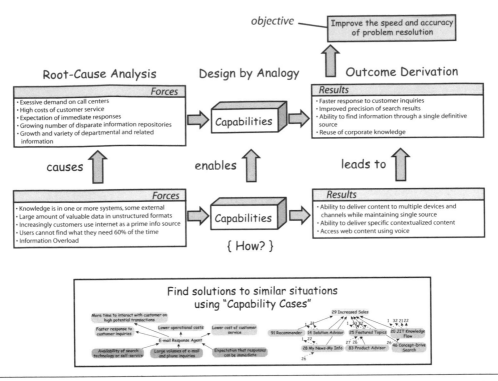

FIGURE 5.10. MATCHING CAPABILITIES USING FORCES AND RESULTS FROM THE BUSINESS SITUATION.

Workproduct I Candidate Capability Cases Portfolio

Candidate Capability Cases Portfolio

A collection of Capability Cases and selected solution stories that serve as inspirations for the envisioned solution. A Portfolio may include fully developed Capability Cases selected from a catalog. It can also include newly identified capabilities. These are identified by their name and a short intent statement.

Activity 12 Explore Future Business Possibilities

BCE-12
Explore Future
Business Possibilities

Using current business activity scenarios (created in Activity 9), create future work scenarios for the enterprise. Transform the existing work scenarios into views of how the business will be able to operate with the new capabilities selected for the solution initiative (as identified in Activity 11). Create narratives and storyboards in conjunction with the scenarios to convey how the work sequence will change for each business activity with the support of these new capabilities.

A vital part of the *Solution Envisioning* approach is the use of creative techniques to help understand and envision future scenarios of how the world can and will be different after the solution is deployed. The creation of *future business work scenarios*, describing typical activities of system stakeholders, is a key step in understanding the business requirements. The nominated capabilities explored in the previous activity usually will stimulate insights into new and better ways of performing certain business processes.

Using the stakeholder activity scenarios established earlier (Activity 9), desired improvements can be identified to meet the new business objectives. This is done by analyzing the scenarios—looking for problem areas, the constraints that cause potential bottlenecks, and process improvement opportunities. To create compelling future scenarios, the work in this activity seeks to ask and answer question such as:

- How is the world changing?
- What are the new ways to win?
- What is it possible for us to become?
- What known solutions can help us decide what we should become?
- What do we want to become?

Finding answers to these questions requires stakeholders, on one hand, to dwell in the problems they are facing and, on the other hand, to disconnect from the current logic and "reach for the future." The resulting, newly envisioned scenarios are effective in giving the team a common perspective on the problem space and a shared vision of the solution.

Stories, storyboards, and metaphors are fundamental thinking blocks used to support this work. They focus attention on the people who will use the solution and the value it will bring. Future scenarios encourage unconstrained thinking. They give concrete focus to the work and get straight to the heart of what needs changing in an empowered way. Sidebar 5.5a highlights "Storyboarding" as a very useful technique for creating the type of essential activity scenarios that we recommend for exploring future business possibilities. Sidebar 5.5b provides an example of such a storyboard extracted from the published paper by one of the authors of this book on the TEPM project at IBM.[12]

---

[12] *Experiences Using Knowledge Model-Driven CBR for Knowledge Enablement of Best Practices Within IBM Global Services*. Ralph Hodgson, Greg L. Baker, Prady Pradhyumnan [Hodgson, 2001].

Workproduct J (transformed) Essential Activity Scenarios

 Essential Activity Scenarios

Storyboards of transformed scenarios (To-Be) for how the business can operate with the new capabilities selected in the solution initiative. These future retrospective stories may include a narrative description of activities that a role in the organization needs to perform. It can be thought of as a "day in the life" story of a person operating in that role in the envisioned future.

Sidebar 5.5a Technique (T4): Storyboarding

Problem Context

When design needs to be anchored in end-user situations.

Understanding the opportunities for innovation by capturing the problems people face in a real-world domain.

Conveying functionality of a proposed solution, product, or service.

Convincing people of the value of a proposed product in a real-world domain, and, by analogy, that it would be valuable in their own settings.

Collecting requirements and generating feedback on how the events and functionalities depicted in the story map to the intended domain.

Helping people understand how they could incorporate a new technology in their own work practice and recognize the value of doing so.

Approach

Scenarios allow free thinking. Divergence within a group of developers is harnessed. Scenarios give concrete focus to work and get straight to the heart of the matter in a connected way.

Stories, storyboards, and metaphors are fundamental thinking blocks. They focus attention on the people who will use the solution and the value it will bring. Stories are rich, fleshed-out descriptions of settings, people, activities, goals, motivations, and values presented in a coherent, causally connected way. The process of creating a story can insure that attention has been paid to the factors necessary to create an effective solution.

Advice and Guidance To prepare a new scenario, we suggest working through the following steps:

Before Starting
- Determine the goals
- Be cognizant of audience needs and dispositions
- Determine a style and medium

Framing the Story
- Features, activities, or the activity area(s) the story will explore
- Select a general setting
- Decide on the protagonist(s)
- Select an overall activity and goal

Create each episode of the story
- Enumerate events
- Consider event flow
- Combine events into a script

Produce the scenario
- Storyboard the script
- Select suitable images and icons
- Review with subject-matter experts
- Package for distribution

When operational scenarios are envisioned, multiple modes of system operation need to be considered as "themes and variations" to envision a system that accommodates all.

Sidebar 5.5b   Example of Using Storyboarding

David Chan was an IT Architect working as a consultant for IBM. He often faced the challenge of navigating the vast array of information sources in IBM. This was always a formidable and time-consuming task for IBM Global Services Practitioners until a KM initiative came along and provided a new project workplace on the WEB.

FIGURE 5.11A.

When David Chan was working on a customer project for Speedy Franks Company, he needed to do some requirements work on short notice. Fortunately, his project manager had decided to make use of a new Project Environment. The Manager was keen to do this because of the potential to reuse relevant work from other colleagues.

Figure 5.11b shows the list of workproducts David was responsible for. He selected Non-Functional Requirements and asked the system to find relevant intellectual capital (IC).

Project: Speedy Frank Logistics Applications ▼   List of Work Products

Work Product	Due Date	Status	Link to Activities	People Assigned	Date Created	Last Revised	Version
Business Context Diagram	11/20/99	Draft	Link	Chan, Didier	11/5/99	11/5/99	1.0
Business Object Model	11/25/99	Draft	Link	Chan	11/4/99	11/5/99	1.1
Capability Model	11/18/99	In Review	Link	Chan	11/2/99	11/5/99	1.3
Non-functional Requirements for Supply Chain Replenishment Systems	11/10/99		Link	Chan			
Detailed Requirements Matrix	12/01/99		Link	Chan			
Application Packages Recommended	12/28/99		Link	Chan, Didier, Melody			

Create New
Revise
Review
Check Out
Check In
Search for IC
Attributes

FIGURE 5.11B.

FIGURE 5.11C.

A profile dialog appears with a number of search attributes.

The system knows that Speedy Frank's is a Logistics Application in a retail company, that Chan was in the role of Requirements Engineer, and that the focus of the current search is Non-Functional Requirements. These allowed the system to set many search attributes. David set some of the other attributes.

In response, the system retrieved relevant assets using similarity-based searching (see Figure 5.11d). The retrieved results were determined by how the assets fit with the profile of the situation-at-hand. For example, the third search result has the value "Wholesale" for the attribute "Industry." Although the search was for "Retail," the taxonomy-based similarity calculation computed a relevant match. Ranking of the results was based on the popularity of the assets with other practitioners. This was done by counting the number of instances of "Reuse" that had occurred.

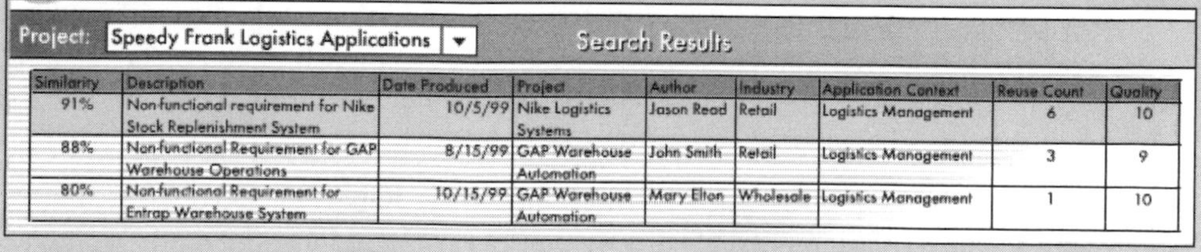

Project: Speedy Frank Logistics Applications ▼   Search Results

Similarity	Description	Date Produced	Project	Author	Industry	Application Context	Reuse Count	Quality
91%	Non-functional requirement for Nike Stock Replenishment System	10/5/99	Nike Logistics Systems	Jason Read	Retail	Logistics Management	6	10
88%	Non-functional Requirement for GAP Warehouse Operations	8/15/99	GAP Warehouse Automation	John Smith	Retail	Logistics Management	3	9
80%	Non-functional Requirement for Entrap Warehouse System	10/15/99	GAP Warehouse Automation	Mary Elton	Wholesale	Logistics Management	1	10

FIGURE 5.11D.

As a result of this Storyboarding effort, the time to do non-functional requirements of the system was reduced by three days.

Activity 13 Explore Technology Options

BCE-13
Explore Technology
Options

Consider established and emerging technologies and known and envisioned solution stories as a means to understanding what might be possible through technology.

This activity further explores the set of technologies that may be used to support future activity scenarios. The intention is to confirm that no promising technology options and potentials have been overlooked and the most promising are in play for consideration—based on the Capability Cases selected. The work often includes a short (approximately half-day) session for business people on the promise (and perils) of new or emerging technologies.

Workproduct K Technology Strategy Outline

Technology Strategy
Outline

A document identifying the set of technologies that may be used to support task scenarios. It takes into account how other organizations, including the company's competitors, may be using technology for competitive advantage.

Activity 14 Perform Stakeholder Benefit Analysis

BCE-14
Perform Stakeholder
Benefit Analysis

Map capabilities to each stakeholder's interests and challenges, expressing a value proposition. Each party has interests that the envisioned solution satisfies; goals and objectives they're trying to accomplish; forces that are addressed by the solution; and barriers that are overcome by the solution. A second task is to elaborate the stakeholder participation matrix to define how each stakeholder needs to be involved in the project.

Stakeholder Impact Summary, shown in Table 5.4, is used to provide input to the creation of the *Stakeholder Benefit Summary*. In addition to the benefit statement, we express the commitment and input required from each stakeholder for a successful project. The ideas of stakeholder participation and benefit align well with the business measurement framework of Performance Prism.

In creating stakeholder-related workproducts, it is important to consider their use later in the project for developing Communication, Education, and Deployment plans.

Workproduct B (component)   Stakeholder Profile and Participation Matrix

 Stakeholder Profile and Participation Matrix   Stakeholder Profile and Participation Matrix (component): Stakeholder Benefit Summary—Links to Business Capability Model and its component maps.

Activity 15   Refine Results

Translate the informal statement of forces into a normalized list. For each result, identify possible measures.

This activity updates and refines the results captured in the Business Capability Model (Workproduct H) in Activity 8 (*Elicit Forces, Barriers, and Results*). When business results are discussed, key points to get clear on are:

- **Measurements**—How results will be evaluated
- **Measurement goals**—The specific measurement values to be attained
- **Strategy alignment**—How identified results support the strategic goals of the business

Figure 5.12 shows an example of a list of *results* from the Capability Exploration phase of a project that focused on an Electronic Records Archive system (see Activity 8 for the list of forces for this project). Figure 5.13 shows possible measures identified for one of these results.

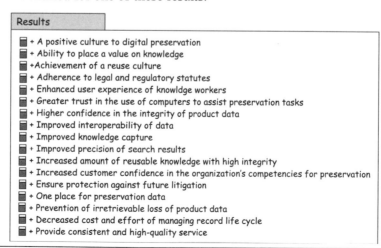

FIGURE 5.12. LIST OF REFINED RESULTS FROM A PROJECT ON ELECTRONIC RECORDS ARCHIVING.

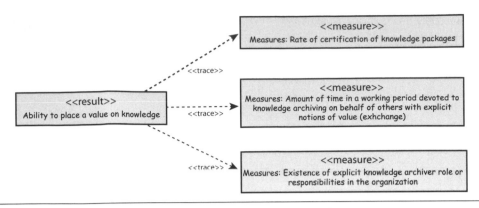

FIGURE 5.13.   EXAMPLES OF MEASURES FOR A RESULT.

Workproduct L   Measures of Effectiveness

 Measures of Effectiveness   A table expressing results and measures for each business activity in the scope of the solution initiative.

BCE ACTIVITIES IV: CONSOLIDATE INITIAL SOLUTION VISION FOR SHARING

This cluster consists of BCE Activities 16–17 (see Figure 5.2 for reference):

16. Map Capabilities to Forces, Barriers, Challenges, and Results
17. Create Solution Vision Presentation

Activity 16   Map Capabilities to Forces, Barriers, Challenges, and Results

BCE-16
Map Capabilities to Forces, Barriers, Challenges & Results

Develop "Cause-Effect/Impact" diagrams depicting how existing and new capabilities are needed in the business context.

Capability maps help to communicate relationships between forces, results, barriers, challenges, activities, and capabilities. The objective of this task is to produce capability maps for each stakeholder. Useful presentations of the maps include the following:

Stakeholder Forces — Capabilities Map

For each stakeholder, a map might illustrate the forces that are affecting the ability to perform their activities.

Stakeholder Results — Capabilities Map

For each stakeholder, this type of capability map shows how capabilities support a stakeholder's activities and how these activities map to the results they are wishing to accomplish. The structure of this type of map is illustrated in Figure 5.14.

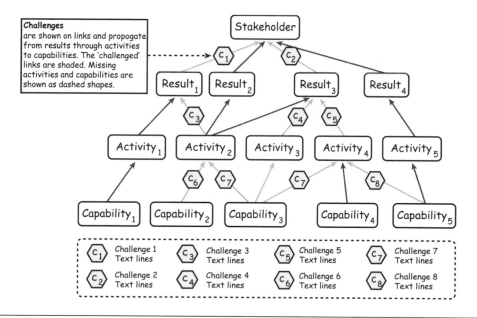

FIGURE 5.14.   STAKEHOLDER RESULTS TO CAPABILITIES MAP.

Challenge Map

This map visualizes importance of a challenge by showing it in the center with connections to other entities. In Figure 5.15, we show the structure for such a map depicting stakeholders and results.

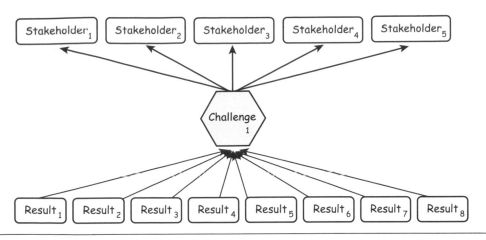

FIGURE 5.15. CHALLENGE MAP STRUCTURE—STAKEHOLDERS AND RESULTS.

Capability Dependency Map

This is a map showing the Capability Cases that are enablers for the desired results.

Workproduct H   Business Capability Model

Business Capability Model

A specification of how the challenges of stakeholders in performing their activities are supported by existing and envisioned capabilities. It includes the following as components:

- Stakeholder Challenges List (see Activity 8)
- Activity Challenges Map—a mapping of the forces, barriers, and results to each activity that is in scope.

Activity 17   Create Solution Vision Presentation

BCE-17
Create Solution
Vision Presentation

Package the work of the phase into a presentation of the vision of the solution. Aspects of the presentation need to address multiple audiences: business executives, system architects, and end-user representatives.

This final activity packages the cumulative outcomes of the Business Capability Exploration phase. This most often takes the form of one or more documents accompanied by presentations. Successful completion triggers the readiness to move to the work of Capability Envisioning, the second phase of Solution Envisioning.

Business Solution Delivery Lifecycle

...need for Change → Business Strategy Development/ Realignment → Solution Initiative Formation → **Solution Envisioning** → Solution Realization & Adoption → ...Business Results

Assessment | Design | Construction | Deployment

Solution Initiative Formation

Business Capability Exploration

Solution Initiative Statement (initial)

Solution Capability Envisioning

Solution Vision Presentation & Shared Space

Solution Concept Document & Capability Model

Software Capability Design

Solution Business Case & Realization Roadmap

Initiate Solution Construction/ Deployment

The overall flow of a complete Solution Envisioning (SE) process can be informally described in terms of these main movements:

Before SE

Pre-a. Formulating a Solution Initiative

Pre-b. Clarifying the business goals and ROI objectives

During SE

1. Confirming business goals and objectives

2. Analyzing the current business situation to understand who is hurting and how

3. Reaching out for someting new – dentifying an initial portfolio of capabilities

4. Consolidating an initial solution vision for sharing with a larger set of stakeholders

5. Preparing for and planning a workshop

6. Conducting envisioning workshop to review a solution vision, touring a gallery of capability cases, evaluating and prioritizing capabilities identified for solution

7. Consolidating a Solution Concept as an integrated set of capabilities

8. Determining infrastructure impact; selecting technologies, vendors and products

9. Developing the technical capability architecture for the solution

10. Confirming the business case; producing an implementation roadmap

After SE

Post-a. Constructing, deploying and adopting the solution

Post-b. Realizing ROI; utilizing foundation established for future enhancement:

SOLUTION ENVISIONING PROCESS: MAIN PHASES AND OUTCOMES.

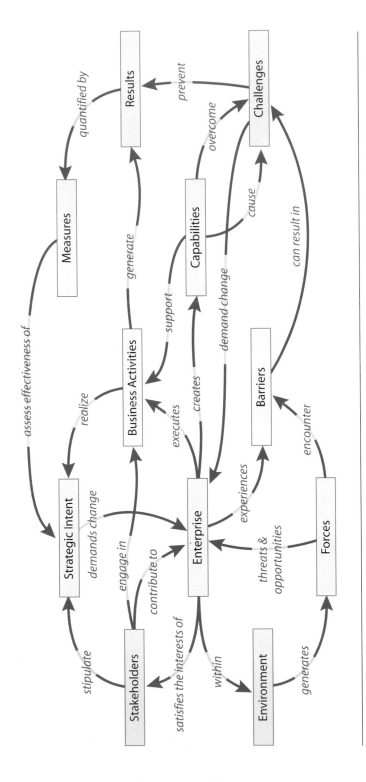

A Vocabulary for Characterizing the Business Context.

CAPABILITY CASES GALLERY AT NASA GODDARD.

USING POSTCARDCAFE AT NASA GODDARD.

ENVISIONING WORKSHOP AT THE UNITED NATIONS FOOD AND AGRICULTURE
ORGANIZATION (FAO).

Ideally, the workshop room has more wall space to hang things than this—notice the creative approach needed for mounting a Capability Case gallery—but this room setting illustrates some important points.

Solution Envisioning needs space—enough space to encourage "walking about" and visiting shared artifacts. Galleries need to be easily accessible and readily re-arranged. It is important that people should not sit at tables—tables encourage personal zones. This workshop at FAO shows a shared table and the chairs arranged so that no one owned a personal space at the table. Participants should be situated so that everyone can see one another and interact. Sitting in a circle is a well established way of establishing an egalitarian atmosphere among people from typically different parts of an organization with different powers and interests.

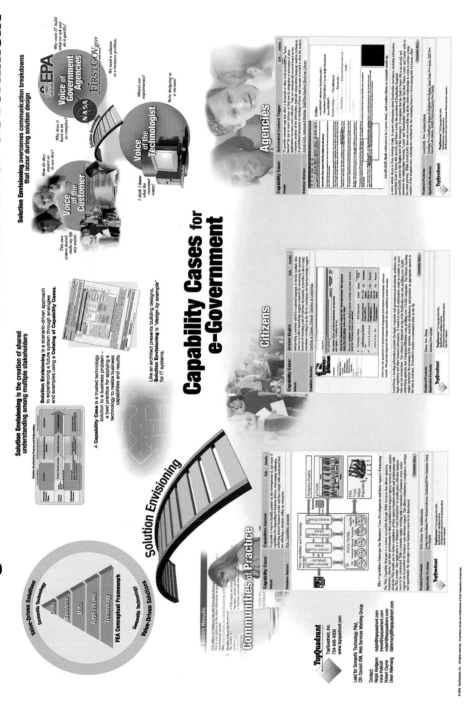

Delivering Value-Driven Semantic Solutions for Government

Capability Case:	# Visual Navigator
Intent:	Effectively present and summarize on one screen large amounts of information by using visualization technologies. Includes ability to navigate and drill down for more details.
Solution Story:	map.net, **The Hive Group's Amazon Product Map**, Smart Money Stock Market Map, Visual Navigation at HighWire Stanford, Infoscape Webmap

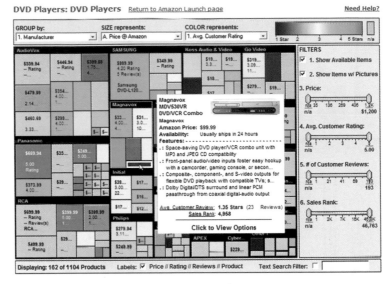

The Hive Group's Visual Map of Amazon Products

Amazon offers a large number of products. Having to make sense of them all when selecting the right one can be overwhelming. Text browsing of categories and product listings does not produce a pleasant shopping experience. The Hive Group solved this problem by allowing shoppers to use visual maps for exploring product categories using visual cues group, size, and color. Shoppers are able to change what group, size, and color represent, thereby selecting the criteria that are important to them. In the image above, products are categorized (grouped) by being organized according to manufacturer. Size of the product rectangle corresponds to its price. Colors indicate the popularity of the product as reflected by the number of sales. Maps can be filtered on how good is the deal offered (percent of discount), product price, and other attributes. Positioning a cursor over a product displays detailed information.

Business Benefits:	Improved user experience, ability to find the right product among a large number of offerings, increased sales, shorter discovery process, ability to intuitively guide users to relevant information.
Featured Products:	Honeycomb from The Hive Group
Other Applicable Products:	BrainEKP from TheBrain Technologies Corporation, DataVista Spectrum from Visualize, Inc., Inxight Star Tree SDK from Inxight Software, Inc., KartOO from KartOO SA, Metis from Computas, WebMap Server from WebMap Technologies

Capability Case:	# Generative Documentation

Intent:	To maintain a single source point for information about a system, process, product, etc., but deliver that content in a variety of forms, each tailored to a specific use. Documentation is generated as needed from the more basic source. The form of the document, and the information it contains, is customized to a particular audience.

Solution Story:	**Automatic Schematic Generation with 3-D Models**, Meeting Minutes Butler for a German Financial Company, Sharing Engineering Knowledge at Ford

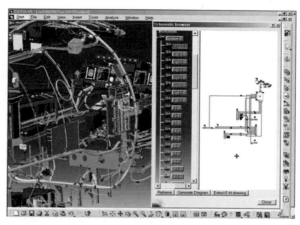

Schematic Diagrams are Generated from Selected Components from a 3D Image.

A Cogito partner has built a systems engineering platform that allows end users to explore a 3D diagram. Cogito links 3D icons to a conceptual ontological model, and generates schematics of the selected components and their surroundings. No schematic diagrams are stored; Cogito generates the schematics from the Knowledge Center, based on the current context.

Business Benefits/ Results:	Derivation of all of the standard schematic drawings from a single source model assures the internal consistency across all derived documents, enables real-time global work group collaboration, and eliminates the cost and errors of document production and configuration management.

Featured Products:	Cogito Knowledge Center from Cogito, Inc.

Other Applicable Products:	Ontobroker from Ontoprise, e2KS from Emergent Systems

Product Design Assistant

To support the innovative product development and design process by bringing engineering knowledge from many disparate sources to bear at the appropriate point in the process. Possible enhancements to the design process include rapid evaluation, increased adherence to best practices, and more systematic treatment of design constraints.

Solution Story:

Audi Semantic Testcar Configurator, Sharing Engineering Knowledge at Ford

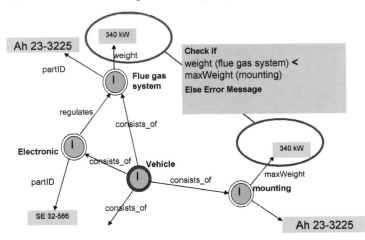

Constraints on possible configurations recorded as rules in an ontology.

Audi manufacturing engineers design, build, and test new prototypes as part of the innovation process. The faster this cycle can be completed, the greater the number of innovations that can be brought to market, and the sooner. AUDI uses a semantic engine from Ontoprise to represent complex design knowledge in electronic form. The engine brings together knowledge from many different sources and draws logical conclusions from the combined information. Audi uses this capability to provide a computational representation of complex dependencies between components of research test vehicles. These dependencies play a key role in the configuration and development of new vehicles. For example, in order for testing to proceed smoothly, the engineer must know if a selected engine can be built into the chosen chassis, if the brakes are sufficient for the engine performance, and that correct electronics are present in the vehicle.

"We expect a shortening of the development cycle, while at the same time improving development quality," said Thomas Syldatke of Audi. "The electronic advisor shall take care of routine tasks, allowing our engineers to concentrate on creative efforts."

Benefits:

Reduced the overall prototyping cycle time for new car designs, improved development quality, automation of routine tasks, increasing innovation as engineers gained time for creative efforts.

Featured Products:

Ontobroker from Ontoprise, OntoEdit from Ontoprise

Applicable Products:

Cerebra Inference Engine from Network Inference, e2KS from Emergent Systems

Workproduct M   Solution Vision Presentation and Shared Space

BCE M Solution Vision Presentation & Shared Space A presentation that provides (a) a summary of the business situation; (b) a vision of one or more possible solution concepts; (c) motivating future scenarios and supporting capabilities; and (d) value propositions that serve as input to making a business case.

THE RESULTS OF BCE AND READINESS TO MOVE TO THE NEXT PHASE

The major deliverable of this phase is an initial Solution Vision. However, that alone is not a sufficient indicator of *doneness*. We recommend using the following checklist to ensure completeness of the work of this phase. If the answer to any of these questions is "No," the work of Business Capability Exploration is not yet complete:

- Have the business challenges been identified?
- Are the business forces listed and supported by evidence?
- Are the business results clearly separated from solution capabilities?
- Has the root cause analysis been performed showing the dependencies between results?
- Can forces, challenges, and results be connected to business scenarios?
- Can each result be measured?
- Are the measurements identified?
- Have the goals for measurements been established?

Before moving forward to the next level of decisions to be made in the next phase, it is essential to reconfirm the scope of the solution initiative. Modeling business situations can either lead to a validation of projected system boundaries or to a realization that the boundaries must be expanded. One indication that the problem, or parts of the problem, lay outside of the currently defined system boundaries is when we are not able to map forces, challenges, and results to scenario steps. In such cases, business scenarios may need to be extended. Executing this step often means taking a model of the business situation and the root definitions of viable solutions to the sponsors in order to obtain an agreement on the expanding or adjusting the scope.

TRAIL MARKER V: BUSINESS SITUATION AND SOLUTION INITIATIVE UNDERSTOOD

Chapter 5 is the first of a three-part practitioner's handbook for practicing Solution Envisioning. It covered Phase I—Business Capability Exploration, and provided a step-by-step guide for understanding the business situation, clarifying the solution initiative that needs to be undertaken, and developing an initial solution vision and concept for realization.

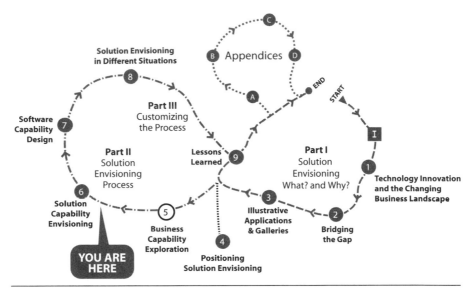

FIGURE 5.16.

You are now ready to proceed to Phase II in Chapter 6, "Solution Capability Envisioning—Phase II of Solution Envisioning."

6

SOLUTION CAPABILITY ENVISIONING—PHASE II OF SOLUTION ENVISIONING

"Some things have to be believed to be seen."
—Ralph Hodgson (Poet, 1871–1962)

FIGURE 6.1.

CHAPTER PREVIEW

The second phase of Solution Envisioning has two key goals:

- Develop a solution concept that addresses the business situation and challenges
- Ensure that it is shared by all key stakeholders

This chapter explains the steps involved, describes some techniques that have proven to be effective, and gives accounts of some real-life Solution Envisioning experiences. Sidebars offer insights into what is at work when solutions are being conceptualized and where further information on theory and practice can be found. A highlight of the chapter is an in-depth coverage of Solution Envisioning workshops.

The chapter draws lessons and insights from a number of projects where Solution Envisioning techniques were applied and workshops conducted:

- e-Banking Project, 1996
- IBM's Technology-Enabled Project Model (TEPM) Project, 1999
- Practitioner Support Network (PSN), 2000
- State Government Search Technology Workshop, 2001
- NASA Digital Shuttle Project, 2002
- Electronic Records Archiving Envisioning Workshop, 2003
- United Nations FAO Solution Envisioning Workshop, 2004
- Enterprise Architecture Portal Envisioning Workshop, 2004
- NASA Goddard Solution Envisioning Workshop, 2004

SOLUTION CAPABILITY ENVISIONING (SCE)—APPRAISING SOLUTION IDEAS

Envisioning requires us to imagine a future state of the world where new solution concepts are in use. This is a creative process that tests the desirability of innovative solution concepts and their enabling technologies.

Before Solution Capability Envisioning (SCE) can happen, there first has to be a shared understanding of the problem situation, opportunities for improvements, and the desired future business model. This was the work of Phase 1, "Business Capability Exploration," as described in Chapter 5, "Business Capability Exploration—Phase I of Solution Envisioning." Phase 2 starts with the following baseline of workproducts:

- Solution Vision
- Candidate Capability Cases

The work of this phase is to take the business ideas of Phase 1 and produce a *Solution Concept* of the required IT solution.

The key activity of the SCE phase is the "Solution Envisioning Workshop." Solution envisioning encourages exploration of possibilities by inviting new ways of speaking about and seeing a business situation. New systems ideas are stimulated by opportunities that present themselves when we are unconstrained in our ability to perceive and define solution concepts. Preoccupation with the constraints of the "current business logic" will block new ideas. The activities of this phase focus on extending and sustaining a dialog of managed conversations among stakeholders in order to: facilitate divergent thinking; encourage exploration of multiple ideas and possibilities; select one or more desirable options; and, ultimately, converge on a "Solution Architecture."

The workshop can be conducted in a number of ways, and preparation needs to frame the deliverables of Phase 1 according to the chosen approach. This and other related topics are discussed in the subsequent sections that cover preparing for and conducting the workshop.

The Work of Solution Capability Envisioning

A consolidated overview of Solution Capability Envisioning key *Activities*, *Workproducts*, and supporting *Techniques* is shown in Figure 6.2.[1]

---

[1] Table D.2 in Appendix D provides a concise reference to the definitions of all the Activities and Workproducts of SCE.

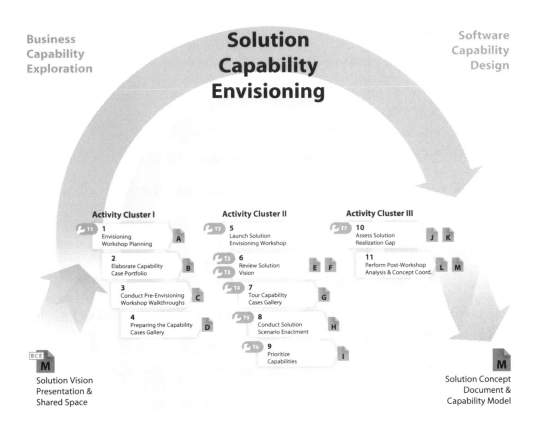

FIGURE 6.2. THE ACTIVITIES AND WORKPRODUCTS OF SOLUTION CAPABILITY ENVISIONING.

The Three Activity Clusters of SCE

The Solution Capability Envisioning (SCE) phase is organized in three activity clusters:

I. Prepare for Solution Envisioning Process—Preparation consists of ensuring that key people will participate (for example, attend the workshop), planning and logistics, the framing of scenarios and capability maps, and the refinement of Capability Cases for the gallery. This cluster consists of Activities 1 through 5.

II. Conduct the Solution Envisioning Workshop—The process of Solution Envisioning involves one or more workshops where scenarios and new capabilities are explored in context with the current and envisaged business situations and prioritization is decided. The process can be iterative when there is a need for periods of reflection and assimilation of new ideas. This cluster consists of Activities 5 through 9.

III. Perform Post-Workshop Analysis and Consolidation of Concepts—This cluster consists of Activities 10 and 11.

This chapter provides a *complete* and *comprehensive* record of all the Activities and Workproducts that may be needed to execute the Solution Capability Envisioning phase. In any given situation, only a subset of these is typically required.

Envisioning and Design as Social Constructions

In design processes, such as the design of technology-enabled business capabilities, the act of creation (the essence of design) is enabled (and limited) by fundamental human capabilities. These include our abilities to envision something new, to share its essential features, and to manage the complexity of documenting a hierarchy of specifications and details in a form that allows the new capability to be realized (implemented).

This means that solution design and development are governed by our individual and group capacities for envisioning, articulation, translation, and communication. If these tasks are performed sufficiently well in an efficient order, they enable a productive hierarchy of decisions within a traceable decision flow process. The result will be a gradual but confident transformation of shared vision into a broader shared understanding and, finally, a shared memory or translation of the vision and understanding into actionable artifacts (plans and specifications).

These results are what allow diverse teams of people at different stages and levels in the process to continue on track with design and implementation. However, a large number of non-technical challenges, barriers, and gaps hinder people from co-operatively engaging in focused envisioning and careful communication that is needed to produce good solution requirements. It is essential to both acknowledge these barriers and to know how to work around them in order to "bridge the gaps" in human communication, intention, and action.

Throughout history, an approach that has consistently helped people overcome communication barriers and gaps is the use and reuse of compelling "stories" or exemplars of success to move toward agreement and action. This is accomplished by using a wide variety of overlapping methods—such as elaborating scenarios, applying patterns or cases, invoking designs by analogy or metaphor, and so on—together with the paths these practices have engendered for success.

With this deeper understanding of the challenges involved in designing and developing business solutions, our goal has been to refine and evolve Solution Envisioning to provide a setting for and a way to manage the strategic conversations about technology. By allowing stakeholders to see technical solutions in action, it forms a bridge between business need and technological promise.

SCE ACTIVITIES I: PREPARE FOR THE SOLUTION ENVISIONING WORKSHOP

This cluster of activities includes the following:

1. Envisioning Workshop Planning
2. Elaborate or Develop Capability Cases
3. Conduct Pre-Envisioning Workshop Walkthroughs
4. Prepare for Capability Cases Gallery

Activity 1   Envisioning Workshop Planning

SCE-1
Envisioning,
Workshop Planning

The Solution Envisioning workshop needs to be an effective experience with the right people participating and willing to devote time to the workshop. For this to happen, critical pre-work must be done. The material produced in *Business Capability Exploration (BCE)* is organized in an appropriate way for use in the workshop. The venue must be carefully chosen and room bookings made ahead of time.

The primary task of planning involves securing participation of the key stake-holders. Their willingness to devote time to the workshop often requires pre-work-shop conversations and briefings. Much material will have been gathered in the previous phase of *Business Capability Exploration*. This will have to be organized in an appropriate way for use in the workshop. New Capability Cases may have to be written and existing ones may need some tailoring. Lastly, the venue must be carefully chosen and preparations for the gallery and the work of the workshop will need to be considered.

The project team must give ample time to preparing materials that will be used in the workshop. In our experience, there is a strong risk for a workshop to fail simply because critical materials have not been made available in the appropriate formats. The venue must be carefully chosen and room bookings made ahead of time.

Planning the envisioning workshop typically involves the following tasks each de-scribed in their own section:

- Identify Participants
- Design the Workshop Approach
- Produce Workshop Agenda and Guidance
- Schedule Workshop
- Invite and Confirm Participants
- Select Scenarios
- Prepare Capability Maps
- Distribute Workshop Briefings

Identify Participants

The Solution Envisioning team should be made up of members that represent all affected areas of the enterprise and sponsored by an executive of the company. The team should be committed to entering into a joint dialog.

The process of identifying workshop participants starts with groups. Stakeholder analysis performed during the previous phase has identified target groups and key individuals inside the groups. Ideally, there will be strong and passionate sponsorship for "making a difference" within the group. Individuals from these groups should participate based on the following criteria:

- Subject matter expertise (of the work done by their group)
- Respected by their peers
- Capable of proactive participation

- Authority to undertake a pilot project
- Interest in technology-enabled business transformation

From the perspective of roles of the participants who are needed and the work to be done, a Solution Envisioning workshop will typically include one or more sponsors, business consultants, IT architects, industry consultants, line-of-business decision makers, IT management representatives, and end user representatives. Some organizations have Centers of Excellence for Technology that will send representatives to the workshop. When emerging technologies are being considered, researchers are often invited.

Design the Workshop Approach

Every Solution Envisioning workshop follows the same basic structure described in this chapter. Similarly, every workshop has some unique elements. In the preparation for the workshop, it is important to identify the techniques and exercises you will use to ensure they are supported by the workshop room and available equipment. Chapter 8, "Solution Envisioning in Different Situations," provides additional guidance on workshop design and tailoring.

Produce Workshop Agenda and Guidance

This task develops a tailored agenda for the workshop. A generic two-day envisioning workshop format is shown in Table 6.1.

TABLE 6.1.   WORKSHOP AGENDA

TIME	SESSIONS	THEMES
Day 1 3 hrs	**The Business Situation** Where we are now? Where we say we want to be	"Rants and Raves" "Business Scenarios and Objectives" "Stakeholders and Expectations"
Day 1 4 hrs	**Visiting the future** Scenario walkthroughs Capability Cases in action Creative exploration Capability model	"Day in the Life" envisioning "What-if" inquiries Technology drivers Capability Cases Metaphors
Day 2 4 hrs	**Setting priorities** Decision criteria Ranking of Capability Cases Decision Model	Shared understanding Business imperatives Feasibility "Run," "Jump," and "Leap" options
Day 2 2 hrs	**Preparing for the roadmap** Deployment horizons Process envisioning	Architectural issues Infrastructure readiness Organizational readiness

A specific agenda may vary depending on the length of the workshop and other factors. Examples of customized agendas are provided later in this chapter and in Chapter 8.

Schedule Workshop

As for all workshops, it is important to consider which times of the day and particular days of the week will be most effective (for example, do not schedule a workshop for a Friday prior to a holiday weekend).

Another key consideration is finding and booking the right room. The workshop room should have the following:

- **Plenty of wall space**—Gallery tours, capability maps, and storyboards require display space.
- **Sufficient room** for participants to comfortably walk around, engage in group discussions, and congregate around wall displays.
- **Breakout space**—When a workshop involves more than six people, the room should either be large enough to accommodate breakout groups or an extra room will need to be booked.

When a team wants to hold a workshop, often at short notice, they typically end up with a conference room. The room is clearly inappropriate—the space is cramped, the table obstructs movement of people. With rooms like this, at best only three or four people get to drive the flow of ideas. Others are spectators. Figure 6.3 illustrates an example of such a room.

On the other hand, the workshop environment at the United Nations Food and Agriculture Organization, shown in Figure 6.4, was much more effective. However, it still had problems with respect to wall space, which is critical to a Solution Envisioning workshop. The area shown in the picture represented about half of the room. The table was significantly less central to the room than the one shown in the previous picture. Participants could interact more readily, access to materials on the wall was unobstructed, and the room allowed small group discussions to take place.

FIGURE 6.3.   PICTURE OF A NON-OPTIMAL ENVISIONING WORKSHOP SETTING.[2]

FIGURE 6.4.   A BETTER WORKSHOP SPACE—UNITED NATIONS FAO ENVISIONING
WORKSHOP.

[2]   From a Solution Adaptation Process Envisioning Workshop that one of the authors participated in.

The workshop may have the need for special tools and, invariably, a projector. Part of the task in booking the room is making sure all the necessary materials are at-hand, including supplies, audio-visual equipment, and refreshments. Considerable delay can happen on the day looking for supplies or a projector.

The importance of having rooms for envisioning is taken very seriously by some companies. One of the best rooms we have seen is at the General Motors Pontiac facility. It devotes a large room to being a permanent workshop space for future IT initiatives.

Invite and Confirm Participants

Attendees should be invited by the solution initiative sponsor or the individual's manager. We find that in most organizations the invitations have to be sent at least two weeks before the workshop. If traveling to the workshop location is re-quired, a longer notice will be needed.

Select Scenarios

In BCE, the activity "Explore Future Business Possibilities" results in future work scenarios for the enterprise captured in the workproduct *Essential Activity Scenarios*. These can be thought of as "Day in the Life" stories of a person oper-ating in that role in the envisioned future. The purpose of this task is to elaborate one or more of these scenarios in preparation for the workshop. Keep in mind that, typically, a one-day workshop will not be able to enact more than about three sce-narios—depending on their complexity.

Prepare Capability Maps

As explained in the previous chapter, Capability Maps help communicate relation-ships between forces, results, barriers, challenges, activities, and capabilities. Different types of maps can be used at the workshop. The objective of this task is to produce capability maps for each key stakeholder.

Most of this work will have been started in the previous phase (BCE). The work now is to select and prepare the maps that will be most useful for the Solution Envisioning workshop.

Figure 6.5 shows an example of a "Challenge Map" from a project with the U.S. Department of Transportation (DOT) to define an IT Enterprise Architecture Portal. The challenge, "How to know which projects are over-budget?" is the center of fo-cus. Above this are the stakeholders who are affected by this challenge. Below the challenge are the collective results that are impacted by the challenge.

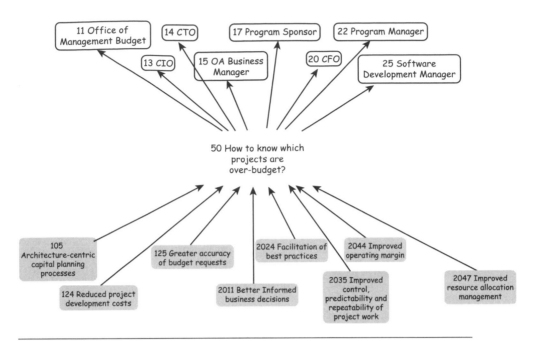

FIGURE 6.5.   "STAKEHOLDERS-CHALLENGE-RESULTS" MAP—U.S. FEDERAL
AGENCY WORKSHOP.

The map was created using the "Cognitive Mapping" technique (see Sidebar 6.1) and a tool that supports that technique, Decision Explorer[3] from Banxia Software. Another form of a capability map, a *Stakeholder-Results-Capability Cases* map, shows Capability Cases that are known to produce results needed by specific stakeholders. This map can show one or more stakeholders in the top layer, results in which they are interested shown in the middle layer, and related Capability Cases in the bottom layer. An example of a Stakeholder-Results-Capability Cases map from a project with a U.S. Federal Agency is shown in Figure 6.6.

Distribute Workshop Briefings

The briefing for the workshop can be sent together with the invitation or shortly thereafter. It should consist of a Workshop Agenda and Guidance document along with a Solution Vision presentation (produced in the previous phase).

---

[3]   Information on Decision Explorer can be found at http://www.banxia.com.

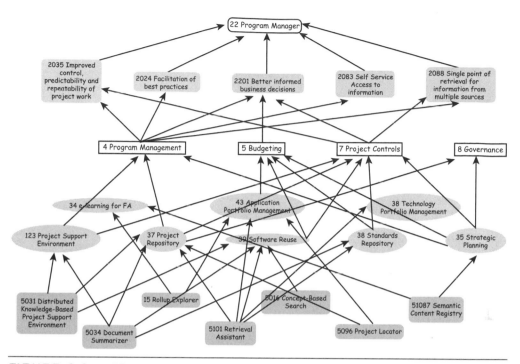

FIGURE 6.6.   "STAKEHOLDER-RESULTS-CAPABILITY CASES" MAP EXAMPLE.

Sidebar 6.1   Technique (T1): Cognitive Mapping

SCE T1   Cognitive Mapping   Cognitive mapping is a form of mind-mapping where diagrams are not constrained to be hierarchical but are networks of ideas. Cognitive mapping is a technique for managing the qualitative information that surrounds complex or uncertain situations. It allows you to capture—in detail—thoughts and ideas, to explore them, and to gain new understanding and insight. A cognitive map is a graph showing relationships between constructs. The relationships usually depict an influence such as "cause and effect" or "impacts" or "because of/therefore" links. The constructs include goals, objectives, "facts," perceptions, and assumptions about the world and constraints.

In Solution Envisioning, we use cognitive mapping to explore relationships—for example, between forces, Capability Cases, and results. In Colin Eden's and Fran Ackerman's book *Making Strategy*, cognitive maps are used to depict relationships between goals (or disastrous outcomes), strategies (or issues), and more detailed considerations. Teardrop diagrams are drawn showing successful levels of explanation. Figure 6.7 illustrates this idea, making the connection with Solution Envisioning constructs.

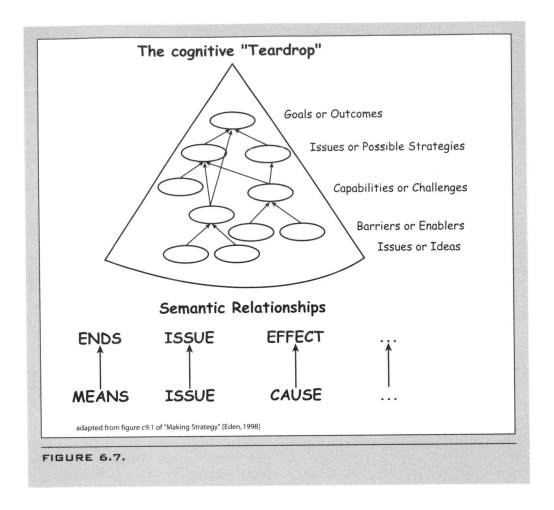

The cognitive "Teardrop"

Goals or Outcomes

Issues or Possible Strategies

Capabilities or Challenges

Barriers or Enablers
Issues or Ideas

Semantic Relationships

ENDS   ISSUE   EFFECT   ...

MEANS   ISSUE   CAUSE   ...

adapted from figure c9.1 of "Making Strategy" [Eden, 1998]

FIGURE 6.7.

Workproduct A   Envisioning Workshop Logistics and Scheduling

SCE A   Envisioning Workshop Logistics and Scheduling   A package that will be distributed to the workshop participants. It includes the following as key components:

- Workshop Agenda and Guidance
- Solution Vision Presentation

Workshop participants should also get access to the shared space.

Activity 2   Elaborate Capability Cases Portfolio

SCE-2
Elaborate Capability
Cases Portfolio

In the "BCE" phase, capabilities were nominated for the solution. Some of these may need to be elaborated to be tailored for the situation-at-hand. New Capability Cases may also have to be written.

In preparation for the workshop, the project team may decide that the solution stories used to illustrate Capability Cases are not compelling enough. They may want to search for a better fitting story or to create a new, envisioned story.

Specializing Capability Cases

In some situations, it could also become important to go one step further and take an inspiration from a generic Capability Case to create a specific and contextualized one. For example, in the Wire Data Management System (WDMS) project at NASA (introduced in Chapter 5), there was a significant interest in the *Semantic Data Integrator* CapCase.

Systems developed in different work practice settings have different semantic structures for their data. Semantic Data Integration addresses the fact that time-critical access to data is made difficult by these differences. The intent of Semantic Data Integrator is to allow data to be shared and understood across a variety of settings. Although this capability was relevant to the situation that the WDMS project needed to address, there was a concern that the engineers in the workshop would have a hard time relating to it unless it was translated into a more specific example.

To address this concern, we created a new CapCase that described a specific instance of semantic data integration between two systems used by electrical engineers: SDS (Shuttle Drawing System) and SIMS (a system that housed photos of the shuttle taken after completion of each engineering change order).

The work resulted in a specialized Capability Case called *Semantic Engineering Artifact Navigator*, which is shown in Figure 6.8.

In the workshop gallery, both Capability Cases were presented—"Semantic Data Integrator" and "Semantic Engineering Artifact Navigator." The first one served as an existence proof to demonstrate the feasibility of the proposed solution.

Capability Case:

Semantic Engineering Artifact Navigator

Intent: To be able to easily locate and compare "as-built" components of an aerospace vehicle— for example, electrical components—with "as-designed" drawings and specifications of the same components.

Solution Story: Integrated Vehicle Drawing and Photo Image Viewer.

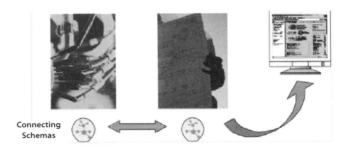

Jeff is an electrical engineer involved in maintenance work on a long service aircraft. He is doing a problem report assessment on electrical wiring. Jeff accesses the vehicle's Engineering Drawing System (EDS) for information on how the harness is configured. Jeff suspects that, given the problem, the design does not make sense—the "as-designed" drawing does not reflect the "as-built" situation. He could also decide that splicing is needed to fix the problem. There is no nearby splicing on the drawing, but he knows that there may be a splice created by the previous repair. Jeff clicks on a "as-built" button, and an image of the most recent digital photograph of this electrical component appears from the Vehicle Image Management System (VIMS). Having a picture immediately reveals the actual view of the component. Jeff can now make a more informed interpretation of the drawing and its associated Engineering Change Notices (ECNs).

How It Works: Semantic Engineering Artifact Navigator uses metadata and associations to relate the information in EDS to the information in VIMS. This metadata can support a simple form of reasoning that allows a query to be constructed for SIMS. A result list of relevant images is returned and the engineer can select the most relevant image.

Benefits: Navigating between systems and manually integrating them was a time-consuming and tedious activity. The engineer needs to know where in VIMS to go to get relevant information and determine how best to make a query using data derived from EDS and the problem report. The new capability's benefits are as follows:

- Time savings
- Improved ability to make quick and accurate decisions
- Higher job satisfaction—less time spent on tedious tasks
- Reduced risk/increased safety through reliable information correlation

Applicable Products: Network Inference's Cerebra Engine, Ontoprise's OntoBroker, Unicorn Solution's Semantic Information Manager.

FIGURE 6.8.   SEMANTIC ENGINEERING ARTIFACT NAVIGATOR CapCase.

Workproduct B   Capability Cases Portfolio

 Capability Cases Portfolio The "Capability Cases Portfolio" is a collection of Capability Cases and selected solution stories that serve as inspirations for the envisioned solution. A portfolio may include fully developed Capability Cases selected from a catalog. It can also include newly identified capabilities. These are identified by their name and a short intent statement.

Activity 3   Conduct Pre-Envisioning Workshop Walkthroughs

SCE-3
Conduct Pre-Envisioning
Workshop Walkthroughs

The purpose of the pre-workshop briefings is to create a familiarity with the materials so that all attendees are equally prepared and there are few derailments on the day.

If this activity is not done, the workshop can run aground for the following reasons:

- Discomfort with business context and scope
- Feelings that "we are already doing this"
- Unanticipated political interests
- Unexpected revelations of related projects and people's interests that de-focus the workshop by "throwing a curve ball"
- Lack of motivation because of misunderstanding of objectives
- Discomfort over why certain people are present and others not

The most effective workshops are the ones that are already underway before the day participants assemble in the same room. The walkthroughs can range from one-on-one sessions to conference calls where several participants use the shared workspace established for the solution to review the materials. Pre-workshop walkthroughs can also take the form of a dry-run with the project sponsor.

Sending out a questionnaire is a good way to prepare for conversations with key people. In our experience, though few questionnaires may get completed, they still fill a useful purpose in helping to prepare the ground for the interviews. For instance, individuals may not fill them out, but after you call them (or conduct an interview in person), they may be more prepared because they at least looked at the questionnaire. One reason may be that there is something concrete in front of them that they can now respond to in conversation with you. Finally, such questionnaires can sometimes be a critical substitute for remote interviews.

Workproduct C   Evidence of Business Situation and Possibilities

SCE C   Evidence of Business Situation and Possibilities   A collection of articles workshop participants are asked to bring to the session. They may be newspaper clippings about technologies and what other organizations are doing, excerpts from internal presentations and speeches, customer letters, or any other items of interest.

Some examples of statements of evidence in support of *forces* are as follows:

- *Customers will not perform transactions they perceive to be complex on the web*
  Evidence: When transactions on the web are complex, abandonment rates go up to 95%.

- *Emergence of semantic web*
  Evidence: According to Gartner, by 2005, Ontologies will be part of 75% of application integration projects.

- *Call-avoidance from customers and staff results in significant savings*
  Evidence: Average cost of a customer-service transaction across multiple channels—$32 by phone, $1.17 using web self-service.
  Evidence: 39% of companies use their website to provide information on specific questions (concerning product, services, or an account).

- *Increasing glut of data and information*
  Evidence: Growth of Internet content with 1 billion static HTML pages in 2001, content doubles every three months.
  Evidence: Recent research indicated that across all sites, visitors couldn't find what they are looking for 60% of the time.

Participants should be asked to package other items, such as news stories and interesting websites in a way that makes them easy to communicate in the workshop. Sometimes, we have used the metaphor of an exhibition booth to arrange people's contributions.

Activity 4   Preparing the Capability Cases Gallery

SCE-4
Preparing the Capability Cases Gallery

SCE D

The gallery will need to be set up ahead of the workshop. The preferred arrangement is to have the gallery in the same room as the workshop so tours can happen informally at different times of the day.

The Capability Cases have been developed or elaborated during Activity 2. This activity focuses on the work necessary to construct the gallery. Capability Cases are printed and framed or mounted so they can be displayed in the gallery. Some Capability Cases will be featured more than once using different solution stories to more fully illustrate their aspects. Each exhibit should be numbered to make it easy to rank and prioritize them. If time permits, a *Tour Guide* outlining each Capability Case is a good thing to have.

It is important that the content of the gallery is known and can be referred to easily. What will happen during the workshop is certain capabilities will start to be seen as more important than others. When the gallery is in the same room as the workshop, it is possible to place markers (usually colored dots) against Capability Cases to indicate their salience. This has the obvious analogy to an art gallery when a picture is sold. As a counterpoint, the workshop should ensure that commitment to ideas does not constrain further exploration of possibilities. By having the dynamic of Capability Cases being continually assessed, the workshop leader can ask very pointed questions about why certain capabilities are being ignored and others promoted.

Finally, a package of materials is printed to be distributed to the workshop participants on the day of the workshop. It includes the following as key components:

- Workshop Agenda and Guidance
- Solution Vision Presentation
- Essential Activity Scenarios—a selected set
- Capability Maps—a selected set

All these components were produced and updated either in the previous phase (BCE) or in preceding Activities in this phase. They should also be available within the online shared workspace that was set up for Solution Envisioning in BCE. If a Tour Guide has been produced, it is also included in the package.

Workproduct D   Gallery of Capability Cases

SCE
D

Gallery of Capability Cases and Gallery Tour Guide

The gallery is a central idea in the Solution Envisioning approach. This is the equivalent of the architect's book of designs. Some time is needed before people arrive to arrange the gallery around the room in an appropriate way. If there is time, a Gallery Tour Guide is a useful thing to produce. This gives an overview of each featured Capability Case, explaining the justification for its inclusion in the gallery.

If a Tour Guide is provided, space should be left next to each Capability Case for the participant to make notes for their use in the workshop. Examples of galleries are shown in Figure 3.4 in Chapter 3, "Illustrative Applications and Galleries" and in photographs in the color insert in the middle of this book.

SCE ACTIVITIES II: CONDUCT THE SOLUTION ENVISIONING WORKSHOP

> *"Solution Envisioning—reconciling the desirable and the possible."*
> —*Ward Cunningham, OOPSLA 1998 Solution Envisioning Workshop*

The Solution Envisioning workshop comprises the following activities (numbered as shown in Figure 6.2):

5. Launch the Solution Envisioning Workshop

6. Review Solution Vision

7. Tour Capability Cases Gallery

8. Conduct Solution Scenario Enactment

9. Prioritize Capabilities

A typical Solution Envisioning workshop ranges from one to two days in duration. Irrespective of the type or length of the workshop, it always follows an orderly sequence of managed interactions as a *directed inquiry*. Table 6.2 provides an overview of how a workshop is framed as a movement through a series of focal points that address key questions. A mapping of the work for each focus is given to the Activities where it is primarily performed and to the Working Artifacts and Methods described in this cluster.

TABLE 6.2.   SOLUTION ENVISIONING WORKSHOP FRAMEWORK

Focal Point	Key Questions	SCE Activity Where Facilitated	Working Artifacts/Methods
Exploring the Present	Where are we now—how did we get here? What are our distinct competencies? What are our vulnerabilities? What do we feel proud of and sorry (rant and rave) about? What are the issues, problems, and complaints we have?	Activity 5	Context Diagram Value Nets Capability Maps
Exploring Change— Analyzing Forces and Trends	How is our world changing? What are the new market conditions and forces? What are the new ways to win? What are others doing? What is threatening us? Who do we want to be like?	Activities 5, 6	Forces Maps Challenges Maps Results Maps Scenarios Capability Cases Solution Stories

TABLE 6.2.   SOLUTION ENVISIONING WORKSHOP FRAMEWORK—CONTINUED

Capability-Based Design—Interplay of Technology and Business Design	What is it possible to be? What are the new ways to work? What do new technologies enable us to become? What opportunities are there for us to do that?	Activities 6,7	Capability Cases Solution Stories Scenarios Storyboards Gallery Tour
Making Commitments	Where do we choose to be? What future do we desire? What are we willing to change in the organization? What is happening in that future?	Activities 7, 8, 9	Future Retrospectives
Future Roadmap	How will we get there? What business and solution capabilities will help us? What will we build/buy? What realization process will we follow?	Activity 9 (After the workshop, continuing in Activity 10)	Decision Models Roadmaps Capability Cases

Activity 5   Launch the Solution Envisioning Workshop

SCE-5

Launch Solution Envisioning Workshop

The workshop is the main activity of this phase. A progression of conversations is managed based on *exploring the present, assessing technology capabilities, future scenarios*, and *realization planning*.

This activity represents an organizing thread that connects the workshop exercises in an approach designed to create a shared concept of the solution. Activities 6 through 9 outline specific work that is carried out during the envisioning sessions.

Preparing the Rooms

Before people arrive, the room needs to be arranged including wall displays of exhibits, such as Capability Case galleries and storyboards. For the workshop exercises, we recommend preparing the walls by papering them with plain paper charts (large, flip chart-sized Post-it Notes work well). The paper can then be sprayed with glue to prepare a surface to which cards and other paper will stick, making it easy to arrange and rearrange them. Another option is to use self-stick cards such as *Oval Maps*.[4]

---

[4] www.ovalmap.com.

Documents and other artifacts the workshop will use are laid on the tables in a tidy manner so people are less likely to start browsing and disarranging things.

Managing Introductions

The workshop starts by first giving a very short idea of what the workshop is about. It is always good to have the initiative sponsor kick off the workshop. The introduction of participants then follows. It can take up to 40 minutes depending on the size of the group. When many of the people do not know each other, ice-breaking techniques, such as *Introductions by Neighbor*, offer a fun way to start the session and build camaraderie.

The workshop leader starts by explaining the agenda and approach. He or she reminds people of the attitudes that block creativity. A good way to do this is to include a slide in the agenda presentation that defuses the situation. Table 6.3 lists attitudes that block creative ideas adopted from *The Whole Brain Business Book* by Ned Hermann [Hermann, 1996].

TABLE 6.3. ATTITUDES THAT BLOCK CREATIVE IDEAS

1. Don't be ridiculous.	13. That's not our problem.
2. We've tried it before.	14. Why change it? It is still working OK.
3. We've never done it before.	15. You are two years ahead of your time.
4. It costs too much.	16. We are not ready for that.
5. That's beyond our responsibility.	17. It isn't in the budget.
6. It's too radical a change.	18. Can't teach an old dog new tricks.
7. We don't have time.	19. Top management will never go for that.
8. We're too small for it.	20. We'll be the laughing stock.
9. That will make other equipment obsolete.	21. We did all right without it.
10. Not practical for operating people.	22. Let's form a committee.
11. The union will scream.	23. Has anyone else ever tried it.
12. Let's get back to reality.	24. Are our competitor's doing it?

The *ConceptCafe* technique (see Sidebar 6.2) provides an approach for facilitating insights and their expression through the use of metaphors. Using this technique helps to build trust and support for people to share their true insights and feelings about the current system(s) they use and the proposed system(s).

A form of ConceptCafe that we find to be particularly useful is called *PostcardCafe* (see Sidebar 6.2, Figure 6.9). A picture of this technique being used at NASA Goddard Space Flight Center is included in the color insert. Excerpts from the comments made reflect some of the reactions and insights triggered in the participants in response to the cards:

"I picked this picture of a woman holding up her arm saying 'we can do it' because this speaks to how much I want to make something happen."

"I choose this postcard of grownups on a merry-go-round because of how it evokes the process we go through each year to get budgets renewed. It is like a merry-go-round because it never stops and people are caught up with the bureaucratic process and no real sense of how things connect to business needs."

"The postcard of circus elephants being taken on a stroll through Manhattan in the 1920s or thereabouts caused me to think about our own efforts of trying to integrate new capabilities with our current IT system—incompatible worlds is what triggered this thought."

Sidebar 6.2   Technique (T2): ConceptCafe

This technique, which we credit to Martine Devos,[5] uses managed dialog to overcome the inhibitions people might have in sharing feelings about the current system and about the system-to-be. The workshop leader poses an issue, an idea, or a question for the team to respond to. Each team member writes out a card and places it in the center of the table or on the floor in the case when the workshop participants are sitting in a circle. When the team is ready to discuss the responses, a team member starts the process by explaining his or her response. The two members to the right write whatever thoughts are invoked by the telling of the stories associated with the card. They then place their cards into the shared workspace. As this happened, the rest of the group is asked to write further thoughts on individual cards. The process proceeds around the circle in this fashion until all ideas have been given time for expression.

One form of the ConceptCafe, useful to surface assumptions, dispositions, and insights, and again credited to Martine Devos, is a "Postcard Cafe." The leader brings to the workshop a pile of postcards featuring a rich variety of images. An example is shown in Figure 6.9. He or she asks workshop participants to go to the pile and pick a postcard that evokes an image that connotes some feeling, idea, or issue they are feeling about the current system or the system-to-be.

The postcards serve as metaphors and facilitate turning what Arieti calls "amorphous cognitions" into concrete forms [Arieti, 1976]. They stimulate the expression of feelings and ideas.

[5] http://c2.com/cgi/wiki?ConceptCafe.

FIGURE 6.9.   POSTCARDCAFE—A FORM OF CONCEPTCAFE.

The group re-forms as a circle and each member tables his or her card, explaining why it was chosen. The postcard is then placed in the center of the table. The process then proceeds as just described.

Sidebar 6.3 gives an example of the focus and agenda for a one-day envisioning workshop.

Sidebar 6.3   Example of a Solution Envisioning Workshop for "Validating a Solution Initiative"

This envisioning workshop was conducted for the Practitioner Support Network (PSN) project at a major professional services organization. By practitioners, we mean consultants in the field. The goal of the project was to explore how the company's consulting engagements are supported and to develop a solution (organizational and IT) that would provide a better support in the resolution of technical problems. The Solution Envisioning workshop was a one-day session with the agenda shown in Table 6.4.

TABLE 6.4. PSN ENVISIONING WORKSHOP AGENDA

9:00 am–9:15 am	Introductions	Motivations, expectations, and working assumptions
9:15 am–9:45 am	Where are we now?—The practitioner's world today	"Three What's" from the practitioner's point of view
9:45 am–10:00 am	Break	
10:00 am–11:30 am	What forces influences us?	Review of market forces, business drivers, technology trends
	How the world is changing, what others are doing, and what are the new ways to work	Gallery Tour
11:30 am –12:30 pm	Where do we want to be?	Scenario Enactment
	The practitioner's world tomorrow and how "systems" will help us	
12:30 pm–1:30 pm	Working lunch	
1:30 pm–2:45 pm	Where do we want to be? (cont'd)	Result Prioritization
		Decision Modeling
2:45 pm–3:00 pm	Break	
3:00 pm–5:00 pm	How do we get there?	Plans and actions

This project provides a useful example of how the following themes are discussed:

Where are we now?

- Practitioner's are like "troops at the frontline 10,000 wide and two people deep."
- "We cannot grow 'redwoods' fast enough."
- "If only the frontline knew what the frontline knew."
- "The customer can call our product support hotline if they have a technical problem with one of our products, but we, company employees, have no way of initiating support requests."

How is the world changing?

- Innovation centers and inbound/outbound/unbound work
- Communities of practice
- Consulting services over the web

What scenarios help us to envision the solution?

- Practitioner hits the wall—the bad old days
- Practitioner hits the wall—the good new days
- A day in the life of a new practitioner expert

- A day in the life of a practice web dispatcher
- A day in the life of a center-based expert
- A pre-planned architecture decision-making workshop

What can technology allow us to be?

- A mediation for virtual environments and communities-of-practice
- A "sense and respond" organization
- A "nerve center" for knowledge bringing tacit and explicit knowledge together
- A learning organization through best practices and experience factories

Activity 6   Review Solution Vision

 SCE-6
Review Solution
Vision

Capability maps and overviews of the to-be scenarios are used to explain the vision of the envisioned solution. The details of how capabilities support the business are worked out later in scenario enactments. The purpose of the review is to justify the reasoning about the current business situation and why certain choices have been made for the to-be business design.

The purpose of the review is either

- To choose a statement for the solution initiative that the group can commit to—this is needed when alternative solution initiative statements are present.
- To refine and fine-tune a solution initiative statement—this is needed when there is single statement—believed to be adequate—going in to the workshop.

Statements of alternative ideas of future systems—so-called *root definitions* in Soft System Methodology[6]—and capability maps with overviews of to-be scenarios are used to explain the vision of one or more envisioned solution initiatives. The solution initiatives are then explored for their feasibility and desirability within the scope of what the group believes is possible to achieve and willing to nominate.

The ConceptCafe technique described earlier (in Sidebar 6.4) can be used in this activity to facilitate obtaining insights into solution vision and expression through the use of metaphors. The results of doing a ConceptCafe at this point in the

---

[6]   See Sidebar 5.1 in Chapter 5 on the use of the related CATWOE technique, [Checkland, 1981].

workshop can refine the expression of "forces," "results," and "challenges" for the selected Capability Cases.

The focus of this activity is to decide between multiple solution initiative statements. It brings attention to the nature of the effort and commitment needed to undertake alternate initiatives.

A principal technique that we use in deciding which of a number of solution options should be pursued is "Three E's Mapping of Solution Initiatives" (see Sidebar 6.4).

Sidebar 6.4   Technique (T3): Three E's Solution Initiative Mapping

 Three E's Solution Initiative Mapping

A 3-by-3 matrix is used to show where alternate Solution Initiatives are positioned according to the nature of the undertaking to which the group must commit. The three distinctions of "efficiency," "effectiveness," and "edge" are used to place each capability in an axis representing the degree of change in the business. These distinctions, described in the book, *Planning IT*, by David Silk [Silk, 1992] are as follows:

- Efficiency is about doing things right from the perspective of the different stakeholders. Capabilities should be utilized to maximize the returns from their deployment. More efficiency might mean reducing costs by doing the same job with fewer resources.

- Effectiveness is about doing the right things. Possible solution initiatives are allocated to those activities that satisfy the needs, expectations, and priorities of the different stakeholders. More effectiveness might mean employing other resources to do a better job.

- Edge is about doing innovative new things.

The vertical axis represents the nature of the organizational intervention needed to make the solution initiative happen. The three levels are defined as follows:

- **Operations**—Commitment to the solution is focused on a business problem that the group has full control over.

- **Tactical Intervention**—Decisions to realize the solution is within existing budgets but needs approval from a higher level of management.

- **Strategic Intervention**—The solution represents a significant strategic change and has wider implications. There will need to be approval from executives of the enterprise and the need for a business case is likely to postpone the solution into the following fiscal year.

Example of Comparing Alternative Solution Initiatives

Figure 6.10 shows relationships among a number of alternate solution initiative statements for a Customer Support system. Arrows indicate a possible roadmap that would allow a staged realization of capabilities.

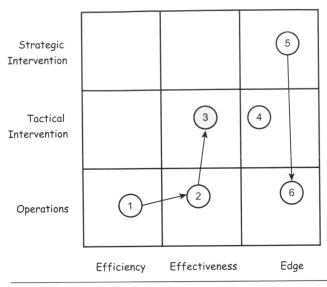

FIGURE 6.10.   A "THREE E'S" DIAGRAM MAPPING SOLUTION INITIATIVES.

Alternative solution initiatives statements for the Customer Support System are described in Table 6.5. The power of this technique is in focusing people on the reality of what can be realistically achieved and on what deliverables are needed if the initiative requires senior management or executive-level commitment. Another benefit is in the support the technique gives to re-factoring solution initiatives to arrive at a roadmap that allows a staged realization of the solution vision.

TABLE 6.5.   Solution Initiatives for a Customer Support Solution

#	Solution Initiative Statements (Alternative Root Definitions)	Results	Intervention	Dependency
1	A system to improve the efficiency of call center Level 1 support staff by improving the current internal search engine with concept-based search capabilities.	Efficiency	Operations	None
2	A system to improve the effectiveness of call center Level 1 support staff through a concept-based search that extends beyond knowledge sources in the organization.	Effectiveness	Operations	Depends on (1) so that external organizations have confidence in adopting the solution
3	A learning system that improves the effectiveness of all levels of call center support staff by providing a knowledge-centric environment that learns over time from the experiences of all support personnel and other expertise in the company.	Effectiveness	Tactical— Needs upper management to commit resources to knowledge modeling	Having (2) done will give upper management proof that knowledge-centric solutions work
4	A self-service system that provides edge over the competition by allowing users to ask questions online by using a knowledgebase.	Effectiveness	Tactical— Needs upper management to initiate other changes to the user's installed software	None—Can be started without the need of any previous system deployments
5	A self-service system that provides edge over the competition by allowing the user system to be remotely diag-nosed and fixed through a knowledge-enabled system that interacts with the user's equipment.	Edge	Strategic— Needs executives to approve of new ways of doing business using remote diagnostics	None
6	A self-service system that provides edge over the competition by allowing the user system to be remotely diag-nosed and fixed through a knowledge-enabled system that interacts with the user's equipment. When automated diag-nostics and remedies fail, the system provides a seamless transfer to Customer Support for remote fixing.	Edge	Operations— Deliver more of the vision expressed in solution (5)	Builds on the success of (5)

Workproduct E   Solution Vision (Revised)

 Solution Vision (Revised)   An elaboration of the solution vision to take account of choices between alternate solution initiatives and to review comments and new insights.

The Solution Vision workproduct was produced initially in the previous phase. In this phase, the vision is elaborated and refined based on the workshop outcomes. There is also work entailed in ensuring that the form of the workproduct will provide a clear and compelling concept of the solution. It can take various forms. Often, a document or presentation is not the best form. We have found a poster, or even a rich postcard, to be more effective. In a few cases, with adequate time and resources available, we have been able to produce a CD or DVD as highly effective ways to communicate and propagate the vision of a solution.

Workproduct F   Solution Initiative Statement (Revised)

 Solution Initiative Statement (Revised)   A specification of the intent of the solution in terms of the problem that is being addressed, who benefits and how, motivations for the solution, constraints that surround the solution, and who is the sponsor. This serves as a concise statement of a program that will create and deploy IT capabilities needed to achieve the required business transformation. NOTE: Variants or alternative solution initiative statements may be produced in BCE. Refinement and selection of a final statement is made in this phase.

Activity 7   Tour Capability Cases Gallery

SCE-7
Tour Capability
Cases Gallery

A guided tour of the gallery of Capability Cases provides an opportunity for attendees to understand the value of selected technologies and to make connections from the solution stories to their situation. Ideas can be sparked by these connections and also be the interplay of ideas and business possibilities.

A guided tour of a gallery of Capability Cases is the main focus of this activity. The primary motivation for guided and impromptu tours of the Capability Case Gallery is to encourage the workshop participants to envision solution possibilities. These tours trigger a shared experience of possibilities and discussions that are stimulated around capabilities (both those directly represented in the gallery, and sometimes new ones invented on-the-fly by the group in reaction to these). This kind of interaction not only sharpens and evolves the solution concept, but plays an important role in forging shared understanding and commitment to an envisioned future.

Grounded in the business context and situation, the team is encouraged to detach itself from what the business is currently doing and to think openly by being unconstrained and triggered by a range of solution concepts. The approach used is based on Capability Cases, which enable participants to understand the value of selected technologies and make connections from solution stories to their own situation. Ideas can be sparked by these connections as they create interplay with new business possibilities.

Chapter 3 provides some gallery tours we have run in selected situations. It includes more detail regarding the experience for stakeholders and how the gallery influences the direction and progress of envisioning. To complement the gallery tour, we use a variety of Creative Exploration Techniques (see Sidebar 6.5). For example, a good tool to combine with the gallery is the "Synectics" creativity technique.

Synectics is an approach to creative thinking that encourages bringing dissimilar concepts into juxtaposition [Gordon, 1961]. The term Synectics comes from the Greek word synectikos, which means "bringing forth together" or "bringing different things into unified connection." Creativity involves putting concepts into new arrangements. In this way, every thought or action involves synectic thinking—the process of discovering the links that unite seemingly disconnected elements. It is a way of mentally taking things apart and putting them together to furnish new insight for all types of problems.

The main tools are analogy and metaphor. The approach works by overcoming attachment or predisposition to existing ideas and commitments so that new concepts might emerge. "Prompts" are used by the workshop facilitator to encourage lateral thinking and new connections between ideas. The prompts are categorized according to modes of thinking. Some examples of using prompts are as follows:

- **Context**—"Have we set the boundary for the solution in the right ways?"

- **Transference**—"How is Customer Relationship Management like Hospital Care?"

- **Fantasy**—"What if electronic products could tell you when they where out of warranty? How would that benefit a manufacturer?"

Sidebar 6.5   Technique (T4): Creative Exploration Techniques

"Creativity is the marvelous capacity to grasp mutually distinct realities and draw a spark from their juxtaposition."

—Max Ernst

 Creative Exploration

Exploration of an unconstrained range of solution possibilities is essential to innovative thinking. We have witnessed so many systems that suffer from the "prescient design" syndrome.[7] This trap happens often when use cases are introduced too early in the system development lifecycle. Grounded in the problem analysis of the Business Capability Exploration phase, creative exploration techniques seek to explore the power of solution ideas to arrive at the essence of a solution. Establishing the nature of the solution is paramount before any use cases detailing the flow of interactions can be specified.

Among the many books and writings on creative techniques, we have found the following techniques to be valuable:

- Metaphor and Analogy
- Storyboarding
- Synectics
- Perfect World—also known as "Camelot"
- Future Retrospective
- ConceptCafe

We have included sidebars that cover several of these creativity techniques in this chapter and previous ones. More on Synectics and the art of Storytelling can found in Appendix B. One example of the use of metaphor and analogy that we have found to be especially useful in conjunction with envisioning is Perfect World–Camelot.

This technique is used to encourage a group to detach themselves from the current business situation and to imagine what would be a "perfect world." They are asked to describe the ideal situation by its attributes and to compare these to the current business situation.

Tools

The software tools we find useful for aiding the creative process are as follows:

- Banxia's Decision Explorer
- Axon Research's Axon tools[8]
- Mind-mapping tools
- Microsoft PowerPoint

---

[7]   We owe the term "prescient design" to our colleague Jack Ring who regularly encourages people to escape from the trap of being committed too early to a design without considering the problem and range of possible solutions (www.jackring.org).

[8]   http://web.singnet.com.sg/~axon2000/index.htm.

Workproduct F   Capability Interest and Value Proposition Scorecard

Solution Initiative
Statement (Revised)

The scorecard is a table that ranks capabilities according to their perceived value and interest to different stakeholders. Each Capability Case is scored by the attendees of the workshop.

Activity 8   Conduct Solution Scenario Enactment

SCE-8
Conduct Solution
Scenario Enactment

Each of the Essential Activity Scenarios that were created is walked through, and the applicability of specific capabilities is explained in context with the envisioned work in the future business model.

Each of the Essential Activity Scenarios created in BCE (and possibly refined in the preparation work of this phase) are presented to the group for a structured walk-through. The applicability of specific capabilities is examined in the context of how work in the future will be performed. The activity uses *Future Retrospective* (see Sidebar 6.6) as well as the other Creative Exploration Techniques (T4) described in Activity 7.

The use of Future Retrospective stories helps people to step into the future, to imagine the solution in use, and to describe what is happening and then how this transformation was accomplished. Such stories paint scenarios that illuminate aspects of the "to-be" world. They allow free thinking and focus attention on the people who will use the solution and the value it will bring. The most effective stories have rich descriptions of settings, people, activities, goals, motivations, and values presented in a coherent, causally connected way. The process of creating a story can insure that attention has been paid to the factors necessary to create an effective solution.

When a number of these stories have been done, the group should be asked to decide which are the most interesting and why. This process is highly effective not only in surfacing assumptions and dispositions about future solutions, but also in seeing where there is still an attachment to the current logic of the business.

After the most interesting and important future scenarios are in focus, diagrams are created for key scenarios that show outcomes for different stakeholders and the relation of selected Capability Cases to supporting steps in the scenarios. Figures 6.17a and 6.17b show an example of these types of diagrams for scenario enactment.

Sidebar 6.6   Technique (T5): Future Retrospective

 A future retrospective asks a group to step into the future, to imagine the solution in use, and to describe what is happening and then how this transformation was accomplished.

Future News Story

An effective way to doing *Future Retrospectives* is to ask each member of the group to step into the role of a journalist and write a news story. The first step is to collect headlines.

FIGURE 6.11.

The idea of a *future interview* is to direct people's attention to future outcomes. The facilitator asks the workshop to project themselves into the future and imagine being in the role of a journalist reporting on the success of the solution. The following is an example of reporting such a story from a workshop that envisioned solutions for archiving electronic records.

"Labs and GOCOs use data archiving middleman"

Government Owned/Company Operated companies (GOCOs) and National Laboratories have an ongoing need to share information. Until recently, these interactions were handled on a case-by-case-basis. At each point, the access rights to the information had to be negotiated.

The recent adoption of the GOCO ERA now allows all access information for any archived artifacts to be negotiated up front with a neutral agent. The archive takes care of validating all packaging information about the information, and adding any authentication information as part of the archiving process.

Requests for information no longer go directly to the GOCOs, but instead can be mediated through the archive. This provides selective access to large amounts of information without having to transfer all this information in a batch to the requesting party. The authenticity of the information can also be verified by the archive.

GOCO has sold several trucks formerly used to ship tons of paper to labs.

—Robin Riat, August 8, 2007

This same project included a further envisioning exercise. The team was asked to envision how the portal featuring the Electronic Records Archiving solution might look in the year 2007 (assuming portals would still be a preferred approach). Figure 6.12 was done with a UML Modeling tool of the envisioned portal. *Breaking News* shows some of the journalist stories.

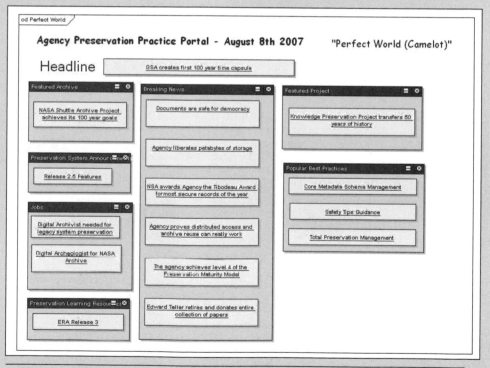

FIGURE 6.12. FUTURE RETROSPECTIVE FOR AN ERA PORTAL—ENVISIONING STORIES FROM 2007.

Workproduct G Solution Enactment Diagram

 Capability Interest and Value Proposition Scorecard

Annotated pictures of how events, actions, and capabilities help stakeholders perform their work in selected activity areas.

The *Solution Enactment Diagram* workproduct documents a number of key scenarios of the envisioned solution. The diagrams can be depictions of interactions between stakeholders and the systems, databases, and other resources within the business context. Figures 6.13a and b show an example.

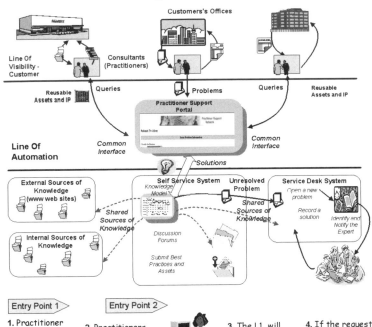

(1) The PSN is a knowledge portal serving consultants in the field at different customer locations by providing a single point of entry for resolving technical problems and improving navigation of knowledge resources and "best practices."

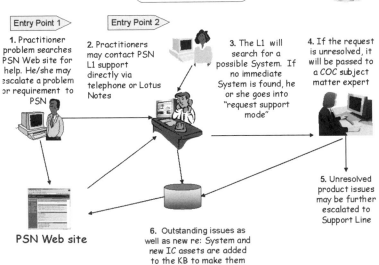

(2) Consultants in the field seek technical support from the PSN system.

FIGURE 6.13A. SCENARIO ENACTMENT FOR THE PRACTITIONER SUPPORT NETWORK (PSN).

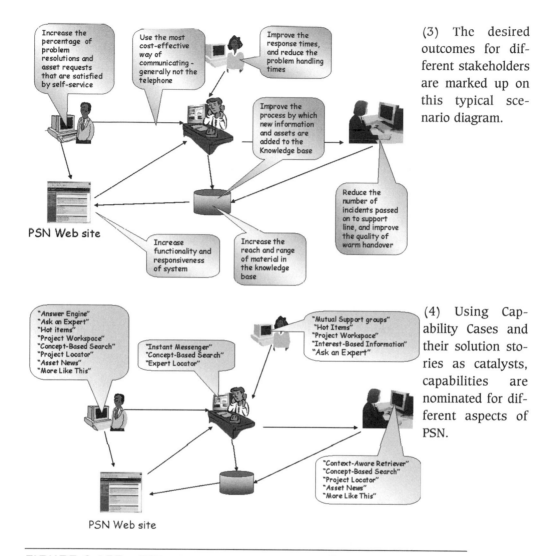

(3) The desired outcomes for different stakeholders are marked up on this typical scenario diagram.

(4) Using Capability Cases and their solution stories as catalysts, capabilities are nominated for different aspects of PSN.

FIGURE 6.13B. SCENARIO ENACTMENT FOR THE PRACTITIONER SUPPORT NETWORK (PSN)—CONTINUED.

Activity 9   Prioritize Capabilities

SCE-9
Prioritize
Capabilities

Capabilities that have been confirmed (in the workshop) to be of the most interest to an organization are examined from three perspectives: *desirability*—the business value, *feasibility*—ease of implementation, and *adequacy*—functional fit. Each capability is prioritized accordingly.

There are a number of techniques for prioritizing capabilities:

1.   Multi-Criteria Decision Analysis

2.   Value Mapping

    a.   Urgent/Important 2-by-2

    b.   Business Value 2-by-2

The techniques we typically use for prioritization are outlined in Sidebar 6.7.

Examples of Using Suggested Techniques to Prioritize Capabilities

Implementation effort and maturity of the capability play a key role in the selection process. Often, enterprises will stage the implementation of the capabilities according to the effort. Some are risk averse and will not consider capabilities that are still in conceptual, research, or early commercialization stages. Others will proactively seek competitive advantage through the use of emerging technologies.

Use of Urgent/Important 2-by-2 for Prioritization

In the NASA AMES *Collaborative Ontology Viewer and Editor (COVE)* project, we used Banxia's Decision Explorer tool to provide a collaborative workshop approach to agreeing on the priority of the system's capabilities. Figure 6.14 shows a screenshot of a 2-by-2 matrix with dependencies between the capabilities. *Ontology-Driven Discussions* emerged as the most critical capability.

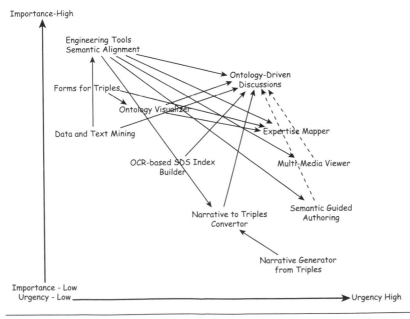

FIGURE 6.14.   URGENT/IMPORTANT 2-BY-2 FOR CAPABILITIES IN THE NASA COVE PROJECT.

Example of Use of Business Value 2-by-2

An example of a business value 2-by-2 from a design of a supply chain collaboration portal for a major manufacturer is shown in Figure 2.14 in Chapter 2, "Bridging the Gap with Solution Envisioning." The diagram shows portal capabilities positioned according to their perceived business value and implementation effort. In some situations, it may be useful to replace the "Effort" axis with a "Risk" axis.

Sidebar 6.7   Technique (T6): Prioritization Techniques

 Multi-Criteria Decision Analysis

A number of decision modeling techniques exist, each supported by tools. Most are based on criteria that are ranked for importance against which alternatives are scored and compared. Because different approaches work better in different situations, we describe three leading techniques:

1.   V.I.S.A. Multi-Criteria Decision Analysis[9]

2.   Bayesian Decision Technique

3.   Analytical Hierarchical Process

These techniques are described fully in Chapter 7 and Appendix B.

Value Mapping

Urgent/Important 2-by-2 Technique

This variant of value mapping is concerned with reaching consensus on a prioritization of proposed system capabilities. The capabilities are placed in a 2-by-2 matrix whose vertical axis denotes importance and horizontal axis urgency. By "importance," we mean relevance to the business situation. "Urgency" can mean a number of things: criticality to driving early value for the business needs or criticality to the interests of the project by earliest demonstration of value. An example of application is shown in Figure 6.14.

---

[9] V.I.S.A. is a decision support tool that compares alternative strategies or options against multiple criteria. The name V.I.S.A. (Visual Interactive Sensitivity Analysis) embodies the design objective of facilitating modeling and analysis in a visual and interactive way, leading to improved understanding, better communication, and consequently, better considered decisions. The tool is available at www.simul8.com/products/visa.htm. Professor Val Belton's and Professor Theodor J. Stewart's book, *Multiple Criteria Decision Analysis: An Integrated Approach*, is a useful reference [Belton 2002].

Business Value 2-by-2 Technique

The intent of this technique is to communicate the value and effort of proposed system capabilities so decisions on prioritization can be made. Capabilities are positioned in a 2-by-2 matrix. The vertical axis denotes business value, low to high, and the horizontal axis denotes the effort to realize the capability. This approach has some similarities with a technique used by eXtreme Programming (XP) practitioners for scoring effort and value on "Story Cards." In our case, we are using Capability Cases that represent one or more solution stories, and we are introducing an insightful way of showing all the scorings in a matrix.

Workproduct I   Capability Prioritization Matrix

 Capability Prioritization Matrix   A table, or equivalent, listing selected capabilities with measures of importance and priority, rough order of magnitude on effort, and desired target dates for realization. Some treatment of dependencies should also be provided.

SCE Activities III—Post-Workshop Assessment and Consolidation

This comprises the following activities:

> 10. Assess Solution Realization Gap
>
> 11. Post-Workshop Analysis and Consolidation of Concepts

Activity 10   Assess Solution Realization Gap

SCE-10
Assess Solution
Realization Gap

Implementing and deploying the solution brings challenges arising from differences between the organization's current competencies and resources, the impact on existing systems, and the readiness of the selected technologies. An assessment of these gaps and the organization's ability to address them produces a risk list and an informed decision model on solution options.

This activity produces two workproducts using primarily the *Root-Cause Analysis* technique (see Sidebar 6.8), and, in some cases, *Decision Belief Mapping* (see Appendix B).

In producing the first workproduct, a Risk Assessment Model, identified risks will be used to inform release planning. The project will either decide to do low-risk capabilities first or face the challenges that surround the highest risk capabilities. In a value-driven approach, the first determination is what functionality is needed to drive value for the business. If there are risks associated with functions, then activities must be planned to overcome those risks. In the XP Agile Method, technical risks are addressed using what is referred to as an "Architecture Spike."

The second, optional workproduct is a Solution Options Decision Model. For the selection of development strategies covered by this model, we refer to Chapter 7, which details these options:

1. Custom Development

   a.   Traditional Lifecycle Software Development

   b.   Agile Development

2. Package-Based Development

   c.   Open Source Software Packages

   d.   Proprietary Software Packages

3. Component-Based Development

   e.   Platform-Oriented Frameworks

   f.   Model-Driven Architecture

   g.   Web Services

   h.   Semantic Web Services

The Solution Options Decision Model uses criteria determined during the workshop. The criteria often used as a starting point are

- Ease of Development
- Ease of Deployment

Sidebar 6.8   Technique (T7): Root-Cause Analysis

 Root-Cause Analysis   The root cause analysis technique explores connections between situations, outcomes, and events by inquiring into dependencies that bring about causality. By asking "How?" and "Why?" questions, root causes are discerned and a network graph showing associations between concepts is drawn. We have found the Decision Explorer tool from Banxia to be very effective for drawing these networks, or "cognitive maps." By studying these networks, the potency of a particular cause can be ascertained from the plurality of its connectivity.

Workproduct J   Risk Assessment Model

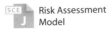

Risk Assessment Model — An identification of risks, their likelihood and impact, and critical dependencies. The model can be presented either in the form of a list, a table, or a database model with each risk correlated to specific capabilities.

Workproduct K   Solution Options Decision Model (Optional)

Solution Options Decision Model (Optional) — The solution option decisions are concerned with technology choices and the selection of a development strategy. Technology choices will be different for platforms, IT infrastructure, application infrastructure, and application software. Standards for the enterprise will constrain choices and this workproduct captures such rationale.

Activity 11   Post-Workshop Analysis and Consolidation of Concepts

SCE-11
Conduct Post-Workshop Analysis & Concept Coord.

The workshop and work of this phase generates new insights, agreements (and potential disagreements) over dependencies, issues, priorities, and commitments to going forward. An analysis of this leads to a refinement of the "Solution Concept" and its associated roadmap.

It is important to conduct a team debrief as soon after the completion of the Solution Envisioning Workshop as possible, while thoughts and perspectives are still fresh. We debrief with the project team discussing the insights each person gained. We also put together a brief summary document of the workshop. This should include the following:

- Introductory material
- List of observations—Problems or challenges (those reflecting major themes from the workshop) are individually linked to business issues
- Recommendations—Best opportunities to pursue (with the business value of each)
- An appendix of the actual workshop output

After preparing a summary document, we recommend either meeting with participants or conducting a conference call to discuss it. This will both validate findings and perspectives and help foster continuing participant involvement and buy-in. This call will attempt to answer questions, such as the following:

- How would they like to go forward?
- What problems do they foresee?
- Where do we (participants and facilitators) start? (Considering the proper scope of the pilot work or research visits.)

In most cases, this interaction yields a validated, finalized version of the summary document of the workshop that takes the participant feedback into account. There may be cases where the organization will not want to proceed beyond this point (for example, due to budgetary constraints). It is therefore important to be sure that the document, and the discussion around it, delivers value in itself.

At this point in the Solution Envisioning process, the capabilities of the solution exist as a collection of capabilities. There is a need to organize these capabilities into a conceptual architecture of the solution.

Capability Modeling

Capability Modeling is the way we organize the capabilities nominated for the solution into a conceptual architecture that is *platform-independent*. The purpose of this architecture is to communicate the vision, functionality, and component structure of the solution to all stakeholders.

A Capability Model organizes capabilities according to the following principles:

- Separation of concerns and conceptual integrity
- Layering, or partitioning, according to dependencies between capabilities
- Parsimony—everything is needed and nothing is redundant
- Component placement—constraining allocations to known components
- Viewpoints—separating different aspects of the architecture for different interests

Separation of concerns should already have happened as a result of the clustering of capabilities afforded by Capability Cases. For layering, two ways of arranging the architecture sketches have been found to be successful: horizontally and vertically. A horizontal depiction shows stakeholders on the left and capabilities in a progressive treatment of enablement to the right, with external systems on the far right. The vertical arrangement is organized in a similar way but from top to bottom. We prefer the vertical depiction because of its connection to early work in Solution Envisioning for depicting IT support for enterprise activities.

Example Capability Models

We cite one example here from a project to create an IT Resource Pool Management System for a professional services firm. In this example, an enterprise view of the capability model is presented as a high-level grouping of capabilities in the form of a table. Each capability is mapped to the stakeholders who benefit and is attributed with a relative percentage for importance. The codes used for the stakeholders are as follows:

- **AS**—Approved Supplier
- **ADM**—Administrator
- **RM**—Resource Manager
- **SA**—Skills Administrator
- **PA**—Procurement Administrator
- **VRDM**—Vendor Resource Deployment Administrator

TABLE 6.6.   Capabilities for the IT Resource Pool Management System

Capability	Stakeholders Benefited	Importance (%)
Resource Request Manager: Defines the needed resources and the price that is acceptable: notifies potential suppliers and manages the request through to a confirmed subcontractor.	VRDM, AS	29
Resource Matcher: Confirms that the candidates offered have the requisite skills, are available in the location needed, and are offered at a suitable price for that location: When there are multiple choices, rank the candidates according to specific criteria (for example, price).	VRDM, AS	27
Supplier Manager: Maintains a list of approved suppliers, and control the rules for dealing with them and their access to requests.	PA	14
Resource Pool Manager: Basic administration of the system, such as maintenance of profiles that describe the standard skill sets needed for each offering and defining the skills and availability of individual subcontractors (probably by the AS).	SA, PA	12
Infrastructure: Security and access control, authentication of suppliers, personalization, and so on.	RM, AS	7
Report Generator: Provides a set of reports that monitor the effectiveness of the system, the tool, and the service providers.	RM, PA	6

TABLE 6.6.   CAPABILITIES FOR THE IT RESOURCE POOL MANAGEMENT SYSTEM—
CONTINUED

Capability	Stakeholders Benefited	Importance (%)
Performance Advisor: Uses historical data for comparison purposes to aid decisions on selecting vendor resources.	RM, VRDM, PA, AS	3
Enterprise Application Integrator: Provides integration with other application suites.	VRDM	2
Total:		100

Workproduct L   Solution Concept Document

 Solution Concept Document

The Solution Concept workproduct conveys the vision of the solution. It is a description of the business context with forces and motivating scenarios; stakeholders and their desired results; capabilities that enable new ways to work; future scenarios that illustrate new ways to work; and a roadmap that addresses risks, impacts, and the options and plans for the solution design work of the next phase.

A "Concept of Operations" (ConOps) document (or presentation) is sometimes a required way to present the results of Solution Envisioning. A ConOps is a widely accepted approach to describing the desired characteristics of a proposed system from the user's (non-technical) point of view. Chapter 8 describes an example project where a ConOps is constructed from Solution Envisioning Workproducts.

Workproduct M   Solution Concept Document and Capability Model

 Solution Concept Document & Capability Model

This is a composite Workproduct that represents the output of the SCE phase. It consists of the Solution Concept Document (Workproduct L) and a Capability Model of the solution. A Capability Model is a conceptual architecture of the solution that guides the architectural design and technology selection. It provides a common vision by telling a story of a solution. It assists design, construction, and deployment of a technology by keeping them on track. It may contain multiple diagrams (viewpoints) for different stakeholders.

The Results of SCE and Moving to the Next Phase

Envisioning gives rise to a vision, first in the mind of the originator, then (through appropriate communication) in the minds of colleagues and other participants. Having the vision is not enough—it must be shared, nurtured, and shepherded to become stronger and more permanent. Through evangelizing, the vision becomes known and shaped by others. Participation brings endorsement but none of this will matter if we have not been equally creative in finding the path to implementation. There must be enough caring to carry it out.

TRAIL MARKER VI: SOLUTION CONCEPT AND ROADMAP ESTABLISHED

Chapter 6 is the second of a three-part practitioner's handbook for practicing Solution Envisioning. It described Phase II—Business Solution Envisioning—in detail. The material covered gives a step-by-step guide to this stage of the envisioning process whose central activity is the *Solution Envisioning Workshop*.

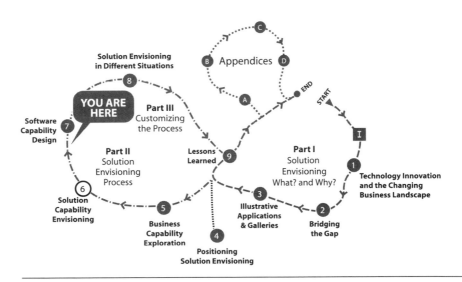

FIGURE 6.15.

Excellent facilitation skills are needed to organize and run high-quality, enjoyable workshops. In addition to this chapter, the case studies covered in Chapter 3 and an extended technique, "Conducting Envisioning Workshops as Theater Play," included in Appendix B, provide insight into how envisioning workshops are conducted.

You are now ready to proceed to Phase III as described in Chapter 7, "Software Capability Design—Phase III of Solution Envisioning."

7

SOFTWARE CAPABILITY DESIGN—PHASE III OF SOLUTION ENVISION

> *"What we call results are beginnings."*
>
> —*Ralph Waldo Emerson*

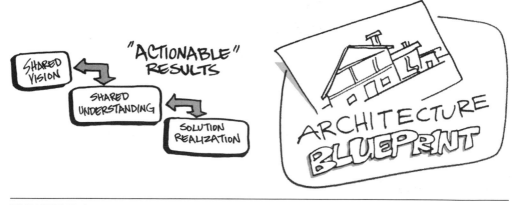

FIGURE 7.1.

CHAPTER PREVIEW

The goal of the third phase of Solution Envisioning is to deliver designs and plans, and optionally a business case, to realize a business IT solution. Capability Envisioning, the previous phase, delivers a *Solution Concept*—motivating scenarios, a set of capabilities, and their prioritization.

The *Capability Model* from the previous phase is elaborated into a *"Capability Architecture."* Detailed work depends on technology choices made during this phase. The *Capability Architecture* can be thought of as the conceptual form of a component model for the solution. In this chapter, we show how the Capability Architecture can be derived from the work of the previous phases. We will discuss aspects of this work that are dependent on the implementation strategy and software development process.

Based on the *Capability Architecture* that is created, this phase delivers a "Solution Realization Plan" and a "Solution Adoption Plan." These plans take into account the prioritization of capabilities and the impact the solution will have on the organization.

In most cases, the sponsorship for the solution initiative will require completion and validation of a "Business Case." The chapter includes guidance and techniques for calculating return on investment (ROI).

SOFTWARE CAPABILITY DESIGN (SCD)— FROM CONCEPT TO REALIZATION

The main work of this phase is to formalize the workproducts of the previous phases to develop a *"Capability Architecture"* of the solution. Anyone doing this final stage of pre-development work on designing and planning a solution— whether using Solution Envisioning or some other approach—will be confronted with the need to compare and choose among multiple development/implementation strategies. Each will present a possible path to realization of the business solution with different advantages and disadvantages. In this book, we cover three prevalent development strategies:

- Custom Development using traditional methodologies (RUP or MSF), as well as one of the most popular agile approaches—eXtreme Programming (XP)
- Package Implementation including customization and integration concerns
- Component-based Development using Web Services and Service Oriented Architecture (SOA), as well as Model-Driven Architecture (MDA).

At this stage in the process, a development strategy and implementation approach may have already been selected. Otherwise, the decision will be made as part of Activity 1 of the SCD *Evaluate Technology Options and Decide Development Strategy*. In writing about this phase, we had to choose the best way to convey the flow of the work and activities of the phase. Most of the work will directly reflect or be strongly influenced by the implementation approach. One alternative was to present all the variants for each of the development strategies in this chapter. Though logically complete, we found this to be unwieldy and too complex a format for introducing the process—it involved following multiple threads and interrupted the flow of the activities.

Instead, we have written about *Software Capability Design* in terms of one selected strategy, as it would be executed in practice. So, this chapter includes all of the material that is common to all strategies, plus the specialized parts for one of those strategies.

In selecting among approaches, we've considered a number of factors and trade-offs, such as: "What are the current trends in development?" versus "What is the most useful and used modeling language?"[1] The development approach we selected to follow is component-based using Web Services and Service-Oriented Architecture (SOA). Activities of SCD that follow Activity 1 assume this to be the selected development strategy. The specialized parts for the other development strategies covered in this book are described in Appendix C, "Software Capability Design Implementation Alternatives."

The Capability Architecture is a model that identifies the high-level components of the system, and the relationships among them. It includes a diagram that shows interactions between components including high-level descriptions of the interfaces. While capability architecture can be (and usually is) developed in a document, increasingly, there are tools that support construction of capability architecture or translation of a document form of capability architecture into a formal (even executable) model.

For example, in one approach, the Capability Architecture can be transformed into the Component Collaboration Architecture (CCA) of Enterprise Distributed Object Computing (EDOC).[2] Other transformations using the Model-Driven Architecture (MDA)[3] approach are also possible. Components are mapped to one (or parts of a) Capability Case.

---

[1]   Because we are now moving into the realm of implementation, this work takes into account that the Unified Modeling Language (UML) is the most popular design technique adopted by the software development community. UML is a graphical language and modeling formalism used to describe the artifacts of distributed object systems. The Object Constraint Language (OCL) is sometimes used in conjunction with UML to improve the semantics of the models by defining constraints on relationships and attributes and pre- and post-conditions on operations.

[2]   EDOC is an initiative of the Object Management Group (OMG). For more details see: www.omg.org/technology/documents/formal/edoc.htm.

[3]   MDA, Model-Driven Architecture, is an initiative of the Object Management Group for deriving software systems from models. See www.omg.org/mda/ for more details.

As a key early design artifact, Capability Architecture has always played an important role in the solution development. It may sometimes be called a high-level or conceptual architecture.[4] In our experience, the absence of such an architectural model, or a poorly developed one, has often served as a warning sign of a project heading for trouble. Yet, until recently, capability architecture only roughly represented how a solution was actually implemented. Components described by it did not always have direct counterparts in the implementation architecture. Producing a capability architecture that would have direct relation to and provide strong guidance for actual realization of the solution has been an imprecise art with little guidance available.

SCD for a Web Services and SOA Development Strategy

Adoption of model-driven development, Web services, and SOAs are changing the role of the capability architecture. For instance, architecture becomes executable code with the use of MDA platforms because they derive all executables from models of the system.[5] Web services encapsulate the internals of systems into large grained components that expose business capabilities.

For Web services–based solutions, the following activities and decisions can be seen as strongly overlapping with the process of designing the capability architecture:

- The process of deciding what Web services are needed
- How the system can be packaged into Web services
- How the lines of business responsibilities are drawn between Web services
- How Web services interact with each other

As Web services mature and their adoption rates grow (see Sidebar 7.1), having a reliable method for deriving capability architectures becomes more and more critical. Solution Envisioning with Capability Cases is designed to address this need. At the time of this writing, Enterprise SOA books were becoming available,

---

[4] High-level architecture is a fuzzy term. It can be used to describe any early architectural model—for example, a high-level technical architecture. By using the word "capability," we are intending to make clear that this is a functional view of the architecture. Conceptual architecture is more akin to the earlier product of Solution Envisioning—the Capability Model. Like the Capability Model, it does not include the interaction and interface specifications of the Capability Architecture.

[5] Chapter 7 includes a section on the way Solution Envisioning with Capability Cases assists the process of implementing model-driven systems.

and the mapping of Capability Cases to SOA was becoming evident to us in the methods that were being proposed for developing an SOA. A good example of this is Dirk Krafzig's book, *Enterprise SOA*, in which layered architectures are described with a strong capability-based treatment [Krafzig, 2005].

Sidebar 7.1   Business Impact of Web Services

Web Services change the way solutions are being developed. By establishing a common architectural framework for promoting, accessing, and dynamically binding to services, integration becomes a matter of configuring services appropriate to the capabilities required by different business areas. Through a directory concept, services have a single common approach to their management. In short, Web Services provide the mechanisms that allow an industry-standard approach to component-based configuration of solutions.

Web Services are a response to a significant shift in the marketplace. Customers are no longer attracted to IT-intensive solution developments. They are interested in agility through IT solutions that allow new kinds of business models and partnerships to happen. Companies want to drive new revenue models based on extended value nets across virtual enterprises. Capabilities become the integration cornerstones. In this new business world, Web Services become the ability to define and reconfigure capabilities in response to business opportunities.

Web Services are seen as the means to enable business customers to become "business capability vendors" by packaging their capabilities into Web Services components. The basic idea of a Web Service is to wrap a software function in a way that enables it to be executed over the Internet. A Web Service is a software application whose interfaces and binding are capable of being defined, described, and discovered through industry-standard XML protocols. For example:

- **SOAP**—The Simple Object Access Protocol is used for direct interactions (using XML-based messages) between Web Services.

- **WSDL**—The Web Service Description Language is used to describe operations Web services can perform and how they can be invoked.

- **UDDI**—The Universal Discovery Description and Integration provides a directory capability.

Using the UDDI, Web Services can be dynamically (meaning at run-time) discovered, combined, and executed to create a composite application that performs its work either alone or with other applications over a network. The full realization of "Composite Applications" requires "Semantic Web Services" described later in this chapter in Sidebar 7.4.

The Work of Software Capability Design

A consolidated overview of Phase 3 of Solution Envisioning, Software Capability Design, and its key *Activities*, *Workproducts*, and supporting *Techniques* is shown in Figure 7.2.[6]

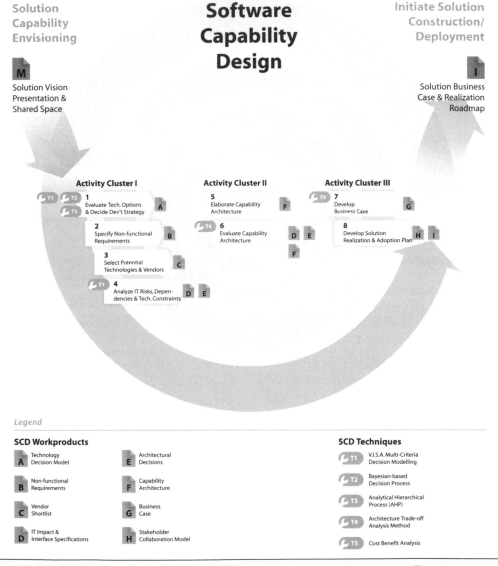

FIGURE 7.2.   THE ACTIVITIES AND WORKPRODUCTS OF CAPABILITY DESIGN.

[6] Table D.3 in Appendix D provides a concise reference to the definitions of all the Activities and Workproducts of SCD.

The Three Activity Clusters of SCD

Software Capability Design (SCD) phase is organized in three Activity clusters:

I.   **Select Implementation Technologies**—This set of activities has the goal of making a decision on the development strategy and implementation approach. In addition to the desired functional capabilities, quality attributes of the system and its components will play a strong influence as will business and technical risks associated with different implementation options for selected capabilities. Another important factor is technology readiness and organizational readiness to adopt the candidate technologies. Top vendors who either have products or technologies are short-listed and a decision model for comparing and choosing options is produced. An additional need is to document IT systems the solution may depend on, replace, or interface with. The cluster consists of Activities 1 through 4.

II. **Develop Software Capability Architecture**—The Capability Architecture identifies high-level components of the system, their dependencies, and illustrates the behavior of the intended system through diagrams that show the interactions between components for the key scenarios of use. Verification and validation is conducted to assess how well the Architecture meets the goals of the stakeholders in delivering functionality and satisfying desired quality goals and measures. The cluster consists of Activities 5 and 6.

III. **Develop Business Case and Solution Roadmap**—The scope and details of a business case will vary according to the mission criticality and size of the solution initiative. The initial business case, developed in the BCE phase, gave a justification for the solution in terms of the business problem being solved, the expected results for key stakeholders, and realized outcomes in the business environment. In this phase, the business case is elaborated further with a statement of commitments, resources, and effort estimates needed to implement, deploy, and support the solution. The business case should also provide a high-level statement of risks and risk mitigation activities. An analysis of costs and return on investment (ROI) completes the business case. Beyond this, a business case might also address organizational impacts, communication, and training needs, as well as the transition plans. The Solution Roadmap calls out the major milestones and capabilities of each release. The cluster consists of Activities 7 and 8.

In subsequent sections, we explain and discuss each of the Activities in some detail. Except where indicated, the definitions are generic and independent of the chosen implementation strategy.

SCD ACTIVITIES I: SELECT IMPLEMENTATION TECHNOLOGIES

This cluster of activities includes (numbered as shown in Figure 7.2):

1. Evaluate Technology Options and Decide Development Strategy
2. Specify Non-Functional Requirements
3. Select Potential Technologies and Vendors
4. Analyze IT Risks, Dependencies, and Technology Constraints

Activity 1   Evaluate Technology Options and Decide Development Strategy

SCD-1
Evaluate Tech. Options
& Decide Dev't Strategy

Make a decision on the development strategy/implementation approach. Develop a decision model for selecting technologies and vendors. Two common approaches to decision modeling are Multi-Criteria Decision Trees and the AHP (Analytical Hierarchical Process) technique. Another approach, which deals with uncertainty, is a Bayesian method using *Belief Maps*. This later technique is described in Appendix B.

Deciding on the implementation strategy is an iterative process. During BCE, an *Overall Technology Strategy* was outlined. At the end of Phase II of Solution Envisioning, implementation options were evaluated and, optionally, a Solution Options Decision Model was developed. Now it is time to select a development strategy and implementation approach as outlined earlier and begin to make decisions on specific technologies and products. Technology Options vary depending on the chosen implementation (development) strategy.

In more detail, the three development strategies that we cover are as follows:

Custom SCD

Custom Development becomes a leading option when the required capabilities are very new and innovative. Building "from scratch" is also necessary when the business process and the end product are unique. A decade ago, nearly all IT projects were about custom development. Today, the number of custom-built solutions is sharply diminished, although they will never completely disappear. Furthermore, fewer development projects are *pure* custom-built as many now include pre-built components; that is, they are a combination of custom and component-based development.

Package-Based SCD

The more mature, stable and *common* the business processes, the more likely it is that there is a good choice of standard packages that include all the necessary capabilities. Examples are Enterprise Resource Planning (ERP), Supply Chain, and Customer Relationship Management (CRM) packages. Many vendors offer industry-specific versions of these packages. However, these solutions are often based on the technology that is a generation (or more) behind current and emerging technologies. So, while there may be a good selection of capable ERP products, only a few, if any, will comply with the SOA and Web services architectures.

Package vendors are usually focused on making their products all encompassing and as capable as possible, as opposed to playing well with other solutions that are part of a given IT infrastructure. That is why implementing a large pre-integrated package often means creating a silo that does not evolve well with the changing business needs. Nevertheless, there are many situations when this choice is seen as most optimal.

Component-Based SCD

This book views component-based development as a process of sourcing and assembling (integrating) solution components from multiple sources. With the growing number of modular capabilities, often implemented as Web services, this is becoming an important option. This option may be used in a combination with the custom-built components.

Components can be realized and integrated in a number of ways. We will describe a Web Services approach to component development. Appendix C includes specific coverage of specialization of subsequent activities of SCD that illustrate how Capability Cases can work with a Model-Driven Architecture (MDA) development framework.

An attractive form of component-based development is a Layered Architecture approach based on Domain Specific Languages. This approach raises the level of software specifications from programming languages to problem-oriented languages by defining progressive layers, and collaborations, of abstract machines. Software Factories are an example of this approach.

Technology Evaluation

Technology evaluation criteria will differ depending on the development strategy and implementation approach. For example, questions commonly asked when evaluating technology options for custom development include:

- Will the solution be built using Microsoft technology or Java-based technology?
- Will this be a Web Services project?
- Will the solution use a Web application server or a portal server?
- Is model-driven development a good fit for this project? If so, what tools will be used?
- How will security, authentication, and single sign-on be handled?
- Will the system be accessed only through a browser or will there be other options such as thick clients and wireless devices?

Existing technology infrastructure, skills, and the set of required capabilities determine which of these questions can be answered quickly and which ones require additional analysis. When multiple options exist, a decision model needs to be created to ensure the fidelity of the selection process.

Package-Based Evaluation Criteria

Many businesses focus too much weight on tactical criteria, such as functionality and cost, while underrating or even overlooking strategic evaluation criteria, such as vendor viability, service, and support capabilities. These evaluation criteria become especially critical when the approach chosen is to implement a single pre-integrated package. Some of the questions to include in the decision model are

- Will the vendor survive as the market evolves?
- Does the vendor have the talent and organization to be successful?
- How committed is the vendor to serving the needs of our industry?
- Is the vendor's technical direction in line with our technical strategy?

Functional fit of a packaged solution can be evaluated by ranking its support for selected Capability Cases. Each Capability Case then becomes a part of the decision model weighted according to its importance and priority.

Component-Based Evaluation Criteria

When the implementation approach is component-based development, reliance on each individual vendor does not need to be as strong. Part of the architectural design should be focused on identifying ways to *unplug* one component and replace it with a different component should the need arise. The strategic questions about vendor evaluation are still part of the decision model, but they should be weighted lower than if a packaged solution option has been selected. Some of the questions to include in the model are as follows:

- What integration strategy should be used?
- How to divide responsibility between components?
- How to ensure plugability of the architecture?

Development Strategy Selected

As stated earlier, we now assume one of the results of Activity I to be selection of the development strategy as Component-based using Web Services and Service Oriented Architecture (SOA). Cluster II Activities (Elaborate Capability Architecture and Evaluate Capability Architecture) are especially dependent on the implementation approach. In the remainder of the chapter, we will describe what is common for all implementation approaches and then focus on a Web Services development and implementation approach. Appendix C provides details on the variations of Cluster II work for:

- Custom Development using traditional methodologies (RUP or MSF) as well as one of the most popular agile approaches—eXtreme Programming
- Package Implementation including customization and integration concerns
- Component-based Development using MDA

This activity produces Workproduct A:

Workproduct A   Technology Decision Model

Technology Decision Model   A list of criteria used to decide on technology options. Each criterion may be given a relative weight. A Decision Model can be implemented as a spreadsheet, although we believe that decision support tools are better suited for this purpose.

A number of decision modeling techniques exist, each supported by tools. Most are based on criteria ranked for importance against the alternatives, which are scored and compared. Decision modeling is important to most activities in this chapter. Since different approaches work better in different situations, we make use of three techniques:

1. V.I.S.A. Multi-Criteria Decision Technique
2. Bayesian Decision Technique
3. Analytical Hierarchical Process (AHP)

The first technique is described in Sidebar 7.2. Descriptions for the other two techniques are available in Appendix B.

Sidebar 7.2   Technique (T1): V.I.S.A. Multi-Criteria Decision Support Technique

SCD **T1** V.I.S.A Multi-Criteria Decision Modelling

Problem Context

How to evaluate and decide on alternatives using multiple criteria refined as a hierarchical tree:
- Without having to do multiple pair-wise comparisons, and
- With the ability to explore the sensitivity of options to ranking and scoring.

Approach and Guidance

The decision-making process used for V.I.S.A. is the same one we recommend using with any of the three decision techniques described in this book. It follows six broad steps:

- Preparation for decision making—At this point in Solution Envisioning, the scope of the decision should be clear. The preparation is limited to orienting the team to the decision method.
- Clarification of the decision space—By clarification, we mean identification of possible decision spaces and the selection of the focus decision space. The decision space for this phase includes selecting development approach, deciding on vendor options, and making choices related to technology, IT constraints, and implementation planning.
- Development of criteria—Evaluation of alternates should be conducted against a finite set of balanced criteria. When this technique is used, criteria are grouped in tree hierarchies.
- Identification of alternative solutions—These will vary depending on the decision space.
- Evaluation of alternatives—Evaluation is the scoring of how each alternate meets each of the criteria and involves these steps.
- Decision about next steps

Example

Figure 7.3 shows an example of a decision model used in selecting an approach and technology for rapid user interface development. Criteria are shown for comparing options. The model uses a tool called V.I.S.A. from Simula8 Corporation.[7] This allows graphical construction of the criteria tree and dynamic sensitivity to weights to be explored. The following alternatives for "Evolutionary Prototyping" were chosen:

1. J2EE—Using a pure Java framework with or without EJBs

2. J2EE with Web Services—Using Web Services to wrapper existing applications
3. J2EE with WebTier—Decisionsmith's Rapid Prototyping environment
4. J2EE with Fablet—A prototyping approach from Fourbit[8]
5. Digital Harbor's PiiE Platform[9]—An example of a high-level construction kit
6. .NET—Microsoft's environment for enterprise-wide computing
7. .NET with Web Services

The criteria we have chosen can be grouped into two sub-trees: development considerations and deployment considerations. Choosing these sub-trees has the benefit of being able to use V.I.S.A.'s two-dimensional graphing to visualize the sensitivity of the criteria. Figure 7.3 shows this for the seven alternatives we selected for the model.

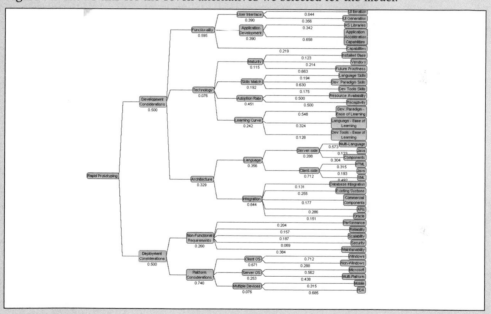

FIGURE 7.3.   V.I.S.A DECISION MODEL EXAMPLE.

The numbers indicate the relative importance of each branch of the tree.

7   www.simul8.com/products/visa.htm.

8   www.fourbit.com (note that, at the time of publishing, Fourbit were no longer in business).

9   www.digitalharbor.com.

Activity 2   Specify Non-Functional Requirements

SCD-2
Specify Non-functional
Requirements

Identify the required quality attributes of the system and its components. This includes performance, availability, security, usability, maintainability, and extensibility. Specify ranges of values from acceptable to desired.

Often referred to as the "-*ilities*" of the system, quality attributes include such factors as performance, usability, reliability, availability, security, understandability, adaptability, and maintainability. The quality attributes of the system and its components are key drivers for the software development process that is to follow. Our method adopts the attribute-driven approach pioneered by Tom Gilb for specifying the quality attributes of the system [Gilb, 1988]. For each quantifiable attribute, we express a range of values: the desired value, an acceptable value, and an undesirable value.

Often non-functional requirements are written as "the system should have high performance" or "the system should be easy to maintain." Without more specific limits or measures, such statements are open to interpretation, misunderstanding, and make it hard to evaluate whether the system meets the requirements. In SCD, we require the designer to specify non-functional requirements as measurable quality attributes. This involves converting a statement like, "The system should have high performance" to more specific and measurable statements, for example, "The system shall be able to process between 50 and 100 transactions per second."

In keeping with a reuse-based philosophy, we use a template called the "Architecture Requirements Checklist" to specify non-functional requirements, as shown in Table 7.1. The template includes many commonly used quality attributes and provides a range of values (service levels) for each attribute. Shaded cells indicate the attribute values selected for the solution in this example.

TABLE 7.1.   Template for Non-Functional Requirements

Non-Functional Requirements Checklist

Ref	Property Stringency:	Service Levels least	..	..	..	most
		Performance				
NFR 1	Transaction size—average	<10K	50–100KB	100–500KB	500KB–1MB	> 1MB
NFR 2	Transaction size—maximum	<10K	100K	1 MB	100 MB	1 GB
NFR 3	Transaction speeds/throughput (billing)	1 per second	1 to 10 per second	10 to 50 second	50 to 100 per second	> 100 per second
NFR4	Transaction concurrency—How many independent sessions can be executing	1	>1 but <5	>4 but <20	>19 but <50	unlimited
NFR 5	Optimization capability	Not Important	Simple Queuing	Optimal Queuing	Dynamic message blocking	Most optimal routing and blocking
		Scalability/Capacity				
NFR 6	Number of connected systems	2	2 to 5	5 to 10	10 to 20	>20
NFR 7	Number of active sessions					
NFR 8	Number of concurrent Integration Objects	Fixed at startup	up to 100 objects	up to 10^3 objects	up to 10^5 objects	10^6 objects
		Availability				
NFR 9	Operational availability	90% 8–5 5 days/wk	95% 8–5 5 days/wk	100% 8–5 5 days/wk		24x7x52
NFR 10	Downtime for installation releases	<1 week	<24 hours	<4hours off-shift	<2 hours	0
		Recoverabilty				
NFR 11	Recovery strategy	None	Manual	Automatic		
NFR 12	Recovery capability	None	Restart Transaction	Restart the Unit-of-Work	Last committed sub-transaction	Last successful byte transferred
		Reliability				
NFR 13	Application integrity	Not Important	Desirable	Critical to Solution		
		Security				
NFR 14	Trusted environment	None	Server(s) only	Servers + Users		All tiers
NFR 15	Audit trail	Not Important	Desirable	Critical to Solution		

TABLE 7.1. TEMPLATE FOR NON-FUNCTIONAL REQUIREMENTS—CONTINUED

Non-Functional Requirements Checklist

	Property	Service Levels				
Ref	Stringency:	least	..	..	..	most
		Adaptability				
NFR 16	Platform neutrality	Not Important	Desirable	Critical to Solution		
		Standards				
NFR 17	De jure and de facto standards	Not important	Desirable	Critical to Solution		
		Maintenance				
NFR 18	Provision of monitoring and supervisory capabilities	Not important	Desirable	Critical to Solution		
NFR 19	Reconfiguration of network topology	Not important	Desirable	Critical to Solution		
NFR 20	Locally Supported. Measured by frequency of need-for/calls-to Vendors	Remote calls < 1/quarter	Remote calls < 1/month	Remote calls < 1/week	On-site as needed	Permanent on-site

Organizing quality attributes into a common framework has become somewhat easier in recent years through the efforts of the ISO/IEC working groups underWG6 of the software engineering subcommittee (SC7).

A number of quality-related measurement standards are relevant for this activity: ISO/IEC 9126—Software product quality, ISO/IEC 14598—Evaluation of software products, IEEE Std.1061-1998, and ISO/IEC 25000 SQuaRE—Software Product Quality Requirements and Evaluation. These standards can be used as a framework of a quality model using the FCM approach—Factors, Criteria, and Metrics. An example of an FCM model is shown in Figure 7.4.

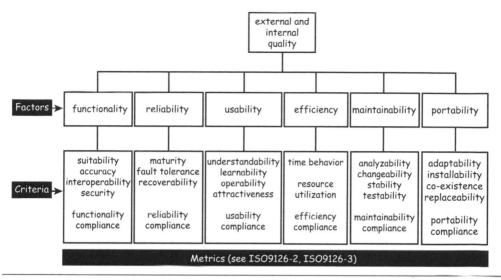

FIGURE 7.4.   ISO 9126 QUALITY MODEL.

Workproduct B   Non-Functional Requirements

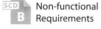

Non-functional Requirements   A document describing non-functional requirements as the quality attributes of the system. They are often stated as constraints on the functional requirements but also could include attributes pertaining to development, deployment, and maintenance. Each non-functional requirement is further clarified by providing a range of values as well as identifying measurements to be used to test conformance to requirements.

Activity 3   Select Potential Technologies and Vendors

SCD-3
Select Potential
Technologies & Vendors

Identify top vendors that can offer technology for building the capabilities. If a definitive decision is not made as to which one of the three implementation options will be taken, the work has to take in to account each of the options under consideration. For example, the Vendor Shortlist may list vendor choices for a Packaged Solution and, separately, for a Component-based Solution.

Evaluation is performed by ranking technologies against the decision model. This activity narrows down the choices to, at most, the top two to three options. For Component-based Development, there could be two to three options per component. Often, the final selection can not be made at this time because technologists need time for hands-on experimentation with the tools. When this is the case, the solution roadmap should allow time for prototyping and include a milestone for making the final decision.

Assessing the applicability of vendor products and technologies is often a managed process that may involve issuing RFIs or RFPs. After data has been gathered, the job of ranking and scoring alternatives is undertaken. In the projects using packaged solutions or component-based development, business community plays a key role in the ranking and selection process because a capability match is one of the most important criteria in the decision model.

With the custom development projects, vendor selection is usually about identifying the right platform and tools for development. As such, it is focused more on the technical merits as opposed to business capabilities. Selection is conducted mainly by IT people with no (or little) involvement from the business community.

Workproduct C   Vendor Shortlist

 Vendor Shortlist   This document identifies two to three top vendor choices, their specific strengths, and solution fit. Solution fit is determined by ranking technology choices against the decision model.

Activity 4   Analyze IT Risks, Dependencies, and Technology Constraints

 **SCD-4**
Analyze IT Risks, Dependencies & Tech. Constraints

Identify the business and technical risks associated with different implementation options for selected capabilities. Consider technology readiness for use as well as organizational readiness to implement the candidate technologies. Document other systems that the solution may depend on, replace, or interface with.

Starting with *Existing IT Systems in Context* (BCE Workproduct F, introduced in Chapter 5), identify a relationship between existing IT systems and the new solution. When integration is important, identify an integration mechanism and strategy for interfacing.

As described in Chapter 2, we find it useful to distinguish between integration mechanisms (ways in which a capability is invoked as a part of the overall solution) and strategy (an architectural approach for integrating capabilities).

Typically, systems use one of the following integration mechanisms:

- **UI Integration**—The simplest form of integration. Examples include making a capability accessible through a link on the Web or as a *portlet* in a portal.

- **Task-centric Integration**—One example of this mechanism is an Instant Helper screen with a *"Can I help you?"* message popping up when a user hesitates at a check out in the e-shop.

- **Data-centric Integration**—Where data is shared, aggregated, or exchanged.

- **Process-centric Integration**—When a capability is triggered by events in a process or has to generate events for other capabilities or processes.

An integration strategy will depend on technologies used for the solution and the systems it needs to integrate with. Common strategies include:

- **Proprietary Plug-ins**—Used when integrating additional capabilities into large-grained functional components that offer some degree of openness through proprietary APIs. The style could operate on multiple levels.

- **Cooperative Applications**—An example is a cooperation of MS Word and Groove where each serves a clearly separate function and operates independently. At the same time, a MS Word document could be stored and version-controlled by Groove.[10] Another example is two custom business applications that serve separate business functions where one sends a weekly data extract to another.

- **Common Integration Framework**—Requires a set of agreed protocols used by different applications to communicate. Examples include Enterprise Application Integration (EAI) platforms, Service Oriented Architectures (SOA) for Web Services, Enterprise Service Bus (ESB), the COM/DCOM, J2EE, and CORBA platform and architecture frameworks. Interoperability is achieved through an application profile.

These high-level integration decisions can be further detailed by selecting a specific style of access for each interface, such as:

- Off-line data migration
- File-based interface

---

[10] Groove (www.groove.net) is a virtual office/collaboration space that supports distributed workers. Groove provides products with different levels of capabilities (for example, Groove Virtual Office File Sharing Edition), but provides all work in conjunction with third-party tools, such as MS Office suite. Ray Ozzie founded Groove Networks in October 1997. Ray is best known as the creator of Lotus Notes, the world's leading groupware product with more than 100 million users worldwide. Groove Networks is now being acquired by Microsoft.

- Message-based
- Program Changes
- Object Wrappers

Although the assumed decision taken regarding development strategy is that the solution will be implemented using Web services, it may still need to interface to other systems using a different approach, for example, just a URL link. These decisions are captured in the IT Impact and Interface Specifications workproduct. We find it useful to present this workproduct as a diagram showing impacted systems. The nature of the impact can be indicated through color coding.

Important decisions about all aspects of the architecture are documented in the Architectural Decisions workproduct. This is a free-form document, but it is a good practice to assign an ID number to each decision. Table 7.2 shows an example of what an Architectural Decisions document may look like. The example deals with the architectural decisions for implementing an order management system.

TABLE 7.2.   Example of Architectural Decisions for an Order Management System

	Architectural Decisions
Ref.	**Notes**
AD 1	The architecture has four layers: Implementation Services (for example, J2EE), Infrastructure Services, Common Business Objects, Applications.
AD 2	Differences between external systems are managed by providing insulation sub-layers and wrappers for heritage systems.
AD 3	Siebel OMS integrated with external ANSC Trigger is the recommended solution. Billing is outside of Siebel OMS. A strong candidate for the Billing System is Oracle Billing.
AD 4	Integration at the infrastructure level is performed using TIBCO.
AD 5	Message-Oriented Middleware is implemented in MQ Series.
AD 6	The eBusiness Application Integration will be implemented using the Unified Application Network (UAN) Standard.

Workproduct D IT Impact and Interface Specifications

 IT Impact and Interface Specifications A document identifying IT systems that the solution will have an impact on. This is best accomplished through a diagram showing impacted systems together with the nature of impact.

Workproduct E Architectural Decisions

 Architectural Decisions A document describing important decisions about aspects of the architecture including technology choices, the structure of the system, the provision and allocation of function, and adherence to standards. Each decision can be described in a free format style with headings like problem statement, resolution, alternatives, and justification.

SCD ACTIVITIES II: DEVELOP SOFTWARE CAPABILITY ARCHITECTURE

This cluster of activities includes (numbered as shown in Figure 7.2):

5. Elaborate Capability Architecture

6. Evaluate Capability Architecture

The Capability Model of the previous phase now needs to be translated into a Software Capability Architecture. How this happens is somewhat dependent on the development strategy that is chosen: Custom Development, Package Implementation, and Component-based approaches. Each brings specific considerations and engineering methods to the activities and workproducts of this stage of work. However, there are common elements of these activities that are not dependent on the chosen realization strategy. We outline the common elements first, then the specializations required for elaborating a capability architecture in SOA projects.

Activity 5 Elaborate Capability Architecture

SCD-5
Elaborate Capability Architecture

The Capability Model of the BCE phase is elaborated into a Capability Architecture. This identifies high-level components of the system, their dependencies, and illustrates the behavior of the intended system through diagrams that show the interactions between components for the key scenarios of use.

Common to all development approaches is the use of capabilities as allocations of functionality. In the case of Custom Development, the identified capabilities set the contexts for use case modeling. For Package Development, capabilities will need to be mapped to package modules. For Component-based Development, capabilities are mapped to components.

Elaborating Capability Architecture in Service-Oriented Architecture Projects

A Service-Oriented Architecture (SOA) is a loosely coupled set of components that provide application functionality. SOAs have an intuitive appeal in the sense that our day-to-day experiences are *service-oriented*:

- Placing your card in an ATM machine—The ATM has a "Cash Dispensing Service"
- Checking in for a flight using an e-Ticket—The kiosk has a "Check-in Service"
- Asking for a quote for a product from a supplier
- Checking the status of an order

The basic idea of SOA is to have common services that can be invoked by other applications. It can involve either simple data passing or multiple services coordinating in an activity (see Sidebar 7.3 for some characterizations of SOA from other sources). Web Services provide the interoperability between the components within an SOA. The skill required is in designing the services so that each is a *unit-of-work* that is reusable across components. Commonality and Variability (CV) analysis is a good technique for determining a partitioning of functionality.

An approach to partitioning is to view an SOA is an "engine" with defined capabilities within an Enterprise Service Bus (ESB) infrastructure [Chappell, 2004]. The value of Capability Cases is that they already offer a good starting point for the partitioning of services.

Translating a Capability Architecture to an SOA implementation[11] is a mapping and allocation exercise. An illustration of mapping and allocation is shown in Figure 7.5.

---

[11] According to Roy Schulte, VP and Research Fellow at Gartner, "A new form of Enterprise Service Bus (ESB) infrastructure—combining MOM, Web services, transformation, and routing intelligence—will be running in the majority of enterprises by 2005. These high-function, low-cost ESBs are well-suited to be the backbone for service-oriented architectures and the enterprise nervous system."

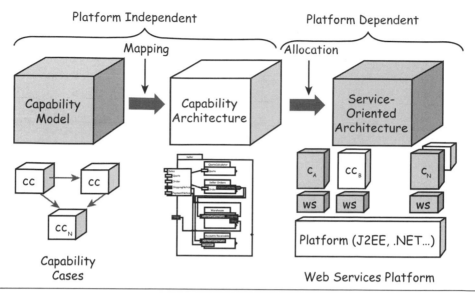

FIGURE 7.5.   MAPPING A CAPABILITY ARCHITECTURE TO WEB SERVICES.

Sidebar 7.3   Characterization of Service Oriented Architecture

"A service-oriented architecture (SOA) defines how two computing entities interact in such a way as to enable one entity to perform a unit of work on behalf of another entity. The unit of work is referred to as a service, and the service interactions are defined using a description language. Each interaction is self-contained and loosely coupled, so that each interaction is independent of any other interaction."

Source: www.whatis.com

...an application architecture in which all functions, or services, are defined using a description language and have invokable interfaces that are called to perform business processes. Each interaction is independent of each and every other interaction and the interconnect protocols of the communicating devices (i.e., the infrastructure components that determine the communication system do not affect the interfaces). Because interfaces are platform-independent, a client from any device using any operating system in any language can use the service.

Though built on similar principles, SOA is not the same as Web services, which indicates a collection of technologies, such as SOAP and XML. SOA is more than a set of technologies and runs independent of any specific technologies."

Source: www.webopedia.com

The steps involved in translating the Capability Architecture into an SOA implementation using an Enterprise Service Bus (ESB) approach, are as follows:

1. Agree on technology standards
2. Identify services categories
3. Specify the Web Services Architecture
4. Map capabilities to service categories and Web services
5. Identify existing systems that provide useful functions and information
6. Allocate service elements to each capability
7. Architect orchestration and process patterns
8. Identify policies governing the access to and use of services and components
9. Define performance and monitoring criteria and standards
10. Define SOA specifications for external procurement of services

In Solution Capability Design, only initial work on some of these tasks is performed—the detail work is done when the solution implementation project starts. The objective we target here is to have a robust solution design and a realistic implementation plan. Appendix C provides more detail on mapping strategies from Capability Cases to components.

Before specifying any Web Services, it is imperative that a Component Architecture is decided. Without an architecture, services will tend to proliferate and the system will become a "sea of services" that are hard to understand, maintain, and evolve. With or without a commitment to MDA, the Component Collaboration Architecture (CCA) of EDOC is a good approach, but any Component-based Development method and architecture is better than none.

An example of a Web Services Infrastructure Architecture is illustrated in Figure 7.6.

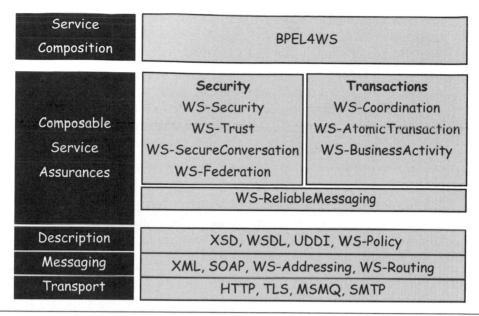

FIGURE 7.6.   THE WEB SERVICES ARCHITECTURE STACK.

At the time of this writing, there is no uniformly agreed upon framework for application-level layers. One example is IBM's *On-Demand Operating Environment Architecture*[12] framework. Its service categories include:

- User Interaction Services
- Information Services
- Business Process Services
- Infrastructure Services
- Different Business Function Services (or Application Services)
- Common Services, such as Community Integration Services

The Federal Enterprise Architecture (FEA)[13] offers another framework for categorization of services in the FEA Services Reference Model (SRM) shown in Figure 7.7. The FEA SRM is one of five models that make up the FEA Reference Model. The other models are a Business Reference Model (BRM) that defines business

---

[12] From Mark Palmer's presentation, *Is SOA Ready for Prime Time?*, at the 2004 Annual Convention of the Chinese Institute of Engineers Dallas-Fort Worth Chapter—www.cie-dfw.org/Is_SOA_Ready_aug2004.ppt.

[13] http://www.feapmo.gov/.

activities; a Performance Reference Model (PRM) that defines measurement areas, categories, and indicators; a Technology Reference Model (TRM) that provides a categorization of technologies; and a Data Reference Model (DRM) intended for harmonization of data element, data types, and information exchange.

Enterprise Architectures, such as FEA, are motivated by the same interests as our work on Solution Envisioning with Capability Cases to provide the semantics for making connections between business needs and technical capabilities.

The categories are useful for organizing the capabilities into architectural layers, and we recommend adopting one of the available frameworks customizing it as necessary.

Capability Architecture in the form of Capability Cases will already have accomplished a first-cut of the componentization of the system. What is needed next is an analysis of interactions across capabilities according to the key use scenarios of the system.

Customer Services

Customer Preferences   Customer Initiated Assistance
Cusromer Relationship Management (CRM)

Process Automation Services

Tracking and Workflow   Routing and Automation

Business Management Services

Management of Process   Supply Chain Management
Organizational Management   Investment Management

Digital Asset Services

Content Management   Document Management
Knowledge Management   Records Management

Business Analytical Services

Analysis and Statistics   Visualization
Business Intelligence   Reporting

Back Office Services

Data Management   Assets/Materials Management
Human Resources   Development and Integration
Financial Management   Human Capital/Workforce Mangement

Support Services

Security Management   Communication
Systems Management   Collaboration
Forms   Search

FIGURE 7.7.   FEA Services Reference Model.

An important step in establishing component architecture is partitioning the capabilities according to the following six principles:

- **Commonality and Variability**—Combining functions that have cohesion around common data and behavior into components, while at the same time making provision for specialization.
- **Interface Consistency**—Standardize interfaces across components.
- **Component Interchange and Plugability**—Exchangeable parts (see #2)
- **Small is Beautiful**—Keep components as small as possible and no smaller.
- **Many Clients, Few Dependents**—Reduce the dependency of one component on others and design components that are useful to many others.
- **Everything is Needed, Nothing is Redundant**—The parsimony principle.

Capabilities (and Capability Cases) exist for different layers of the Web Services architecture. In many cases, Capability Cases will map directly to Web Services. Table 7.3 provides an example from a B2B Project. In this example, we are using IBM's On-Demand framework for architectural layers.

TABLE 7.3.   CAPABILITIES TO WEB SERVICES MAPPING

Capability Case	Architecture Layer	Web Service	Responsibilities (Functions)
Order Status Tracker Intent: Provide a reliable single point for tracking the progress of a purchase order.	Business Function Services	Order Status Tracker Service	Receive Order Status Request Obtain Order Status (warehouse, shipment, courier) Notify Status
Payment Approver Intent: Provide a trusted single point of clearance for all payment processing.	Utility Business Services	Payment Approver Service	Receive Payment Information Check Payment Authorization Make Payment Notify Payment Status Issue Receipt
Bill Presentment Intent: Enable bills to be consolidated and paid from one place according to customer preferences: email, mail, fax, or EDI.	Utility Business Services	Bill Presentment Service	Receive Payer Billing Preferences Receive Payee Bill Instructions Consolidate Bills Present Bills to Payer Accept Payments Notify Payee

TABLE 7.3.   Capabilities to Web Services Mapping—continued

Capability Case	Architecture Layer	Web Service	Responsibilities (Functions)
Concept-Based Search Intent: Provide precise and concept-aware search capabilities specific to an area of interest using knowledge representations across multiple knowledge sources both structured and unstructured.	Information Management Services	Search Service	Know knowledge sources Relate knowledge to an ontology Extract concepts from query Query knowledge sources Collate relevant knowledge Provide search results

SOA solutions must ensure high-performance, reliable, extensible, scalable, and open standards-based communication and integration for service provisioning and use. To satisfy these goals, enterprises should ensure their Web services have guarantees of service quality. This entails performing active performance management and continuously monitoring the end-point integrity of Web services. Overheads of using the Web Services standards must be carefully considered as well as latency and dependence onthe Service Level Agreements (SLAs) of external Web Services providers.

The work of this phase is to identify criteria and standards for assuring service-level characteristics. Testing is a key consideration and thought is given to such concerns as availability, performance (both throughput and latency), load testing, reliability, scalability, fault tolerance (fail-over for high availability), and transaction integrity.

In the world of Web Services, there is a strong commitment to the idea of an open market of Web Services provisioning. For an enterprise, this brings a critical need to specify expectations of Service Level Agreements from service providers. The work of this task is not to define detailed specifications but to set out the principles and approach that will be used in the detailed design work.

Some examples of available Web Services are given in Table 7.4.

TABLE 7.4.   EXAMPLES OF PUBLISHED WEB SERVICES

Service Category	Provider	Web Services	Remarks
e-Commerce Services	Amazon www.amazon.com	Amazon Simple Query Service Amazon e-Commerce Service	Amazon Web Services (AWS) provides software developers with direct access to Amazon's technology platform and product data.
Information Services	Alexa www.alexa.com	Alexa Web Information Service (AWIS)	The Alexa Web Information Service (AWIS) provides developers with programmatic access to the information Alexa Internet (www.alexa.com) collects from its Web Crawl, which, at the end of 2004, encompassed more than 100 terabytes of data from over 4 billion Web pages. Developers and website owners can use AWIS as a platform for finding answers to problems on the Web and incorporate them into their Web applications.
Business Utility Services	Concord www.concordefs-net.com	EFSnet Web Payment Services	Payment services include credit-card processing and debit: PIN services, gift cards, EBT, and other types of purchase cards.
Information Services	Salesforce.com www.sforce.com	Sforce Web Services	Sforce defines core application services such as authentication, data management, document management, and text search.

In closing, the description of this activity, it is important to note some challenges in fulfilling the promise of Web services that are currently being addressed by utilizing semantic Web technology[14] to support discovery, composition, and the orchestration of Web services (see Sidebar 7.4).

---

[14] See http://www.w3.org/2002/ws/swsig/ for W3C Semantic Web Services Interest Group, and http://www.xml.com/pub/a/2000/11/01/semanticweb/ for a Semantic Web primer.

Workproduct F   Capability Architecture (SOA Projects)

Capability Architecture identifies the high-level components of the system and the relationships among them. It includes a diagram that shows interactions between components including high-level descriptions of the interfaces. It can also include an identification-level use case model.

Specialization for SOA

The Capability Architecture in an SOA project is a model that maps capabilities to Web Services and defines how the services will be orchestrated by an SOA platform.

Sidebar 7.4   Semantic Web Services

Semantic Web Services promise a new level of functionality of executable services over the Internet. The current technology of Web Services around UDDI, WSDL, and SOAP provides only limited support in facilitating service recognition and comparison, service configuration, and service composition. As a result, it is hard to realize complex workflows and business logics with current Web Services.

In a business environment, the promise of flexible and autonomous Web services is automatic cooperation between enterprise services. An enterprise requiring a business interaction with another enterprise should be able to automatically discover and select the appropriate optimal Web Services relying on selection policies. Services are invoked automatically and payment processes initiated. Mediation is based on data, process, and policy ontologies, with semantic interoperation providing the run-time orchestration. An example would be supply chain management where an enterprise manufacturing limited lifetime goods must frequently seek suppliers as well as buyers dynamically. Instead of employees constantly searching for suppliers and buyers, the Web service infrastructure does it automatically within defined constraints.

Web Services on their own lack the expressive constructs needed for the automatic discovery and composition of services. Current technology around UDDI, WSDL, and SOAP provides only limited support in mechanizing service recognition, service configuration and combination, service comparison, and automated negotiation.

Dynamic service composition and interoperability requires a precise profile of the service, its process model, and how it is to be invoked. These needs are addressed by the Semantic Web Services work that led to the standard OWL-S.[15] Locating services is fundamentally a problem of semantics—matching the meaning of requests with the meaning associated with a service in its intent, behavior, and results. In OWL-S, the description of a Web service is organized into three specifications: what a service does (the service profile), how the service works (the process model), and how the service is implemented (the grounding).

---

[15] For more information, see www.daml.org/services/owl-s/1.0/owl-s.html.

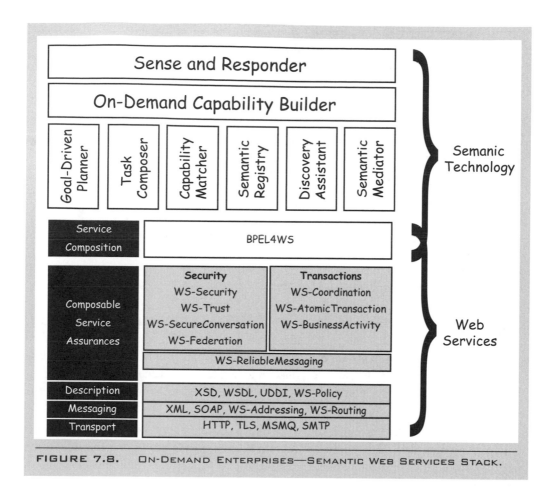

FIGURE 7.8.   ON-DEMAND ENTERPRISES—SEMANTIC WEB SERVICES STACK.

Activity 6   Evaluate Capability Architecture

SCD-6
Evaluate Capability
Architecture

The Capability Architecture is evaluated to assess how well the Architecture meets the goals of the stakeholders in delivering functionality and satisfying desired quality goals and measures.

Solution Envisioning is a capability-based method that uses the business forces, challenges, and results of the business situation to identify and validate capabilities. This provides a strong assurance of the needed functionality. To validate this functionality, we use an approach based on Architecture Trade-Off Analysis

Method (ATAM), developed by the Software Engineering Institute at Carnegie Mellon University (see Sidebar 7.5).

Because the work of SCD is still early in the solution implementation cycle, an ATAM-like approach can only be used in *discovery mode* to confirm and validate the architectural decisions made so far and to identify additional architectural decisions. At this point in the solution envisioning process, some of the ATAM steps have already been accomplished:

- The business context and drivers are already identified (from BCE)
- Scenarios (of use) have been developed
- Quality attributes have been identified

The additional work of this activity involves identifying and selecting additional scenarios and analyzing different architectural approaches.

Identifying Additional Scenarios

This task focuses on growth and exploration scenarios, but it is likely that additional use scenarios will also be identified. Growth scenarios represent anticipated changes to the system—for example, double the number of records in the database while maintaining the same response time. Exploratory scenarios represent unanticipated changes the system has not been designed to handle. They expose the limits of the current design.

Growth and exploratory scenarios are akin to Doug Bennett's Change Cases, which can be used to specify how the architecture has made provisions for anticipated new requirements for a system or modifications to existing requirements [Bennett, 1997].

The scenarios are associated to the quality attributes they could impact. For example, the database growth scenario can be connected to performance (transaction speed), but also recoverability. This can be done by adding a scenario description to the appropriate row of the *Non-Functional Requirements* produced in Activity 4. If it is necessary to explore more than a handful of scenarios, we suggest creating a list of scenarios and cross-indexing them.

A more sophisticated representation of scenario-attribute connection is achieved using a *utility tree*. To create a utility tree, follow these steps:

1. Start the tree with *utility* as its root.

2. Form the second level of the tree by using the categories of non-functional requirements, such as performance, security, and availability, shown in bold in Table 7.1.

3. Form the third level of the tree by using the individual non-functional requirements (quality attributes).

4. Attach scenarios as the fourth and final level as shown in Figure 7.9. It is best to have at least a couple of scenarios for each attribute. However, not having scenarios for one of the attributes may be fine. It usually means that the attribute is not very important.

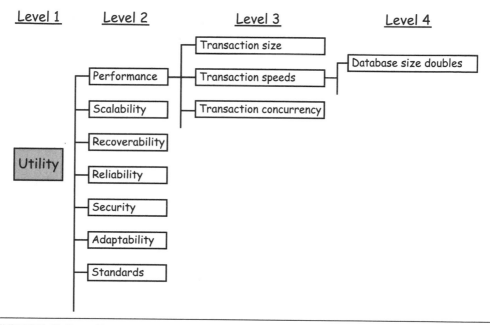

FIGURE 7.9.   PARTIALLY POPULATED UTILITY TREE.

Selecting Scenarios for Evaluation

Prioritization happens across all scenarios positioned in the utility tree—use, growth, and exploration. Each scenario is ranked (high, medium, low) according to two criteria: its importance to the success of the system and its technical difficulty. Consequently, each scenario has two ratings, for example (H, M)—*high* importance to success, *medium* technical difficulty.

ATAM suggests two iterations—first, analysis for all scenarios, followed by analysis of the highest ranking scenarios. Because Solution Envisioning is a rapid method, we typically perform a single iteration of analysis—only on the high-ranking scenarios. These are scenarios ranking high in at least one criterion: importance or technical difficulty. If a project team finds itself ranking every scenario high, we recommend using the Analytical Hierarchical Process Technique (T3) (pair-wise comparison) described in Appendix B, "Additional Techniques."

Optionally, a full ATAM can be undertaken. We recommend doing this for all life-critical systems and for some mission-critical systems (where architectural decisions workproduct indicates that a lot of technical uncertainties and issues are present). At this stage of Solution Envisioning, many architectural decisions still remain to be done. One exception is package-based development. When a decision is made to purchase a package, its functionality comes together with an entire architectural framework. For that reason, we suggest a more robust evaluation approach for package implementation projects as described in Appendix C.

Sidebar 7.5   Technique (T4): Architecture Trade-Off Analysis Method (ATAM)

Problem Context	Evaluating how well an architecture satisfies quality goals and understanding how the goals interact (trade off) with each other. ATAM is recommended for projects greater than four person-years.
Approach and Guidance	Detailed description of ATAM is provided in [Clements 2002b]. ATAM has nine main steps:

Presentation

1. Present the evaluation method.

2. Present the business drivers.

3. Present the architecture, focusing on how it addresses business drivers.

Investigation and Analysis

4. Identify the architectural approaches.

5. Generate quality attributes down to the level of scenarios.

6. Analyze the architectural approaches.

Testing

7. Prioritize scenarios using a voting process involving all stakeholders.

8. Analyze the architectural approaches—re-iterate Step 6, but using the highly ranked scenarios from Step 7.

Reporting

9. Present the results—present findings to assembled stakeholders.

Architectural approaches are evaluated from the following perspectives:

- **Risks**—Potentially problematic architectural decisions.
- **Non-risks**—These are good decisions that rely on assumptions that are frequently implicit in the architecture.
- **Sensitivity**—A sensitivity point is a property of one or more components (or component relationships) that is critical for achieving a particular quality attribute response.
- **Trade-offs**—A trade-off point is a property that affects more than one attribute and is a sensitivity point for more than one attribute.

The documenting of risks and non-risks consists of:

- An architectural decision (or a decision that has not been made)
- A specific quality attribute response that is being addressed by that decision along with the consequences of the predicted level of the response
- A rationale for the positive or negative effect that decision has on meeting the quality attribute requirement

Analyze Architectural Approaches

This step identifies architectural decisions that can ensure the scenario will not impact quality attributes of the system. Some architectural decisions have already been identified in Activity 3. Expect that additional decisions will be identified during this activity. Some previously made decisions may be reversed or questioned.

Prioritization of scenarios and identification and analysis of alternative approaches are best performed in the workshop mode. This ensures that different stakeholders can contribute and participate in the evaluation process. We recommend running the architecture evaluation workshop in two sessions. For example:

- First session is used to prioritize scenarios (2 to 3 hours)
- Second session is used to analyze architectural decisions (3 to 4 hours)

Often the process results in identifying viable alternatives that will be decided on later in the implementation process. Another outcome is identifying the types of decisions that will need to be made in the future.

Workproduct D   IT Impact and Interface Specifications (revisions)

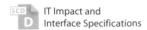 IT Impact and Interface Specifications   Update may be needed to reflect additional architectural decisions and risks identified during the evaluation activity.

Workproduct E   Architectural Decisions (revisions)

 Architectural Decisions   Results of the Capability Architecture evaluation are added to the Architectural Decisions document as follows:

- Additional architectural decisions identified during the workshop are added to the list of architectural decisions.
- Lists of analyzed (or deferred because of low priority) scenarios is included in an additional section, as well as the architectural alternatives that will be decided on during the later phase.

Workproduct F   Capability Architecture (revisions)

 Capability Architecture   The Capability Architecture is updated to reflect any additional architectural decisions and risks identified during the evaluation activity.

SCD ACTIVITIES III—DEVELOP BUSINESS CASE AND SOLUTION ROADMAP

This cluster of activities includes (numbered as shown in Figure 7.2):

7. Develop Business Case
8. Develop Solution Realization and Adoption Kit

Activity 7   Develop Business Case

Identify resources needed to implement the solution. Develop financial and return on investment (ROI) numbers. Analyze risks and identify risk mitigation activities.

This activity uses several workproducts from the previous phases, including:

- Business Capability Model (Workproduct F) and Measures of Effectiveness (Workproduct L) developed during the BCE phase
- Risk Assessment Model (Workproduct J) developed in the SCE phase

Much of the information that is typically in the Business Case has already been produced during the previous activities, including answers to the following questions:

- What is the opportunity/problem you are trying to solve?
- What is the desired result you are looking for?
- What is the nature of the improvement?
- What are the direct quantifiable benefits, such as spending reductions, revenue improvements, or profit improvements?
- What are the indirect benefits and leading indicators, such as customer satisfaction and cycle time improvements that will result in the direct benefits?
- What are the concerns or risks and how will they be addressed?

What remains to be determined is the amount of investment necessary to accomplish the desired result as well as the new operational costs. These amounts, together with the expected direct benefits, will serve as the basis of the cost-benefit calculation. The following steps should be taken:

Establish Baseline Operational Costs

Costs may be derived from the number of people currently assigned to the process. Dollars paid to any outside vendors should also be included. These costs should then be adjusted by factoring in inflation and other expected increases or decreases to determine the baseline view cost that will be used for comparison with the costs of the new system.

Establish Baseline Benefits

These are the ongoing benefits that the business receives from the current system. Calculate baseline values for the measurement indicators you will be using to measure performance of the new solution. Adjust the values because it is safe to assume that no system will stay static. Often, companies expect to continue receiving the same stream of revenue even without making any investments. Rarely does this happen. Make some reasonable assumptions as to what would happen to revenues if nothing is done. Document these in the business case and use them to make adjustments to the baseline measures. Finally, connect measurement indicators to the direct quantifiable "bottom-line" benefits such as costs, profits, or revenue. For example, the bottom-line connection can be made in the following ways:

- If you are using customer profitability as a measurement and are proposing to increase it, you may want to use the formula that calculates profits of the unit as the average profit-per-customer times the number of customers.
- If you are using self-service index as a measurement, you need to find a formula that connects the cost of operating a help desk to the self-service index.

Make sure to document your assumptions on how measurements that are expected to be impacted by the solution relate to the bottom line.

Estimate Expected Benefits

These should be estimated based on the expected value of the measurements after the solution is deployed. Calculate future benefits using formulas utilized for the baseline benefits.

It is useful (and prudent) to perform analysis for a range of possible outcomes, for instance, by using best-case, worst-case, and expected-case figures.

Estimate One-Time Project Costs

These reflect the total cost of implementing the solution. They are often broken down by phases and cost categories (such as labor, hardware, software, and so forth).

If this project is a re-attempt or replacement for another initiative that did not complete successfully, "sunk" costs (previously incurred expenses) should not be included in the calculations. However, the actual salvage value of equipment that may be retired and sold can be used to offset project costs.

Estimate Expected Operational Costs

Estimating operational costs requires answering the question: "How much will it cost to operate the process in the future?" If your business case is built entirely on cost savings, this step can be skipped because it is already covered in the step that estimates expected benefits.

Perform Cost-Benefit Analysis

A number of indicators can be used. Specific indicators are often mandated by the company policy. The *Cost-Benefit Analysis* technique (see Sidebar 7.6) describes some of them including *Net Present Value*, the most commonly used indicator.

This section would not be complete without mentioning Real Options Analysis as an approach for evaluation of technology investments. In an increasingly complex and uncertain world, conventional valuation approaches described in the Cost-Benefit Analysis technique may not adequately reflect the sophisticated decisions many businesses have to make when they are considering whether or not to add new and innovative capabilities.

Real options analysis applies the cutting-edge tools of financial options theory to the assessment of business decisions. The mechanics of real options analysis is explained in the book *Real Options: Managing Strategic Investment in an Uncertain World.*[16] Five types of decision situations are listed where options theory is appropriate, and conventional NPV analysis can give misleading results.

These include the following:

1. Wait-to-invest options
2. Growth options
3. Flexibility options
4. Exit options
5. Learning options

In certain capital-intensive industries, operating under great uncertainty, such as mining, petroleum, and space flight operations, real options are frequently used. In other industries, this technique is less commonly known and used.

---

[16] Martha Amram and Nalin Kalatilaka. *Real Options: Managing Strategic Investment in an Uncertain World* [Amram, 1999].

Sidebar 7.6   Technique (T5): Cost-Benefit Analysis

 Cost Benefit Analysis

Definitions

The following financial indicators can be used to analyze costs and benefits of IT investment:

Return on Investment (ROI) is a simple formula originally developed in 1913 by an engineer in DuPont's treasury department. It is calculated by dividing the return, or incremental gains that will be received from an investment, by the costs that were required to achieve that gain.

Net Present Value (NPV) is a difference between expected returns and investment calculated taking into account cost of capital. It is determined by multiplying a stream of net future cash flows by a discount rate representing external cost of capital then subtracting the initial investment in the project. NPV is one of the most frequently used analytical tools to value a project.

Payback Period is the number of years it takes to recover the initial investment in the solution.

Internal Rate of Return (IRR) is the return earned on a given investment. It is the rate that makes net present value of all cash flows equal to zero. Technically, IRR is a discount rate: the rate at which the present value of a series of investments is equal to the present value of the returns on those investments. Investments (or cash outflows) could be quarterly (monthly, yearly) spending on the solution implementation; returns (inflows) could be quarterly benefits from the solution. The internal rate of return assumes cash inflows are reinvested at the internal rate.

Sometimes, one or two of these indicators are used, but often business cases contain all four.

Approach and

ROI can be expressed as a ratio or as a percentage where the benefit-to-cost ratio is multiplied by 100. Example: a 3.5, or 3.5:1, or 350% ROI are numerically equivalent.

Guidance

Microsoft Excel has an NPV formula that returns the net present value of an investment based on a series of periodic cash flows and a discount rate. The discount rate used in calculating NPV should be the external cost of capital obtained from the office of the CFO. This is the rate that a company will pay if they raise money through the capital markets.

To clarify the concept of a present value: it is what the currency value of capital, received at a future date, is equivalent to in today's dollars. Present value is based on the "time value of money" concept, which states that $1 today is worth more than $1 in the future. For example, the present value of $11,000 to be received one year from now is equal to $10,000, assuming a discount rate of 10%.

A shorter payback period usually means a higher rate of return. Decreasing the payback period also means decreased risk and higher liquidity. Payback is calculated by allocating the cost against the stream of benefits and determining the time frame in which the number reaches zero. A more sophisticated approach to calculating payback is to take into account the "time value of money" concept.

Businesses expect the IRR to be equal to or exceed the "required" rate of return. The required rate is typically a company's cost of capital. Microsoft Excel has an IRR formula that gives the internal rate of return for a series of cash flows.

Cost-benefit analysis usually include several calculations taking into account different scenarios and also comparing the calculations on the pre-tax/post-tax basis.

Example

The example below shows the business investing $500,000 in a solution over the course of two years. These are cash outflows shown as negative numbers. Investments are frontloaded, meaning that moneys were invested in the beginning of each year.

The business receives back one and a quarter million dollars spread across three years, as shown in the table. Return has been calculated prior to entering it into the table as a difference between *Expected Benefits* and *Baseline Benefits* for each year. Calculations assume that return is received at the end of each year. As you can see, the Net Present Value of this investment is $383,689.64.

	A	B	C	D
1	10% Annual Discount Rate			
2				
3				
4		Year 1	Year 2	Year 3
5	Investment	-$400,000	-$100,000	
6	Return	$50,000	$200,000	$1,000,000
7				
8	Net present value of the investment	$383,689.64		

To experiment with the numbers, you can enter this example into an Excel spreadsheet. Be sure to replace the number in cell A8 with the following formula: = *NPV(A1,C5, B6,C6,D6) +B5*.

Why did we place the first-year investment outside of the NPV formula? The NPV calculation is based on future cash flows. If the first cash flow occurs at the beginning of the first period, there is no point in applying the discount rate to it. This number, therefore, must be added to the NPV result, not included in the values arguments.

Because cash inflows and outflows are estimates and we are assuming the cost of money will not change, it is important to explore several scenarios when doing cost-benefit analysis. For example:

- If the discount rate was 8%, the NPV would go up to $444K.
- If the project costs exceeded estimates by 25%, and the expected return fell short by 25%, then the NPV (using a 10% discount rate) would go down dramatically to just under $43K, but it would still remain positive.
- If, in addition, the cost of money went up by 25%, making the discount rate 12.5%, then the NPV would become negative at minus $7.5K.

The questions to consider when exploring different scenarios are:

- What events and circumstances could cause the numbers to change?
- How likely are they to happen?
- What can we do to prevent the events and circumstances that negatively impact the NPV?

Because IRR is the rate at which NPV goes down to 0, then:

- Using our original numbers, IRR is about 29.5%.
- Using a scenario where cost goes up by 25% and returns go down by 25%, IRR is roughly 12 and 1/8 or 12.11%.

Even though this project offers an attractive return, the payback does not occur until Year 3. Today, most companies want shorter payback periods. It is likely the project team will be asked to assess whether the implementation plan can be adjusted to yield earlier returns.

The outcome of this activity, a business case, is a detailed investment proposal. It puts the investment decision into a strategic context, and it positions the business objectives and options that will affect both the decision and the investment itself. It provides the information necessary to make a decision about whether a project should proceed.

Workproduct G   Business Case

 Business Case   A document that substantiates the request for solution funding by establishing the:

- Need for funding
- Benefits to be derived
- Corporation's ability to implement the solutions
- Solution's ability to provide expected benefits and financial return

A business case may also include a spreadsheet with the ROI calculations.

As a document, the business case packages several workproducts produced in the previous activities and also includes results of financial calculations that are the focus of the work in this phase. A business case is usually presented as a PowerPoint Presentation or MS Word document. A spreadsheet with the cost-benefit analysis calculations is often attached.

Table 7.5 provides a Business Case template we have used, depending on the situation, to produce a document in the range of 6.5 to 16.5 pages. The Source heading references workproducts from this and previous activities from which the material can be drawn.

TABLE 7.5.   BUSINESS CASE TEMPLATE

Business Case Section	Description	Size (pages)	Source
Executive Summary	A short summary of the key points made in each of the sections.	.5–1.5	This activity
Approach	Identify the team that produced the business case and give an overview of the activities and the methodology.	.5–1	This activity
The Needs and the Benefits (this section may also be called Project Rationale or Value Proposition)	Explain why the company would want to undertake this project. Frame the need for the solution and relate it to corporate or business unit priorities and strategies. Describe major decision drivers and how they influence the need for the initiative. Describe the benefits and urgency for the solution.	1–2	■ Solution Vision ■ Business Capability Map ■ Evidence of Business Situation and Possibilities

TABLE 7.5.   Business Case Template—continued

Business Case Section	Description	Size (pages)	Source
Project Description	Include succinct description of the initiative. Describe capabilities of the solution. Explain and identify how the proposed capabilities will meet the needs of the business unit that will derive the benefit.	1–3	▪ Solution Concept ▪ Solution Initiative Statement ▪ Capability Architecture ▪ Technology Decision Model ▪ Vendor Shortlist
Broader Context	Position the initiative in the broader organizational context. Explain how this project addresses larger corporate goals. Connect it to what is being done by the competition or what other departments may be doing. Describe how this project interacts with other corporate initiatives. For example, will it advance the development of a related initiative?	.5–1.5	▪ Business Context Model ▪ IT Impact and Interface Specification
Implementation Plan	Address all key issues surrounding deployment of the solution. Include a synopsis of major events that must occur prior to deployment. Describe: Transition plans and issues. Training and documentation needs. Organizational impacts. Provide description, quantification, and timelines for the major resource requirements of the project.	1–3	▪ Capability Prioritization Matrix ▪ Stakeholder Profile and Participation
Financial Analysis	Provide summaries that include the highlights of the cost-benefit analysis and a description of the factors that influenced the sensitivity analysis. Provide a clearly articulated and identifiable set of assumptions. Refer to attached spreadsheet.	1–3	This activity

TABLE 7.5.   BUSINESS CASE TEMPLATE—CONTINUED

Business Case Section	Description	Size (pages)	Source
Dependencies and Risks	Identify any dependencies on vendors, suppliers, or other departments within the organization. Describe business and technical risks, the impacts they could have, and the plans to mitigate them.	.5–2	▪ Risk Assessment Model ▪ Architectural Decisions ▪ IT Impact and Interface Specification ▪ Stakeholder Profile and Participation
Performance Measurement Plan	Describe how costs and benefits will be measured as the project progresses. Address the exit strategy if an initiative is not yielding expected return on investment.	.5–1	Measures of Effectiveness

Activity 8   Develop Solution Realization and Adoption Plan

SCD-8
Develop Solution
Realization & Adoption Plan

Develop a roadmap for implementing the solution. Identify major milestones. Address organizational impacts, communication, and training needs, as well as transition plans.

A solution moves from a conceptual form through a design form to a solution implementation—executable code. Still, we are not done until the solution is adopted and operational. The Solution Realization Roadmap is more than a project plan. It must also include enough details on the architecture, the goals for incremental releases,[17] and a presentation of the Solution Concept and Business Case. The Solution Concept presentation need only summarize the business case. It is usually sufficient to have just a high-level project plan to describe the implementation steps.

A solution is more than executable code. The adoption of the solution by the enterprise and its associated parties will need a strategy and plan. The Adoption Plan defines migration plans and the incremental rollout of the solution to different constituencies. Migration plans are concerned with data integrity and migration issues and the strategies for cut-over to the new solution. The incremental rollout of the solution defines the training and support needed for each constituency of users. Communication and education plans will be needed for orientations. For

---

[17] In recognizing the nature of incremental development and the insights that occur, details of the first increment and outlines of subsequent releases only are all that are needed.

operational needs, help desk and web-based e-Support capabilities will need to be considered. A Solution needs continued commitment from stakeholders. The *Stakeholder Collaboration Model* sets out expectations of key stakeholders for the solution realization.

The workproducts of this activity provide a strong orientation to any new people that will form the realization team. This is especially important in outsourced development.

Workproduct H   Stakeholder Collaboration Model

Stakeholder
Collaboration Model

A document, often a table, identifying specific input, resources, and other contributions expected from the various solution stakeholders. It builds on the Stakeholder Profile and Participation Matrix developed in BCE.

Workproduct I   Solution Realization Roadmap

Solution Business Case
& Realization Roadmap   A package of deliverables that typically includes:

- Solution Architecture (Vendor Short List, Architectural Decisions, IT Impact and Interface Specification, and Non-Functional Requirements)
- Solution Concept in presentation format with outlined Business Case
- Adoption Plans with training and support needs and migration strategy
- Solution Roadmap with outline plan (for example, a high-level MS Project plan)

THE RESULTS OF SOFTWARE CAPABILITY DESIGN

In the design of software solutions, three aspects of evaluation happen: solution desirability, feasibility, and adequacy. Each can be associated with the deliverables of this phase.

The expression of "desirability" is accomplished by the envisioning of the conceptual nature of the solution. Initially, this takes the form of the *Capability Model*. In this phase, this is elaborated into a *Capability Architecture*. It is the basis of the technical architecture—the blueprint that will give strong guidance to the developers for the realization of the solution.

Feasibility is addressed by looking at the solution from two points of view: the qualities the solution must possess and the organization's ability to build and adopt it. Technical feasibility is determined by non-functional requirements and technical risks. Organizational feasibility is determined by available skills and willingness to commit to financial risks. These plans take into account the prioritization of capabilities. Feasibility is expressed as the "Solution Realization Plan" and "Solution Adoption Plan."

Adequacy is determined by stakeholder decision making with trade-offs for comparing and choosing among solution options. Quantitative decision support techniques and a shared experience of consensus and commitment building are essential to arriving at a sustainable outcome.

Each aspect of evaluation completes an important part of the solution blueprint: "What the Solution is—the Capability Architecture," "How the solution will be realized—the Plans," and "How the decisions were made," as evidenced in the *Architectural Decisions and Stakeholder Collaboration Models*. Collectively, these results provide a firm foundation for solution realization, and metaphorically, they comprise the "solution charrette" of Software Capability Design.

FIGURE 7.10.   SOLUTION CHARRETTE—AN "ARCHITECTURE METAPHOR."[18]

[18] The French word *charrette* means "cart" and is often used to describe the final, intense work effort expended by art and architecture students to meet a project deadline. This use of the term is said to originate from the Ecole des Beaux Arts in Paris during the 19th century, where proctors circulated a cart, or "charrette," to collect final drawings while students frantically put finishing touches on their work" (as described at www.charretteinstitute.org/charrette.html).

MOVING FROM SOLUTION ENVISIONING TO SOLUTION REALIZATION

With the final phase of Solution Envisioning complete, several questions come to mind. What happens with the workproducts created in Solution Envisioning now that we are ready to implement the solution? Having been adequately translated into designs, can they now be entirely left behind with the next stage of the work centered on bringing more detail to the Architecture and decomposing the implementation plan into more granular tasks? To answer these questions, we turn to a story we have recently heard about a small village that lays high in the Savoy Mountains of France.[19]

> *Close to Mount Blanc, the natural beauty of the place has always drawn skiers and other vacationers. The village had many attractive buildings made of native granite and wood, but until about a hundred years ago, there were no hotels. This is when two local brothers—Alphonse and Antoine—each decided to open an inn. Today, these two very different inns face each other on the bustling main street of the village.*
>
> *Alphonse was always in love with this corner of France. He never found it necessary to leave his home village. Alphonse's inn is built in the traditional style with hand-carved furniture and rustic wood. The younger brother, Antoine, wanted to see the world. He left the village when he was a young lad and returned to build his inn many years later. It is called Hameau du Glacier and has clean, elegant lines, large windows, and a surprisingly contemporary look influenced by Scandinavian Architecture.*

The story just related is a recounting of the make-believe story used by the developers of Le Village resort. Although the inns are open, the rest of the village is still being constructed, and Alphonse and Antoine exist only in the imagination of the people who designed and are building this resort. The elaborate story was created to ensure that every corner of the village has an authentic feel. It has been used as a guide for creating blueprints and building plans. Now that the village (*Le Village*, in French) is in progress, the story is continually consulted by architects, interior designers, and the staff who will operate the inns and other businesses in the village.

We find the creative process of realizing Le Village is analogous in a central way to using Solution Envisioning with Capability Cases. Solution Envisioning makes it possible to create and tell a story that captures the essence of the business

---

[19] This is our retelling of a story as it was related in the December 2004 issue of *Travel + Leisure* magazine: http://www.travelandleisure.com/invoke.cfm?objectid=B4C29B2C-8A25-4ABA-AE3D0E4F3BBCD0F8.

solution. As the story evolves, it gets translated into design concepts and, eventually, blueprints such as the Capability Architecture. When the implementation project starts, the Capability Architecture is used to create more detailed designs and, ultimately, the infrastructure and implementation code that realizes the solution.

Yet, no matter how good the detailed design artifacts are, they will never be complete in conveying the essence of the solution. Many decisions have to be made along the way to implementation. People making these decisions need to be guided by the spirit of the solution. This is why builders of Le Village consult the story of Alphonse and Antoine even though they have detailed building plans. And this is why the Solution Concept created during Solution Envisioning must live on—to guide continued development, alongside other artifacts, such as a Use Case Models, Object Models, and Component Architectures.

TRAIL MARKER VII: BUSINESS CASE AND ROADMAP FOR IMPLEMENTATION

Chapter 7 is the third and final part of a practitioner's handbook for practicing Solution Envisioning. It covered Phase III—Software Capability Design. A step-by-step guide was outlined for establishing a Capability Architecture and Technology Strategy for an implementation, as well as a Business Case and Solution Realization Roadmap.

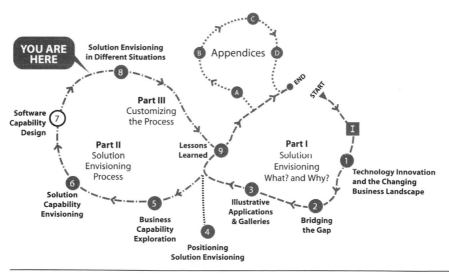

FIGURE 7.11.

The key concerns of Phase III have been:

- The importance of decision-making techniques for making informed technical choices
- Full consideration of the choices in development strategy and the impacts on implementation
- How the results of this and previous phases can be translated into workproducts that are useful to the implementation team
- Developing a business case with cost-benefit analysis
- The importance of Solution Adoption strategy and planning as key to assuring a successful project

Chapter 8, "Solution Envisioning in Different Situations," will show some examples of how Solution Envisioning can be customized to specific situations.

PART III

CUSTOMIZING AND USING SOLUTION ENVISIONING

CONTENT

PURPOSE

To provide additional guidance for planning the set-up, tailoring, customizing, and implementation of the Solution Envisioning process in a specific organizational setting.

KEY QUESTIONS ADDRESSED

How do we set up, tailor, and implement solution envisioning as a practice? How do you apply it in different situations? How do you introduce and communicate about it within an organization to convey its value?

ORIENTATION

The Solution Envisioning approach is flexible and has been adapted to the specific constraints of different business situations and their problems.

Though the most benefit will usually be gained where it is possible to go through the whole process—often in a tailored, somewhat condensed form—constraints sometimes require using Solution Envisioning in shorter sessions. Parts of the process can be used effectively and independently, for example, as mini-envisioning exercises or engagements or within envisioning workshop intensives.

The chapters in Part III, read in conjunction with either Part I, Part II, or both, show how the Solution Envisioning approach can be adapted to specific business situations. Examples and case studies demonstrate that it is especially useful where tough challenges demand breakthrough solutions and return on investment, but that it is also effective for problems needing incremental improvement.

The final chapter, Conclusion, closes this book with reflections on what works and does not work in practicing Solution Envisioning and the particular *mind-set* it requires. We present some insights and plans for continuing to evolve the approach and discuss how aspects of Solution Envisioning relate to key obstacles in the design process. For those interested in experimenting with envisioning and Capability Cases, we suggest some practical steps to get started. We announce our website, which will be available as a community sandbox and repository for Capability Cases. The website will also provide companion materials (for example, templates) for the Solution Envisioning process and updates related to this book.

PRIMARY AUDIENCE

Change agents, champions, and other personnel charged with implementing best practices in the business or organization and developing and deploying new solutions to address today's challenges.

8

SOLUTION ENVISIONING IN DIFFERENT SITUATIONS

"Agility is the ability to both create and respond to change in order to profit in a turbulent business environment."

—*Jim Highsmith*

FIGURE 8.1.

CHAPTER PREVIEW

When technologies must be considered for addressing business needs, an opportune context is presented for using Solution Envisioning with Capability Cases. Different types of business situations arise where there is a need to bring business stakeholders and technology providers into effective communication. In Chapter 1, "Technology Innovation and the Changing Business Landscape," we introduced nine situations where use of Solution Envisioning with Capability Cases has proven to be of value. In Figure 8.2, these situations are positioned according to organizational focus area and the place in the business solution lifecycle where they become especially relevant.

Other important factors that require different application of Solution Envisioning are the size of the project and the phasing approach an organization takes in conducting the envisioning work. For these reasons, tailoring Solution Envisioning becomes important.

Four representative projects are described in this chapter. They cover different applications of the process and range in duration from less than two weeks to over two months. The chapter addresses tailoring considerations related to the project type as well as to the need to work alongside technology or development strategy choices, such as Model Driven Architecture, Quality Function Deployment, and Rapid Prototyping.[1]

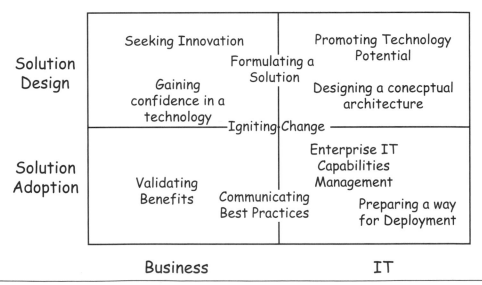

FIGURE 8.2.   TEN SITUATIONS WHERE CAPABILITY CASES HAVE PROVEN TO BE OF VALUE.

---

[1]   For a more thorough treatment of how the Software Capability Design phase of Solution Envisioning is tailored to connect with specific development approaches, please consult Chapter 7 and Appendix C.

Solution Envisioning as a Customizable Framework

How can the process support a variety of situations and contexts? In practice, we use the process and methods of Solution Envisioning with Capability Cases (as presented in Chapters 5–7) as a flexible framework. The work of envisioning should not be viewed as a fixed sequence of steps. It is better when understood and conducted in a goal-driven manner. Outcomes are accomplished by organizing activities and deliverables in ways that are *tuned* to the context and needed pace.

The structure of the framework is decision-centric. Major phases are aligned with three essential outcomes that need to connect in an actionable way:

1. An understanding of the business (problem) situation for which a solution is sought

2. Creation of the solution concept based on desired business capabilities

3. Development of a blueprint for the realization the solution

The starting place and amount of time and effort a given initiative or project needs to spend in each phase varies according to its individual circumstances and context. Progress through the phases is not strictly sequential, but iterative and opportunistic. The overall flow is governed only by what is not known, what needs to be known at a given time, and dependencies. Specific methods and their accompanying techniques are selected for use and tailored to the situation. Table 8.1 provides matching and tailoring guidance to the Solution Envisioning process for each of the situations identified in Figure 8.2.

TABLE 8.1.   GUIDANCE FOR MATCHING AND TAILORING SOLUTION ENVISIONING TO SITUATIONS OF USE

Situation	Desired Outcome	Role of Capability Cases	Stakeholder Involvement	Process Tailoring Suggestions[2]
Seeking Innovation	Ideas on how new technologies can be used to create specific business value	Presenting innovative ways of using technology in different business domains Triggering creativity	IT and Business Solution Sponsors	BCE key phase SCE typically deferred SCD typically deferred

---

[2] The modes referred to for running the Solution Envisioning Workshop—with an *exploration*, *validation*, or *commitment* focus—are described in the next section "Different Situations—Different Approaches."

TABLE 8.1. Guidance for Matching and Tailoring Solution Envisioning to Situations of Use—CONTINUED

Situation	Desired Outcome	Role of Capability Cases	Stakeholder Involvement	Process Tailoring Suggestions
Formulating a Solution	Specific capabilities that will support well-defined objectives of the business	Translation of business needs into capabilities Ensuring comprehensive coverage of the possible solutions space	IT and Business Solution Sponsors	All three phases are equally important, customization depends on the project size and implementation strategy
Promoting Technology Potential	Technology adoption	Identification of specific business problems that technology can solve	Technology Evangelist or Technology Vendor	BCE—key phase SCE—can be abbreviated, runs in an exploration mode SCD—deferred
Gaining Confidence in a Technology (or Exploring Technology Potential)	Assessment of technology readiness Determination of value Technology Adoption plan	Identifying readiness Developing an initial business case	CTO, Technology Strategist, Senior Architect	BCE—often abbreviated SCE—key phase, usually runs in an exploration mode, often in conjunction with technology training SCD—typically deferred
Designing Conceptual Architectures	A conceptual architecture for the solution that is implementable	Identifying, clustering, and arranging capabilities	Solution Architect	BCE—runs in a validation mode SCE—often abbreviated, runs in validation or commitment modes SCD—key phase
Communicating Best Practices	An organizational memory of reusable solutions	A registry of best practices and available business components	Solution Owner, Enterprise Architect	BCE—runs in a validation mode SCE—key phase SCD—not applicable
Enterprise IT Capability Management	Document existing IT capabilities in the context of their use.	Communication of the intent and status of IT capabilities	Enterprise Architect	All phases run in the validation mode

TABLE 8.1.   GUIDANCE FOR MATCHING AND TAILORING SOLUTION ENVISIONING TO SITUATIONS OF USE—CONTINUED

Situation	Desired Outcome	Role of Capability Cases	Stakeholder Involvement	Process Tailoring Suggestions
Igniting Change	Top Management commitment for change	Inspiration, over-coming compla-cency, instilling confidence	Change Agent—can be from busi-ness or IT; the desired effect is the identification of a "solution champion"	BCE—often abbreviated SCE—key phase, runs in an explo-ration mode SCD—typically differed
Validating Benefits	Confirmed capabili-ties with associated measurements and business case	Translation of busi-ness needs into ca-pabilities Proof of existence and value	Business Solution Sponsors	BCE—runs in vali-dation mode SCE—runs in a validation mode SCD—runs in vali-dation mode
Preparing the Way for Deployment of a Solution	Audience is prepared for the solution	Communication of solution goals and capabilities	Solution Owner	BCE—runs in vali-dation mode SCE—key phase, runs in a commit-ment mode SCD—not applicable

As indicated in the table, not only is the overall process customized, but the way Solution Envisioning workshops are run must be carefully tailored to the situation. The motivation for and approach to customizing workshops is covered in the next section.

FOCUSING THE SOLUTION ENVISIONING WORKSHOP

The Solution Envisioning workshop is often the central focus and watershed event in the process. It also requires the largest commitment of time and resources in the preparation and participation of key stakeholders whose time is at a premium.

Therefore, it demands careful consideration and shaping to maximize benefit for the effort invested.

The design of the workshop depends on the overall intent of the Solution Envisioning work. Three kinds of workshops are distinguished:

1. **Solution Validation**—Group validation of a candidate or decreed solution
2. **Solution Commitment**—Gaining "buy-in" for an already decided solution concept
3. **Solution Exploration**—An inquiry into innovative solutions

For the first two kinds of workshop, the solution is already decided for the most part. In the third type of workshop, the work is highly creative and inclusive of the differing views. In our experience, the project might start as a Validation or Commitment workshop, but on exposure to more stakeholders, it becomes a Solution Exploration workshop. Figure 8.3 shows the comparative position of these three types of workshops within an *Advocacy/Inquiry Map*.

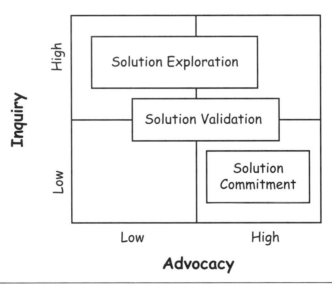

FIGURE 8.3.   Types of Envisioning workshops.

The preferred tools and techniques used for the *Solution Envisioning workshop* depend on the workshop type, length, expected audience, and the complexity of the situation-at-hand.

In Chapter 6, "Solution Capability Envisioning—Phase II of Solution Envisioning," we described the preparation period and the workproducts produced ahead of the Solution Envisioning workshop. This description is more in line with workshops run in the validation or commitment modes. In this chapter, we focus on the typical flow of a two-day Solution Exploration workshop. All the workshops follow the same generic framework, as presented in Table 6.2, but the exploration workshops are different in the following ways:

- Typically, the BCE phase and workshop preparation period are highly abbreviated, often lasting no more than a week and as little as a day.
- Often, there is no Solution Initiative Statement at the start of the workshop—the workshop creates one.
- By its nature, these workshops are more dynamic and fluid.

At minimum, the following is needed to start the workshop:

- **Agenda**—It will need to be carefully reviewed with the workshop sponsor.
- **A set of candidate Capability Cases**—This preliminary set is selected or created based on the understanding of the general problem or a business area that will be explored at the workshop.

The business area being explored guides the selection of Capability Cases. One Solution Exploration workshop we ran focused on better management of information. At another workshop focus was on how to improve operations for a call center at a large financial services company. A third workshop explored capabilities in the supply chain management. When the workshop is conducted to "Gain Confidence in Technology" or "Promote Technology Potential," the technology under consideration provides another viewpoint for selection of the Capability Cases. In these situations, it is common for the candidate Capability Cases to be from a variety of industry and business areas.

It is helpful if some forces, results, and challenges can be identified before the workshop. If not done beforehand, the information will then need to be elicited during the workshop. It is likely that business activity scenarios will not be prepared before the workshop.

If there is no time to do a full stakeholder analysis before the workshop, important stakeholders may not be present. We recommend spending some time with the workshop sponsor to do a brief analysis. One technique useful in this situation is the "Value Net" (see Sidebar 5.2). When the workshop participants come from different parts of the organization, we recommend starting the workshop with this technique. It is equally useful when the workshop leader is not familiar with the roles and responsibilities of everyone in the workshop. Draw the diagram showing how participants and their respective work relates to one another, asking, "Who is whose customer?" and "Who is collaborating with whom?" For attendees, this technique establishes a shared context. For the facilitator, it helps with getting to know the team.

With context scoped, Forces, Challenges, and Results are the next things to uncover. The *Three What's* technique, described in Sidebar 5.3, offers a way to discover this information. It also sets up the stage for using CATWOE (described in Sidebar 5.1). When the workshop starts without a Solution Initiative Statement, CATWOE becomes a key technique. It is expected and encouraged that a number of "Root Definitions" or alternative ideas about future systems will be identified.

If time allows, we have found a role-playing exercise to be useful in conjunction with CATWOE. For each Solution Initiative Statement, we ask participants to play the roles of "Customer," "Agent," and "Owner." It is useful to have people act in the "Environment" and "Worldview" roles. At least one Technology Exponent is needed to pay attention to the relevance of the nominated Capability Cases and look out for new capabilities. As needed, the workshop facilitator(s) may also act as Technology Exponent(s). They will need to say when they are stepping in and out of this role.

Here is how the "play" goes. Each participant with a Root Definition is asked to play the role of "Solution Provider" and to sell the solution to the "Problem Owner"—the Customer. At times, the facilitator should intervene and get reactions from other participants. From time to time, players of main roles are asked by the facilitator to step out of character to express insights they may be getting.

Through this process, the root definition and CATWOE are refined as well as the forces, results, and challenges of the business situation. Technology exponent(s) will at times recognize the value of other Capability Cases. Typically, what results from this exercise is two or three Solution Initiative Statements for further exploration.

After these exercises, in our experience, attendees are very receptive to appreciating solution ideas. A "Gallery Tour" can be conducted at the end of Day 1. Alternatively, it can be left until the morning of Day 2. Other techniques and exercises described in this book that are useful for Day 1 include:

- **Future Retrospective**—Imaging the work done and describing what the future world is like and how the organization got there.

- **Camelot**—Imagine the ideal world, describe how things happen, how future work is done, and how technology is an enabler. This technique is used often in future search conferences.

- **ConceptCafe**—The use of imagery and metaphor to surface assumptions, unexpressed feelings, and to explore possibility.

Experienced facilitators draw on a repertoire of their favorite, reliable techniques to use in response to team dynamics and other situations at hand. A comprehensive website with creativity techniques is hosted by Mycoted Ltd.[3] Some of the techniques we use at Solution Envisioning workshops are described there. It is likely the reader will be able to select and adopt a few additional useful workshop techniques from this site. We also recommend the book by James M. Higgins on creativity techniques [Higgins, 1994].

Whatever techniques are used at the end of Day 1, a minimum requirement is to have one or more root definitions framed as a solution initiative statement. Because there is likely to be a certain amount of work done to prepare for Day 2 of the workshop, we recommend an early finish on Day 1 by running no more than a 6-hour session.

What kind of preparation is needed for Day 2? The information gathered during the Three What's technique is formalized into forces, challenges, and results. These serve to supplement any forces, challenges, and results prepared ahead of the workshop. Capability Cases will need to be reviewed and extended. The gallery of candidate Capability Cases must be prepared before the workshop. After Day 1, you may decide to remove some and add others. There will be little time to create new ones—at best one or two can be created or specialized.

After a brief review of the preparation work, Day 2 often starts with the creation of business activity scenarios. Following that, attendees are asked to select and rank Capability Cases. In the exploration workshops, the ranking techniques are often informal and even playful. For example, attendees may be given red ("I want it"), yellow ("I may want it") and blue ("I don't care for it") stickers and asked to place them on the Capability Cases.

At one workshop, the ranking exercise happened right after the team returned from a joint lunch in a restaurant. The workshop facilitator pretended to be a waiter. He went to each person in the room saying, "I have the following capabilities on the menu, which ones would you like?" Each attendee could pick two. Figure 8.4 shows how the voting went for a subset of Capability Cases.

---

[3]   http://www.mycoted.com/creativity/techniques/index.php.

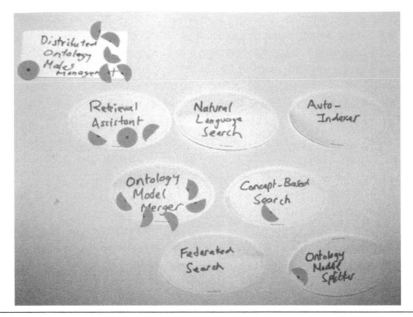

FIGURE 8.4.   Capability Case priorities at the FAO workshop.

Enacting envisioned scenarios is a good exercise to do next. The value and utility of selected Capability Cases is examined in the context of business activity scenarios. To set the stage for the planning session, we find the "Three Es" technique (see Sidebar 6.4) useful.

Each Capability Case is examined from the perspective of where it falls in the spectrum of efficiency, effectiveness, and edge. Participants are asked to identify what organizational support they would need to realize the capabilities—identifying which ones they:

- Could just go ahead with because they already have the mandate and resources
- Would need to go to their immediate boss to authorize
- Would need to get broader organizational support for

The planning session is the next exercise of the workshop. This is followed by agreeing on action items which concludes the workshop. These may include:

- Identifying other stakeholders who need to be informed of the workshop results
- Assessing synergies that have been discovered during the workshop
- Ensuring commitment from management for going forward

Additional techniques we find useful for Day 2 include:

- **Experienced Envisioners Panel**—Ask a subset of the attendees to imagine themselves at a future conference where they are panel members in a discussion about a solution they have implemented. Ask each to prepare a short (no more than 10 minutes) presentation on solution concepts, why they were chosen, and how they built it.
- **Synectics**—An approach to creative thinking that encourages bringing dissimilar concepts into juxtaposition.

At our first Solution Envisioning workshops, we explained the main concepts, vocabulary, and techniques used to the workshop participants. We soon learned that this was not always effective. In hindsight, we do not recommend spending more that a few minutes in the beginning of the exploration workshop to do this. Usually, attendees expect to be in the workshop mode and do not appreciate starting with a long presentation or discussion of the process. Moreover, it takes precious time away from other activities.

We have found that the best way to familiarize the team with the terminology and methods is by just using them and explaining them in the situation as needed. One exception to this rule may be when the workshop team is highly analytical and accustomed to very structured ways of working. Such groups may need to preview the method ahead of time to become comfortable with it and able to engage in a creative dialog.

While the workshop experience is an important result in its own right, the workshop is most effective when its results are documented and "packaged" for broader distribution. It is not likely for an exploration workshop to gather enough details to produce a Solution Concept. Its deliverable is more likely to be a Solution Vision presentation and an initial Business Case for one or more Solution Initiatives.

DIFFERENT SITUATIONS—DIFFERENT APPROACHES

Given the highly context-dependent nature of envisioning work and the various possible uses of Capability Cases, we do not offer nor recommend a recipe for customizing and applying Solution Envisioning. In practice, one of the first steps taken is to determine and communicate a way of working with Solution Envisioning and Capability Cases that is sufficiently suited to the specific opportunity.

Instead of a formula for tailoring, we give several illustrative accounts of the use of Solution Envisioning and Capability Cases that should prove helpful. We cover the following categories or situations of use introduced earlier:

A. Formulating a Solution

B. Promoting Technology Potential

C. Gaining Confidence in a Technology

Together with the tailoring suggestions given in Table 8.1, insights from these examples may provide initial guidance to those who would wish to consider how to customize or use parts of the process in their specific situations.

A. Formulating a Solution

A.1 Using Solution Envisioning to Formulate a Concept of Operations

The solution formulation phase is sometimes called *Solution Design* or *Requirements Definition*. We have used Solution Envisioning to document the design as a *Concept of Operations* (ConOps).

ConOps efforts are a widely accepted approach to describing the desired characteristics of a proposed system from the user's (non-technical) point of view. The central purposes and motivations of a typical ConOps effort are to:

- Determine the future system's characteristics with all stakeholders for the envisioned solution
- Communicate the vision to other parties
- Build consensus among diverse user groups, contractor organizations, and several developers

The audience for a ConOps may include a wide range of people, for instance:

- Users might use it to determine whether their needs and desires have been correctly specified.
- A buyer might use it to acquire knowledge of the users' needs.
- Developers typically use it as a basis for system development activities and to familiarize members of the development team with the problem domain and the system to which the ConOps applies.

A number of standards are available for ConOps documents. Key sources of guidance and a standard template for ConOps documentation are IEEE and ANSI/AIAA standards:

- IEEE Std. 1362-1998, IEEE Guide for Information Technology-System Definition-Concept of Operations (ConOps) Document

- ANSI/AIAA G-043-1992, Guide for the Preparation of Operations Concept Documents

The *standard* ConOps development process has a number of potential drawbacks. For instance, standard processes and associated deliverables may not provide enough support to reflect and integrate the goals and interests of Solution Designers, Developers, and Adopters. Table 8.2 pairs some significant pitfalls of standard ConOps approaches with capabilities from the Solution Envisioning approach that respond to them.

TABLE 8.2.   PITFALLS OF STANDARD CONOPS APPROACHES ADDRESSED BY SOLUTION ENVISIONING

Potential ConOps Challenge/Pitfalls	Solution Envisioning Response
The "Voice of the Customer" may not be adequately represented. Adopters of the solution addressed by the ConOps should participate in the Solution Envisioning and planning for development and deployment.	Reinforce the ConOps process and documentation by further engaging and strengthening the voice of the customer through scenarios of use.
Without substantial engagement of adopter-stakeholders, there is a high risk that some functional requirements will be too specific or missing.	Enable stakeholders from all stages of the solution lifecycle to forge and communicate a shared understanding of the intended solution.
Little operational help is provided on what the customer must do to secure successful adoption—for example, in addressing questions and issues such as, "How are the proposed changes going to affect my work?"	Structure a shared cause-effect framework composed of simple sentences that express important causes and related effects about stakeholders, results, challenges, forces, and strategies pertaining to a proposed solution and its adoption.

Figure 8.5 shows how we tailored Solution Envisioning to develop a ConOps document for the Wire Data Management System (WDMS) introduced in Chapter 5, "Business Capability Exploration—Phase I of Solution Envisioning." Naming of the phases was adapted to suit the context and preferences of the project sponsors.

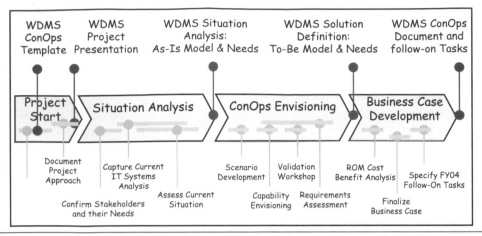

FIGURE 8.5.   WDMS PROJECT ACTIVITIES, TASKS, AND DELIVERABLES.

Throughout the work, Capability Cases provided an essential kernel around which a more effective ConOps and adoption cycle could coalesce. In particular, Capability Cases served as name-branded *handles* for understanding and encapsulating core capabilities by their name. They:

- Created an implementation-independent vocabulary for envisioning a future state of operations and documenting what the solution must be able to do, not how it should be developed and realized

- Were readily understood and appreciated by a wide range of stakeholders from business executives to electrical engineers who were solution users to IT developers

- Were effective in connecting a capability to both business value and IT realization, thus supporting articulation of a cause-effect rationale within a decision flow analysis

All phases of Solution Envisioning were important in this situation. Business Capability Exploration and Solution Capability Envisioning were executed in full. Due to the nature of a ConOps project, which stops short of a developing a technical architecture and implementation plan for the solution, only select components of Software Capability Design phase were performed with emphasis on cost-benefit analysis and a business case. With reference to major phases shown in Figure 8.5, correspondence to the phases of Solution Envisioning is as follows:

- **Project Start** represented a short start up activity during which the extended team was made familiar with the Solution Envisioning process and its complementary fit with the goals of ConOps work. From this, the Project Approach was confirmed and documented. Use of an integrated ConOps Template (incorporating IEEE and ANSI standards, see Table 8.3) was also confirmed.

- **Situation Analysis** in Figure 8.5 represents the Business Capability Exploration phase. During this phase, activities drawn from BCE were performed. They included:

  - *Confirm Stakeholders and their Needs:* 14 people were interviewed.

  - *Capture Current IT Systems Analysis:* Existing systems were understood. Analysis discovered more 20 relevant systems.

  - *Assess Current Situation:* As-Is activity scenarios were developed showing the current overall process for unexpected repairs (problem fixes) and scheduled maintenance.

- **ConOps Envisioning** represents the Solution Capability Envisioning phase. During this phase, activities drawn from SCE included:

  - *Scenario Development:* Activity scenarios were developed to explore causes for bottlenecks and unnecessary steps or complexity. Selected future operational scenarios were created to illustrate the role of the new or modified system, its interaction with users, and its interface to other systems.

  - *Capability Envisioning:* Possibilities for improvement for selected activity scenarios were explored using relevant capabilities that could better support or streamline work tasks. Eleven Capability Cases were developed. Some were selected from a portfolio of existing Capability Cases that had solution stories that provided real examples of using the capability in different settings. Due to the specialized nature of WDMS context and work, a majority were specialized versions or adaptations of existing capabilities. One of these is featured in the section on specializing Capability Cases in Chapter 6, "Solution Capability Envisioning—Phase II of Solution Envisioning"—Semantic Engineering Artifact Navigator (see Figure 6.8). Others were newly created Capability Cases with envisioned stories of how the capability would work to deliver value for the Space Shuttle program.

  - *Validation Workshop and Requirements Assessment:* Capabilities were presented to WDMS stakeholders in a requirements assessment workshop. From this session and from individual interactions with stakeholders, four capabilities were given priority for the first release of WDMS, five capabilities are currently deferred, and two capabilities were merged based on a clearer understanding of the related task.

- **Business Case Development** represents selected performance of activities drawn from the *Software Capability Design* phase of Solution Envisioning. These primarily included:

  - *ROM Cost Benefit Analysis:* Summaries of operational and organizational impacts/benefits and expected impacts on stakeholders during development were produced. Rough order of magnitude (ROM) costs for development, maintenance, and cost of use were established.

- *Finalize Business Case:* In addition to linking the cost-benefit analysis and costs-to-business objectives, the business case included an analysis of the proposed system with summaries of advantages and disadvantages/limitations, and the alternatives and trade-offs considered.

- *Specify FY04 Follow-on Tasks:* The project concluded successfully with completion of the ConOps deliverables. The work stopped short of recommendations for the realization of the proposed system, so the sponsors requested a roadmap for follow-on tasks to explore realization alternatives and implementation considerations, such as making final decisions about technology selection.

Table 8.3 shows a template used for the ConOps document with a mapping to the workproducts of Solution Envisioning as sources for the concepts and content of each section. The template is an integrated outline drawn from both the IEEE 1362-1998 and ANSI/AIAA G-043-1992 standards.

TABLE 8.3. CONOPS TEMPLATE WITH MAPPING TO CONTENT FROM SOLUTION ENVISIONING

A "Concept of Operation" Outline and Templates	Solution Envisioning Source
1 Scope	
1.1 Identification—This paragraph shall contain a full identification of the system to which this document applies, including, as applicable, identification number(s), title(s), abbreviation(s), version number(s), and release number(s).	
1.2 Scope of the Document—This section shall explain the goals and focus of the project work and the purpose of this deliverable.	Solution Initiative Statement
1.3 Motivational Scenarios—Scenarios take two forms: event scenarios that hypothesize different future conditions, and process scenarios that are examples of the "current pain" and envisioned stories that motivate the solution.	Stakeholder Challenges List Essential Activity Scenarios (transformed)
1.4 System Overview—This shall briefly state the purpose of the system to which this document applies. It shall describe the general nature of the system; summarize the history of system development, operation, and maintenance; identify the project sponsor, acquirer, user, developer, and support agencies; identify current and planned operating sites; and list other relevant documents.	Solution Vision Presentation Solution Initiative Materials Inventory Stakeholder Profile and Participation Matrix

TABLE 8.3. CONOPS TEMPLATE WITH MAPPING TO CONTENT FROM SOLUTION ENVISIONING—CONTINUED

A "Concept of Operation" Outline and Templates	Solution Envisioning Source
1.5 **Document Overview**—This shall summarize the contents of this document and shall describe any security or privacy considerations associated with its use.	
2 **Reference Documents**—This section shall list the number, title, revision, and date of all documents referenced in this document. This section shall also identify the source for all documents not available through normal government sources.	Solution Initiative Materials Inventory
3 **Situation Analysis**	
3.1 **Background, Objectives and Scope**—This paragraph shall describe the background, mission or objectives, and scope of the current system or situation.	Business Context and Activity Areas
3.2 **Current Stakeholders**—This paragraph shall describe current stakeholders of the system including its users, developers and maintainers.	Stakeholder Profile and Participation Matrix
3.3 **Operational Policies and Constraints**—This paragraph shall describe any operational policies and constraints that apply to the current system or situation.	
3.4 **Current Capabilities**—This shall provide a description of the current system or situation, identifying differences associated with different states or modes of operation (for example, regular, maintenance, training, degraded, emergency, alternative-site, wartime, and peacetime). The distinction between states and modes is arbitrary. A system may be described in terms of states only, modes only, states within modes, modes within states, or any other scheme that is useful. If the system operates without states or modes, this paragraph shall so state, without the need to create artificial distinctions. The description shall include: a. The current operational environment and its characteristics b. Major system components and the interconnections among these components c. Interfaces to external systems or procedures d. Capabilities/functions of the current system e. Charts and accompanying descriptions depicting inputs, outputs, data flow, and manual and automated processes sufficient to understand the current system or situation from the user's point of view. f. Performance characteristics, such as speed, throughput, volume, and frequency g. Quality attributes, such as reliability, maintainability, availability, flexibility, portability, usability, and efficiency h. Provisions for safety, security, privacy, and continuity of operations in emergencies	Business Context and Activity Areas Essential Activity Scenarios (initial version) Existing IT Systems in Context

TABLE 8.3. ConOps Template with Mapping to Content from Solution Envisioning—continued

A "Concept of Operation" Outline and Templates	Solution Envisioning Source
3.5 Support Concept—This section shall provide an overview of the support concept for the current system, including, as applicable to this document, support agency(ies); facilities; equipment; support software; repair/replacement criteria; maintenance levels and cycles; and storage, distribution, and supply methods.	Stakeholder Profile and Participation Matrix
4 Justification For and Nature of Change **4.1 Forces, Desired Results, and Challenges**—This paragraph shall: Describe new or modified aspects of user needs, threats, missions, objectives, environments, interfaces, personnel, or other factors that require a new or modified system Summarize deficiencies or limitations in the current system or situation that make it unable to respond to these factors	Stakeholder Challenges List Activity Challenges Map
4.2 Future Stakeholders—This should state who the stakeholders will be in the future. The effect of the system will probably cause a difference on the group of stakeholders for the current system(s).	Stakeholder Profile and Participation Matrix
4.3 Desired Changes—This paragraph shall summarize new or modified capabilities/functions, processes, interfaces, or other changes needed to respond to the forces, results, and challenges identified in 4.1.	Business Capability Model Measures
4.4 Priorities Among the Changes—This paragraph shall identify priorities among the needed changes. It shall, for example, identify each change as essential, desirable, or optional, and prioritize the desirable and optional changes.	Capability Prioritization Matrix
4.5 Changes Considered but Not Included—This paragraph shall identify changes considered but not included in 4.3, and the rationale for not including them.	Capability Cases Portfolio Capability Interest and Value Proposition Scorecard
4.6 Assumptions and Constraints—This paragraph shall identify any assumptions and constraints applicable to the changes identified in this section.	Technology Strategy Outline
5 New System Concept—This section shall be divided into the following paragraphs to describe a new or modified system.	
5.1 Background, Objectives, and Scope—This paragraph shall describe the background, mission or objectives, and scope of the new or modified system.	Solution Vision Presentation Business Context and Activity Areas

TABLE 8.3. CONOPS TEMPLATE WITH MAPPING TO CONTENT FROM SOLUTION ENVISIONING—CONTINUED

A "Concept of Operation" Outline and Templates	Solution Envisioning Source
5.2 Operational Policies and Constraints—This paragraph shall describe any operational policies and constraints that apply to the new or modified system.	
5.3 New Capabilities—This shall provide a description of the new or modified system, identifying differences associated with different states or modes of operation. The distinction between states and modes is arbitrary. A system may be described in terms of states only, modes only, states within modes, modes within states, or any other scheme that is useful. If the system operates without states or modes, this paragraph shall so state, without the need to create artificial distinctions. The description shall include, as applicable: a. The operational environment and its characteristics b. Major system components and the interconnections among these components c. Interfaces to external systems or procedures d. Capabilities/functions of the new or modified system e. Charts and accompanying descriptions depicting inputs, outputs, data flow, and manual and automated processes sufficient to understand the new or modified system or situation from the user's point of view f. Performance characteristics, such as speed, throughput, volume, and frequency g. Quality attributes, such as reliability, maintainability, availability, flexibility, portability, usability, and efficiency h. Provisions for safety, security, privacy, and continuity of operations in emergencies	Solution Concept Document Capability Model
5.4 Support Concept—This paragraph shall provide an overview of the support concept for the new or modified system, including, as applicable, support agency(ies); facilities; equipment; support software; repair/replacement criteria; maintenance levels and cycles; and storage, distribution, and supply methods.	IT Impact & Interface Specification
6 Future Scenarios—This section shall describe one or more operational scenarios that illustrate the role of the new or modified system, its interaction with users, its interface to other systems, and all states or modes identified for the system. The scenarios shall include events, actions, stimuli, information, interactions, and so forth, as applicable. Reference may be made to other media, such as videos, to provide part or all of this information.	Solution Enactment Diagram

TABLE 8.3. ConOps Template with Mapping to Content from Solution Envisioning—continued

A "Concept of Operation" Outline and Templates	Solution Envisioning Source
7 **Summary of Impacts**—This section shall be divided into the following paragraphs	Risk Assessment Model
7.1 **Operational Impacts**—This paragraph shall describe anticipated operational impacts on the user, acquirer, developer, and support agency(ies). These impacts may include changes in interfaces with computer operating centers; change in procedures; use of new data sources; changes in quantity, type, and timing of data to be input to the system; changes in data retention requirements; and new modes of operation based on peacetime, alert, wartime, or emergency conditions.	Solution Realization Roadmap
7.2 **Organizational Impacts**—This paragraph shall describe anticipated organizational impacts on the user, acquirer, developer, and support agency(ies). These impacts may include modification of responsibilities; addition or elimination of responsibilities or positions; need for training or retraining; and changes in number, skill levels, position identifiers, or location of personnel in various modes of operation.	Solution Realization Roadmap Stakeholder Collaboration Model
7.3 **Impacts During Development**—This paragraph shall describe anticipated impacts on the user, acquirer, developer, and support agency (ies) during the development effort. These impacts may include meetings/discussions regarding the new system; development or modification of databases; training; parallel operation of the new and existing systems; impacts during testing of the new system; and other activities needed to aid or monitor development.	Solution Realization Roadmap
8 **Analysis of the proposed system**	
8.1 **Summary of Advantages**—This paragraph shall provide a qualitative and quantitative summary of the advantages to be obtained from the new or modified system. This summary shall include new capabilities, enhanced capabilities, and improved performance, as applicable, and their relationship to deficiencies identified in 4.1.	Business Case
8.2 **Summary of Disadvantages/Limitations**—This paragraph shall provide a qualitative and quantitative summary of disadvantages or limitations of the new or modified system. These disadvantages and limitations shall include, as applicable, degraded or missing capabilities, degraded or less-than-desired performance, greater-than-desired use of computer hardware resources, undesirable operational impacts, conflicts with user assumptions, and other constraints.	Business Case

TABLE 8.3. ConOps Template with Mapping to Content from Solution Envisioning—continued

A "Concept of Operation" Outline and Templates	Solution Envisioning Source
8.3 Alternatives and Trade-offs Considered—This paragraph shall identify and describe major alternatives considered to the system or its characteristics, the trade-offs among them, and rationale for the decisions reached.	Solution Options Decision Model
9 Implementation Considerations	
9.1 Realization Alternatives—This section shall describe implementations and technology options including decisions already made and to be made in the future, as well as their decision rationale.	Technology Decision Model Vendor Shortlist
9.2 Estimation of Costs	Business Case
Appendices—Appendixes may be used to provide information published separately for convenience in document maintenance (for example, charts, classified data). As applicable, each appendix shall be referenced in the main body of the document where the data would normally have been provided. Appendices may be bound as separate documents for ease in handling. Some recommended appendices include: Appendix A—Acronyms and Glossary Appendix B—Capability Architecture and Capability Maps Appendix C—Business Rules Appendix D—Feedback Form	

Although the WDMS sponsors were satisfied with the ConOps Document that resulted from the project, they quickly realized the work performed had produced more results and value than could be adequately captured in this document.

They idea of a CD developed. The results of the WDMS study project could be communicated through a CD to a broader set of constituents and decision makers. With the objective to stimulate conversation about the need and possibilities for change, a CD would prepare the ground for decisions, commitments, and funding for follow-on projects. Figure 8.6 shows a view of the front page of the CD. Its content included:

- Presentations of the project background, findings, recommendations for future capabilities, and a business case for implementing the solution
- The ConOps Document
- An additional, rich set of resources, references, and tools that were produced as part of the Solution Envisioning activities and workproducts for documenting the current situation and needs

FIGURE 8.6.   WDMS CD FRONT PAGE—A RICH RECORD OF CHALLENGES AND POSSIBILITIES.

In conclusion, our experience in tailoring Solution Envisioning to produce ConOps deliverables demonstrated its effectiveness for supporting and enhancing this type of work. Beyond this, as its central goal, Solution Envisioning stimulates and facilitates strategic conversations to forge shared understanding, vision, and commitment for action. A richer workproduct, such as a CD, provides a more effective means for communicating the solution initiative, vision, concepts, and business case.

A.2   Finalizing a Solution Design

We now consider projects where solution design has already been started and is well under way using approaches different from Solution Envisioning. It has been our experience in such cases that the decision-making process often runs into obstacles because of short-comings in traditional methods.

A general characteristic of these situations is that significant work has already been done, and it can't be repeated. Solution Envisioning has to take into account and reuse, to the extent possible, results of this work. On the positive side, much of the foundation may already be in place, making it possible to run the first two steps of Solution Envisioning, not as full phases, but focused on validation.

The specifics of tailoring Solution Envisioning for use in such situations are highly dependent on the context. Receptivity and the ability of the team to reconsider some of the decisions made are key factors. While tailoring and integrating for a project-in-progress poses many challenges, it is usually possible to tailor Solution Envisioning so it can make a substantial, positive difference in the project that is already underway. These situations often have some common characteristics:

- First, it is likely that requirements have been defined without being sufficiently informed by what is possible.
- Second, a framework for making decisions may not be in place, impacting the project team's ability to make progress.
- Third, the framing of business requirements through a capability-level analysis that can be connected in a traceable way to the technical requirements is missing.

It is the combination of these characteristics that is important, in the following sense: A process that takes them into account will articulate the business needs in a compelling and actionable way. At the same time, it will leave open their specific fulfillment to discovery of alternatives—a *least-commitment* strategy.

Solution Envisioning offers a rich set of activities and resources that can be selected and tailored to provide these elements. What do we mean by capability analysis and exploration? To answer this question, we reiterate points made in Chapter 4, "Positioning Within the Solution Delivery Cycle," and Chapter 5 about the key aspects of the envisioning approach that are missing from most methodologies:

- **Situation analysis**—Determining what matters to the enterprise
- **Capability analysis**—Linking what matters to what can be done

Capability Cases support capability analysis and exploration by describing a real solution (what to do) and how it applies to a real situation (what matters) while still being sufficiently general to encourage a range of interpretations/modifications (exploration) by the stakeholders. The project described next is an example of using capability-level analysis to improve the team's ability to converge on the right solution design.

Illustrative Example

This example is drawn from our participation in the design of a new order management system for a manufacturing company. The project team developed a large document accompanied by several spreadsheets of detailed requirements that the new system had to support. It included many features needed for order entry, tracking, invoicing, and customer management processes. The company initiated a twelve-week project for defining the requirements and the new business processes

(To-Be) at a detailed level. There were approximately 10 process scenarios, and requirements line-items numbered over 500.

It became time to match the requirements to the available package solutions. None of the packages in the marketplace met the requirements exactly as specified. Did it mean the available solutions didn't meet the company's goals? On this point, the project team was not completely sure or in agreement.

Each of the evaluated solutions differed from the detailed requirements in its own way. Still, a number of options looked attractive. While they didn't support some of the features exactly as defined, they generally offered an alternative way to accomplish the same result. In many cases, the process flows didn't match all the "To-Be" descriptions that the team had just completed. One of the solutions offered interesting features the team had not thought of before.

At this point, two questions were on the minds of people on the team:

1. How important was it to stay exactly to the specifications?
2. Were the process flows from the solution alternatives viable?

The team, being pre-occupied with defining, describing, and, later, evaluating detailed functions and features, had not realized it was lacking a decision framework. It was not until choices had to be made and substantiated to the project sponsors that this omission became apparent.

When asked to help with the selection process, we introduced the following key elements from a Solution Envisioning perspective to help make decisions:

- Conceptual architecture of a solution described as a set of capabilities
- Connections between capabilities and business objectives
- Technology selection criteria

Because considerable analysis of the business situation, process scenarios, and requirements work had already been done, we were able to quickly derive missing information. Therefore, the BCE and SCE phases of Solution Envisioning were run as short validation phases, taking about 5 and 10 days, respectively, to complete. The SCD work included architecture activities, decision modeling, and vendor interviews and was completed within four weeks.

One of the Capability Architecture views of the new system is shown in Figure 8.7. Because Capability Cases derive solution design from the business objectives, they offer an effective way to identify business and component selection requirements.

With the capability model and selection criteria in place and agreed to by the project stakeholders, a decision became possible. The company designed a solution that combined a packaged application, an integration hub, a business rules engine, and two custom-made components.

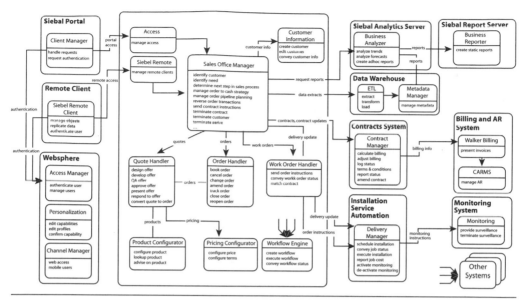

FIGURE 8.7. CAPABILITY ARCHITECTURE OF AN ORDER MANAGEMENT SYSTEM.

Reflecting on the work of this project, the process scenarios and process architecture were certainly the most useful in identifying capabilities. Requirements at the detail level were not so useful because they prematurely constrained people's view of the future solution, making it harder to appreciate the new capabilities the vendors were offering. What was needed to make decisions was a high-level statement of requirements in the neutral form of business capabilities conveying results needed and corresponding measures of effectiveness. Had this been done initially, it would have made the work of assessing the vendor offerings more productive. It is precisely here that Capability Cases offer their value—they abstract requirements into a neutral language of capabilities.

B. Promoting Technology Potential

Technology products are getting more sophisticated, and solution portfolios more complex. At the same time, technology buyers are more demanding in their need to know how business will benefit from an investment. In this environment, many technologists find themselves in a position of solution sellers.

They may be IT or research people who have created a good solution in one context and want to communicate how it could help in other situations. They may be technology evangelists wanting to communicate a vision. They may be technology vendors looking to position their products. They understand the technology well and see the potential it has to solve many business problems. The key challenge becomes how to provide a common ground for managing a conversation between solution providers and "problem owners." If this challenge is not met, technology ideas and their potential cannot be realized.

Communicating solution value is about positioning solution capabilities within customer-specific business scenarios. Solution Envisioning accelerates this process by providing tools and methods to:

- Rapidly explore with the customer key business scenarios
- Connect business value propositions to solution features in a compelling way
- Position existing success stories and references within specific business context

Because this is an exploration of a potential rather than a design of a solution, the use of Solution Envisioning will typically draw primarily on Capability Cases and elements from the first phase of the envisioning process—Business Capability Exploration.

A powerful example of this process at work was a one-day event we designed in September, 2003. This exploration of the potential use of semantic technologies for e-government took place at the White House Conference Center and was attended by more than 130 people representing over two dozen government agencies as well as some of the largest government contractors.[4]

The recurring question from the attendees was, "How can we better understand the business value of this technology?" At the same time, when solution providers were quizzed with respect to what their products could *not* do, several identified the following key issue: "We can't create new capabilities without having a clear understanding of needs—what we offer can only be as good as the requirements we receive from potential customers." This is a common impasse for emerging technology fields because it is difficult for a problem owner to formulate good requirements in advance of well-understood technology capabilities.

To respond to this need, the day was designed as a mini-envisioning experience with a panel discussion between *Problem Owners* and potential *Solution Providers* as a central feature of the day's activities. By *problem*, we simply mean a business situation that requires an IT solution. Concise statements of business needs, problems, or challenges related to government agencies or contexts were solicited ahead of time using a small template with the following requests:

---

[4]   Proceedings and highlights of the 2003 e-Gov Semantic Technology conference are available at www.topquadrant.com/conferences/tq_proceedings.htm.

1. Please describe (in one paragraph) the nature of the problem or challenge you are facing.

2. What business forces are making this problem especially critical or important? (For example, new regulations? Changes in expectations for services provided?)

3. Describe what you are currently doing to address the problem/challenge (2–5 bullets).

4. In your ideal world, how could the advances in information management and technology help solve your problem?

5. Please list any websites that provide additional information or context for question #1.

Some problem statements were chosen for discussion on the panel. Prior to the panel discussion, participants viewed a gallery of solution stories from nine vendors in the format of Capability Cases. The idea was to encourage viewers to browse through different solutions, getting ideas that help to understand their own requirements, as well as the current capability of the technology. Solutions presented in the gallery ranged over automotive design, airport security, intelligence research, technical documentation integration, and publishing. All solutions were organized in a *gallery brochure* in which each solution was summarized and classified according to the business capability it provides, further facilitating the process of comparing, contrasting, and evaluating the solutions.

The conference topic and format were appealing to far more people than the venue could accommodate. Though we stretched the number to the limit (a bit beyond, actually), when the day of the conference arrived, we had to turn away requests to attend that were about half beyond the number of those who were admitted. As a result, the conference was held again in 2004 with twice the number of attendees (approximately 260). With the interest level continuing to grow, expectation is that it will now be an annual event for some time to come.

C. Gaining Confidence in a Technology

Typically, these types of projects are one- to two-weeks in duration. Called *Solution Envisioning Lite*), they are often combined with training on a specific technology. The motivation for these projects is to understand the applicability of technology and its readiness. The combination of Solution Envisioning with emerging technology training is powerful for the reasons described in Sidebar 8.1. What often follows these small projects is a full-blown Solution Envisioning. This is especially if the focus of the *Lite* project is an initial business case.

The specific example we now describe is the tailoring of Solution Envisioning Lite for an international agricultural organization (abbreviated for the purposes of our discussion as IAO). IAO was interested in training on semantic Web technology. Project sponsors emphasized the need to understand how others have applied this technology and where it could be used best. They were already experimenting with the Semantic Web tools to provide better access to a variety of databases containing reports, articles, and statistical information. A number of people believed that this emerging technology had a significant potential, but they could not quite pinpoint or explain its business value to others. Combining training with Solution Envisioning was obviously the right approach.

The project had a short BCE phase performed remotely using conference calls as the way to conduct interviews and planning sessions. Teleconferences established the stakeholders, the business context, and our knowledge of what was already being built. The preparation period took nearly one week during which a stakeholder map was developed; forces, results, and barriers were identified; and relevant Capability Cases were selected. Where needed, new Capability Cases were developed.

It was decided to conduct the workshop as a two-day event attended by 12 to 14 people representing a diverse mix of stakeholders. The workshop was framed as a solution exploration and communicated to the attendees as follows:

AIMS:

In this workshop, we want to explore the business situation by a process of inquiry into the challenges-at-hand. From an analysis of the situation, we want to explore desirable future outcomes and the capabilities that will enable new ways of working. We want to explore the applicability of known solutions to similar situations by understanding documented solution stories and their "Capability Cases." With this knowledge, we want to assess how we might adopt and adapt these solutions in our own work.

OBJECTIVES:

The objectives of the workshop are to:

- Confirm the IAO working context and stakeholders
- Agree on forces, desired results, and challenges
- Inquiry into desired futures
- Determine key capabilities
- Explore relevant Capability Cases
- Understand, in-depth, a subset of key Capability Cases
- Investigate how to adopt and adapt Capability Cases
- Explore what might be done next

Sidebar 8.1   Making Sense of Emerging Technologies with Solution Envisioning

The problems Solution Envisioning addresses are key to the success of any technology project. However, we note that there is a set of projects where these problems are especially critical—in fact, they dominate the effort. These are the projects that target creation of new technology-enabled business capabilities through the adoption of emerging or *breakthrough* technologies. In these cases, which are becoming more of the norm than the exception with the increasingly rapid evolution of technology, understanding what technology can do for the business requires creativity and facilitated conversations between technologists and business people.

In the Introduction, we noted that Semantic Web Technology is an example of a significant, emerging technology, and throughout the book, we have included discussions of several Solution Envisioning projects and numerous Capability Cases focused on semantic technology. In conducting trainings on semantic technology—both at the conceptual level (for executives and managers), and hands-on tutorials and exercises in Semantic Web languages (OWL and RDF/S, for developers)—we experienced a demand to include a mini-envisioning session.

Although the training material already includes a substantial review of semantic technology-based Capability Cases and cases studies, attendees expressed a need for a structured, highly-interactive session that would facilitate:

- Situating semantic technology in their own context
- Framing their own challenges
- Envisioning how semantic technology could provide specific solutions

It is easier to combine such a mini-envisioning session with private trainings, where all the attendees share the same or strongly related context. However, even in public trainings there still was a keen interest to envision how to make the technology work and ground it in real circumstances.

We cite an example of a four-day, public semantic technology training session conducted in March, 2004. By request, we dynamically revised the agenda to include a three-hour, mini-envisioning session on the last afternoon. We solicited three or four candidate problem contexts from the students. Respective *problem owners* briefly described their situation and hopes/expectations for how semantic technology might apply. After voting and selecting a single context, the remainder of the session became a condensed envisioning workshop. Even though the students did not all share the background, they stated that they got significant value from this exercise.

To us, this experience has revealed the inadequacy of emerging technology training without envisioning. This has encouraged us to explore ways of embedding envisioning techniques into common practices.

Figure 8.8 shows the workshop agenda as distributed to the participants. During the workshop, two *Solution Initiative Statements* were defined and explored. One of the initiatives was implemented shortly after the workshop.

This agenda has proven to be a highly reusable structure for conducting intense technology-based envisioning workshops.

Day 1	Solution Envisioning Workshop
Part 1	Welcome and Introductions

9:30	Welcome
9:35 – 9:50	Goals and Approach of the workshop The Solution Envisioning Method and main techniques
9:50 – 10:15	Introductions – motivations and expectations

Part 2	Situation Analysis

10:15 – 10:45	FAO Context and Stakeholders FAO context that is considered in-scope, stakeholders and their interests.
10:45 – 11:15	Exploration of Critical Issues and Opportunities for change The forces present in the FAO environment. How is the world of FAO is changing, what new ways are there to work? How does this gives rise to challenges and act as obstacles to desired results? What are we sure of? What are we uncertain of?
11:15 – 11:45	Future Retrospective What stories from the future can we envision? Who have we benefited? How were those benefits evident? How does this help us to define success?
11:45 – 12:30	Activity Areas and Scenarios Key activities that the semantic solution should support for what stakeholders
12:30 – 1:30	Lunch
1:30 – 2:30	Situation Analysis Maps Validation and Elaboration Categorization, clustering and causal mapping of forces, challenges, results and other assertions with connection to activities and stakeholders.
2:30 – 3:00	Solution Initiative Definition "A Solution that provides X to Y for the purpose of achieving Z" Exploration and agreement on root definitions of the solution initiative.
3:00 – 3:15	Break
3-15 – 4:15	Exploration of capabilities "We need a way to do X" Information, processes, technologies and tools needed to support the agreed activities.
4:15 – 5:00	Quick Tour of Semantic Technology Capability Cases What are others doing? How can technology help us?
5:00	Close of Day 1

9:30 – 9:45	Start of Day 2
9:45 – 10:15	Process Check – where we are in the Solution Envisioning method

Part 3	Solution Capability Envisioning

10:15 – 10:30	Thoughts and Issues
10:30 – 10:45	Selection of Capability Cases for Detailed Review
10:45 – 12:30	Semantic Capability Cases in Depth - detailed description of selected capability cases. Review of similar solutions, scenarios and capabilities.
12:30 – 1:30	Lunch
1:30 – 2:00	Capability Map Mapping capability cases to the business situation. Initial prioritization.
2:30 – 3:15	Design Fest How to adapt the capability cases for the FAO needs
3:15 – 3:30	Break
3:30 – 4:00	Prioritization and Next Steps

Part 4	Wrap-Up

4:00 – 4:30	Reflection on how this was useful, what actions are needed, how to go forward

FIGURE 8.8.   SOLUTION ENVISIONING LITE WORKSHOP AGENDA.

THE COMPLEMENTARY ROLE OF SOLUTION ENVISIONING

Incorporating Solution Envisioning into QFD

Quality Function Deployment (QFD) was developed to overcome the growing distance between producers and users of a product by linking the needs of the customer (end user) with design, development, engineering, manufacturing, and service functions that produce a product.[5] QFD introduced notions of *Voice of the Customer* and the *Voice of the Engineer*. Another well-known QFD concept is *The House of Quality*—an assembly of several deployment hierarchies and tables.

While QFD approach is highly customized, it usually includes a relationship matrix where:

1. Each row describes a need (*demanded quality* in QFD terms). This represents the voice of a relevant customer.

2. Each column describes a solution (measurable *response* to the demanded quality—something that the solution provider would propose to drive and measure to satisfy requirements. This represents a response of an *engineer*.

3. Each cell is used to describe a relationship between the intersecting row and column.

With this brief introduction of QFD, we present a few key points and insights that emerged from a two-week project that took ConOps and Requirement documents as input for a digital archiving solution and validated them. In the project, the validation process became an integration of QFD with Solution Envisioning. Our client[6] identified the following issues:

- QFD isn't aligned well with software development.

---

[5]   QFD was developed in Japan in the late 1960s by Professors Shigeru Mizuno and Yoji Akao. The purpose of Professors Mizuno and Akao was to develop a quality assurance method that would design customer satisfaction into a product before it was manufactured. Prior quality control methods were primarily aimed at fixing a problem during or after manufacturing. The introduction of QFD to America and Europe began in 1983 when the American Society for Quality Control published Akao's work in *Quality Progress* and Cambridge Research (today Kaizen Institute) invited Akao to give a QFD seminar in Chicago.

[6]   We are indebted to John Zimmerman for the opportunity to align Solution Envisioning with the goals and processes of QFD and for the specific insights reflected in Figure 8.9.

- When trying to use it to go from a strategy to requirements, a critical gap becomes apparent—it is not clear how to move from "business functions" to "software features."

Solution Envisioning plays a complementary role for producing QFD workproducts. Moreover, it fills one central gap in the linkage in the QFD process from customer needs to software capabilities. This gap between *Business QFD* and *Technology QFD* is illustrated in Figure 8.9. This is the same gap that motivated the creation of Solution Envisioning with Capability Cases. In the context of QFD, the gap is addressed by using Capability Cases to connect projected business needs with software features or system specifications. Capability Cases represent *capability enablers* that support answering the question, "*What does the solution have to be for the business?*" (see *Solution What* in Figure 2.6.)

Following an introduction to Solution Envisioning concepts, the project sponsor asked us to make the QFD process *complete* by tailoring it to accomplish Business Capabilities Design, as shown in Figure 8.9. The work was conducted as an intensive two-week envisioning workshop with the following goals:

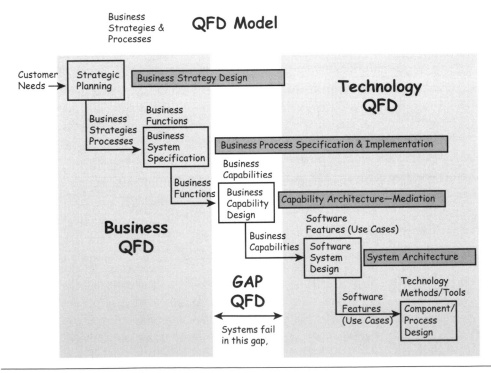

FIGURE 8.9.   USING SOLUTION ENVISIONING TO PERFORM BUSINESS CAPABILITIES DESIGN IN QFD.

- Understand use of the digital archiving solution (described by the ConOps) at a typical government agency
- Understand business impact of the solution on an agency
- Make issues concerning digital archiving solution concept easily communicated to all stakeholders
- Make research issues related to digital archiving technology visible in a way that speaks to the business stakeholders
- Develop a business case for adoption of the solution concept
- Articulate future scenarios that connect preservation needs to the digital archiving solution capabilities through compelling stories
- Bridge any gaps between the provider, the business, and IT

Along with required QFD matrixes, the process has resulted in:

- Identification of a capability-based Solution Concept for digital archiving
- Elaboration of an integrated set of Capability Cases for the Solution Concept

In validating ConOps and Requirements documents, the process revealed a number of *holes* and resulted in discovery of missing capabilities. The results were well-received by the program manager responsible for this very large scale archiving solution. Some highlights of the feedback were:

- Given the extensive effort that went into the ConOps work, the customer was surprised that a very brief integrated QFD and capability-based analysis had uncovered missing requirements.
- A high-ranking customer executive expressed the view that this work represented the most complete response they had received from anyone reviewing the ConOps and requirements.
- Capability Cases came across as a strong vehicle to support understanding by business sponsors and potential adopters of the solution.
- The vocabulary of Solution Envisioning—forces, challenges, results, and capability cases—was recognized as providing a basis for a shared cause-effect framework.
- Strong suggestions were made that the presentation become the basis for a workshop for an extended group of stakeholders to further explore solution capabilities and the contribution this approach might make to easing adoption issues.

Enterprise Architecture and Solution Envisioning

By enterprise architecture (EA) work, we mean the activities focused on the understanding all of the different elements that go to make up the enterprise and how those elements interrelate.[7] According to the Institute for Enterprise Architecture Developments,[8] these elements include, but may not be limited to, strategies, business drivers, principles, stakeholders, units, locations, budgets, domains, functions, activities, processes, services, products, information, communications, applications, systems, and infrastructure. Figure 8.10 is an illustration of enterprise architecture layering that we find useful in Solution Envisioning. For clarity, only some of the relationships between elements are shown.

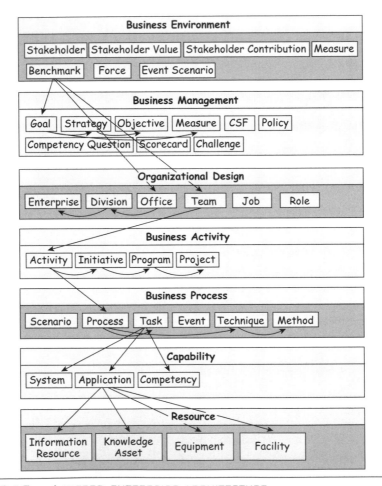

FIGURE 8.10.   LAYERED ENTERPRISE ARCHITECTURE.

---

[7]   The definition is adopted from the Institute for Enterprise Architecture Developments.

[8]   http://www.enterprise-architecture.info/index.htm.

Solution Envisioning explicitly models elements such as business drivers, stakeholders, activities, and strategies. In practice, we use it to identify (and link to) a common set of capabilities—application, data, and infrastructure components—needed to support different enterprise activities.

A number of architecture frameworks and reference models have been developed for describing enterprise architecture. Among them are ISO RM-ODP,[9] IEEE STD 610.12, the DoD Architecture Framework (DoDAF),[10] Zachman's Enterprise Architecture Framework [Zachman, 1987],[11] and the US Federal Enterprise Architecture (FEA) model.[12] The interest in connecting software architecture with business needs has caused the software development community to look for ways to reach further upstream. For example, Grady Booch's work on the *Handbook of Software Architecture*[13] extends Kruchen's 4+1 Model View[14] with constructs for stakeholders, a concept of *environment* and *forces*. At the time of writing, these ideas were not far enough developed to allow us to comment on how our Solution Envisioning approach could be compared. Suffice to say, we were motivated by similar insights and goals for connecting the worlds of business and IT. For the purposes of illustrating points of connection to Solution Envisioning, we limit our discussion to just two established standards: DoDAF and ISO RM-ODP.

What most frameworks and models have in common is a separation of concerns according to different viewpoints. Each viewpoint serves the interests of particular stakeholders. In doing so, enterprise architecture must specify relationships that express "fitness for purpose." Measures of effectiveness need to be established up front, in conjunction with a concept of operations. These measures of effectiveness become the objective function for evaluating alternative architectures through each viewpoint.

Solution Envisioning and DoDAF

DoDAF's overall purpose is to facilitate interoperability of DoD systems in contexts of operations. DoDAF is not a description of a specific architecture. Instead, it

---

[9] RM-ODP or Reference Model for Open Distributed Processing is an ISO standard reference model for specifying the architecture of a system.

[10] http://www.defenselink.mil/nii/doc/DoDAF_v1_Volume_I.pdf   and   http://www.defenselink.mil/nii/doc/DoDAF_v1_Volume_II.pdf

[11] Zachman, J.A., "A Framework for Information Systems Architecture," IBM.

[12] http://www.feapmo.gov/.

[13] http://www.booch.com/architecture/index.jsp.

[14] Phillipe Kruchen's Model View appeared in an IEEE computer paper [Kruchen, 1995].

establishes a common way of describing, presenting, and comparing DoD enterprise architectures and facilitating the use of common principles, assumptions, and terminology. DoDAF is structured around four viewpoints:

1. **All Views (AV)**—Contains framework products relevant to all views.

2. **Operation View (OV)**—Products describing the tasks and activities, operational elements, and information exchanges required to accomplish DoD missions.

3. **System View (SV)**—A set of graphical and textual products that describes systems and interconnections providing for, or supporting, DoD functions.

4. **Technical View (TV)**—The minimal set of rules governing the arrangement, interaction, and interdependence of system parts or elements.

The framework defines 26 products that fall into the four viewpoints just described. The mapping of DoDAF to Solution Envisioning workproducts is shown in Table 8.4.

TABLE 8.4.   MAPPING OF DoDAF TO SOLUTION ENVISIONING WORKPRODUCTS

Applicable View	Framework Product	Framework Product Name	General Description	Solution Envisioning Workproduct
All Views	AV-1	Overview and Summary Information	Scope, purpose, intended users, environment depicted, analytical findings	Solution Initiative Statement
All Views	AV-2	Integrated Dictionary	Architecture data repository with definitions of all terms used in all products	Solution Initiative Glossary as a starting point
Operational	OV-1	High-Level Operational Concept Graphic	High-level graphical/textual description of operational concept	Business Context and Activity Areas; Essential Activity Scenarios; Solution Enactment Diagram
Operational	OV-2	Operational Node Connectivity Description	Operational nodes, connectivity, and information exchange need lines between nodes	Downstream from Solution Envisioning

TABLE 8.4.   Mapping of DoDAF to Solution Envisioning Workproducts—
          continued

Applicable View	Framework Product	Framework Product Name	General Description	Solution Envisioning Workproduct
Operational	OV-3	Operational Information Exchange Matrix	Information exchanged between nodes and the relevant attributes of that exchange	Downstream from Solution Envisioning
Operational	OV-4	Organizational Relationships Chart	Organizational, role, or other relationships among organizations	Stakeholder Profile and Participation Matrix; Stakeholder Collaboration Model
Operational	OV-5	Operational Activity Model	Capabilities, operational activities, relationships among activities, inputs, and outputs; overlays can show cost, performing nodes, or other pertinent information	Capability Architecture as an input
Operational	OV-6a	Operational Rules Model	One of three products used to describe operational activity—identifies business rules that constrain operation	Downstream from Solution Envisioning
Operational	OV-6b	Operational State Transition Description	One of three products used to describe operational activity—identifies business process responses to events	Downstream from Solution Envisioning
Operational	OV-6c	Operational Event-Trace Description	One of three products used to describe operational activity—traces actions in a scenario or sequence of events	Solution Enactment Diagram
Operational	OV-7	Logical Data Model	Documentation of the system data requirements and structural business process rules of the Operational View	Downstream from Solution Envisioning

TABLE 8.4.   MAPPING OF DoDAF TO SOLUTION ENVISIONING WORKPRODUCTS— CONTINUED

Applicable View	Framework Product	Framework Product Name	General Description	Solution Envisioning Workproduct
Systems	SV-1	Systems Interface Description	Identification of systems nodes, systems, and system items and their interconnections, within and between nodes	Capability Architecture; IT Systems in Context
Systems	SV-2	Systems Communications Description	Systems nodes, systems, and system items and their related communications lay-downs	Downstream from Solution Envisioning
Systems	SV-3	Systems-Systems Matrix	Relationships among systems in a given architecture; can be designed to show relationships of interest, for example, system-type interfaces, planned versus existing interfaces, and so on.	IT Impact & Interface Specification
Systems	SV-4	Systems Functionality Description	Functions performed by systems and the system data flows among system functions	Downstream from Solution Envisioning
Systems	SV-5	Operational Activity to Systems Function Traceability Matrix	Mapping of systems back to capabilities or of system functions back to operational activities	Byproduct of SE process—transformation of Capability Model to Capability Architecture
Systems	SV-6	Systems Data Exchange Matrix	Provides details of system data elements being exchanged between systems and the attributes of that exchange	Downstream from Solution Envisioning

TABLE 8.4.   MAPPING OF DODAF TO SOLUTION ENVISIONING WORKPRODUCTS—
CONTINUED

Applicable View	Framework Product	Framework Product Name	General Description	Solution Envisioning Workproduct
Systems	SV-7	Systems Performance Parameters Matrix	Performance characteristics of Systems View elements for the appropriate time frame(s)	Non-functional Requirements
Systems	SV-8	Systems Evolution Description	Planned incremental steps toward migrating a suite of systems to a more efficient suite, or toward evolving a current system to a future implementation	Solution Realization Roadmap
Systems	SV-9	Systems Technology Forecast	Emerging technologies and software/hardware products that are expected to be available in a given set of time frames and that will affect future development of the architecture	Technology Strategy Outline; Solution Options Decision Model
Systems	SV-10a	Systems Rules Model	One of three products used to describe system functionality—identifies constraints that are imposed on systems functionality due to some aspect of systems design or implementation	Architectural Decisions—provides a starting point
Systems	SV-10b	Systems State Transition Description	One of three products used to describe system functionality—identifies responses of a system to events	Downstream from Solution Envisioning

TABLE 8.4. MAPPING OF DODAF TO SOLUTION ENVISIONING WORKPRODUCTS—
CONTINUED

Applicable View	Framework Product	Framework Product Name	General Description	Solution Envisioning Workproduct
Systems	SV-10c	Systems Event-Trace Description	One of three products used to describe system functionality—identifies system-specific refinements of critical sequences of events described in the Operational View	Downstream from Solution Envisioning
Systems	SV-11	Physical Schema	Physical implementation of the Logical Data Model entities, for example, message formats, file structures, physical schema	Downstream from Solution Envisioning
Technical	TV-1	Technical Standards	Profile Listing of standards that apply to Systems View elements in a given architecture	Architectural Decisions and Technology Decision Model provide a starting point
Technical	TV-2	Technical Standards Forecast	Description of emerging standards and potential impact on current Systems View elements, within a set of time frames	Technology Strategy Outline—provides a starting point

DoDAF's concept of architecture capabilities aligns with capabilities in Solution Envisioning. The capability-based approach is valuable for mapping or transforming from business-level concepts (or models) to technical models in Enterprise Architecture work.

Solution Envisioning and ISO RM-ODP

ISO RM-ODP is based on the principle that to satisfy the needs of different stakeholders—solution sponsors, solution users, and solution developers—architecture must provide multiple viewpoints of the solution. RM-ODP defines five architectural viewpoints, shown in Figure 8.11, that address views of different categories of stakeholder:

1. **Enterprise Viewpoint**—The business perspective

   This is the manager's and user's view of the system and its environment that focuses on the purposes, policies, and scope of the business solution.

2. **Information Viewpoint**—Semantics and information perspective

   The information viewpoint considers the solution and its environment in terms of the information and information processing performed.

3. **Computational Viewpoint**—System functionality

   The computational viewpoint describes the essence of the solution in terms of governing principles, features, key concepts, and mechanisms. It answers the question, "What are the design ideas behind solution architecture?"

4. **Engineering Viewpoint**—System distribution

   The engineering viewpoint is a viewpoint of the system and its environment that focuses on the infrastructure and functions required to support distributed interaction between components in the system.

5. **Technology Viewpoint**—Technology and products

   This is the viewpoint of the system that focuses on governing mechanisms, technology choices, and how these technologies support the execution and integration of the system components.

Architectural models defined during Solution Envisioning projects directly map to the RM-ODP architecture viewpoint specification framework. Figure 8.12 shows how the workproducts produced during the three phases of Solution Envisioning projects provide either early versions of the RM-ODP architectural viewpoints or direct input for creating them.

There is one more significant viewpoint that we consider essential, although it is not a part of RM-ODP. We call it a *development viewpoint.*

The development viewpoint considers the solution in terms of software workproducts (artifacts), engineering methods, and recommended processes. As covered in Chapter 7 and Appendix C, the implementation option decisions made during the Software Capability Design phase of Solution Envisioning govern the nature and the evolution of the development viewpoint.

How does the system fit with business policies and deliver business value?

Business Managers, IT Managers

What is the statement-of-fit with our requirements and what are the implications that the system will bring?

IT Managers, Business Analysts

What are the key design concepts and mechanisms and what technologies are involved?

Enterprise View

Information View

System

Computational View

Technology View

Engineering View

Architects, Developers, Technologists

Will the system run on our platforms, comply with our architecture constraints and satisfy our required service level characteristics?

Developers, Release Managers

What will we have to change and how easy will it be to understand the design of the system?

Architects, System Managers

FIGURE 8.11. VIEWPOINTS OF A SYSTEM.

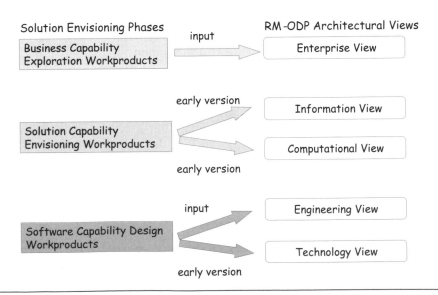

Solution Envisioning Phases		RM-ODP Architectural Views
Business Capability Exploration Workproducts	input →	Enterprise View
Solution Capability Envisioning Workproducts	early version ↗ ↘ early version	Information View / Computational View
Software Capability Design Workproducts	input ↗ ↘ early version	Engineering View / Technology View

FIGURE 8.12. EVOLVING SOLUTION ENVISIONING OUTPUTS INTO A DETAILED ARCHITECTURE

Solution Envisioning and Development Paradigms

Chapter 7 mentioned a number of development paradigms. It is appropriate in this chapter to revisit these and describe the relationship between Solution Envisioning and two development paradigms: *Rapid Prototyping* and *Model-Driven Architecture*. We limit our discussion to just these two because both have a special affinity to Solution Envisioning.

Solution Envisioning and Rapid Prototyping

Why Rapid Prototyping? A number of purposes are served by prototypes:

1. Sharing a vision of a proposed solution
2. Building consensus for a solution
3. Resolving areas of technical uncertainty
4. Evolving how the user interface should be constructed
5. Mitigating risks of implementation
6. Overcoming areas of architectural difficulty

Solution Envisioning with Capability Cases reduces the need to use prototypes for the first two purposes. However, this still leaves four valid reasons for building a working prototype. We often use prototyping to check the feasibility of a solution. This work can be particularly useful in Activities 1, 2, 3, and 6 of the Software Capability Design phase in Chapter 7. Executable prototypes are done for proof of technical feasibility, for which object-oriented techniques and environments are very effective.[15]

However, with prototyping there comes a danger. This we call the "Demo Syndrome"—the prototype becomes the solution. To ameliorate the "Demo Syndrome" some environments and platforms enable a special kind of development called "Evolutionary Prototyping." A computation model is at the center of these environments and the tools provide models that are directly executable by an engine. One example is the PiiE platform from Digital Harbor.[16]

Typically, these environments are built on the principle of *Layered Abstract Machines*, where one layer of the system raises the computational power by offering services to upper layers. Each layer raises the level of abstraction closer to the problem domain and away from the computational engine.

---

[15] A good reference on such prototyping is the book by Philippe Krief, *Prototyping with Objects* [Krief, 1996].

[16] www.digitalharbor.com.

Solution Envisioning works well with evolutionary prototypes for the following reasons:

- The prototypes can be built concurrently with the Solution Envisioning work and reflect and influence the ideas as they are happening.

- Stakeholders have immediate confidence in the direction that the project is taking.

- Prototyping is focused by the solution envisioning workproducts. Without this, there is the danger that developers will prototype in isolation from the real needs and strategic goals of the enterprise.

- Evolutionary prototyping needs a fast and dynamic approach to defining solution concepts. Traditional requirements approaches, including detailed use case modeling, do not integrate well with this mode of working. Capability Cases convey the essence of what is being sought and embody a story about a solution concept. The detailed implementation of the Capability Case becomes the prototyping effort.

Solution Envisioning and Model-Driven Architecture

Model-Driven Architecture (MDA) is an approach to system specification, portability, and interoperability based on the use of formal and semi-formal models. The MDA derives all executable code from models of the system.

Capability Cases can be viewed as a model-based approach to specifying solution concepts. The models bridge business and IT by being expressions of how business drivers (forces), outcomes (results), and challenges relate to specific capabilities. Although the models are not behavioral, they organize structural and functional components of the solution with traceability.

Doing development using MDA requires architects to create the system specification independent of any implementation considerations. This is called a *Platform Independent Model* (PIM). Formal or semi-formal transformation rules translate the PIM to one of many possible target platforms (such as Java [J2EE], Microsoft [.NET] or Web Services), creating *Platform Specific Models* (PSMs). By applying further constraints and mechanisms, the PSMs are translated into the executable systems in the form of *Platform Specific Implementations* (PSIs).

There is an interesting variant of the MDA approach called *Enterprise Distributed Object Computing*, or EDOC.[17] This specifies a general component model called ECA

---

[17] OMG, UML Profile for Enterprise Distributed Object Computing Specification, Enterprise Collaboration Architecture (ECA), formal/04-02-01 v1.0, http://www.omg.org/technology/documents/formal/edoc.htm.

(Enterprise Collaboration Architecture). ECA allows recursive definition of components that are inter-connected using conversational ports that are bi-directional and defined in a precise way using protocol choreographies. EDOC works well for representing the functionality of a distributed system. The constructs in EDOC are closer to the problem domain and map well to Capability Cases.

Connection between Solution Envisioning with Capability Cases and model-driven development is based on exploring how capabilities map to components and how scenarios used for the solution envisioning become collaborations in the Component Collaboration Architecture of the EDOC. Integration is achieved by:

- Mapping Capability Cases to components in a PIM.

- Using Essential Activity Scenarios to inform the design of interactions that define the collaborations needed among the components.

By having already delineated functionality and behavior, Capability Cases provide a powerful starting point for the architecture of the solution. Appendix C provides more detail on how a Capability Architecture is elaborated and evaluated for MDA-based solutions.

TRAIL MARKER VIII: SOLUTION ENVISIONING TAILORED TO SITUATION

This chapter used examples to illustrate how Solution Envisioning is intended to be a flexible process that can be adapted to the unique circumstances of varying situations. While Chapters 5–7 detailed three phases for applying the *standard* process, Solution Envisioning is highly customizable to the situation at hand.

Readers who have taken either the long route or a shorter tour through the book may be happy to finally arrive at the nice, short, final chapter. Our last chapter, "Conclusion—Lessons Learned and Looking Ahead with Envisioning," concludes the main part of this book with reflections on Solution Envisioning from practice and some suggestions for getting started. For those who still want more—well, there are several Appendices to go through....

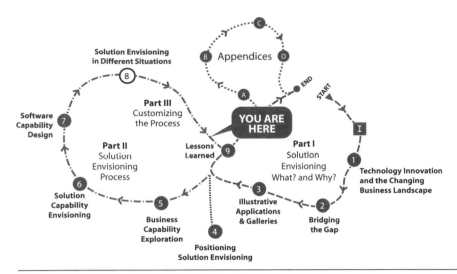

FIGURE 8.13.

9

CONCLUSION—LESSONS LEARNED AND LOOKING AHEAD WITH ENVISIONING

"Good ideas are not adopted automatically. They must be driven into practice with courageous patience."

—Hyman Rickover

FIGURE 9.1.

Reflections on Solution Envisioning

Formulating a solution requires interplay between needs and design. In this book, we have shown that Solution Envisioning views design as a creative act that explores and often stimulates need. With at least 20 years' experience with Solution Envisioning among us, we are able to report some insights into what works and does not work in this approach. The following ten points provide a top-ten list of insights into Solution Envisioning. In Sidebar 9.1, we shed some light on the mindset embodied in the practice of envisioning.

1. Envisioning Comes Natural to Certain Kinds of People

There are left-brain and right-brain people—creative types and analytical types. Solutions are frequently conceived by individuals rather than groups. Often, a solution architect, after "living the problem,"[1] recommends a solution—from a personally known solution space. In many cases, this solo-envisioner is a *seasoned* practitioner with a portfolio of past systems experiences on which to draw. However, there may be drawbacks to this approach, as exemplified by the following in Point 2.

2. Envisioners Can Be Blind-Sided, Too

Natural envisioners may think they are fine with what they know and have no need for Solution Envisioning activities or for bringing others along. However, even the most experienced and visionary practitioners can be guilty of conjuring solutions without complete understanding of the problem or possible solutions. It is easy for a single person to be unaware of certain technical options or to misunderstand certain aspects of the situation and challenges that need to be addressed.

3. Envisioners Need to Be Enthusiastic Communicators

A vision may be inspired and compelling, but failure to communicate it yields little results. When one or more individuals envision a system solution, they are still required to convey their vision to a large number of stakeholders who have diverse perspectives and interests (see Point 7). The rare exception to this is when the envisioner will be the one and only implementer of the solution.

---

[1] We are indebted to Kal Ruberg who, at an OOPSLA workshop in 1996, made the powerful statement, "You have to be the problem to become the solution." Simply put, this is about gathering requirements by experiencing the problems first-hand.

4. Envisioning Is Often Blocked by Complacency

We end up with ineffective and outdated solutions because we stick with the "devil we know." With technology options growing every day, keeping up-to-date and assessing what is "ready for prime time" is time-consuming. The bias toward "what worked in the past" is a severe barrier to effective envisioning. By bringing Capability Cases to bear on the problem, we ensure a more complete solution space is appreciated.

5. Detachment from the Present Is Crucial

Successful envisioning requires pulling all the spatial and temporal constructs together in a *sketch* of the final system. Experience shows that, for the envisioner, it is a critical skill to have the ability to remove oneself from the logic of the current situation and see the possibility of a different future.

6. Envisioning Is About Making Connections

The envisioner looks at a problem from different perspectives and makes connections between seemingly dissimilar domains. The "aha" moments come from making creative leaps to solution concepts. Some "ahas" happen by seeing the root causes behind the challenges the business is facing. Others happen by seeing ways of taking ideas from one space into a different space. Capability Cases for the workshop should be selected on two bases. The primary set will be those that directly connect to forces, challenges, and results. Another, smaller set is chosen to serve as a catalyst for creative thinking. Depending on the breadth of the problem space, this set can be very diverse. In practice, it is usually governed by some correspondence to the business capability area. Selection is not a precise science; intuition is very much at work.

7. A Vision Without Commitment Has a Short Half-Life

In any enterprise, the outcomes of envisioning are dependent on the quality of the communication and collaboration involved. For the vision to become compelling and useful, that is, accepted and actionable, it must be adopted by all stakeholders such that they can each *make it their own*. Solution Envisioning is inherently a group process with a critical need to build a committed team.

8. Envisioning Can Start Anywhere, but Workshops Need One Physical Space

Much of the work through the three phases of Solution Envisioning can be done in a remote, distributed fashion. However, an Envisioning Workshop must be conducted in a co-located setting, and ideally in a different place from the normal workplace. Strong facilitation skills are needed to organize and run high-quality, enjoyable workshops. For this reason, the facilitator should not be the person acting as scribe or be too busy generating the shared artifacts for the workshop.

9. Capability Cases Can Be Long-Lived

Given careful thought and abstraction over several solution stories, Capability Cases have been found to be relevant and valuable over a number of years. Our oldest Capability Cases were created four years ago, and all of them are still in use.

10. Solution Envisioning Combines Familiar Ideas in New Ways

Many aspects of the Solution Envisioning process and supporting methods will already sound familiar to you and others—you may say "we already do these things." Our contribution is in bringing together a number of powerful techniques and a simple framework for discussing business settings (forces, challenges, results, and scenarios) and solution concepts (Capability Cases).

Sidebar 9.1 The Mindset of Solution Envisioning

The activity of envisioning a solution, of any type or complexity, involves a particular mindset. Aspects of this mindset include the following:

- **Anticipation**—Seeing the future now, story-telling about future scenarios, sometimes called *Imagineering* or, as Gareth Morgan calls it, "Imaginization" [Morgan 1993].

- **Discovery**—Surfacing of assumptions, deep understanding of need, and analogical reasoning

- **Creativity**—Innovation through new possibilities and connections between ideas

- **Belief**—Embracing possibility, suspension of disbelief, detachment from the current business logic, making leaps of faith

- **Holistic thinking**—Living in the problem space; seeing the whole system not just parts

- **Metaphorical exploration**—Finding powerful metaphors that inspire the conceptual basis of the solution and capture the user experience

- **Dialog**—Establishing a setting for constructive conversations by adopting the principles of the suspension of assumptions, tolerance of the tension of opposites, active or

generative listening, a disposition to inquiry (as opposed to advocacy), and deriva-
tion of meanings or *ladder of inference.*[2]

- **Acting with conviction**—Making and keeping commitments, having the courage to break down barriers, staying with the vision, evangelizing

PLANS FOR EVOLVING SOLUTION ENVISIONING

In practice, using the process and associated methods of Solution Envisioning is enhanced by having reusable assets beyond Capability Cases. For instance, the work is able to progress much faster when existing lists of forces, results, challenges, and capability maps are used. In the beginning, we created Capability Cases as PowerPoint presentations. That worked reasonably well early on, but as our base of solution design assets grew, we realized that a structured repository was needed. So, we built a knowledge environment called TopDrawer[3]—using a semantic network datastore—to work with them.

The new environment opened the possibility of adding a number of important tools that support the Solution Envisioning process, including:

- Tools for exploring the semantic network and dynamically building different views of capability maps
- Intelligent advisors that find and recommend capabilities based on the business focus, industry focus, and desired results

We have also been experimenting with other ideas that represent a natural complement to these, as well as the integration of decision support and simulation tools.

Looking to the future, we want to improve our tooling for use over the Web (see www.capabilitycases.org) and to stimulate people's thinking and assist in decision making within the workshops. Capability Cases could also be evolved to support live demos and even a multimedia experience.

---

[2] For insights into the nature of dialog, see Robert Levi's *Information on the Dialogue Process* reported by Mary Margaret Palmer at http://world.std.com/~lo/bohm/0002.html in 1995. David Bohm's work on dialog is at http://www.muc.de/~heuvel/dialogue/dialogue_proposal.html. Peter Senge's work on systems thinking in *The Fifth Discipline Fieldbook* also provides a treatment of dialog [Senge, 1994].

[3] TopDrawer is an environment for creating, viewing, and dynamically working with Capability Cases.

We are also exploring simple steps that would improve the accessibility of the Solution Envisioning process and methods. One idea is to investigate the value of having a plug-in tool for the RUP Methods Browser.

FOSTERING ADOPTION AND PRACTICE OF A NEW APPROACH

Any new approach in the world faces an uphill battle. This is why many new things are often described in a tongue-in-cheek way as "a 10-year overnight success." No matter how much it may be needed, or well thought out, any new invention, process, or technology is likely to go through a similar adoption cycle to the one described in the book *Crossing the Chasm* [Moore, 2002].

A Rose by Any Other Name...

We find that while early adopters readily embrace the new concepts and terminology of Solution Envisioning and Capability Cases, others are more cautious. *Solution Envisioning* may sound a bit too creative and "off the wall" for structure-oriented IT people. Indeed, we have found that to some people, it suggests a scenario where the participants are just having fun and not enough real work is getting done or results accomplished!

So, why didn't we choose a more easily acceptable name? For one, because Solution Envisioning describes well what happens in the early stages of solution realization. For another, we believe that any reaction to "envisioning" in the name is only surface-deep.

Aside from the name, there is sometimes a knee-jerk disposition to mislabel or pigeonhole the concept and intent of Solution Envisioning. We sense that this is based on the tendency in all of us to react to something new with a "sounds like..." statement, as in "it sounds like rapid application development" or "it sounds like joint application development." The software development industry is dominated by cycles of this kind. Anything new needs time to be understood, absorbed, and then embraced or rejected based on its true merits. Our hope is that when Solution Envisioning becomes a better-known concept in the world, any issues with the name or intent will fade away.

In the meantime, we acknowledge there have been situations where using "envisioning" in the name of the project was perceived as a problem. The people who wanted to work with it typically asked us to call it something else, something that sounded more familiar—for example, a "pilot project," a "solution definition project," or even a "discovery project." In all these cases, we ended up facilitating exactly the same work—applying Solution Envisioning.

Because the process described in this book is flexible and tailorable to a number of situations (see Chapter 8, "Solution Envisioning in Different Situations"), we don't have an issue with qualifying the name by adding more familiar terms to it, for instance, calling it "a pilot solution project using Solution Envisioning." After all, when use cases were moving through a similar adoption curve, people often said something like, "We are doing requirements using use cases." These days, it is more common just to hear, "We are doing use cases." The word "requirements" is assumed, but the original way of speaking remains more accurate.

Winning the Right to Do Solution Envisioning

It is probably safe to assume that readers of this book are interested in new ways to ensure more effective use of IT. If the ideas and practices in this book make sense to you, you may find yourself wanting to introduce them into your organization. Some readers may be able to just decide to begin practicing Solution Envisioning. Others will first need to convince their colleagues and managers that it is a practical and cost-effective thing to do. They may need to educate key decision makers about the main concepts, activities, and results of Solution Envisioning.

Because Solution Envisioning is something new in the world, we have found ourselves often working with change agents who are looking for a more effective process to improve their chances of success. These experiences motivate us to make two key recommendations on best ways to introduce a new approach:

- **Identify the right first project**—A number of criteria can be stated for selecting the first project on which to use Solution Envisioning:

  1. Multiple stakeholders are involved or will need to participate.
  2. A project manager realizes that the project vision is not shared across the team.
  3. Key people express strong opinions about the quality of the functional or technical decisions being made.
  4. The project has high visibility and is critical to an organization.
  5. The technology selection process is complicated.
  6. The system is new, as opposed to extensions to an existing system.

- **Adopt an iterative approach**—To win the right do Solution Envisioning in full, you may need to do some aspects of the work in Business Capability Exploration. This often entails clarifying and connecting to the business strategy and helping formulate and obtain funding for the solution initiative. Usually, the best way to accomplish this is through a one- to two-week *Solution Envisioning Lite* project—a condensed, tailored version as introduced in Chapter 8. A key concern of this type of introductory project is demonstrating the nature of the process, its soundness, and its promise to business decision makers, particularly those in a position to fund a solution initiative. After its value is understood and communicated within an organization, a full Solution Envisioning project can take place.

Making the Business Case to Do Solution Envisioning

Making the case—highlighting the value of Solution Envisioning—must include both of the following briefs:

- Observing the possible consequences and risks of failure in doing the things the same old way
- Communicating the unique features and benefits that enhance prospects of success by explicitly conducting a Solution Envisioning phase

1. The Escalating Costs of Failure

As noted in the Preface and throughout this book, there is great importance as well as significant challenge in getting the right supporting technology capabilities in place for a business. To reinforce this point, initially, we thought to distill a representative sampling of the extensive statistics on technology project failures. With the current focus on ROI (return on investment) and business cases, we elected instead to draw attention to studies that go beyond assessing only how well IT projects met their budget. The associated research shows that poor communication and so-called "bad" requirements are the major reasons for failures.[4] Correspondingly, such studies show that improving these aspects of the solution realization process has shown significant return on investment. We quote from one such informative study.

In January 2003, AMR Research published a study on success of CRM (Customer Relationship Management) initiatives. It asked the top 12 CRM vendors to provide a list of reference accounts that the vendor believed had created value from their

---

[4] Some studies find that poor communication between responsible parties causes 57% of all issues.

CRM implementation. It deliberately avoided defining "value" so that "the vendors could determine what value meant."

This is what AMR found:[5]

- **Project failure:** 12 percent of CRM projects fail to go live
- **Dead on arrival:** 47 percent of CRM projects go live, and the technology aspects of the project are considered a success, but business change and adoption fail
- **Survived, but the value unknown:** 25 percent of CRM projects succeed in delivered and adopted systems but still cannot quantify a specific quantified business benefit
- **Delivered value:** 16 percent of projects reach the Promised Land and measurably influence business performance

Underlying all such studies is the lack of synergy—communication and coordination—between the IT and business sides of organizations. Few projects define what success means. Not surprisingly, few achieve it.

In making a business case do more upfront exploration, planning, and communication—as facilitated in some form of the Solution Envisioning process—you may find the need to consult studies on the frequency and causes of IT project failures. In Sidebar 9.2, we give some sources and general guidance for assessing and making use of this type of information.

2. Solution Envisioning Responses—Features and Benefits

On the positive side, there are common insights emerging from the studies cited above:

- Communication and coordination, or synergy, between business and IT are not technical, but human interaction issues. Establishing a common language has proven to be the most effective way of gaining mutual understanding. More and more often, a key point of advice is to establish a common project vocabulary.[6]

---

[5]   http://techrepublic.com.com/5100-6298_11-5034681.html.

[6]   For a relevant example on the importance of a common project vocabulary and other best practice advise for implementing content management systems, see http://www.cms-watch.com/Features/OpinionWatch/FeaturedOpinion/?feature_id=116.

- All recent studies stress that having a clear idea of the benefits of a solution will yield improved success rates. Communicating the business value widely and effectively seems to be a core factor.

- Spending time on understanding and analyzing business needs pays off; so does the time invested in understanding solution options and doing a thorough job in selecting technologies.[7]

- The benefits of flexibility and the practice of *delayed decision management* are getting more attention.[8]

In alignment with these insights, we have outlined throughout the book how Solution Envisioning enhances prospects for success by overcoming key obstacles in solution design that create risks early on in the solution lifecycle. Addressing these obstacles places requirements on any process that will be used to define business solutions. Though it has multiple dimensions, three main aspects of Solution Envisioning can be differentiated in this regard:

- Creativity

- Solution Conceptualization

- Communication

Table 9.1 gives a summary that may be useful for presenting the value of doing Solution Envisioning.

---

[7] In many ways, this has always been a well-known fact. Not surprisingly, one of Abraham Lincoln's most often repeated quotes is: "If I had eight hours to chop down a tree, I'd spend six hours sharpening my ax." Following this advice in an organizational setting requires shared commitment as well as understanding and trust in the process.

[8] Delayed decision management acknowledges that it is not feasible to make all decisions early in the process. It is important, however, to know which decisions must be made at which point and to make the best decisions. There are some very key decisions that must happen early in the solution development cycle. If made incorrectly, these decisions are guaranteed to severely damage the project. This is why Solution Envisioning puts such emphasis on establishing a decision framework. See this article: http://www.sdbestpractices.com/documents/s=8696/sdm0308a/ and [Poppendieck, 2003] for some discussion on this topic.

TABLE 9.1.   HOW SOLUTION ENVISIONING ADDRESSES KEY OBSTACLES IN SOLUTION DESIGN

Aspect	Obstacle	Solution Envisioning Response
Creativity	Being too grounded in the "as is" world	Using Future search techniques
	Not realizing what is possible through the use of technology	Using Capability Cases to spark ideas Analogical Reasoning
Solution Conceptualization	Misunderstanding the nature of the problem	Assessing and modeling the Business Situation
	Getting too deep into details before laying out a solution concept	Expressing the essential nature of the Conceptual Architecture before detailed design
	Not knowing how to decide among multiple options	Managing divergent and convergent thinking Making technology choices and building consensus using decision models
	Missing key options	Exploring a broad solution space using a variety of Capability Cases
	Not taking into account changes that the solution will bring about	Thinking about problems and solutions as systems
Communication	Lack of common language	Using Capability Cases to establish a common vocabulary of solution components
	Lack of knowledge or sharing of "pain points"	Focused story telling to get clear on the present and to explore desirable future outcomes
	Differences in knowledge and experiences	Representing solution capabilities through rich pictures Providing a rationale for the solution through a traceable decision flow from business objectives to solution capabilities

Sidebar 9.2   What Do Statistics on Project Failure Show?

Statistics on project failure are widely available and can motivate the need for change in the way IT solution projects are initiated and conducted. We include some guidance and cautions on finding, interpreting, and presenting this type of information:

- **The numbers are easy to find**—We quote a few in Chapter 1, "Technology Innovation and the Changing Business Landscape." A simple web search will find many additional sources of statistics.[9] Several books already list and dissect these numbers.

- **Failure statistics can be perceived as extremely discouraging**—The findings are pretty bleak. Some indicate that less than 20% of IT investments deliver value. Is the problem so difficult that nothing can be done? Should companies just stop spending money on IT? Of course, this is not an option—business and technology today go hand in hand. The bottom line is that even though disproportional amounts of money go to waste, it is possible to get better results while spending less.

- **The findings are so discouraging that they may not be believed**—With numbers so bad, it is easy to say, "This can not be true." Or it may be true elsewhere, but it does not happen here because we have sound project management, or because we have good people, or we only do short projects, or (pick your favorite reason).

The truth is that many studies have found it somewhat difficult to clearly determine success and failure criteria. Aggregating information and separating symptoms from causes can also be challenging. Nevertheless, the numbers are reasonably consistent across all studies, industries, and types of solutions. Certainly, better project management practices of the past decade have brought welcomed improvements. Smaller projects seem to do better, and this makes perfect sense. However, according to some studies, 64% of smaller (less than a year long) projects still don't do well. And it is not always possible to keep a project small—even with staging—so companies sometimes have to undertake large strategic initiatives.

Most studies we have seen focused on costs: sunk cost (projects closed before completion), cost of defects that could have been prevented in the requirements phase, and overall cost and schedule overruns. Another commonly measured factor is partial or incomplete implementations—features planned for, but not delivered. While these numbers certainly bear relationship to the business success of the project, they do not necessarily directly reflect the business value actually obtained or not, not to mention lost opportunity costs. We have seen projects declared a technical success—completed on schedule and budget—yet, for a variety of reasons, they didn't do anything (or as much as expected) for the business. We have also seen projects and project ideas with good business potential closed down or never funded.[10]

---

[9]   Some examples include OASIG Study (1995), The Bull Survey (1998), KPMG Canada Survey (1997), and Chaos Report (1995), all cited at http://www.it-cortex.com/Stat_Failure_Cause.htm.

[10]   In 1998, one such example was the unsuccessful attempts of Sergey Brin and Larry Page of Google to get Yahoo!'s interest in their ideas and plans. Yahoo! executives thought that no one needed a better search engine; instead, they convinced themselves that Yahoo! should develop and sell enterprise portals. Google's founders got a similar reception at other portal vendors. Reluctant as they were, they had no choice but to start their own company. The rest is history, and "google" is now a verb.

Some Practical Next Steps

If you are considering experimenting with Solution Envisioning or Capability Cases, some steps you might want to take are

- If you are an IT person, take time to understand and appreciate business strategy methods and techniques. Do not try to extend your favorite software development method into the world of business. Instead, extend your comfort zone and learn new ways of working.

- If you are a business person involved with technology projects, help your technical colleagues create a space where you can jointly envision and implement your company's future.

- One of the hardest tasks in understanding solution requirements is separating *what is needed* from already pre-conceived ideas on *how it can be implemented*. Use Solution Envisioning language (forces, results, challenges, capabilities) to separate *what* from *how*.

- Integrate Solution Envisioning with your current solution lifecycle methodologies—applying the approach during the inception or envisioning phases.

- Think capabilities—create your first Capability Case.

We expect that one of the first questions a beginning practitioner of Solution Envisioning may have is, "Where do I get Capability Cases?" With that in mind, we have started a community website—www.CapabilityCases.org. All the Capability Cases in this book (and more) are available on the site. Our vision and plans for the website are discussed in the next section.

Readers may be able to re-use existing Capability Cases directly or specialize them as described in Chapter 7, "Software Capability Design—Phase III of Solution Envisioning." Chapter 2, "Bridging the Gap with Solution Envisioning," offers guidance and templates (also downloadable from the website) for creating Capability Cases, as well as techniques for writing solution stories. Additional techniques for story writing are available in Appendix B.

Until five or six years ago, it was not as easy to write Capability Cases. Today, the Internet is full of examples, ideas, and readily accessible applications and capabilities. In addition, we found the following tips useful in creating and using Capability Cases:

- Take care in naming Capability Cases and in describing their intent. Finding several examples of a capability really helps capture its essence.

- Try to keep the summary-level view of a Capability Case down to a single page.

- Print the summary page and place it in a plastic sleeve in a three-ring binder. This way, you will begin to assemble your portfolio. It is important for Capability Cases to be tactile—for people to be able to flip through and pass them around.

- Put any additional (elaborated information) on the back side of the Capability Case summary page.

- Share your work with others—submit it to CapabilityCases.org.

- We found that lists of forces, results, challenges, and measures can be both highly re-usable and helpful when creating Capability Cases. For that reason, they are also available on the website. The need for specialization applies to these assets as well. For instance, instead of using a generic result like "Improve productivity," some readers will find it necessary to make it more specific to be meaningful in their situation.

A Community Sandbox—CapabilityCases.org

Our plan is to create a site—www.capabilitycases.org—that will support the growth of a community interested in the potential and use of envisioning and Capability Cases. Additionally, the site will provide companion materials (for example, templates) for the Solution Envisioning process and updates related to this book.

Initially, we will be presenting Capability Cases there, both individually and in galleries—collections of Capability Cases that reflect various interests and purposes. The Capability Case templates featured in the book—summary and extended views—will be available for inspection and download. We will also provide a way to upload and index new Capability Cases.

We would also like to offer community features—wikis,[11] discussion threads, and chat, as well as a way to create and store Capability Cases online.

---

[11] From Wikipedia, the free encyclopedia (http://en.wikipedia.org/wiki/Wiki): "A **Wiki** or **wiki** is a website that allows users to add content, as on an Internet forum, but also allows anyone to edit the content. "Wiki" also refers to the collaborative software used to create such a website."

END OF TRAIL: SOLUTION ENVISIONING

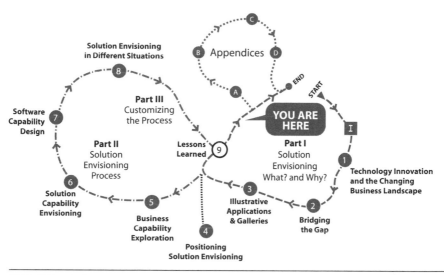

FIGURE 9.2.

The upstream of the software development lifecycle, like all *headwaters*, are very challenging places to be—perhaps, the last under-explored world of software development. We have attempted to chart this territory, putting down some maps for how to envision solutions. Even with several years of practice culminating in this book, we know that we have only begun to map this space. As with any pioneering effort, there will be many opportunities for new discoveries, improvements, and insights.

We look forward to connecting with others who want to explore the headwaters and make connections between all of the communities that need to be respected, heard from, listened to, and served in this process.

If there is a final thing to say about the importance of Solution Envisioning, perhaps it is the thought that solutions are really the introduction of new systems[12] in a complex environment where they co-exist with many other systems. They work only if the nature of the problem is understood and the solution is adopted by those who are affected by the problem (and the solution). Envisioning should anticipate the effects of the solution in the future world that is being envisioned.

---

[12] Our colleague, Jack Ring, calls them "Problem Suppression Systems," and we are indebted to him for these remarks and many other insights regarding the envisioning of solutions.

The act of introducing a new solution changes the original problem and introduces new problems.

Looking ahead as envisioners, we anticipate there will continue to be plenty of envisioning work to be done for some time to come.

History and Design of Solution Envisioning

The X-Model and Object-Oriented Development

Solution Envisioning with Capability Cases has evolved as a result of the authors' work on software development projects across multiple industries going back to the early '90s.

At that time, there was a quest for the *best* approach to develop object-oriented software and many methods proliferated. Objects were highly motivated by the desire to have systems that "modeled the real world," which resulted in more extensible and modifiable software that could be built with higher quality and faster development processes through the reuse of classes and frameworks.

These interests caused many people to examine and improve their software development processes. Traditional waterfall models, predicated on the notion of "analysis *then* design *then* coding," were felt by many to be inappropriate. Iterative models were designed to allow early experience and validation of design decisions and a more informed discovery of requirements.

Recognizing that there is an act of designing involved in arriving at viable solution concepts—design before analysis (of specification requirements)—led to the need for having a way to explore concepts early in the lifecycle. The mood was very much about reuse and the sentiment was: "If programmers have libraries, and designers have classes and frameworks, then what can we provide business people and solution architects so they can think better about problems and solutions?" This marked the early motivations for Solution Envisioning and led to the X-Model for an Object-Oriented Development process [Hodgson, 1991].

The X-Model builds on the V-Model of Software Development, which shows the life-cycle as a decent into more detailed work follows by an ascent towards delivery, with implied horizontal relationships across different levels of the V [Ould, 1990]. What happens in the X-Model is a second V that is drawn inverted below the original V. In this inverted V, activities and artifacts relating to building reusable components, frameworks, and models are depicted. The implication of vertical meanings between the two Vs is at the core of the intuitive appeal of the visualization.

We show a version of the X-Model for Capability Cases in Figure A.1. Each activity in the solution development process is reuse-driven. Capability Cases influence solution concepts; architectures and patterns inform the structuring of the solution; components and Web Services contribute to the building of the solution.

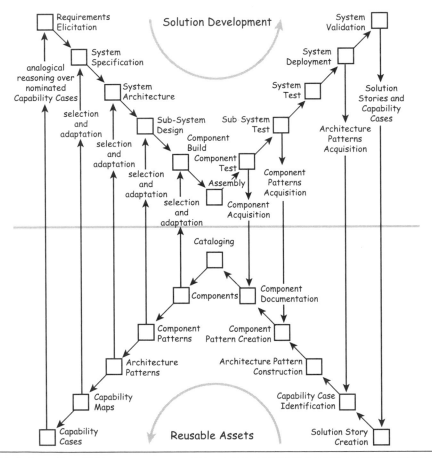

FIGURE A.1.   THE X-MODEL OF SOLUTION DEVELOPMENT USING CAPABILITY CASES.

DESIGN BY ANALOGY AND THE ARCHITECTURE HANDBOOK

The X-Model was influenced by ideas on *Analogical Reasoning, Domain Modeling*, and early work with Bruce Anderson on the *Architecture Handbook* [Anderson, 1992], a pre-cursor to the *Design Patterns* movement.

OOPSLA WORKSHOPS—(1996–2000)

Important ideas about system envisioning evolved in a series of workshops on System Envisioning conducted at the annual OOPSLA Conference between 1996 and 2000. The workshops participants, Bruce Andersen, Alistair Cockburn, Marine Devos, and many others listed in the Acknowledgments, contributed to formulating a repeatable and practical set of methods for facilitating this crucial upstream envisioning process. At the same time, a System Envisioning Wiki site was established at http://c2.com/cgi/wiki?SystemEnvisioning.

Since then, Solution Envisioning has matured to embrace recent thinking on business strategy, such as Balanced Scorecard and Performance Prism, and approaches to software development, such as Web services, component-based development, and Agile Development methods.

OTHER SEMINAL INFLUENCES

Lastly, the influence of Checkland's Soft Systems Methodology [Checkland, 1981], *Future Search Conferences*, storytelling techniques, and the patterns community should not go without mention.

Figure A.2 shows a timeline of the main influences.

We will elaborate more on the influences of these methods and approaches in terms of their contribution to the origins and the continuing evolution of Solution Envisioning.

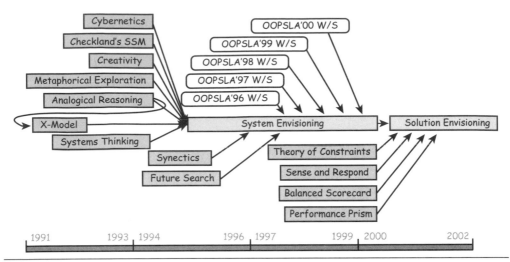

FIGURE A.2.   BACKGROUND OF MAJOR INFLUENCES ON SOLUTION ENVISIONING.

SOLUTION ENVISIONING AND CREATIVITY

Creativity comes from the interplay of ideas. Arthur Koestler[1] called this *bisociation*—the emergence of new insights from making connections between dissimilar ideas. In Solution Envisioning, we encourage the juxtaposition of ideas through the use of Capability Cases. They create a language for a design dialog.

Creativity as an aesthetic pursuit was well described in Arieti's writings in *Creativity—The Magic Synthesis* [Arieti, 1976]. Here, a phenomenon called the *Amorphous Cognition* is described. *Amorphous* because the idea or realization first emerges by being felt internally with no form—no representation in language or imagery, but nonetheless a cognition. To distinguish these ideas from *Concepts*, Arieti calls them *Endocepts* from the Greek "endo" meaning "inside." Think of Endocepts as "Ahas"—insights that suggest ways out of a problem situation. In Solution Envisioning, we see this happening when the stories associated with Capability Cases spark people's imagination. What is at work is the connection of elements from one solution idea to elements of another and to elements within the problem context, so-called analogical reasoning.

Osborn's work in 1953 on creativity enumerated a 7-step process. Parallels can be made to Solution Envisioning:

---

[1]   Arthur Koestler. *The GHOST in the MACHINE* [Koestler, 1967].

1. **Orientation**—*Pointing up the problem:* Forces, results, barriers, and challenges

2. **Preparation**—*Gathering pertinent information:* Business Capability Exploration

3. **Analysis**—*Breaking things down:* Business situation analysis

4. **Ideation**—*Generating alternate ideas:* Capability Cases

5. **Incubation**—*Letting up to invite illumination:* Solution Envisioning Workshop

6. **Synthesis**—*Putting ideas together:* Conceptual Design

7. **Evaluation**—*Judging the ideas:* Capability Prioritization and Gap Analysis

In thinking about solutions, we might often have insights on the nature of a solution, but we struggle to have a physical representation. Articulating these insights is key to successful innovation—a central idea in Solution Envisioning.

For interested readers, more models of the creative process can be found in Gentner's work on Analogical Reasoning [Gentner, 1989]; Boden's work on creativity types [Boden, 1990]; Finke's Geneplore Model [Finke, 1992] and [Finke, 1996]; Csikszentmihalyi's work [Csikszentmihalyi, 1997]; Ken Robinson's book *Learning to Be Creative* [Robinson, 2001]; and Thomas Ward's work "Creative Cognition" [Ward, 1999].

For example, Margaret Boden, one of the leading experts in cognitive science, has argued that creativity can be explained as a process combining exploration (search) and recognition. She distinguishes three types, or degrees, of creativity, each categorized by a different type of search.

The simplest type of creativity occurs when one explores permutations and combinations of familiar ideas, hoping for an inspired change. For example, when one artist succeeds at capturing the imagination of the public with pictures of small children with big eyes, another artist may attempt to do the same thing by painting children with big ears.

The second degree of creativity involves exploring an unknown space, that is, a dimension or variable not used before. Boden gave the example of Christopher Columbus who set sail not knowing what he might find—and then misrecognized North America as "The Indies" when he did get there. Although this example involves a *physical* space, Boden usually means conceptual spaces when she discusses space. The more clearly *conceptual* spaces can be defined, the better we can identify creative ideas.

The third and highest degree of creativity occurs when one explores a space that has been transformed in new ways. This type of creativity brings dramatic changes making possible what was once considered impossible. An example is the discovery of the transistor. Prior to 1950, it was considered a given that all electronics and information processing systems had to work at relatively high and dangerous levels of electrical voltage. The invention of the transistor changed this so dramatically that power distribution through wires may no longer be necessary in the next few years. This type of creativity often is possible by connecting concepts or images. Einstein did it by linking mass and energy. Another example given by Boden is Kekule's discovery of the ring structure of benzene[2] while thinking about a ring of snakes chasing each others tails. He had actually seen such a ring some years before.

WHY METAPHORS ARE POWERFUL

Metaphors are a form of imagery. Through images we arrive at insights and share ideas. Metaphors and analogies free one's imagination, creating a new space for people to enter and explore connections.

Metaphors draw attention to new ways of seeing things and new possibilities. Through metaphor, we share insights into the essential elements of a problem situation and the key features of a solution. In this way, metaphors shape the thinking of a group. According to Hill and Levenhagen, "Metaphors and other mental models provide a means for individuals and, ultimately, organizations to create and share understanding. These mental models establish images, names, and an understanding of how things fit together. They articulate what is important and unimportant ... the models must be articulated and accepted in the organization for them to be effective ... In the context of such models, believing is seeing."[3]

---

[2]   From http://encyclopedia.laborlawtalk.com/benzene_ring: "The chemist Friedrich August Kekulé von Stradonitz was the first to deduce the ring structure of benzene. After years of studying carbon bonding, benzene, and related molecules, he dreamt one night of a snake eating its own tail. Upon waking, he was inspired to deduce the ring structure of benzene." From http://www.answers.com/topic/benzene: "The simplest picture of the benzene molecule, proposed by the German chemist Friedrich Kekulé (1865), is a hexagon of six carbon atoms joined by alternating single and double bonds and each bearing one hydrogen atom, symbolized by ⬛. However, modern studies have shown that the six carbon-carbon bonds are all of equal strength and distance; thus, the double-bond electrons do not belong to any particular bonds but rather are delocalized about the ring, with the result that the strength of each bond is between that of a single bond and that of a double bond."

[3]   Hill, R. C. and M. Levenhagen. *Metaphors and Mental Models: Sense Making and Sense Giving in Innovative and Entrepreneurial Activities* [Hill, 1995].

In Figure A.3, a storyboard from a workshop on the "Nature of the Future Organization," we see the use of a number of metaphors.[4] A DNA metaphor likens the organization to a living organism. An army metaphor emphasizes the need for readiness to adapt to changing conditions.

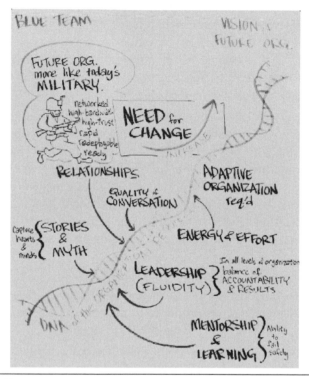

FIGURE A.3.   TWO METAPHORS AT WORK IN A "VISION OF THE FUTURE
ORGANIZATION" EXERCISE.

CAPABILITY CASES AND PATTERNS

To help understand what Capability Cases are, we first give the following brief history of the pattern movement. Several decades ago, an architect, Christopher Alexander, wrote a book describing the types of capabilities that make living spaces (towns, neighborhoods, and houses) habitable [Alexander, 1979]. His goal

---

[4] The Advanced Thinkers Forum on future organizational models was organized by Andy Snider of Snider Associates and held at IBM in New York, November 2003.

was to communicate through the architectural patterns, what he called "the quality without the name," and what we often call *best design practices*, to the rest of the architectural community. Because talking about something that doesn't have a name presents an understandable challenge, Alexander gave a name to each pattern. The book catalogs and describes each of them.

A number of years later, computer professionals were facing a similar challenge. Many of them were experienced architects of computer systems and had assembled a good amount of "best practices" proven to work. Yet, the software community as a whole was still struggling to solve the same problems over and over again. Christopher Alexander's approach to communicating through a language of patterns was embraced as a means to solve this problem.

Many patterns now exist—software architecture patterns, design patterns, organizational patterns, even anti-patterns describing "worst practices" (the approaches that don't work). In each case, the goal of the individual using them (an experienced software architect, designer or technical manager) was to communicate to the rest of his community. Basically, a pattern gives a name to a best practice, provides a concise description of a problem context and a solution it offers, and illustrates this description with a concrete example of the best practice in use. Patterns have established a shared vocabulary for commonly used programming, design, and architecture ideas.

Patterns are written by software architects for software architects, by experienced system testers for other system testers, and so on. Why do these people need a special pattern language to communicate to the rest of their community, to professionals who arguably already speak the same language?

The main reason is that the topics they talk about are highly conceptual, abstract, and illusive—having "the qualities without the name." When looking through pattern catalogs, the communication made possible by applying the same description template to a large set of possible solutions is very powerful.

The most widely used design patterns are the *Gang of Four Design Patterns* [Gamma, 1994]. The GOF book changed the way software designers talked about their designs. It gave the software community a standard vocabulary for recurring solutions to design problems. Patterns like "Factory," "Composite," "Proxy," "Iterator," "Mediator," and "Visitor Pattern" became part of the programming vernacular. The GOF book established a new culture for talking about reusable software design ideas in a concise way using a standard template. The pattern template always expresses the intent of the idea, the context in which the solution is applicable, and examples.

Templates for patterns vary somewhat for each domain because the template itself represents a best practice of communicating a certain type of a solution. Therefore, a template for communicating best practices of organizational design may vary from the templates for communicating best programming or infrastructure solutions. Alexander's patterns need to speak to architects and planners, the GOF patterns need to speak to software designers, and so on.

Since the GOF book, numerous patterns have been published for architecture, analysis, process [Berczuk, 2002], innovation [Manns, 2004], and user interfaces [van Duyne, 2002]. The PLoP communities[5] have published four volumes of patterns. The tradition of documenting patterns in software architecture and design has seen no interruption. In 2002, Martin Fowler's *Patterns of Enterprise Application Architecture* [Fowler, 2002] offered more than forty commonly used patterns, described in platform-independent ways, for building object-oriented applications for information and transaction-based systems.

This book continues the tradition of using patterns in a new design/decision space, earlier in the software engineering lifecycle—to support the upstream work of deciding on the conceptual nature of a software solution. This is the spot where solution concepts have to be evaluated in context with business situations, opportunities, and desired futures—that is, precisely where the "gap" between business and IT occurs.

---

[5]   In August of 1993, Kent Beck and Grady Booch sponsored a mountain retreat in Colorado where a group converged on foundations for software patterns. Since then, the Hillside Group has been incorporated as an educational non-profit. It has sponsored and helped run various conferences and has been responsible for getting the Pattern Languages of Program Design series of books put together and published. More information is available at http://hillside.net/. Since then, there has been an explosion in pattern books. We are only referencing a few books, not because there are no other books worth mentioning, but because the number of good books that took pattern ideas on board is so large.

Sidebar A.1 Reflecting on the Relationship Between Capability Cases and Patterns

Upon reflection on the different types of patterns and the different ways of using them, we came to conclude there are at least two types of patterns:

- **Best Practice Patterns**—Intended for use within a single community. Some examples are Design Patterns and Architecture Patterns.

- **Bridging Patterns**—These may be intended for and have use as *Best Practice Patterns*, but they also exhibit a strong potential to serve as communication tools between two (or more) communities. We believe some User Interaction Design Patterns, for example the ones on http://www.welie.com/patterns/index.html, fall into this category and so do Capability Cases.

What are the key differences between these two types of patterns?

One important difference is in what's needed to use them successfully. In the case of *Best Practice Patterns*, a reference library seems to be sufficient. *Bridging Patterns*, on the other hand, need a process for their use. The process could be fairly simple, like a technique for using User Interaction Design Patterns in a web design meeting or more elaborate like Solution Envisioning.

Patterns typically require three examples of use. While this is a strong requirement for *Best Practice Patterns*, it may not need to be an equally strong requirement for the *Bridging Patterns*. This is because their goal is somewhat different. In fact, we recognize a special category of Capability Cases—the ones that are at an early inception stage. There may be no examples quite like them or only one or two research prototypes. Nevertheless, we find it useful to formalize them as Capability Cases to give them a name and to discuss their business value and applicability.

Finally, *Bridging Patterns* must have a stronger emphasis on storytelling. All patterns include some elements of storytelling in the examples of use, but we believe a good story is especially critical for *Bridging Patterns*.

It would seem to make sense for *Bridging Patterns* to be explicit in defining what communities they are trying to "bridge." Correspondingly, their pattern language should reflect interests of each community as well as the "bridging" qualities of the pattern. In designing a template for Capability Cases, we have tried to take this into consideration by:

- Bringing in the Performance Prism framework with its multi-stakeholder orientation
- Including fields of interest to business leaders and technologists

THE IMPORTANCE OF THE "RIGHT" DELIVERABLES

Often, solution design documents, such as requirements specifications, concept of operations, and solution concept definitions contain tens or even hundreds of pages of material. Regardless of any value to their notorious *thunk factor* (the impressive, physical size and weight of the requirements, or specs), when a solution progresses to the next stage of the lifecycle and new people get involved, it is more typical than not for there to be confusion and a frenzied search to understand "what this solution is about." As a result, inordinate amounts of time and effort are spent on "getting on the same page," revisiting decisions, and redoing the work.

Large requirements and concept documents make necessary information difficult to find and, once found, difficult to comprehend. Frequently, their format and style is much harder to penetrate and can easily conceal the fact that some critical information is missing. The size of a document is often in a reverse proportion to its effectiveness as a communication vehicle. We've observed that brief, concise definitions coupled with grounding a solution in the business context significantly increase the completeness and effectiveness of communication.

To give an example, on one of our recent projects, we found it necessary to distill over 200 pages of text to about 20 pages of business solution concepts, which we graphically depicted and succinctly described. As a result, the solution "revealed" itself. It became visible and more easily understood. This enabled the team to identify important aspects of the solution that had been overlooked in the original requirements.

This experience, and others of a similar nature, has lead to important decisions on the format and content of Solution Envisioning deliverables:

- **Deliverable content must be parsimonious**—It should only contain information both necessary and sufficient to communicate the solution concept.

- **Deliverable format should take in to account the way people process information**—The content must be interconnected to show the linkages between technical decisions and capabilities and capabilities and the work context. It should strike the balance between visual and textual presentation. If we believe that a picture is worth a thousand words, the right balance should err on the side of the visual content.

- **Deliverables must show an integrated view of the "whole" system**—After the main concept of the system is communicated, the details can be presented.

Beyond capturing the important solution design decisions, the goal of the deliverables is to enable the next group of people to pick up and carry out the solution implementation without an undue amount of special instructions and interactions.

ADDITIONAL TECHNIQUES

CREATIVITY TECHNIQUES

Using Storytelling for the Creation of Future Scenarios

This technique is specifically noted in Chapter 6, "Solution Capability Envisioning—Phase II of Solution Envisioning," as one of the SCE techniques (see Technique 4), but we also found it useful during some of the BCE (Business Capability Exploration) activities.

Addendum A to Technique (T4): Guidance on the Art of Practical Storytelling

Through stories, we share meaning about the world. We make and exchange sense of the experienced world, and we create the future through stories. Story telling is an integral part of what it means to be a human being.

The following points are taken from a presentation by Kathleen McShea called "Evaluating Innovation Strategies."

Bad Lecturing Is Tiring:

"Let me explain..."

"Let me show you a chart..."

"These are the requirements we have for your problem..."

"We have the solution to your problems..."

Storytelling is energizing, refreshing, and interesting:

Storytelling is a "dance" that ignites creativity.

"Imagine a world"...No winners or losers.

You don't impose ideas—you invite participation in the solution.

The following quotes come from from Steve Song's presentation on storytelling [Song, 2002]:

"Stories are the secret reservoir of values: change the stories individuals or nations live by and tell themselves, and you change the individuals and nations."

"Great leaders understand the power of the stories they project to their people," he writes. "They understand that stories can change an age, turn an era around."

"When we have made an experience or a chaos into a story, we have transformed it, made sense of it, transmuted experience, domesticated the chaos."

Stories illuminate:

They create a space in which people can share an understanding or envision a new reality.

We identify with each other through stories.

A story becomes powerful when the listener identifies with the story, enters into its world, and makes his or her own understandings and connections that transcend the story.

In Chapter 2, "Bridging the Gap with Solution Envisioning," we referenced Denning's book, *The Springboard: How Storytelling Ignites Action in Knowledge-Era Organizations*. The 12 Denning Steps to guide creation of a Springboard Story are

1. What change are you seeking?

2. Think of an incident where the change was in part or in whole implemented.

3. Who is the single protagonist in the story?

4. Is the single protagonist archetypal for your specific audience?

5. When did the incident happen?

6. Where did the story happen?

7. How fully does the story embody the change idea?

8. Can the story be extrapolated to more fully embody the idea?

9. Does the story make clear what would have happened without the change idea?

10. Has the story been stripped of unnecessary detail?

11.   Does the story have an authentically happy ending?

12.   Does the story link to the purpose to be achieved in telling it?

Sidney Bailin offers the following advice for framing a story and designing how it unfolds [Bailin, 2000; Bailin, 2003]:

An essential essence in a story is the notion of "setup and payoff"-"question and answer":

- The story engages people by making them wonder about things—raising questions then providing answers.

- To enhance dramatic tensions and interest, the story might include answers to questions which raise other questions, or that only partially answer the previous questions.

This controlled release of information is the shape of the story:

- *Aspects of the story make the questions important or interesting*—For example, characters and their world—invoking a sense of identification on the part of the consumer with a character, a situation, challenges, or aspirations.

- *A world*—It comprises information that allows the reader to immerse herself in the story—to place herself within the story world—by identifying with one or more characters or, as an observer, with the narrator's voice.

- Equivalent to *context* in design—The narrative concepts of world and voice are closely related to the ideas of perspective and view in visual design.

- *Forward movement*—The causal structure that drives the story. The main character of a story has a goal, just as in design. To achieve the goals, he takes certain actions, which cause a change of state for better or worse—perhaps causing other actions by other characters in response—necessitating further actions by the main character. The characters do not know the outcome in advance, and for the most part, neither does the reader.

- *Shape*—The storyteller, who controls the release of information by using techniques such as mystery, suspense, and surprise, keeps the reader engaged. The resulting patterns of rising and falling tension—teasing versus gratification, a preponderance of questions versus a preponderance of answers—give the story its shape.

- *Design a headline*—The headline helps you get clear on the goal.

- *Pick some challenges the story overcomes*—These are the motivations for the story.

- *Set the scene*—The context of the story.

- *Decide on the protagonist*—This could be one or more stakeholders.

- *Make sure the story is simple*—It needs to be understood by readers with different backgrounds.

- *Make sure it has a happy ending*—A solution to the challenges.

- *Celebrate what was good about the solution*—Explain what it did for the business.
- *Reflect on the story*—Emphasize its strong points, and mention possible follow-ups to the storyline.

The following is some miscellaneous advice we've culled from our own experience and have absorbed from many other sources:

Envisioned Versus Real Stories

As the story is clearly not an objective description of an actual situation, you are at liberty to be entirely subjective:

- You can make things happen as you want them to.
- You can present things in particular ways just because they "feel right" that way.
- You can note what has to happen to make you feel comfortable and how you react to things that make you uncomfortable.

You are definitely not saying that "This is what will happen," but you are, tentatively, holding it up as a mirror to yourself:

- Noting the sorts of beliefs, expectations, feelings, judgments, anxieties, reactions, and so forth that you may well find yourself bringing to such a situation.

Using Stories to Gain Insights

Examining how you instinctively react in a given situation could be a path to understanding feelings and thoughts you find difficult to put into words.

Creating stories can

- Give insight into your own deeper motives.
- Provide warning signs of personal anxieties and frailties that may affect how well you can respond.

This could be accessed by creating or finding a story or parable that is clearly fictional, but nevertheless has some parallels to a real situation you are facing.

Last Tips

There are no requirements for a technical skill in story writing:

- Stick figure drawings or amateur narration are ample.
- Authors can review their own stories.

Synectics

The use of synectics during Solution Envisioning workshops is mentioned in Chapter 6, Technique 4. Here, we provide additional details on synectic prompts.

Addendum B to Technique (T4): Some Synectic Technique Prompts[1]

Addition	Analogy	Animation	Context	Combination
Extend or expand the solution.	Draw associations.	Mobilize the visual and psychological tensions.	Make subject areas bigger or smaller.	Bring things together—ideas, materials, and techniques.
Augment the source ideas.	Seek similarities between things that are different.	Control the pictorial movements and forces.	Increase the stakeholders.	Connect, arrange, link, unify, mix, merge, rearrange.
What else can be included in your idea?	Compare with elements from different domains, disciplines.	Apply factors of repetition and progression.	Think of a bigger problem that subsumes this problem.	Bring together dissimilar things to produce synergistic integrations.
	What can I compare my subject to?	Can we anthropomorphize the solution—what human qualities does the subject have?		What else can you connect to your subject?
	Make logical or illogical associations.			Connect different sensory modes, frames of reference, disciplines.

[1]   Adapted from the checklists in Axon2005, the tool from Axon Research.

Contradiction	Fantasy	Parody	Symbols	Transference
Deny the subject's original function visually and intellectually, yet remain structurally integrated.	Fantasize your ideas to trigger surreal, preposterous, outlandish, bizarre thoughts.	Apply ridicule, mimicry, mockery, burlesque, or caricature to ideas.	How can the source ideas be imbued with symbolic qualities?	How can the source ideas be converted, translated, transfigured?
Laws of nature, such as gravity, time, human functions.	Topple mental and sensory expectations.	Make fun of ideas—find a joke or pun that illuminates them.	A visual symbol stands for something other than what it is.	Move source idea into a new situation.
Normal procedures, social conventions, rituals.	How far out can you extend your imagination?	Find similes that act as insights.	Works of art are often integrations of both public and private symbols.	Adapt, transpose, relocate, dislocate.
Optical and perceptual harmony (for example, illusions).	What would happen if people did not have to search for information and information was smart enough to find people?		Turn your subject into a symbol (public or private).	Adapt source idea to a different frame of reference.
			Private symbols are cryptic, have special meaning to its originator.	Move source idea out of its normal environment.
			Public symbols are cliché, well-known, and understood.	Transpose to a different historical, social, geographical setting.

DECISION SUPPORT TECHNIQUES

Decision support techniques are used throughout SCE and SCD activities. This appendix contains two techniques that we use in addition to Technique (T1): V.I.S.A. Multi-Criteria Decision Support Technique described in Chapter 7, "Software Capability Design—Phase III of Solution Envisioning."

Technique (T2): Bayesian Decision Modeling Technique

Problem Context   How to make a selection among different alternatives while taking into account uncertain knowledge and the variation of knowledge and opinions in the decision-making team.

Approach   Bayesian decision theory works well in situations characterized by uncertainty and risk. In these situations, the available information is imprecise, incomplete, and even inconsistent. Decision outcomes can be uncertain and the decision-maker's attitude towards them can vary widely.

This technique is best suited for situations when there is a strong need to build a consensus among multiple participants or there is a need to accommodate uncertainty.

The Bayesian decision model has three elements:

1. A set of beliefs about the decision space

2. A set of decision alternatives

3. A preference over the possible outcomes of action

Belief modeling must, first of all, be simple and intuitive. Complex models that require vast amounts of precisely specified information may be theoretically attractive, but are useless to the busy practitioner. We begin with the premise that teams have objectives. These may be ill-understood initially, but nonetheless, they are of prime importance. More specifically, the beliefs we model are team member beliefs about how decision alternatives impact objectives.

The other major component of this approach is the preference model. A preference model corresponds, roughly, to a set of objectives. In its most general form, a decision-theoretic preference model can represent any consistent set of user preferences. However, the general form is very difficult to describe and harder to understand.

When using this technique, evaluation of alternatives involves these steps:

1. Measurement of the team's knowledge about the alternatives

2. Determination of the confidence/belief that the alternative satisfies the criterion

3. Determination of the team's overall evaluation of the alternatives

Example

A belief map (see Figure B.1) was constructed using Robust Decision's tool Accord.[2] It shows option rankings as rated by several people in the team.

The X-axis indicates the knowledge of how an alternative ranks for the selected criterion, and the Y-axis indicates the confidence that the option will meet the "good" value of the criterion. Each axis is divided into degrees of knowledge or confidence: "VL" for very low, "L" for low, "M" for medium, "H" for high, and "VH" for very high.

Circled numbers in the diagram represent different options. Each person has his or her own color.

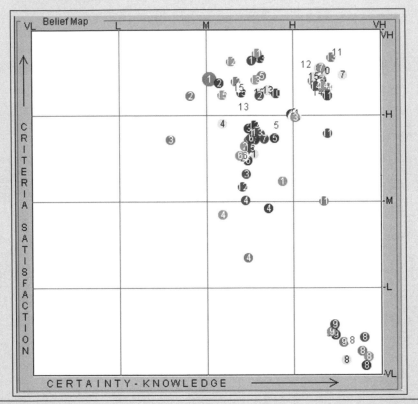

FIGURE B.1. PROBABILISTIC DECISION MODEL EXAMPLE.

2 Accord is a decision support tool from Robust Decisions: www.robustdecisions.com. A paper on Robust Decisions' decision support method is available at http://www.robustdecisions.com/BayesianMethodDecisions.pdf.

We can see from the diagram that there is a consistent opinion about options 8 and 9 (in the bottom-right corner). The team has good knowledge of how the criteria can be assessed and does not give them a very good score. The picture is different for option 1. It seems that people who are knowledgeable like it more than people who are not certain of their knowledge. The converse is true for option 4.

By accommodating different perspectives and areas of expertise, this decision approach can explore the basis of a decision more effectively than assigning a discrete value to a ranking. Ranking is done in a joint meeting (either phase-to-phase or using a real-time collaboration technology, such as WebEx). An interesting feature of the Accord tool is the ability to do Monte Carlo analysis on the probabilities of solution alternatives.

Technique (T3): Analytical Hierarchy Process (AHP)

Problem Context   Decision making in the context of multiple criteria and the need to determine the sensitivity of ranking, such as "How much importance do you give to criterion X over criterion Y?," and the scoring of options by answering questions like, "With respect to criterion X, how much do you prefer alternate A over alternate B?".

Approach   Create a hierarchical decomposition of criteria and a list of options. Perform pair-wise ranking of the criteria starting at the leaf-level of the tree and working upwards to the root. For each criterion at the leaf-level, make a pair-wise assessment of each option. The AHP method rolls these valuations up to each sub-root and to the overall root of the tree. The answers at the root of the criteria tree are the overall assessment of the options. A downside of pair-wise comparison is that it requires time. Assigning weight to 8 criteria is just 8 operations. Pair-wise comparing 8 criteria amounts to 28 operations.

Examples   We used this technique on a project where the team was concerned about integrating their solution with the other systems already present. Many conversations centered on this topic. When the team was presented with a flat list of eight criteria and asked to assign a weight to each one, integration was ranked as "very important" with the highest weight. We then went through a pair-wise comparison asking questions like, "What is more important: integration with other systems or functionality?" or "What is more important: integration or time to implement?". Surprisingly, after this exercise, integration ended up being one of the least important criteria. The tool we used was ExpertChoice.[3]

[3]   www.expertchoice.com.

ExpertChoice's support for sensitivity analysis is illustrated in the following example. A decision had to be made on the best next steps for a Knowledge Worker Desktop (KWD) Initiative.

In Figure B.2, the left side of the screen shows recommendations for achieving the goal of developing and deploying KWD. Options on the right are for what to do next. After the scoring has been completed, sensitivity can be analyzed. For example, when "Confirm business commitment to implementing KWD" is a top objective with 44.4%, and "Start the pilot implementation" is given only 14.3% weight, "Envisioning" comes up as the highest scoring alternative. If "Start the pilot implementation" is given more importance, then "KWD Intranet" will become the top alternative.

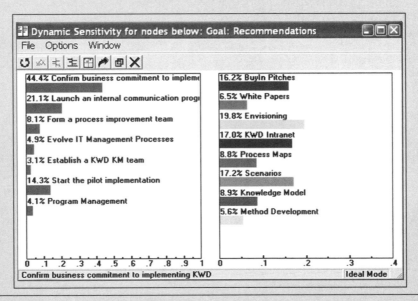

FIGURE B.2. PROBABILISTIC DECISION MODEL—SENSITIVITY ANALYSIS.

The ExpertChoice tool supports sensitivity analysis by allowing users to dynamically adjust the weights of each goal. The power of such tools is in giving immediate feedback to how sensitive options are to criteria ranking and scoring. We have found it is only really possible to use the pair-wise comparison technique without a tool only if the number of criteria is less than 10 or 12.

CONDUCTING ENVISIONING WORKSHOPS AS "THEATER PLAY"

The envisioning workshop leader must be a good facilitator. It is the leader's responsibility to create a special atmosphere in the workshop—an atmosphere that makes it possible to create, discuss, and design the solution in a group setting. This section is intended as additional guidance to workshop leaders on how to ensure the right atmosphere in the workshop.

Creative work requires the group to engage in a dialog, and certain dispositions have to be collectively in place for the group to make progress:[4]

1. Disposition to inquiry
2. Suspension of disbelief
3. Tension of opposites
4. Generative listening
5. Ladder of inference

The leader should be cognizant of, and remind participants of, the following:

1. We each should be attentive to four levels of individual knowing: what we know, what we know we don't know, what we don't know we don't know, and what we know isn't so.
2. Recognizing and building a vocabulary of ideas.
3. Establishing symbols and notations that are mutually understood.
4. Seeing the essential ideas in solution examples—not what is, but the *essence* of what is.
5. Exercising the interplay of the brain's right and left lobe.
6. Diversifying your learning styles (mitigating the tendency to resist cognitive dissonance).
7. Learning to help others see the vision—learning to see what they don't see, why they don't see it, and what they have to realize in order to see it.

Envisioning as a Five Act Play

Many times, the Solution Envisioning workshop follows the metaphor of a play with five acts:

1. **Exposition**—Establishing the context and the motivating scenarios

---

[4]   Bohm, David. "On Dialogue." Edited by Lee Nichol, Routledge, 1996.

2. **Elicitation**—Free expression of refutations and confirmations

3. **Exploration**—Business capability exploration through scenarios

4. **Validation**—Validation through enacting the envisioned solutions

5. **Closure**—Planning and commitment to the road ahead

In this way, it is shaped as a dialog that follows a sequence of interaction episodes, each paying attention to the right theme at the right time.

Workshop Act I—Exposition

The main objective of exposition is to present results of the BCE phase. The presentation is framed by using Solution Envisioning themes of *Where are we now?*, *How is the world changing?*, *Why do we need to change?*, *What scenarios help us envision the change?*, and *How can technology help us?*

A useful way of setting the context and scope for the workshop is to present Figure B.3, adapted from John Friend's "The Strategic Choice Approach" chapter in *Rational Analysis for a Problematic World* [Rosenhead, 1989].

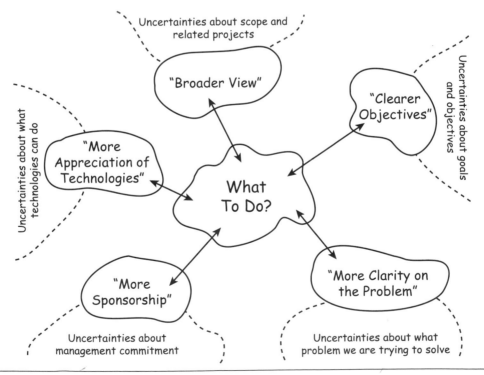

FIGURE B.3.   UNCERTAINTY BUBBLES—DRAWING OUT CONCERNS.

Workshop Act II—Elicitation

The elicitation solicits participants input that confirms, rebuffs, or shades a different light on the findings of the BCE. The main goal of elicitation is to ensure the group shares a common view of the current situation and is committed to designing a solution. For that to happen, the workshop must provide a space for participants to freely talk about their views, experiences, and opinions. The elicitation is designed to overcome the following key barriers on the road towards a solution:

- Conflict:
    a.   Different interests in different parts of the organization
    b.   Unshared vision of organizational future
    c.   Hidden agendas
- Denial:
    d.   We see only what we have cognition of
    e.   What fits with our plans
    f.   What we have pre-arranged in our minds

The *Three Whats* technique, introduced in Sidebar 5.3, and its use in conjunction with envisioning workshops further described in Chapter 6, can be effectively used in the workshop setting to overcome aspects of conflict and denial. We also use *Rants and Raves* exercises, where each person is asked to contribute one or more rants about what is not working and one or more raves about what is.

Prouds and Sorries, borrowed from *Future Search* conferences [Weisbord, 1992; 1999], is a related exercise. Unlike *Rants and Raves*, it is more focused on an individual or the department he belongs to as opposed to an organization at large. People get to share their experiences, perceptions, and accomplishments by answering the question, "What am I proud of or sorry about?".

Workshop Act III—Exploration

Exploration is performed in a series of envisioning cycles. Each cycle works through the themes of "Where are we now?", "How is the world changing?," "What is it possible to be?", "What do we want to be?", "What capabilities will help us?", and "How will we get there?", with the following pattern:

- Present some aspect of the business context
- Review the relevant work of BCE
- Choose a stakeholder and activity area
- Confirm with the group that the workshop can move on
- Select a scenario
- Review relevant capability maps

- Conduct a gallery tour (see Activity 7 of the SCE Phase, see Chapter 6)
- Enact the scenario (see Activity 8 of the SCE Phase, see Chapter 6)

The Capability Maps prepared for the workshop play are large role in the exploration act. They are used to review BCE work. Projecting Capability Maps is a powerful way to explore other Capability Cases related by either being able to respond to a common force or by contributing to a common business result.

Workshop Act IV—Validation

Validating the Solution Concept is concerned with the stakeholders':

- Agreement over how well the business situation was expressed in the forces, results, and challenges that were connected to envisioned capabilities in the Capability Map
- Confidence on the selected business context and business areas
- Shared understanding of proposed capabilities
- Confirmation that the scenarios chosen for "Solution Enactment" were relevant and comprehensive
- Commitment to the capability prioritization and solution option decisions

The process of seeking validation should allow sufficient time for review not only by all workshop participants but also the sponsors and other key people who have been identified. Do not forget during planning the time that needs to be allocated to soliciting and incorporating feedback in the workproducts.

Workshop Act V—Closure

The Solution Vision and Capability Model are the key deliverables that "close" this phase. We think of this as a *charrette*—the heroic effort needed to complete a design.[5]

---

[5]   Martin Aurand of the Carnegie Mellon University Architecture Archives' Charrette Digital Project: "The term 'charrette' evolved from a pre-1900 exercise at the Ecole des Beaux Arts in France. Architectural students were given a design problem to solve within an allotted time. When that time was up, the students would rush their drawings from the studio to the Ecole in a cart called a *charrette*. Students often jumped in the cart to finish drawings on the way. The term evolved to refer to the intense design exercise itself. Today, it refers to a creative process akin to visual brainstorming that is used by design professionals to develop solutions to a design problem within a limited timeframe." [Aurand, 2003].

FIGURE B.4.   CHARRETTE—SOLUTION ENVISIONERS OF OLDE.[6]

[6] Image, op. cit.

SOFTWARE CAPABILITY DESIGN IMPLEMENTATION ALTERNATIVES

Some alternative approaches to implementation were not fully covered in Chapter 7, "Software Capability Design—Phase III of Solution Envisioning." This appendix details variations on the work in Cluster II (Activities 5 and 6) of SCD for:

1. Custom Development using traditional methodologies, as well as one of the most popular agile approaches—eXtreme Programming

2. EDOC Component-Based Development for Model-Driven Architecture (MDA)

3. Package Implementation including customization and integration concerns

SCD FOR CUSTOM APPLICATIONS

By traditional development, we mean any custom development project that uses a development process or methodology framework, such as the Rational Unified Process (RUP) or the Microsoft Solutions Framework (MSF).

One popular development process or methodology in use today is RUP—a software development process designed by the authors of UML and offered by Rational Software Corporation (now part of IBM). The RUP consists of four phases:

1. Inception

2. Elaboration

3. Construction

4. Transition

A second development method we cover is MSF. This is described on a page at the Microsoft's website[1] as follows:

> *"The Microsoft Solutions Framework (MSF) provides people and process guidance—the proven practices of Microsoft—to help teams and organizations become more successful in delivering business-driven technology solutions to their customers. MSF is a deliberate and disciplined approach to technology projects based on a defined set of principles, models, disciplines, concepts, guidelines, and proven practices from Microsoft. ... MSF is called a framework instead of a methodology for specific reasons. As opposed to a prescriptive methodology, MSF provides a flexible and scalable framework that can be adapted to meet the needs of any project (regardless of size or complexity) to plan, build, and deploy business-driven technology solutions."*

Referring to Figure 7.2, Cluster II work of SCD includes these Activities:

   Activity 5: Elaborate Capability Architecture

   Activity 6: Evaluate Capability Architecture

Subsequent sections contain specializations of these activities and associated workproducts for the RUP and MSF development strategies previously listed.

Custom Application Using RUP and MSF

SCD Activity 5   Elaborate Capability Architecture

SCD-5
Elaborate Capability
Architecture

Elaborating the Capability Architecture for RUP and MSF

Solution Envisioning with Capability Cases maps directly to the initial phases of RUP and MSF. In RUP, there is an "Inception Phase" defined as a phase that *ensures a project is both worth doing and possible to do*. In MSF, there is a phase called "Envisioning." This is defined as a phase that addresses one of the most fundamental requirements for project success—*unification of the project team behind a common vision*. The Solution Envisioning method we describe has a set of techniques for performing these early phases of the software development lifecycle. Exit criteria for the first phase of RUP and MSF are met by the results of a Solution Envisioning project. This can be seen in RUP in the following criteria used to evaluate the completion of the RUP Inception Phase:

---

[1]   http://msdn.microsoft.com/vstudio/enterprise/msf/.

- Is the scope well-defined?
- Is the Candidate Architecture found?
- Are critical tasks found and manageable?

Both RUP and MSF specify the user behavior of the software using use cases. A key focus of the SCD Activities II cluster is to prepare for the implementation work by deriving Uses Cases from the Capability Cases.

A Capability Case is a distinct area of functionality. As *subject areas*, these should still be thought of as proto-components leading to packages or large-grained objects of the solution. In doing this, each Capability Case encompasses one or more use cases. For the most part, these are high-level use cases, but selective use cases, usually between 10 to 20%, typically need to be done at the detail level. We recommend readers who are interested in guidance on writing use cases refer to Alistair Cockburn's book, *Writing Effective Use Cases* [Cockburn, 2002].

In Activity 5, Capability Cases and their implied use cases identify components and their high-level interactions. Interfaces and interactions between components are described in either a sequence diagram or a collaboration diagram. If the UML approach is used, it is a good practice to represent each Capability Case as a package.

Workproduct F   Capability Architecture (RUP and MSF Projects)

 Capability Architecture **Specialization for RUP and MSF**

The Capability Architecture identifies the high-level components of the system and the relationships among them. It includes a use case model and a diagram that shows interactions between components including high-level descriptions of the interfaces. Capability Architecture can be presented in a number of views, for example, views identified in RM-ODP (see Chapter 7, "Software Capability Design—Phase III of Solution Envisioning").

Mapping Solution Envisioning to RUP

Figure C.1 shows key artifacts produced by the development projects using RUP methodology. Table C.1 discusses the mapping between Solution Envisioning deliverables and RUP artifacts.

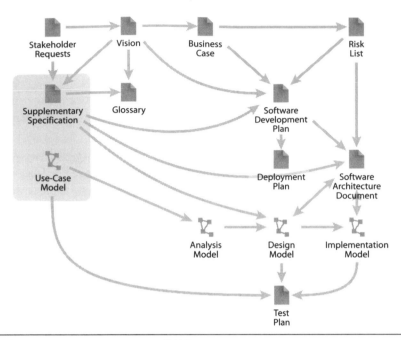

FIGURE C.1.   KEY ARTIFACTS OF RUP.

Solution Envisioning offers a collaborative and business goals–driven approach for performing the work of the Inception phase. Today, most projects employ iterative development processes and RUP mandates iterations. By focusing on prioritizing capabilities, Solution Envisioning directly assists in building incremental development plans. As you can see from the mappings in Table C.1, Solution Envisioning with Capability Cases integrates well with RUP.

TABLE C.1.   Mapping RUP and Solution Envisioning Workproducts

RUP Artifact	RUP Phase	Solution Envisioning Workproduct	SE Phase	Comment
Vision	Inception	Solution Vision	BCE, refined in SCE	RUP says a vision document should contain a general vision of the core project's requirements, key features, and main constraints.
Business Case	Inception, revised at the end of the Elaboration phase	Business Case	SCD	
Glossary	Inception	Glossary	BCE	
Risk List	Inception, revised at the end of the Elaboration phase	Risk Assessment Model	SCE	
Software Development Plan	Inception, revised at the end of the Elaboration phase	Solution Realization Roadmap	SCD	Solution Realization Roadmap contains an initial version of the Development Plan. RUP says the project plan developed during the inception phase should show phases and iterations. It is expected to evolve and become more detailed as the implementation progresses.
Deployment Plan	Inception, revised at the end of the Elaboration phase	Solution Realization Roadmap	SCD	Solution Realization Roadmap contains an initial version of the Deployment Plan. It is expected to evolve and become more detailed as the implementation progresses.

TABLE C.1. MAPPING RUP AND SOLUTION ENVISIONING WORKPRODUCTS—CONTINUED

RUP Artifact	RUP Phase	Solution Envisioning Workproduct	SE Phase	Comment
Software Requirements Specification (Supplemental Specification and Use Case Model)	Inception, extended during the Elaboration phase	Capability Model (list of Capabilities) Capability Prioritization Matrix	SCE	If the development team plans to use RUP, Capability Architecture includes a list of use cases derived from the Capability Cases.
		Non-functional Requirements Capability Architecture	SCD	RUP specifies that only an initial use-case model (10%–20% complete) should be completed during the inception phase.
Software Architecture Document	Limited in the Inception phase Most work is done in the Elaboration and Construction phases	Capability Architecture Architectural Decisions	SCD	RUP says the design activities are centered on the notion of architecture. The production and validation of this architecture is the main focus of early design iterations. Architecture is represented by a number of architectural views. These views capture the major structural design decisions.
Analysis Model	Limited in the Inception phase Most work is done in the Elaboration and Construction phases	Capability Architecture	SCD	

TABLE C.1.   MAPPING RUP AND SOLUTION ENVISIONING WORKPRODUCTS—
CONTINUED

RUP Artifact	RUP Phase	Solution Envisioning Workproduct	SE Phase	Comment
Design Model	Limited in the Inception phase Most work is done in the Elaboration and Construction phases	Technology Decision Model Vendor Short List IT Impact & Interface Specification	SCD	Eventually, the design model becomes a set of design classes structured into design packages and design subsystems with well-defined inter-faces, representing what will become components in the implementation. It also contains descriptions of how objects of these design classes collaborate to perform use cases.
Implementa-tion Model	Construction phase, limited version in the Elaboration phase	N/A		Out of scope for Solution Envisioning
Test Plan	Elaboration and later phases	N/A		Out of scope for Solution Envisioning

Mapping Solution Envisioning to MSF

The output workproducts of the MSF Envisioning and Planning phases can be read-ily aligned with Solution Envisioning workproducts:

- Vision/scope document (Envisioning phase)
- Risk assessment document (Envisioning phase)
- Project structure document (Envisioning phase)
- Functional specification (Planning phase)
- Risk management plan (Planning phase)
- Master project plan and master project schedule (Planning phase)

Showing how business objectives trace all the way down to software is an important concept in the MSF methodology. Because of its focus on connecting business goals to solution capabilities to software design, Solution Envisioning works well.

SCD Activity 6   Evaluate Capability Architecture

SCD-6
Evaluate Capability
Architecture

Evaluating Capability Architecture for RUP and MSF Projects

The Architecture Trade-Off Analysis Method described in Chapter 7 works equally well for RUP and MSF Projects. No additional specific tailoring needs to be made.

SCD in eXtreme Programming (XP) Projects

SCD Activity 5   Elaborate Capability Architecture

SCD-5
Elaborate Capability
Architecture

Elaborating   Capability   Architecture   in eXtreme Programming (XP) Projects

A requirement of extreme programming is for the solution stakeholder (the customer in XP speak) to be readily available and function as a permanent member of the development team. All phases of an XP project require constant communication with the customer, preferably face-to-face, on site.

This requirement can be satisfied by assigning one or more customers to the development team. Here, however, often lies the biggest risk of XP. In many situations, businesses cannot afford to permanently assign their best people to the project. Because of this, they may often be tempted to pass off an inexperienced person (or a low performer) as an expert. When this is the case, an XP project will fail because it relies heavily on the customer's involvement and continuing guidance. Assigning a customer to be part of the development team does not automatically guarantee a good relationship or shared vision as reported by one member of an XP team:

> *"One [customer representative] sat in our midst and still managed to avoid us all."*[2]

---

[2] From "Jack Be Agile but Not Too Hasty." Karl Wiegers; *Better Software Magazine*, August 2004.

Furthermore, different stakeholders often have different perspectives on the system. In our experience, it can be hard to get one customer expert assigned to the development team. There is little chance multiple people will be available on a permanent basis. By having a short and intense period of joint development of the solution concept, Solution Envisioning accomplishes several goals critical to the success of XP projects:

- It establishes a shared language between customers and developers.
- It exposes the development team to a variety of viewpoints.
- It builds a strong relationship between solution customers and developers.
- It enables the developers to better understand the customer team and become savvy about areas of expertise and contribution from each customer representative.

The importance of these goals and a search for the new approaches to accomplish them is evidenced in some recent writings from the members of an XP community-of-practice [Matts, 2003]:

> "Currently, the agile methodologies are incomplete because they only focus on the development and project management of individual software systems. In order to solve business problems effectively and ensure that the software solution solves key aspects of the business problem, a business coach is required. The business coach seeks to overcome the many barriers within organizations that threaten the success of a development project. The business coach will ensure that the development team focuses on the correct business goals. ... One of the key ways that the business coach can assist in the communication between the development team and the business, and also between different areas of the business, is to establish a common language."

The following activities are performed to make the output of Solution Envisioning directly usable for an XP team:

- Write user stories for high priority Capability Cases.
- Organize them into release increments.

Extreme Programming does not use formal design documents; instead, Class, Responsibilities, and Collaboration (CRC) cards[3] are used to design the system.

---

[3] See http://c2.com/cgi/wiki?CrcCards for the origins of CRC cards, www.extremeprogramming.org/rules/crccards.html for an XP overview, and http://alistair.cockburn.us/crystal/articles/ucrcc/usingcrccards.html for an informal guide on using them.

Workproduct F   Capability Architecture (XP Projects)

 **Specialization for XP**

XP projects are lighter in their documentation. A Capability Architecture for XP development may not be a formal document, but a collection of user stories and CRC cards. There will be a set of user stories per Capability Case; a definition of release increments; and optionally CRC cards. Other key Solution Envisioning deliverables, such as Solution Concept and Capability Model are needed by XP projects just as much as they are needed by any other development project. Therefore, they are implemented the same way.

SCD Activity 6   Evaluate Capability Architecture

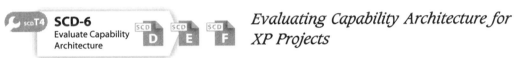

Evaluating Capability Architecture for XP Projects

Even the lightweight version of Architecture Trade-Off Analysis Method we have adapted for SCD is too heavy for XP projects that tend to be relatively small in size. Instead, technical issues should be examined to identify tough technical or design problems. In XP, these problems are explored by creating *Spike Solutions*.

A Spike Solution is a top-to-bottom exploration of an aspect of functionality to investigate requirements, architecture, and design issues.[4]

Workproduct E   Architectural Decisions (revisions)

 Specialization for XP

Updated to document XP Architecture Spike definitions.

---

[4]   See http://c2.com/cgi/wiki?SpikeDescribed for discussions on the "Architecture Spike" of XP.

SCD in EDOC-Based Component Development

SCD Activity 5   Elaborate Capability Architecture

SCD-5
Elaborate Capability
Architecture

Elaborating Capability Architecture in EDOC Projects

The section on MDA (Model-Driven Architecture) in Chapter 8, "Solution Envisioning in Different Situations," outlined the MDA approach based on the EDOC Component Collaboration Architecture (CCA). Sidebar C.1 gives additional, general recommendations regarding the use of MDA with Solution Envisioning.

A key benefit of a model-driven approach is the independence of system specifications from potential target implementation platforms, including middleware platforms, operating systems, and programming languages. The core of the MDA is made up of a number of already available OMG standards that are supported industry-wide. The core infrastructure of the MDA is defined in terms of these standards:

- Unified Modeling Language (UML)
- Meta Object Facility (MOF)
- XML Metadata Interchange (XMI)
- Common Warehouse Metamodel (CWM)

Translations between three model types used with MDA are summarized in Figure C.2.

PIMs (Platform Independent Models) play a number of important roles in the model-driven development:

- They can be used for verification and simulation purposes and to automate testing activities by deriving test cases.
- For systems interoperability, use of PIMs facilitates the creation of different Platform Specific Models (PSMs) corresponding to the same set of PIMs, resulting in easier integration.
- PIMs also improve ability to reuse legacy applications and COTS components. In such cases of reuse, integration is done at a platform-independent level, using PIMs that represent the existing applications and components.

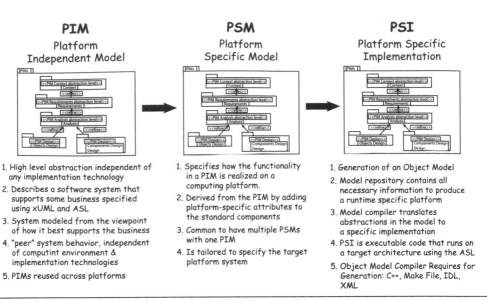

PIM
Platform
Independent Model

1. High level abstraction independent of any implementation technology
2. Describes a software system that supports some business specified using xUML and ASL
3. System modeled from the viewpoint of how it best supports the business
4. "peer" system behavior, independent of computint environment & implementation technologies
5. PIMs reused across platforms

PSM
Platform
Specific Model

1. Specifies how the functionality in a PIM is realized on a computing platform.
2. Derived from the PIM by adding platform-specific attributes to the standard components
3. Common to have multiple PSMs with one PIM
4. Is tailored to specify the target platform system

PSI
Platform Specific
Implementation

1. Generation of an Object Model
2. Model repository contains all necessary information to produce a runtime specific platform
3. Model compiler translates abstractions in the model to a specific implementation
4. PSI is executable code that runs on a target architecture using the ASL
5. Object Model Compiler Requires for Generation: C++, Make File, IDL, XML

FIGURE C.2.   THE   MODELS   OF   THE   MODEL-DRIVEN   ARCHITECTURE   (MDA)
APPROACH.[5]

As mentioned in Chapter 8, the constructs in EDOC are closer to the problem domain and map well to Capability Cases. CCA is also compatible with the ebXML[6] Business Process Specification Schema, which specifies B2B collaborations.

Consider the CCA example from the Data Access Technologies ComponentX tool. Figure C.3 shows a "Seller" component. Each of the methods of the objects shown can be mapped to Capability Cases. For example, the *CustBean* object's *checkCredit* method might invoke a *CreditChecker*, and *checkCustomer* could use a *ConsolidatedCustomerView* Capability.

As a further example, Figure C.4, which has been taken from the EDOC standard,[7] shows an example of a component that has a *QuoteCalculator*. This would correspond directly to a Capability Case.

[5]   Adapted from a presentation by Tom Massie. "An Analysis of Model Driven Architecture (MDA) and Executable UML (xUML)." The MITRE Corporation, February 19, 2004.

[6]   "Electronic Business Using eXtensible Markup Language"; see http://www.ebxml.org/geninfo.htm.

[7]   OMG: UML Profile for Enterprise Distributed Object Computing (EDOC), www.omg.org/technology/documents/formal/edoc.htm.

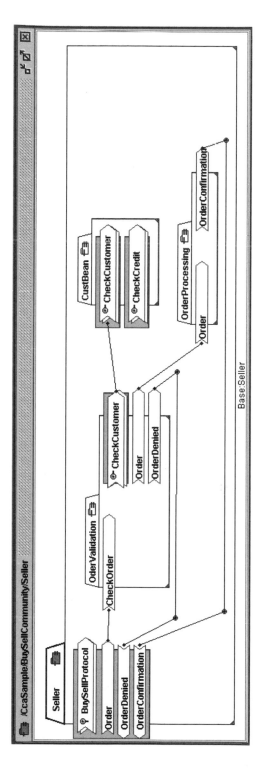

FIGURE C.3.   CCA MODEL FOR A SELLER IN A "BUYSELLCOMMUNITY."

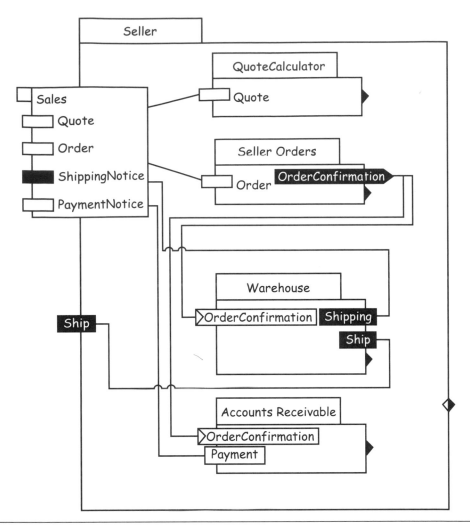

FIGURE C.4. EXAMPLE OF A CAPABILITY CASE WITHIN AN EDOC COMPONENT.

In terms of the Solution Envisioning process, Capability Cases will already have been established and the CCA models are built with these mappings in mind.

Transforming the Capability Architecture to the ECA is done by applying a "CapCase to ECA" (*CC-to-ECA*) mapping using specialization operations. The process is summarized in Figure C.5. Our notation is based on that used by the Pegamento project at the Australian Distributed Systems Centre (DSTC).[8]

---

[8] The Pegamento project is work at the Australian Distributed Systems Technology Centre, based at the University of Queensland, Australia: www.dstc.edu.au/Research/ Projects/Pegamento/ [Duddy, 2004].

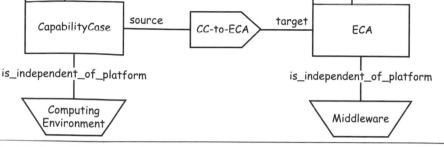

FIGURE C.5.   CAPABILITY CASE MAPPING TO EDOC ECA.

A closely aligned project to Pegamento is the Elemental project, also at the DSTC. We use the Business Contracts Architecture from Elemental, illustrated in Figure C.6, to provide an example of Capability Case mapping.

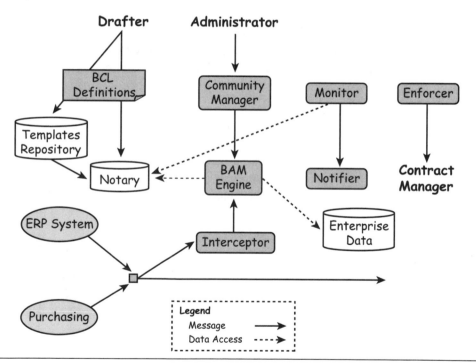

FIGURE C.6.   BUSINESS CONTRACTS ARCHITECTURE FROM ELEMENTAL, A SISTER PROJECT TO PEGAMENTO.

Based on the published paper, the Business Contract Architecture can be summarized as follows:

> *At the heart of the Business Contract Architecture is a Business Activity Monitoring (BAM) component, which manages internal states related to contracts. Non-intrusive interception of business messages exchanged between trading partners for contract monitoring are carried out by an 'Interceptor'. The BAM processes these events and provides access to various enterprise data sources needed by the Contract Monitor for policy evaluation.*

> *Contract policies determine whether the signatories have fulfilled their obligations or whether there are violations to the contract. The Contract Monitor uses the BAM component for event alerts and state processing and sends appropriate messages to a Notifier component. The Notifier sends human readable notification messages to contract managers. Examples of notifications are reminders about the tasks that need to be performed, warnings that some violation event may arise, or alarms that a violation has already happened.*

> *A 'Templates Repository' stores standard contract templates, and optionally standard contract clauses as building blocks for drafting new contract templates. A Notary stores evidence of agreed contracts (and their relationships) created during the negotiation process. This prevents any of the parties repudiating it.*

We now consider the portfolio of Capability Cases that we might have used in a Solution Envisioning approach to derive this conceptual architecture. Two Capability Cases would have been *PolicyEnforcer* and *RepudiationAgent*. The Capability Case *PolicyEnforcer* becomes ECA Component *ContractEnforcer*. The functionality of the Capability Case maps directly, as shown in Figure C.7.

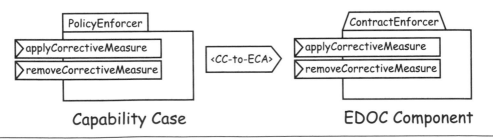

FIGURE C.7.   CAPABILITY CASE MAPPING: POLICYENFORCER TO CONTRACT-ENFORCER.

RepudiationAgent transforms into a component called *Notary* with specializations of the operations *recordEvidenceOfEvent* and *obtainEvidenceOfEvent* into *notarizeDocument* and *obtainNotarizationEvent*, respectively.

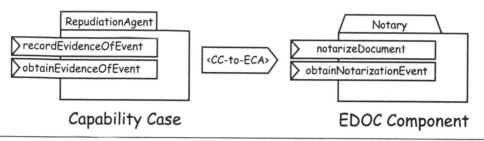

Capability Case

EDOC Component

FIGURE C.8.   CAPABILITY CASE MAPPING: REPUDIATIONAGENT TO NOTARY.

An alternate to MDA translation is to use a reflective architecture. Using the principle of layered abstract machines, EDOC models are directly executable with an underlying computational model. Integrating an ontology-based approach and Semantic Web services with an executable EDOC model has interesting possibilities for adaptive systems.

Workproduct F   Capability Architecture (MDA Projects)

 Capability Architecture   **Specialization for MDA**

The Capability Architecture in an MDA project is a Platform Independent Model and a High-Level form of the Platform-Specific Model.

A Component Collaboration Architecture (CCA) is built from the Capability Model. This expresses the high-level behaviors.

SCD Activity 6   Evaluate Capability Architecture

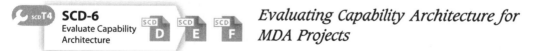

SCD-6
Evaluate Capability
Architecture

Evaluating Capability Architecture for MDA Projects

The Architecture Trade-Off Analysis Method described in Chapter 7 works equally well for MDA Projects. No additional specific tailoring needs to be made.

Sidebar C.1   Recommendations for Using MDA with Solution Envisioning

We recommend that enterprises considering the MDA approach should make the following considerations:

- Technical Feasibility
- Development Feasibility
- Architectural Integrity

Technical Feasibility—Many platforms exist in a typical enterprise IT environment: J2EE, .NET, Legacy Systems, layers of middleware (for example, Tibco, Vitria, Tivoli), and enterprise application systems (for example, SAP, ORACLE and PeopleSoft). All have numerous APIs, often poorly documented—they can be non-conformant with execution behavior and also constantly evolving. The notion of a stable Platform Specific Model (PSM) for these situations is untenable. MDA proponents respond to this by saying that MDA can generate template code from the models, and leave the specifics of the APIs to the developers. In other words, the "devil in the details" is the job of the developer to face. Round-trips back to the models are needed to keep the overall integrity of the system specifications.

Development Feasibility—The MDA approach requires skills and competency development that most IT organizations will have some difficulties attaining. The business side will have an issue with the latency time needed to achieve the necessary competence. Business stakeholders rarely ask for models that describe their business. They do care about having IT systems that are able to change to meet the changing needs of the business. But the business stakeholders need these systems to be built in an agile way without too much investment in models. This is especially so when it might take months to construct such systems without a guarantee that they won't be too brittle to respond to future needs.

Architectural Integrity—To deliver the vision of MDA, like object-oriented development, solutions need to follow sound architectural principles for encapsulation, modularity, control flow, and uniformly applied design patterns. Without these disciplines, solutions will have poor integrity and viability. In other words, if an enterprise commits to MDA, it should also commit to employing best practices in object-oriented and component-based development for building well-partitioned and layered sets of capabilities

The Agile Development community has responded to some of these considerations with an approach that Scott Amber calls "Agile MDD (Model Driven Development) or AMDD."[9] He writes:

"It is important that you look beyond MDD Modeling tools to make MDA work ... I'm also a firm believer in something that I call Agile Model Driven Development (AMDD). An agile model is just barely good enough—it meets its goals and no more. Because 'just barely

---

[9]   www.agilemodeling.com/essays/agileMDA.htm.

good enough' is relative, you can consider a sketch, a Unified Modeling Language state-chart, or a detailed physical database model as an agile model in the right situations. Following an AMDD approach, I typically use very simple tools, such as whiteboards and paper, when I work with users to explore and analyze their requirements. Simple tools are easy to work with, inclusive (my stakeholders can be actively involved with modeling), and flexible, and they're not constraining. They're exactly what I need when I'm exploring the problem domain and identifying my system architecture."

SCD AND PACKAGE IMPLEMENTATION

SCD Activity 5   Elaborate Capability Architecture

SCD-5
Elaborate Capability
Architecture

Elaborating   Capability   Architecture   in Package-Based Projects

In most situations, a Package needs to be customized and integrated with external systems and databases. A Customer Solution is a determination of the *Statement-of-Fit* to the capabilities offered by the Package Vendor. A central idea is determining the gap between the system required and the base Vendor Package. Identifying this gap means quantifying the deltas in capabilities through to components and on to implementations.

In Figure C.9, the *Statement-of-Fit* is shown along with a *Statement-of-Work* and a *Statement-of-Redundancy*.[10]

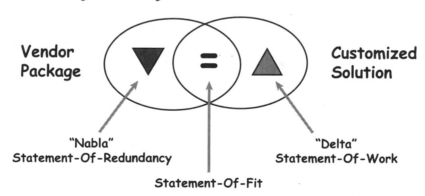

FIGURE C.9.   DELTA-DRIVEN DEVELOPMENT.

[10] This view of the "Delta-Driven Approach" was created by Jean-Piere Pallet and Ralph Hodgson on a project in 1996 for the IBM VisualBanker Package Solution Methodology.

Although most packages have customization strategies, most vendors prefer their customers make as few changes as possible. Changes bring complexity when new releases of the package need to be delivered. To minimize functionality changes, a customer has to consider business process change and organizational change. The tradeoff is simple: either change the package or change your process.

Gap analysis and customization are key to implementing a package-based solution. An important technology selection criterion is the extent to which the vendor provides design documentation that supports the process of determining functional fit and tailoring to the customer-specific business and IT context.

For Package-based development, the steps involved in elaborating Capability Architecture are as follows:

1. Review the capabilities in the capability architecture with the package vendor(s).
2. Map the capability architecture to package modules.
3. Determine the gaps on each capability.
4. Assess any impact of upgrade changes from previous adaptations.
5. Specify and estimate the additional functionality.
6. Determine integration requirements.
7. Define technical strategy for implementation.
8. Document adaptation work.

Not only does this work have to happen the first time, but also with new releases of the Package. If the vendor has made changes to components, then these changes need to be considered in light of any customer-specific changes. The Package should be viewed within a customization lifecycle of managed software assets.

Downstream from Solution Envisioning, more consideration of gaps will be needed. Mapping will involve matching the package's data model against the organization's enterprise data model, identifying issues with entities, attributes, and relationships.

With the advent of Semantic Web Services, there is hope for better integration of packages. In fact, SAP announced their research in this area during a conference presentation given by Dr. Lutz Heuser, the vice president of SAP Research at SAP AG.[11] The project is called *DIP—Data, Information, and Process Integration with Semantic Web Services*[12] and the vision is expressed as:

---

[11] Dr. Lutz Heuser gave this presentation at ICWE2004 which is available at www.icwe2004.org/download/heuser_icwe.pdf.

[12] The DIP project has a website at http://dip.semanticweb.org/.

"DIP's mission is to make Semantic Web Services a reality, providing an infrastructure (i.e. an architecture and tools) that will revolutionize data and process integration in eWork, eGovernment, and eCommerce as the web did it for human information access."

Workproduct F   Capability Architecture (Package-Based Projects)

 Capability Architecture **Specialization for Package-Based Development**

The Capability Architecture must include high-level package modules of the system. This should show interactions between package modules including high-level descriptions of the interfaces. Also needed are the mapping of capabilities to Package modules, a record of the functional gap analysis, and a record of adaptations of the vendor Package and customer-specific changes from previous releases.

SCD Activity 6   Evaluate Capability Architecture

 **SCD-6** Evaluate Capability Architecture

Evaluating Capability Architecture for Package-Based Projects

Package implementations share many of the risks common to custom application development efforts. Because purchasing the package often involves the purchase of an entire application architecture, data model, and development tools, certain types of risks, such as inadequate design, are front-loaded onto the project.

An architectural evaluation is an important part of the application selection process. Special attention should be paid to the integration and customization issues as well as to growth and exploration scenarios.

The evaluation activity described in Chapter 7 should be followed; however, this implementation approach calls for a more rigorous evaluation of architectural decisions that follows the Architecture Trade-Off Analysis Method (ATAM) approach. Two reasons account for this:

1. ATAM is justified in cases where projects are of a complex and expensive nature. Both tend to be true for Packages.

2. Because many technical decisions come with the package, the specifications are available for a full ATAM evaluation.

The Package-based ATAM approach we suggest is summarized as follows:

1. Identify scenarios for a comprehensive set of quality attributes according to package specifications.

2. Construct the Utility tree.

3. Evaluate each architectural decision from the perspective of risks, non-risks, sensitivity, and trade-off points as described in ATAM Technique (Chapter 7).

4. Identify additional decisions.

5. Evaluate addition decisions.

The ATAM workshop typically takes three days and the involvement of as many as 10–20 people—architects and other system stakeholders. Because we are doing ATAM in the discovery mode, and the previous activities of Solution Envisioning already provided inputs necessary for ATAM, the workshop can be performed in one day. The amount of time needed to prepare for the workshop also goes down significantly.

We recommend running the architecture evaluation workshop in two sessions:

1. Prioritize scenarios (3 to 4 hours)

2. Analyze architecture (5 to 6 hours)

To prepare for the first session, all that is required is the repurposing of Non-Functional Requirements into a utility tree. The second session will need the following templates:

- Scenarios (prepared before the session)
- Technical risks
- Technical non-risks
- Sensitivity points
- Trade-offs
- Scenario Analysis of the Architectural Approach Sheet (one per scenario being analyzed; sheets should be partially pre-populated)

For definitions of risks, non-risks, sensitivity points, and tradeoffs, see Sidebar 7.5 (the ATAM technique). Lists can use the same simple template as the Architectural Decisions (shown in Table 7.2 in Chapter 7), along with a reference ID number and a textual description. Because risks, non-risks, sensitivity points, and tradeoffs are identified within the context of scenarios, they can be cross-referenced to the list of scenarios. An additional column is used for this cross-referencing.

A template for the Scenario Analysis of the Architectural Approach, adapted from work by Clements [Clements, 2002b], is shown in Table C.2.

TABLE C.2.   SCENARIO ANALYSIS OF THE ARCHITECTURAL APPROACH

Architecture Evaluation Template

Scenario Ref. (This is a scenario reference ID from Scenario List. Populate this field before the workshop.)   **Scenario Text** (Populate this field before the workshop.)

Attribute(s) (List attributes this scenario is connected to; populate this field(s) before the workshop)

Environment (Use this line to list any assumptions about the operating environment of the system during the scenario and any special conditions. In our example of database growth, this would be "Normal operations." Another often-used description of environment is "During routine maintenance." Populate this field before the workshop.)

Stimulus (This is an event that causes a scenario to happen. It could be a business event—in our example a database could grow because company acquires a competitor—it could also be a technical event, for example CPU failure. Populate this field before the workshop.)

Response (This is the value a quality attribute must have—taken from the Non-Functional Requirements. Populate this field before the workshop.)

Architectural Decisions	**Risk**	**Non-Risk**	**Sensitivity**	**Tradeoff**
List an Architectural Decision relevant to this scenario. Use a textual description instead of the reference number. Some decisions could be pre-populated before the workshop; others are discovered during the workshop.	Any risk this decision could bring. Use a reference number from the risk list. These are identified during the workshop.	Any other implications of this decision. Use a reference number from the non-risk list. These are identified during the workshop.	Use a reference number from the sensitivity list. These are identified during the workshop.	Use a reference number from the tradeoff list. These are identified during the workshop.

Continue listing Architectural Decisions...

Reasoning (Capture relevant rationale and workshop discussions here)

Architectural Diagram (Optionally, a diagram could be included)

Workproduct D   IT Impact and Interface Specifications (revisions)

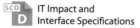 Specialization for Package-Based Development

Updates may be needed to reflect additional architectural decisions and risks identified during the evaluation activity.

Workproduct E   Architectural Decisions (revisions)

[SCD E] Architectural Decisions   **Specialization for Package-Based Development**

The results of the Capability Architecture evaluation are added to the Architectural Decisions document as follows:

Additional architectural decisions identified during the workshop are added to the list of architectural decisions.

Lists of analyzed (or deferred because of low priority) scenarios, risks, non-risks, sensitivity points, and tradeoffs are captured as additional sections.

Scenario Analysis Sheets are included as an appendix (or an additional section).

Workproduct F   Capability Architecture (revisions)

[SCD F] Capability Architecture   **Specialization for Package-Based Development**

The Capability Architecture is updated to reflect any additional architectural decisions and risks identified during the evaluation activity.

Conclusion

The central idea in Solution Envisioning is the expression of a solution architecture as a set of capabilities. In this appendix, we have shown how this idea can be mapped to both custom developments and package-based implementations. The intent is not detailed design, but detailed specification of the functional intent of the solution. Thinking in terms of capabilities provides a common language for mapping to components or to package modules.

D

SOLUTION ENVISIONING ACTIVITIES AND WORKPRODUCTS— SUMMARY TABLE FOR EACH PHASE

THE ACTIVITIES AND WORKPRODUCTS OF PHASE I—BUSINESS CAPABILITY EXPLORATION

	Activities	Workproducts
1	**Establish Solution Initiative Shared Space** Create an accessible shared space and "marketing channel" for project information.	**Solution Initiative Shared Space** A shared workspace such as a website, portal, or collaboration space that provides information and news about the project.
2	**Establish Key Stakeholders** Stakeholders are the different parties who have an interest in the solution— those that benefit from the solution and those affected by the solution. Stakeholders can be customers, partners, users, sponsors, and other affected parties. The first part of this activity is to identify a core set of key stakeholders in relation to the initiative. A second part of this activity is to define how each stakeholder participates (is affected by) the initiative, and whether they need to be involved.	**Stakeholder Profile and Participation Matrix (initial version)** This is a composite workproduct that will eventually cross-index the list of stakeholders with a specification of how each stakeholder benefits and is impacted by the solution initiative (see Activities 10 and 14). The initial version may contain only a list of each stakeholder identified, their role in relation to the business, whether the initiative is likely to affect them, and if they should be solicited for involvement.

3	**Clarify Solution Initiative Statement** Clarify the business transformation being considered by (1) establishing the current business context, (2) assessing related activities and stakeholders, and (3) agreeing on the solution initiative framing.	**Confirmed Solution Initiative Statement** A specification of the intent of the solution in terms of the problem that is being addressed, who benefits and how, motivations for the solution, constraints that surround the solution, and who the sponsor is. This serves as a concise statement of a program that will create and deploy IT capabilities needed to achieve the required business transformation.
4	**Establish Inventory of Reference Materials** Create an inventory of artifacts relevant to the Solution Initiative. These typically include reports, presentations, white papers, memos, and memorandums of understanding, statements of work, and other reference materials.	**Solution Initiative Materials Inventory** The collection of reference materials relevant to the project. The inventory should either be placed in the solution initiative shared space or be accessible from links in the workspace. It is useful to be able to support discussions about inventory materials.
5	**Clarify Business Context** Before Solution Envisioning work can begin, there is a need to explore or validate the business environment and the future intent of the business as seen by a number of key stakeholders. The activity establishes the business context related to the Solution Initiative and identifies relevant activity areas.	**Business Context Model and Activity Areas** A model of the business environment that depicts the key activity areas in a value-net showing the relationships between business units.
6	**Assess Use of Current IT Capabilities** Assess how current applications, systems, and databases are used to support the activities of different organizational units affected and within the scope of the solution initiative.	**Existing IT Systems in Context** A specification of the dependencies of current business activities to existing IT systems indicating which systems and databases need to be considered as *IT givens* for the solution initiative.
7	**Establish a Glossary for the Initiative** Create a readily accessible list of definitions of terminology for project personnel and other interested parties.	**Solution Initiative Glossary** Definition of terms used by the project and pointers to where to find more information if necessary.

8	**Elicit Forces, Barriers, Results** For each stakeholder, determine the underlying forces, barriers, and results that surround the business transformation under consideration. Force is a new or existing condition that is affecting the business. Barrier is an obstacle within the business context that prevents business objectives from being realized. Result is a change in the state of the business that allows business transformation to take place. Forces and barriers must be supported with marketplace evidence.	**Business Capability Model (component)** Stakeholder to Challenges List—A list of the forces, barriers, and results relevant to each stakeholder, along with evidence from the marketplace and business environment. This workproduct will be later transformed into one of the Capability Maps within the "Business Capability Model."
9	**Identify Business Activities in Scope** Identify business activity scenarios in the current business (As-Is) that are in-scope for the solution initiative for all stakeholder roles. Capture the work sequence at the generic level for each activity by creating essential activity scenario diagrams. The scenarios should reflect the essential sequence of work steps that characterize the business activities.	**Essential Activity Scenarios (initial version)** Stakeholder essential business activities are identified by Name and Brief Description. The identified activities are detailed to a useful level as scenario diagrams. Later, these scenarios are used as the basis for creating storyboards of transformed scenarios (To-Be) for how the business can operate with the new capabilities selected in the solution initiative. See Activity 12 for more details.
10	**Perform Stakeholder Impact Analysis** For each stakeholder, information is collected to profile him or her with respect to the solution initiative. A description of the impact on the stakeholder is captured based on how his world will potentially change as a result of the initiative.	**Stakeholder Profile and Participation Matrix (component)** Stakeholder Impact Summary—A tabular specification of how each stakeholder is impacted by the solution initiative. A template is used to document the following information about the stakeholder with respect to the initiative: Attitude, Temperature, Influence, Risk Tolerance, Expectations, and Impact.

11	**Nominate Capabilities** Based on essential business activity scenarios (created in Activity 9), nominate organizational and IT capabilities that could support the enterprise of the future.	**Candidate Capability Cases Portfolio** A collection of Capability Cases and selected solution stories that serve as inspirations for the envisioned solution. A Portfolio may include fully developed Capability Cases selected from a catalog. It can also include newly identified capabilities. These are identified by their name and a short intent statement.
12	**Explore Future Business Possibilities** Using current business activity scenarios (created in Activity 9), create future work scenarios for the enterprise. Transform the existing work scenarios into views of how the business will be able to operate with the new capabilities selected for the solution initiative (as identified in Activity 11). Create narratives and storyboards in conjunction with the scenarios to convey how the work sequence will change for each business activity with the support of these new capabilities.	**Essential Activity Scenarios (transformed)** Storyboards of transformed scenarios (To-Be) for how the business can operate with the new capabilities selected in the solution initiative. These future retrospective stories may include a narrative description of activities that a role in the organization needs to perform. It can be thought of as a "day in the life" story of a person operating in that role in the envisioned future.
13	**Explore Technology Options** Consider established and emerging technologies and known and envisioned solution stories as a means to understanding what might be possible through technology.	**Technology Strategy Outline** A document identifying the set of technologies that may be used to support task scenarios. It takes into account how other organizations, including the company's competitors, may be using technology for competitive advantage.
14	**Perform Stakeholder Benefit Analysis** Map capabilities to each stakeholder's interests and challenges, expressing a value proposition. Each party has interests that the envisioned solution satisfies; goals and objectives they're trying to accomplish; forces that are addressed by the solution; and barriers that are overcome by the solution. A second task is to elaborate the stakeholder participation matrix to define how each stakeholder needs to be involved in the project.	**Stakeholder Profile and Participation Matrix (component)** Links to Business Capability Model and its component maps.

15	**Refine Results**	**Measures of Effectiveness**
	Translate the informal statement of forces into a normalized list. For each result, identify possible measures.	A table expressing results and measures for each business activity in the scope of the solution initiative.

16	**Map Capabilities to Forces, Barriers, Challenges, and Results**	**Business Capability Model**
	Develop "Cause-Effect/Impact" diagrams depicting how existing and new capabilities are needed in the business context.	A specification of how the challenges of stakeholders in performing their activities are supported by existing and envisioned capabilities. It includes the following as components: • Stakeholder Challenges List (see Activity 8) • Activity Challenges Map—a mapping of the forces, barriers, and results to each activity that is in scope.

17	**Create Solution Vision Presentation**	**Solution Vision Presentation and Shared Space**
	Package the work of the phase into a presentation of the vision of the solution. Aspects of the presentation need to address multiple audiences: business executives, system architects, and end-user representatives.	A presentation that provides (a) a summary of the business situation; (b) a vision of one or more possible solution concepts; (c) motivating future scenarios and supporting capabilities; and (d) value propositions that serve as input to making a business case.

THE ACTIVITIES AND WORKPRODUCTS OF PHASE II—SOLUTION CAPABILITY ENVISIONING

	Activities	Workproducts	Source
1	**Envisioning Workshop Planning** The Solution Envisioning workshop needs to be an effective experience with the right people participating and willing to devote time to the workshop. For this to happen, critical pre-work must be done. The material produced in *Business Capability Exploration (BCE)* is organized in an appropriate way for use in the workshop. The venue must be carefully chosen and room bookings made ahead of time.	**Envisioning Workshop Logistics and Schedule** A package that will be distributed to the workshop participants. It includes the following as key components: • Workshop Agenda and Guidance • Solution Vision Presentation Workshop participants should also get access to the shared space.	Workshop agenda is produced in this phase. Other components are created in BCE and elaborated in this phase.
2	**Elaborate Capability Cases Portfolio** In the "BCE" phase, capabilities were nominated for the solution. Some of these may need to be elaborated to be tailored for the situation-at-hand. New Capability Cases may also have to be written.	**Capability Cases Portfolio** The "Capability Cases Portfolio" is a collection of Capability Cases and selected solution stories that serve as inspirations for the envisioned solution. A portfolio may include fully developed Capability Cases selected from a catalog. It can also include newly identified capabilities. These are identified by their name and a short intent statement.	Created in BCE and elaborated in this phase.
3	**Conduct Pre-Envisioning Workshop Walkthroughs** The purpose of the pre-workshop briefings is to create a familiarity with the materials so that all attendees are equally prepared and there are few derailments on the day.	**Evidence of Business Situation and Possibilities** A collection of articles workshop participants are asked to bring to the session. They may be newspaper clippings about technologies and what other organizations are doing, excerpts from internal presentations and speeches, customer letters, or any other items of interest.	Produced in this phase.

4	**Preparing the Capability Cases Gallery** The gallery will need to be set up ahead of the workshop. The preferred arrangement is to have the gallery in the same room as the workshop so tours can happen informally at different times of the day.	**Gallery of Capability Cases** The gallery is a central idea in the Solution Envisioning approach. This is the equivalent of the architect's book of designs. Some time is needed before people arrive to arrange the gallery around the room in an appropriate way. If there is time, a Gallery Tour Guide is a useful thing to produce. This gives an overview of each featured Capability Case, explaining the justification for its inclusion in the gallery.	Produced in this phase.
5	**Launch the Solution Envisioning Workshop** The workshop is the main activity of this phase. A progression of conversations is managed based on *exploring the present*, *assessing technology capabilities*, *future scenarios*, and *realization planning*.		
6	**Review Solution Vision** Capability maps and overviews of the to-be scenarios are used to explain the vision of the envisioned solution. The details of how capabilities support the business are worked out later in scenario enactments. The purpose of the review is to justify the reasoning about the current business situation and why certain choices have been made for the to-be business design.	**Solution Vision (Revised)** An elaboration of the solution vision to take account of choices between alternate solution initiatives and to review comments and new insights.	Starts in BCE; evolved in this phase.
		Solution Initiative Statement (Revised) A specification of the intent of the solution in terms of the problem that is being addressed, who benefits and how, motivations for the solution, constraints that surround the solution, and who is the sponsor. This serves as a concise statement of a program that will	Initial statement is input to BCE. It is reviewed and elaborated in BCE, and further extended in this phase.

		create and deploy IT capabilities needed to achieve the required business transformation. NOTE: Variants or alternative solution initiative statements may be produced in BCE. Refinement and selection of a final statement is made in this phase.	
7	**Tour Capability Cases Gallery** A guided tour of the gallery of Capability Cases provides an opportunity for attendees to understand the value of selected technologies and to make connections from the solution stories to their situation. Ideas can be sparked by these connections and also be the interplay of ideas and business possibilities.	**Capability Interest and Value Proposition Scorecard** The scorecard is a table that ranks capabilities according to their perceived value and interest to different stakeholders. Each Capability Case is scored by the attendees of the workshop.	Produced in this phase.
8	**Conduct Solution Scenario Enactment** Each of the Essential Activity Scenarios that were created is walked through, and the applicability of specific capabilities is explained in context with the envisioned work in the future business model.	**Solution Enactment Diagram** Annotated pictures of how events, actions, and capabilities help stakeholders perform their work in selected activity areas.	Produced in this phase.
9	**Prioritize Capabilities** Capabilities that have been confirmed (in the workshop) to be of the most interest to an organization are examined from three perspectives: *desirability*—the business value, *feasibility*—ease of implementation, and *adequacy*—functional fit. Each capability is prioritized accordingly.	**Capability Prioritization Matrix** A table, or equivalent, listing selected capabilities with measures of importance and priority, rough order of magnitude on effort, and desired target dates for realization. Some treatment of dependencies should also be provided.	Produced in this phase.

10	**Assess Solution Realization Gap** Implementing and deploying the solution brings challenges arising from differences between the organization's current competencies and resources, the impact on existing systems, and the readiness of the selected technologies. An assessment of these gaps and the organization's ability to address them produces a risk list and an informed decision model on solution options.	**Risk Assessment Model** An identification of risks, their likelihood and impact, and critical dependencies. The model can be presented either in the form of a list, a table, or a database model with each risk correlated to specific capabilities.	Produced in this phase.
		Solution Options Decision Model (optional) The solution option decisions are concerned with technology choices and the selection of a development strategy. Technology choices will be different for platforms, IT infrastructure, application infrastructure, and application software. Standards for the enterprise will constrain choices and this workproduct captures such rationale.	Produced in this phase.
11	**Post-Workshop Analysis and Consolidation of Concepts** The workshop and work of this phase generates new insights, agreements (and potential disagreements) over dependencies, issues, priorities, and commitments to going forward. An analysis of this leads to a refinement of the "Solution Concept" and its associated roadmap.	**Solution Concept Document and Capability Model** The Solution Concept workproduct conveys the vision of the solution. It is a description of the business context with forces and motivating scenarios; stakeholders and their desired results; capabilities that enable new ways to work; future scenarios that illustrate new ways to work; and a roadmap that addresses risks, impacts, and the options and plans for the solution design work of the next phase.	Produced in this phase.
		Capability Model This is a composite Workproduct that represents the output of the SCE phase. It consists of the	Produced in this phase.

Solution Concept Document and a Capability Model of the solution. A Capability Model is a conceptual architecture of the solution that guides the architectural design and technology selection. It provides a common vision by telling a story of a solution. It assists design, construction, and deployment of a technology by keeping them on track. It may contain multiple diagrams (viewpoints) for different stakeholders.

THE ACTIVITIES AND WORKPRODUCTS OF PHASE III—SOFTWARE CAPABILITY DESIGN

	Activities	Workproducts	Source
1	**Evaluate Technology Options and Decide Development Strategy** Make a decision on the development strategy/implementation approach. Develop a decision model for selecting technologies and vendors. Two common approaches to decision modeling are Multi-Criteria Decision Trees and the AHP (Analytical Hierarchical Process) technique. Another approach, which deals with uncertainty, is a Bayesian method using *Belief Maps*.	**Technology Decision Model** A list of criteria used to decide on technology options. Each criterion may be given a relative weight. A Decision Model can be implemented as a spreadsheet, although we believe that decision support tools are better suited for this purpose.	Input to technology options come from several work products of previous phases, including: • Technology Strategy Outline prepared in the BCE phase • Capability Cases identification of Applicable Technologies • Solution Options Decision Model created in the SCE Phase
2	**Specify Non-Functional Requirements** Identify the required quality attributes of the system and its components. This includes performance, availability, security, usability, maintainability, and extensibility. Specify ranges of values from acceptable to desired.	**Non-Functional Requirements** A document describing non-functional requirements as the quality attributes of the system. They are often stated as constraints on the functional requirements but also include attributes pertaining to development, deployment, and maintenance. Each non-functional requirement is further clarified by providing a range of values as well as identifying measurements to be used to test conformance to requirements.	Produced in this phase.

3	**Select Potential Technologies and Vendors** Identify top vendors that can offer technology for building the capabilities. If a definitive decision is not made as to which one of the three implementation options will be taken, the work has to take in to account each of the options under consideration. For example, the Vendor Shortlist may list vendor choices for a Packaged Solution and, separately, for a Component-based Solution.	**Vendor Shortlist** This document identifies two to three top vendor choices, their specific strengths, and solution fit. Solution fit is determined by ranking technology choices against the decision model.	Uses as an input Applicable Technologies identified in the Capability Cases.
4	**Analyze IT Risks, Dependencies, and Technology Constraints** Identify the business and technical risks associated with different implementation options for selected capabilities. Consider technology readiness for use as well as organizational readiness to implement the candidate technologies. Document other systems that the solution may depend on, replace, or interface with.	**IT Impact and Interface Specifications** A document identifying IT systems that the solution will have an impact on. This is best accomplished through a diagram showing impacted systems together with the nature of impact.	Started in BCE as Existing IT Systems in Context and elaborated in this phase.
		Architectural Decisions A document describing important decisions about aspects of the architecture including technology choices, the structure of the system, the provision and allocation of function, and adherence to standards. Each decision can be described in a free format style with headings like problem statement, resolution, alternatives, and justification.	Produced in this phase.
5	**Elaborate Capability Architecture** The Capability Model of the BCE phase is elaborated into a Capability Architecture. This identifies high-level components of the system, their dependen-	**Capability Architecture (SOA Projects)** Capability Architecture identifies the high-level components of the system and the relationships among them. It includes a diagram that shows interactions	This phase. Builds on the Solution Concept Document developed during the SCE phase.

cies, and illustrates the behavior of the intended system through diagrams that show the interactions between components for the key scenarios of use.

between components including high-level descriptions of the interfaces. It can also include an identification-level use case model.

| 6 | **Evaluate Capability Architecture**
The Capability Architecture is evaluated to assess how well the Architecture meets the goals of the stakeholders in delivering functionality and satisfying desired quality goals and measures. | **IT Impact and Interface Specifications**
Update may be needed to reflect additional architectural decisions and risks identified during the evaluation activity.

Architectural Decisions
Results of the Capability Architecture evaluation are added to the Architectural Decisions document as follows:
• Additional architectural decisions identified during the workshop are added to the list of architectural decisions.
• Lists of analyzed (or deferred because of low priority) scenarios is included in an additional section, as well as the architectural alternatives that will be decided on during the later phase.

Capability Architecture
The Capability Architecture is updated to reflect any additional architectural decisions and risks identified during the evaluation activity. | Produced in this phase. |
| 7 | **Develop Business Case**
Identify resources needed to implement the solution. Develop financial and return | **Business Case**
A document that substantiates the request for solution funding by establishing the: | Builds on the several Workproducts from the previous phases, including: |

on investment (ROI) numbers. Analyze risks and identify risk mitigation activities.	• Need for funding • Benefits to be derived • Corporation's ability to implement the solutions • Solution's ability to provide expected benefits and financial return A business case may also include a spreadsheet with the ROI calculations.	• Business Capability Model and Measures developed during the BCE phase • Risk Assessment Model developed in the SCE phase
8	**Develop Solution Realization and Adoption Plan** Develop a roadmap for implementing the solution. Identify major milestones. Address organizational impacts, communication, and training needs, as well as transition plans.	**Stakeholder Collaboration Model** A document, often a table, identifying specific input, resources, and other contributions expected from the various solution stakeholders. It builds on the Stakeholder Profile and Participation Matrix developed in BCE.	Builds on the Stakeholder Profile and Participation Matrix developed in BCE.
		Solution Realization Roadmap A package of deliverables that typically includes: • Solution Architecture (Vendor Short List, Architectural Decisions, IT Impact and Interface Specification, and Non-Functional Requirements) • Solution Concept in presentation format with outlined Business Case • Adoption Plans with training and support needs and migration strategy • Solution Roadmap with outline plan (for example, a high-level MS Project plan)	Produced in this phase.

LIST OF FIGURES

LIST OF TABLES

LIST OF TECHNIQUES

GLOSSARY

Agile Methods   Lightweight software development methodologies that emphasize close collaboration between the programmer team and business experts; face-to-face communication (as more efficient than written documentation); frequent delivery of new deployable business value; tight, self-organizing teams; and ways to craft the code and the team such that the inevitable requirements churn is not a crisis. [1]

Analytical Hierarchy Process (AHP)   Developed in the 1970s by Dr. Thomas Saaty at Wharton School of Business, this is the most widely used decision making theory supported by a number of tools. It requires structuring a decision into smaller parts, proceeding from the goal to objectives to sub-objectives down to the alternative courses of action. Decision makers then make pair-wise comparisons throughout the hierarchy to arrive at overall priorities for the alternatives.

Architecture Trade-Off Analysis Method (ATAM)   An approach for evaluating how well an architecture satisfies quality goals and understanding how the goals interact (trade off) with each other. ATAM has been developed by the Software Engineering Institute at Carnegie Mellon University.

Balanced Scorecard   An approach to strategic management through measuring organizational performance developed in the early 1990s by Drs. Robert Kaplan (Harvard Business School) and David Norton [Kaplan, 1996]. The balanced scorecard suggests that we view the organization from four perspectives and develop metrics, collect data, and analyze it relative to each of these perspectives. These perspectives are (1) Customer; (2) Financial; (3) Business Process; and (4) Learning and Growth.

---

[1]   The Agile Alliance website is www.agilealliance.org/home.

Barrier   An obstacle that stands in the way of a business achieving objectives. Questions such as "What are the issues, problems, and complaints that we have?" are used to directly identify barriers. Barriers, together with the new possibilities that the business wants to develop, combine to cause key Challenges that the business must overcome. Just as Forces, Barriers must be supported with marketplace evidence.

Business Capability Exploration   Phase I of Solution Envisioning. Its purpose is to establish the existing context of the business and to support a select, core-team of stakeholders who are initially driving the initiative as they produce a pre-liminary Solution Vision.

Business Case   A justification for investing in something. This book provides a template and a process for creating a business case for IT solutions.

Business Driver   See *Force*.

Business Objective   See *Result*.

Business Use Case   See *Essential Use Case*.

Capability   The capacity or quality of having the potential to provide one or more functions or services. In the context of this book, capabilities relate to how a business IT solution can deliver specific results.

Capability Architecture   Identifies the high-level components of the system and the relationships among them. It includes a diagram that shows interactions between components including high-level descriptions of the interfaces. It can also include an identification-level use case model.

Capability Case   A solution idea that, by anchoring solution concepts in a business situation, makes the "business case for a capability." A Capability Case definitively identifies an IT Solution Concept as a cohesive group of software functions that deliver business value. Each Capability Case can be viewed as a reusable software component for achieving business results.

CATWOE   A technique from the Soft Systems Methodology (SSM) used in Solution Envisioning to formulate and analyze Solution Initiative Statements. CATWOE is a mnemonic that stands for **Customer** (the beneficiary of the business system), **Actor** (the people who perform the tasks in the system), **Transformation** (the core activity of the system, or the primary change brought about as a result), **Worldview** (the underlying belief about the system, whether it is the priority, the type of system, or the objective of the system), **Owner** (the person or body that has the power to approve/cancel the system), **Environment** (the factors outside the system that might impose constraints on how it operates).[2]

---

[2]   For more on SSM, see the Business Open Learning Archive (BOLA) at www.brunel.ac.uk/~bustcfj/bola/information/ssm.html and see [Checkland, 81; Checkland, 90; Wilson, 84].

Challenge   A challenge is often used as a euphemism for *problem* (as in, "We don't have problems, we have challenges"). In the Solution Envisioning approach, a challenge expresses, in a succinct way, the essence of the obstacles or barriers that the enterprise needs to overcome to counteract forces and accomplish business results.

Component-Based Development   An approach to the design and implementation of software applications where systems are assembled using components from one or more sources. The components may be written in different programming languages and run on different platforms. Components exist at different levels of granularity—from a re-usable calendar gadget to a fully featured CRM (Customer Relationship Management) module. What is common is their ability to be *composable*. A software component is any self-contained, independently viable, and deployable grouping of services whose services can be invoked by many different types of clients.

Decision Model   A list of criteria used to decide on technology options. Each criterion may be given a relative weight. A Decision Model can be implemented as a spreadsheet, although we believe that decision support tools are better suited for this purpose.

Design Pattern   Design patterns describe solutions to recurring problems in software development. A solution description is presented in a formal template using a pattern language. The template typically describes the problem, the solution, when to apply the solution, and its consequences as well as examples. The pattern presents a general form of a solution that is then customized and implemented to solve the problem in a particular context. The concept of Design Patterns was first formalized in the 1990s [Gamma, 1995].

Essential Business Activity Scenario   A situated account of a key business activity, in the form of a story or high-level process diagram. Scenarios are carefully selected to provide the most powerful and communicative illustrations of key aspects of enterprise activities that need new IT support.

Essential Use Case   A simplified, abstract, generalized use case that captures the intentions of a user in a technology-independent and implementation-independent manner [Constantine, 1999]. A fully documented essential use case is a structured narrative describing one task or interaction in a simplified, abstract, technology-free and implementation-independent way.[3] An essential use case is sometimes called a *business use case,* although RUP gives this term a slightly different (but very close) meaning. A business use case in the RUP sense is often more focused on the business process and existing technology concerns are often brought into it.

---

[3]   See Scott Ambler's website: www.agilemodeling.com/artifacts/essentialUseCase.htm.

This positions business use cases in between essential and system use cases, but closer to the essential end of the spectrum.

eXtreme Programming (XP)   A software development methodology that is set up for a small team of programmers (usually two to 12) working on projects dynamic in nature where high change in requirements is expected. XP has a number of distinguishing characteristics of which pair programming is, perhaps, the best known. Other XP practices include very small iterations with frequent builds, close teaming with customers eliminating the need for formal documentation, and the "test before code" principle where developers design tests before they write code.[4]

Force   A force is a business driver, internal or external, to the business that requires a response. By force, we mean a new or existing condition that is affecting the business. A force can be an issue, where the business is failing in some way, or an opportunity to realize new benefits.

Future Search   An approach to planning meetings developed by Marvin Weisbord. The purpose of future search is to help large, diverse groups of people discover their common values, goals, and interests and to provide them with a way to create a desired future together that they can start implementing right away. Future search is most beneficial in uncertain, fast-changing situations. It typically involves large groups including many different perspectives (60–80 people) and lasts about 2 1/2 days [Weisbord, 1999].

Internal Rate of Return (IRR)   The return earned on a given investment. It is the rate that makes net present value of all cash flows equal to zero. Technically, IRR is a discount rate—the rate at which the present value of a series of investments is equal to the present value of the returns on those investments.

Joint Application Development (JAD)   A structured (in the sense that it has a pre-defined agenda and goal) workshop session that brings together business people and IT professionals for the purpose of designing an IT system. JAD sessions are often facilitated by professional facilitators. A Solution Envisioning Workshop is a special kind of a JAD session.

Knowledge Model   See *Ontology*.

Measure   A parameter used to quantify the effectiveness of the business result.

Microsoft Solution Framework (MSF)   A well-adopted system development method from Microsoft.[5]

Model Driven Architecture (MDA)   An approach to system specification, portability, and interoperability based on the use of formal and semi-formal models. The

---

[4]   XP has a home page at www.extremeprogramming.org/index.html.

[5]   MSF is described at http://msdn.microsoft.com/vstudio/enterprise/msf/.

MDA derives all executable code from models of the system built using UML and other associated OMG (Object Management Group) standards.[6] The models are built in a platform-independent way. Platform-specific code and executables are generated using MDA-compliant tools.

Net Present Value (NPV)   The difference between expected returns and investment calculated taking into account cost of capital. NPV is one of the analytical tools most frequently used to value a project.

Ontology   A model of how to specify a subject area of interest in which concepts, their attributes, and relationships (associations between concepts) are explicitly named and distinguished. Constraints stipulate distinctions that differentiate concepts, governing how they participate in relationships, and how implicit knowledge is made explicit through qualifiers that allow inferencing over relationship properties. A standard language for representing an ontology on the web is the W3C standard OWL.

Packaged Solution   A ready-made software offering developed for mass distribution and use. Today there are packages that support a wide variety of business functions. The more standardized and commoditized the process, the better fit it is for pre-built, off-the-shelf software. For example, the first widely used business packages were typically accounting modules, such as general ledger. Packaged solutions offer a varying degree of customization to better support business needs.

Payback Period   The number of years it takes to recover the initial investment.

Performance Measure   See *Measure*.

Performance Prism   A second generation performance measurement and management framework that addresses all of an organization's stakeholders   principally, investors; customers and intermediaries; employees; suppliers; regulators; and communities. It does this in two ways: by considering what the wants and needs of those stakeholders are and what the organization wants and needs from its stakeholders. The Performance Prism then addresses the strategies, processes, and capabilities needed to satisfy the wants and needs [Neely, 2002].

Porter's Five Force Model   A business context analysis framework developed by Michael Porter. It models an industry as influenced by five forces: competitors within an industry, potential competitors, suppliers, buyers, and alternative solutions to the problem being addressed [Porter, 1985].

Quality Function Deployment (QFD)   A quality assurance method developed in Japan in the late 1960s by Professors Shigeru Mizuno and Yoji Akao. The main objective of the method was to design customer satisfaction into a product before it was manufactured.

---

[6] OMG MDA website is located at www.omg.org/mda/.

Rapid Application Development (RAD)   The Rapid Application Development methodology was developed to respond to the need to deliver systems very fast. RAD compresses the analysis, design, build, and test phases into a series of short, iterative development cycles. This has a number of distinct advantages over the traditional sequential development model. RAD projects are typically staffed with small integrated teams comprised of developers, end users, and IT technical resources.

Rapid Prototyping   An approach to building demonstrators of solution ideas using software techniques, tools, and environments that support extremely fast and highly iterative development cycles.

Rational Unified Process (RUP)   A widely used software development method created by Rational Corporation, which is now a part of IBM.[7]

Result   A business result is a statement of a desired outcome—something the business wants to accomplish. A result is a change in the state of some aspect of the business or in the impact of the business in its environment.

Return on Investment (ROI)   A simple formula for evaluating profitability of an investment. It is calculated by dividing the return, or incremental gains that will be received from an investment, by the costs that were required to achieve that gain.

Semantic Model   Another way of referring to Ontology, usually used in the context of IT solutions that employ an ontology at execution time.

Semantic Web   An evolution of the Web to a web in which meanings can be exchanged and mediated to provide machine-to-machine and more effective human-to-machine interaction. Described by W3C as "a common framework that allows data to be shared and reused across application, enterprise, and community boundaries. It is a collaborative effort led by W3C with participation from a large number of researchers and industrial partners. It is based on the Resource Description Framework (RDF), which integrates a variety of applications using XML for syntax and URIs for naming."[8]

Semantic Web Technology   Semantic Web Technology is the technology that is enabling the Semantic Web and refers to technologies such as RDF,[9] RDFS,[10] and OWL.[11]

---

[7]   http://www-306.ibm.com/software/awdtools/rup/.

[8]   The Semantic Web is described on the W3C site at www.w3.org/2001/sw/.

[9]   RDF, www.w3.org/RDF/.

[10]   RDF Schema, www.w3.org/TR/rdf-schema/.

[11]   WEB Ontology Language, www.w3.org/2004/OWL/.

Service-Oriented Architecture (SOA)   A Service-Oriented Architecture (SOA) defines how two computing entities interact in such a way as to enable one entity to perform a unit of work on behalf of another entity. The unit of work is referred to as a service, and the service interactions are defined using a description language. Each interaction is self-contained and loosely coupled, so that each interaction is independent of any other interaction.

Soft Systems Methodology (SSM)   A framework of techniques for investigating, understanding, and identifying a problem and purposeful activities to arrive at a solution developed by Peter Checkland of Lancaster University. SSM is based on systems thinking. Among its main techniques are CATWOE, Root Definitions, informal Rich Pictures, and Conceptual Models [Checkland, 1981; Checkland, 1990; Wilson, 1984].

Software Capability Design   Phase III of Solution Envisioning. Software Capability Design work is the conversion of the results of envisioning—the Solution Concept—into an actionable set of high-level designs and plans for building the solution. Its purpose is to complete the development and documentation of a Solution Realization Roadmap.

Software Package   See *Packaged Solution*.

Solution   In general, any undertaking that resolves a problem or responds to a need. In the context of this book, a business IT solution can be a combination of hardware, software, and information (data and content) needed to respond to a business problem or satisfy a business need.

Solution Capability Exploration   Phase II of Solution Envisioning. The purpose of Solution Capability Envisioning is to identify the main functionality blocks for the solution by nominating, evaluating, and prioritizing an integrated set of capabilities that will collectively support the business vision.

Solution Concept   The main deliverable of Phase II of Solution Envisioning, Solution Capability Exploration. It is a description of the business context with forces and motivating scenarios; stakeholders and their desired results; capabilities that enable new ways to work; future scenarios that illustrate new ways to work; and a road-map that addresses risks, impacts, and the options and plans for the design work of the next phase.

Solution Envisioning   A business value-driven approach to designing a system that uses Capability Cases and scenarios to foster innovation, achieve connections between Business and IT stakeholders, and to validate and increase confidence in the solution. Solution Envisioning integrates concepts and techniques from both best-of-breed business strategy methods and software development methods. It is a flexible problem-discovery, situation-assessment, and solution-planning process that can be applied in a variety of situations.

Solution Realization Roadmap   Main deliverable of Phase III of Solution Envisioning, Software Capability Design. This is a package of deliverables. It includes: Solution Architecture (comprised of the Vendor Short List, Architectural Decisions, IT Impact and Interface Specification and Non-Functional Requirements) and Business Case (a presentation that provides (a) a summary of the business case; (b) a roadmap to implementation; and (c) description of key risks and risk mitigation decisions). In addition, the implementation plan may also be packaged as a high-level Microsoft Project plan.

Solution Vision Presentation   Main deliverable of Phase I of Solution Envisioning, Business Capability Envisioning. This is a presentation that provides (a) a summary of the business situation; (b) a vision of one or more possible solution concepts; (c) motivating future scenarios and supporting capabilities; and (d) value propositions that serve as input to making a business case.

System Use Case   A sequence of actions describing a way in which a real-world actor interacts with the system. A System Use Case, often called Use Case for short, can be written in both an informal and formal manner. The goal of a Use Case is to describe in some detail the interaction between a user and the system—to capture both normal or successful flows of interaction events where the user's goals are successfully accomplished (happy use case) and any abnormal or exceptional flows of events as alternative paths through the use case. System Use Cases are created after implementation decisions are made. Therefore, unlike Essential Use Cases, System Use Cases are not technology independent.

Systems Thinking   Systems Thinking has its foundation in the field of systems dynamics founded in 1956 by MIT professor Jay Forrester. Professor Forrester developed an approach to testing new ideas about social systems based on how engineering systems were tested. Unlike other analytical approaches that focus on the element being examined, Systems Thinking focuses on the interactions between the element and other constituents of a larger system. This makes it especially effective in finding the best solutions to complex problems that involve many interdependent elements.[12]

Taxonomy   A tree-like hierarchical structure of information. Taxonomies are often used by Internet portals (such as Yahoo!), online catalogs, and Web stores to categorize information and to offer consistent navigation. Taxonomical hierarchies provide an ordered connection between each item in the structure and the item or items below it.

---

[12] The Principia Cybernetica website is an excellent resource for finding out more on Systems Thinking: http://pespmc1.vub.ac.be/CSTHINK.html.

Unified Modeling Language (UML)   Developed by the Object Management Group,[13] UML is a visual language for specifying and documenting models of software systems, including their structure and design. UML is supported by many development tools.

Use Case   See *System Use Case*.

Web Service   A software application whose interfaces and binding are capable of being defined, described, and discovered through industry-standard XML protocols, such as SOAP, WSDL, and UDDI.

---

[13] www.omg.org/.

REFERENCES

[Anderson, 1992] Bruce Anderson. *Towards an Architecture Handbook*. Conference on Object-Oriented Programming Systems Languages and Applications in Vancouver, British Columbia, Canada. ISBN:0-89791-610-7. ACM, 1992: 109–113.

[Alexander, 1979] Christopher Alexander. *The Timeless Way of Building*. Oxford University Press, 1979.

[Amram, 1999] Martha Amram and Nalin Kalatilaka. *Real Options: Managing Strategic Investment in an Uncertain World*. Harvard Business School Press, 1999.

[Arieti, 1976] Silvano Arieti. *Creativity—The Magic Synthesis*. ISBN 0-465-01443-7. Basic Books, Inc., Publishers, New York, 1976.

[Aurand, 2003] Martin Aurand, Carnegie Mellon University, AASL. "The Charette Digital Project: An Historic Pittsburgh Architectural Journal Goes Online." Unpublished, March 2003. Available: www.library.cmu.edu/Research/ArchArch/Charette/CharetteAASL.ppt.

[Avison, 2003] D.E. Avison and G. Fitzgerald. *Information Systems Development*, 3rd Ed. McGraw-Hill, 2003.

[Bailin, 2000] S. Bailin, M. Simos, L. Levine, and R. Creps. *Learning and Inquiry-Based Reuse Adoption (LIBRA)*. ISBN 0-7803-6009-5. IEEE Press, 2000.

[Bailin, 2003] Sidney Bailin. Private Communication, 2003.

[Barry, 2003] Douglas K. Barry. *Web Services and Service-Oriented Architectures*. ISBN 1-55860-906-7. Morgan Kaufmann Publishers, 2003.

[Beck, 1999] Kent Beck. *Extreme Programming Explained: Embrace Change*. Addison-Wesley, 1999.

[Bennett, 1997] Douglas Bennett. *Designing Hard Software—The Essential Tasks*. Manning, 1997.

[Belton, 2002] Professor Val Belton and Professor Theodor J. Stewart. *Multiple Criteria Decision Analysis: An Integrated Approach*. ISBN 0-7923-7505-X. Kluwer Academic Publishers, 2002.

[Berczuk, 2002] Stephen P. Berczuk, Brad Appleton. *Software Configuration Management Patterns: Effective Teamwork, Practical Integration*. Addison-Wesley, 2002.

[Boden, 1990] Margaret A.Boden. *The Creative Mind: Myths and Mechanisms*. Weidenfeld & Nicholson, 1990.

[Boehm, 1988] Barry Boehm. "A Spiral Model of Software Development and Enhancement." *IEEE Computer*, 21(5): May 1988, 61–72.

[Brooks, 1974] Frederick P Brooks. *The Mythical Man-Month and Other Essays on Software Engineering*. Dept. of Computer Science, University of North Carolina at Chapel Hill, 1974.

[Brooks, 1987] Fred Brooks. "No Silver Bullet, Essence and Accidents of Software Engineering." *Computer Magazine*, April 1987.

[Brown, 2000] John Seely Brown and Paul Duguid. *The Social Life of Information*. Harvard Business School Press, 2000.

[Bussler, 2002] C. Bussler, R. Hull, S.A. McIlraith, M.E. Orlowska, B. Pernici, and J. Yang (eds.) *Web Services, E-Business, and the Semantic Web*. CAiSE 2002 International Workshop. Revised papers. LNCS 2512, ISBN 3-540-00198-0. WES 2002. Springer-Verlag, 2002.

[Buzan, 1993] Tony Buzan. *The Mind Map Book*. ISBN 0-563-86373-8. BBC Books, 1993.

[Carroll, 1995] J.M. Carroll (ed.) *Scenario-Based Design*. John Wiley & Sons, 1995.

[Chappell, 2004] David A. Chappell. *Enterprise Service Bus*. ISBN 0-596-00675-6. O'Reilly, 2004.

[Checkland, 1981] Peter Checkland. *Systems Thinking, Systems Practice*. John Wiley & Sons, 1981.

[Checkland, 1990] P.B. Checkland and J.Scholes. *Soft Systems Methodology in Action*. John Wiley & Sons, 1990.

[Clements, 2002a] Paul Clements, et al. *Documenting Software Architectures: Views and Beyond*. Addison-Wesley, 2002.

[Clements, 2002b] Paul Clements, et al. *Evaluating Software Architectures: Methods and Case Studies*. Addison-Wesley, 2002.

[Cockburn, 2001a] A. Cockburn. *Writing Effective Use Cases*. ISBN 0-201-70225-8. Addison-Wesley, 2001.

[Cockburn, 2001b] A. Cockburn. *Agile Software Development*. Addison-Wesley, 2001.

[Cockrell, 2005] Jim Cockrell and Ralph Hodgson. *Proposed Wire Data Management System Improvements for Space Shuttle Orbiter Ground Operations*. Aging Aircraft 2005 Conference, Palm Springs, CA, 2005.

[Cohen, 2001] Don Cohen and Laurence Prusak. *In Good Company: How Social Capital Makes Organizations Work*. Harvard Business School Press, 2001.

[Csikszentmihalyi, 1997] Mihaly Csikszentmihalyi. *Creativity: Flow and the Psychology of Discovery and Invention*. Harper Collins, 1997.

[Daconta, 2003] Michael C. Daconta, Leo J. Obrst, and Kevin T. Smith. *The Semantic Web: A Guide to the Future of XML, Web Services, and Knowledge Management*. ISBN 0-471-43257-1. John Wiley & Sons, 2003.

[De Bono, 1971] E. De Bono. *Lateral Thinking for Management*. McGraw-Hill, 1971.

[De Bono, 1985] E. De Bono. *Six Thinking Hats*. Little, Brown & Company, 1985.

[De Bono, 1992] E. De Bono. *Serious Creativity: Using the Power of Lateral Thinking to Create New Ideas*. Harper Collins, 1992.

[Denning, 2001] Stephen Denning. *The Springboard—How Storytelling Ignites Action in Knowledge-Era Organizations*. ISBN 0-7506-7355-9. KMCI, Butterworth-Heinemann, 2001.

[Dettmer, 1997] H. William Dettmer. *Goldratt's Theory of Constraints*. ISBN 0-87389-370-0. ASQC, 1997.

[Dove, 1999] Rick Dove. *Solutions Looking for Problems*. Automotive Manufacturing and Production. July 1999.

[Duddy, 2004] K. Duddy, M.J. Lawley, and Z. Milosevic. *Elemental and Pegamento: The Final Cut—Applying the MDA Pattern*. In Proc. 8th IEEE International Enterprise Distributed Object Computing Conference, EDOC 2004. Monterey, USA. 240–252. September 2004.

[Eden, 1998] Colin Eden and Fran Ackermann. *Making Strategy—The Journey of Strategic Management*. ISBN 0-7619-5224-1. SAGE Publications, 1998.

[Erl, 2004] Thomas Erl. *Service-Oriented Architecture—A Field Guide to Integrating XML and Web Services*. ISBN 0-13-142898-5. Prentice Hall, 2004.

[Ferranti, 2003] Marc Ferranti. *Success Requires Routine Reinvention. CIO Magazine*, Special issue. Fall/Winter 2003.

[Finke, 1992] R. A. Finke, et al. *Creative Cognition: Theory, Research and Applications*. MIT Press, 1992.

[Finke, 1996] R. A. Finke. *Imagery, Creativity and Emergent Structure*. Consciousness and Cognition (5). 1996, 381–393.

[Fowler, 2002] Martin Fowler. *Patterns of Enterprise Application Architecture*. ISBN 0-3211-2742-0. Addison-Wesley, 2002.

[Frankel, 2003] David S. Frankel. *Model-Driven Architecture: Applying MDA to Enterprise Computing*. John Wiley & Sons, 2003.

[Gamma, 1994] Erich Gamma, Richard Helm, Ralph Johnson, and John Vlissides. *Design Patterns: Elements of Reusable Object-Oriented Software*. Addison-Wesley, 1994.

[Gentner, 1989] D. Gentner. *The Mechanisms of Analogical Learning*. From *Similarity and Analogical Reasoning*. S. Vosniadou & A. Ortony (Eds.) Cambridge University Press, 1989. (Reprinted in Knowledge Acquisition and Learning, 1993, [673–694]).

[Gharajedaghi, 1999] Jamshid Gharajedaghi. *Systems Thinking—Managing Chaos and Complexity—A Platform for Designing Business Architecture*. ISBN 0-7506-7163-7. Butterworth-Heinemann, 1999.

[Gilb, 1988] Tom Gilb. *Principles of Software Engineering Management*. Addison-Wesley, 1988.

[Gordon, 1961] W. J. J. Gordon. *Synectics*. Harper & Row, 1961.

[Gottesdiener, 2002] Ellen Gottesdiener. *Requirements by Collaboration: Workshops for Defining Needs*. Addison-Wesley, 2002.

[Haeckel, 1999] Stephan H. Haeckel, Adrian J. Slywotsky. *Adaptive Enterprise: Creating and Leading Sense-and-Respond Organizations*. Harvard Business School Press, 1999.

[Heijden, 1996] Kees Van de Heijden. *Scenarios—The Art of Strategic Conversation*. John Wiley & Sons, 1996.

[Hill, 1995] R. C. Hill and M. Levenhagen. *Metaphors and Mental Models: Sense Making and Sense Giving in Innovative and Entrepreneurial Activities*. *Journal of Management* 21(6): 1057–1074, 1995.

[Higgins, 1994] James M. Higgins. *101 Creative Problem Solving Techniques*. The New Management Publishing Company, 1994.

[Highsmith, 1999] James Highsmith. *Adaptive Software Development: A Collaborative Approach to Managing Complex Systems*. Dorset House Publishing, 1999.

[Highsmith, 2002] Jim Highsmith. *Agile Software Development Ecosystems*. Addison-Wesley, 2002.

[Hodgson, 1991] Ralph Hodgson, *The X-Model: A Process Model for Object-Oriented Software Development*, Proceedings of the Fourth International Software Engineering Conference. ISBN 2-906 899-68-2, Toulouse, France, 713–728, 1991.

[Hodgson, 1994] Ralph Hodgson. *Contemplating the Universe of Methods*. In *Object Development Methods*. Andy Carmichael (ed.) Advances In Object Technology Series archive. ISBN 0-9627477-9-3. SIGS Books, 1994.

[Hodgson, 1998] Ralph Hodgson. *Workshop Summary: System Envisioning.* OOPSLA 1998, Vancouver, British Columbia, Canada, ISBN 1-58113-286-7. ACM, 1998.

[Hodgson, 2001] Ralph Hodgson, Greg L. Baker, and Prady Pradhyumnan. *Experiences Using Knowledge Model-Driven CBR for Knowledge Enablement of Best Practices Within IBM Global Services.* ICCBR-2001, International Conference on Case-Based Reasoning, Vancouver, British Columbia, Canada.

[Husch, 1987] Tony Husch and Linda Foust. *That's a Great Idea.* 10 Speed Press, 1987.

[Jacobson, 1994] Ivar Jacobson, Maria Ericsson, and Agneta Jacobson. *The Object Advantage, Business Process Reengineering with Object Technology.* Addison-Wesley, 1994.

[Kalakota, 2003] Ravi Kalakota and Marcia Robinson. *Services Blueprint: Roadmap for Execution.* ISBN: 0-32115-039-2. Addison-Wesley, 2003.

[Kaner, 1996] Sam Kaner, *Facilitator's Guide to Participatory Decision-Making.* ISBN 0-86571-346-4. New Society Publishers, 1996.

[Kaplan, 2001] Robert S. Kaplan and David P. Norton. *The Strategy-Focused Organization— How Balanced Scorecard Companies Thrive in the New Business Environment.* ISBN 1-57851-250-6. Harvard Business School Press, 2001.

[Kaplan, 2004] Robert S. Kaplan and David P. Norton. *Strategy Maps—Converting Intangible Assets into Tangible Outcomes.* ISBN 1-59139-134-2. Harvard Business School Press, 2004.

[Kawasaki, 1999] Guy Kawasaki. *Rules for Revolutionaries.* Harper Business, 1999.

[Koestler, 1967] Arthur Koestler. *The GHOST in the MACHINE.* Hutchinson & Co., 1967.

[Krafzig, 2005] Dirk Krafzig, Karl Banke, and Dirk Slama. *Enterprise SOA—Service-Oriented Architecture Best Practices.* ISBN 0-13-146575-9. Prentice Hall, 2005.

[Krief, 1996] Philippe Krief. *Prototyping with Objects.* ISBN 0-13-014713-3. Prentice Hall, 1996.

[Kruchen, 1995] P. Kruchen. *The 4+1 Model View. IEEE Computer* 12 (6): November 1995.

[Levi, 1995] Robert Levi. *Info on Dialogue Process.* Unpublished, 1995. (Reported by Mary Margaret Palmer). Learning Organization. http://world.std.com/~lo/bohm/0002.html.

[Macaulay, 1996] Linda A. Macaulay. *Requirements Engineering.* ISBN 3-540-76006-7. Springer, 1996.

[Manns, 2004] Mary Lynn Manns and Linda Rising. *Fearless Change: Patterns for Introducing New Ideas.* Addison-Wesley, 2004.

[Matts, 2003] Chris Matts and Andy Pols. *The Agile Business Coach.* Unpublished, 2003. White paper available: http://www.pols.co.uk/business-coach/index.html.

[McDavid, 1999] Doug McDavid and Ralph Hodgson. *System Envisioning: An Essential Step in Building Software Systems*. Chapter 13, 1–15, *Handbook of Object Technology*. Saba Zamir (ed.) ISBN 0-8493-3135-8. CRC Press, 1999.

[Morgan, 1983] Gareth Morgan. *More on Metaphor: Why We Cannot Control Tropes In Administrative Science*. *Administrative Science Quarterly* (28): 1983, 601–607.

[Morgan, 1986] Gareth Morgan. *Images of the Organization*. Sage Press, 1986.

[Morgan, 1993] Gareth Morgan. *Imaginization—The Art of Creative Management*. ISBN 0-8039-5299-6. Sage Press, 1993.

[Neely, 2002] Andy Neely, Chris Adams, and Mike Kennerley. *The Performance Prism—The Scorecard for Measuring and Managing Business Success*. ISBN 0-273-65334-2. Pearson Education, 2002.

[Osborn, 1953] A. F. Osborn. *Applied Imagination*. Revised Edition. Scribner's, 1953.

[Papanek, 1985] Victor Papanek. *Design for the Real World: Human Ecology and Social Change*. Academy Chicago Publishers, 1985.

[Passin, 2004] Thomas B. Passin. *Explorer's Guide to the Semantic Web*. ISBN 1-932394-20-6. Manning Publications, 2004.

[Pollock, 2004] Jeffrey T. Pollock and Ralph Hodgson. *Adaptive Information: Improving Business Through Semantic Interoperability, Grid Computing, and Enterprise Integration*. ISBN 0-471-48854-2. John Wiley & Sons, September 2004.

[Poppendieck, 2003] Mary Poppendieck and Tom Poppendieck. *Lean Software Development: An Agile Toolkit for Software Development Managers*. ISBN 0-321-15078-3. Addison-Wesley, 2003.

[Porter, 1985] Michael E. Porter. *Competitive Advantage—Creating and Sustaining Superior Performance*. ISBN 0-02-925090-0. The Free Press, 1985.

[Pree, 1994] Wolfgang Pree. *Design Patterns for Object-Oriented Software Development*. Addison Wesley, 1994.

[Putman, 2000] Janis R. Putman. *Architecting with RM-ODP*. ISBN 0-13-019116-7. Prentice Hall, 2000.

[Reason, 1988] Peter Reason. *Human Inquiry in Action*. ISBN 0-8039-8089-2. Sage Publications, 1989.

[Robinson, 2001] Ken Robinson. *Out Of Our Minds—Learning to Be Creative*. Capstone Publishing, 2001.

[Rosenhead, 1989] Jonathan Rosenhead (Ed.). *Rational Analysis for a Problematic World*. ISBN 0-471-92285-4. John Wiley & Sons, 1989.

[Schön, 1983] D. A. Schön. *The Reflective Practitioner*. Basic Books, Inc., 1983.

[Schrage, 2000] Michael Schrage. *Serious Play, How the World's Best Companies Simulate to Innovate*. ISBN 0-87584-814-1. Harvard Business School Press, 2000.

[Senge, 1990] Peter M. Senge. *The Fifth Discipline*. Doubleday/Currency, 1990.

[Senge, 1994] Peter M. Senge, et al. *The Fifth Discipline Fieldbook: Strategies and Tools for Building a Learning Organization*. Doubleday, 1994.

[Senge, 2001] Peter Senge. *The Systems Thinker Newsletter*. Available: www.pegasus-com.com/tstpage.html.

[Shapiro, 2001] Steven M. Shapiro. *24/7 Innovation: A Blueprint for Surviving and Thriving in an Age of Change*. McGraw-Hill, 2001.

[Silk, 1992] D.J. Silk. *Planning IT—Creating an Information Management Strategy*. ISBN 075-6-08323. Butterworth-Heinemann, 1992.

[Simmons, 2000] Annette Simmons. *The Story Factor: Secrets of Influence from the Art of Storytelling*. Perseus, 2000.

[Simon, 1981] Herbert A. Simon. *The Sciences of the Artificial*. Second Edition. ISBN 0-262-19193-8. The MIT Press, 1981.

[Song, 2002] Steve Song. *The Role of Storytelling in Knowledge Sharing and Organizational Change*. KM Champions in Africa, Maputo, Mozambique 29, May 2002.

[Sterman, 2000] John D. Sterman. *Business Dynamics: Systems Thinking and Modeling for a Complex World*. ISBN 0-07-231135-5. McGraw-Hill, 2000.

[Sternberg, 1991] Robert J. Sternberg. *Handbook of Creativity*. ISBN 0-521-57604-0. Cambridge University Press, 1991.

[Stowell, 1995] Bob Galliers. *Re-orienting Information Systems Strategy: Integrating Information Systems into the Business*. In *Information Systems Provision: The Contribution of Soft Systems Methodology*. Frank A. Stowell (ed.) McGraw-Hill, 1995.

[Tsoukas, 1991] H. Tsoukas. *The Missing Link: A Transformational View of Metaphors in Organizational Science*. *Academy of Management Review* 16(3): 1991, 566–585.

[Ullman, 2001] David G. Ullman. *12 Steps to Robust Decisions—Building Consensus in Product Development and Business*. ISBN 1-55212-576-9. Trafford Publishing, 2001.

[van Duyne, 2002] Douglas K. van Duyne, James A. Landay, and Jason I. Hong. *The Design of Sites: Patterns, Principles, and Processes for Crafting a Customer-Centered Web Experience*. Addison-Wesley, 2002.

[Wallnau, 2002] Kurt C. Wallnau, Scott A. Hissam, and Robert C. Seacord. *Building Systems from Commercial Components*. ISBN 0-201-70064-6. Addison-Wesley, 2002.

[Ward, 1999] Thomas Ward. *Creative Cognition*. In *Handbook of Creativity*. R. J. Sternberg (ed.) Cambridge University Press, 1999.

[Weill, 2004] Peter Weill and Jeanne W. Ross. *IT Governance*. ISBN 1-59139-253-5. Harvard Business School Press, 2004.

[Weisbord, 1992] Marvin R. Weisbord. *Discovering Common Ground—How Future Search Conferences Bring People Together to Achieve Breakthrough Innovation, Empowerment, Shared Vision and Collaborative Action*. ISBN 1-881052-08-7. Berrett-Koehler, 1992.

[Weisbord, 1999] Marvin R. Weisbord and Sandra Janoff. *Future Search—An Action Guide to Finding Common Ground in Organizations & Communities*. ISBN 1-881052-12-5. Berrett-Koehler, 1999.

[Wiegers, 1999] Karl E. Wiegers. *Software Requirements*. Microsoft Press, 1999.

[Wilson, 1984] Brian Wilson. *Systems: Concepts, Methodologies and Applications*. John Wiley & Sons, Chichester, 1984.

[Zohar, 1997] Danah Zohar. *Rewiring the Corporate Brain: Using the New Science to Rethink How We Structure and Lead Organizations*. ISBN: 1576750221. Berrett-Koehler, 1997.

[Zander, 2001] Ben Zander and Ros Zander. *The Art of Possibility Video*. Groh Publications, February 2001.

INDEX

THIS BOOK IS SAFARI ENABLED

INCLUDES FREE 45-DAY ACCESS TO THE ONLINE EDITION

The Safari® Enabled icon on the cover of your favorite technology book means the book is available through Safari Bookshelf. When you buy this book, you get free access to the online edition for 45 days.

Safari Bookshelf is an electronic reference library that lets you easily search thousands of technical books, find code samples, download chapters, and access technical information whenever and wherever you need it.

TO GAIN 45-DAY SAFARI ENABLED ACCESS TO THIS BOOK:

- Go to **http://www.awprofessional.com/safarienabled**
- Complete the brief registration form
- Enter the coupon code found in the front of this book on the "Copyright" page

If you have difficulty registering on Safari Bookshelf or accessing the online edition, please e-mail customer-service@safaribooksonline.com.